SERVICE FROM THE SEA

We would like to acknowledge the help of the Royal New Zealand Navy Museum staff in the making of this book – in particular Commander David Wright, Claire Freeman, Paul Restall, Katherine Bol and Hayley Gledhill. Thanks also to Richard Jackson.

VIKING
Published by the Penguin Group
Penguin Group (NZ), 67 Apollo Drive, Rosedale,
North Shore 0632, New Zealand (a division of Pearson New Zealand Ltd)
Penguin Group (USA) Inc., 375 Hudson Street,
New York, New York 10014, USA
Penguin Group (Canada), 90 Eglinton Avenue East, Suite 700, Toronto,
Ontario, M4P 2Y3, Canada (a division of Pearson Penguin Canada Inc.)
Penguin Books Ltd, 80 Strand, London, WC2R 0RL, England
Penguin Ireland, 25 St Stephen's Green,
Dublin 2, Ireland (a division of Penguin Books Ltd)
Penguin Group (Australia), 250 Camberwell Road, Camberwell,
Victoria 3124, Australia (a division of Pearson Australia Group Pty Ltd)
Penguin Books India Pvt Ltd, 11, Community Centre,
Panchsheel Park, New Delhi – 110 017, India
Penguin Books (South Africa) (Pty) Ltd, 24 Sturdee Avenue,
Rosebank, Johannesburg 2196, South Africa

Penguin Books Ltd, Registered Offices: 80 Strand, London, WC2R 0RL, England

First published in 2008
1 3 5 7 9 10 8 6 4 2

Photography of objects by Paul Restall
Initial design concept by Athena Sommerfeld
Prepress by Image Centre Ltd
Printed in China by Everbest Printing Co., Ltd.

Publisher: Jeff Atkinson
Managing Editor: Andrea Coppock
Editor: Emma Beckett

ISBN: 978-0-67-007240-8

A catalogue record for this book is available from the National Library of New Zealand.

www.penguin.co.nz

Navy
NAVY MUSEUM
Te Waka Taonga o Te Taua Moana o Aotearoa
PENGUIN
VIKING

SERVICE FROM THE SEA

NGĀ MAHI NŌ TE MOANA

New Zealand Naval history told through the collections of the Royal New Zealand Navy Museum

KELLY ANA MOREY

ABL 0024

CONTENTS

CHIEF OF NAVY,
REAR ADMIRAL DAVID LEDSON, ONZM

The sea has always been central to the New Zealand story.

Until recently the only way people and trade could arrive in – and travel from – New Zealand was by crossing the sea. Even today, while most people travel by air, around 90–95 per cent of our trade is moved by ships across all the world's oceans. So the sea has been very important to our development as a country. And it remains important to both our prosperity and our security.

The sea is also the medium upon which the Navy's ships do their work around the world, and from which our sailors serve their country, protecting our citizens, our resources and our national interests.

Service from the Sea tells the Navy's story and highlights the important role the Royal New Zealand Navy Museum plays in enabling that story to be told. But the Museum is far more than just a backdrop to the story, it provides those essential elements that bring the story to life, make it interesting and relevant, and illustrate that the Navy is about more than ships – that people lie at the heart of the story.

My congratulations to Penguin Books (NZ), the Museum staff and all those who have contributed to this project. Their efforts have created an outstanding book.

Navy

DIRECTOR OF THE NAVY MUSEUM, COMMANDER DAVID WRIGHT, MNZM

In many respects New Zealand has been defined by its military history and its experience of war and conflict. Our military heritage has played a major part in helping build New Zealand as a nation with its own identity, culture and ethos. In this regard, telling the story of New Zealand's military history provides a significant service and contribution to society and the nation.

For the last 25 years the Royal New Zealand Navy Museum has faithfully told the story of our navy, our sailors, their families and the communities from which they came.

Every object and photograph in the Museum tells a story of adventure, courage and, in some cases, sacrifice – they tell the story of long absences from home, appalling conditions and mate-ship. Above all, though, they tell the story of people – not just our heroes, but the ordinary men and women who day in and day out do extraordinary things.

The role of the Museum within the Navy, within the local community and within the nation is an important one and we trust this magnificent book by Penguin Books (NZ) will make a major contribution to telling our Navy's story.

NAVY MUSEUM
Te Waka Taonga o Te Taua Moana o Aotearoa

INTRODUCTION

With over 15,000 kilometres of coastline and an interior that is in places still almost impenetrable, it is no surprise that New Zealand, from the beginnings of human settlement, has been a nation of seafarers both commercial and military in character.

Small ceramic vases with painted scene of HMS New Zealand *at anchor.* GEI 0020 & GEI 0021

Brass deck clock complete in brass-bound wooden case. ICA 0004

Surveyor's sextant. IBC 0023

The New Zealand navy found its first embodiment in the mighty waka of Maori raiding parties who used these traditional ships of war to travel to coastlines held by other tribes and wage war. In 1769 New Zealand was discovered for the northern hemisphere by Lieutenant James Cook, Royal Navy (RN), and subsequently New Zealand harbours became resting places for the various RN ships that ventured this far south on their epic journeys. From this time forth, navy in New Zealand became synonymous with the British tradition. During the Land Wars of the 1860s between the settlers and various Maori tribal groups, the Royal Navy came in support of Britain's far-flung colony, bringing its ships and sailors south to quell the native rebellion. With this influx of fighting men to New Zealand shores came developments of a defensive nature on land. Down on the shoreline in Devonport on the Waitemata Harbour a naval base began to develop. By 1864, two and a half decades after William Hobson had earmarked the area as a likely site for a naval base, the facilities included a blacksmith's forge, a two-storeyed barracks at Sandspit and a slipway.

Peace between the coloniser and the Maori finally arrived in the early 1870s and New

Zealand began to look outward, realising that the coastline of this land that had been so hard won needed to be protected from invaders. In the early 1870s the enemy was the Russians and by 1914, with the outbreak of the First World War, it was the Germans. Although the Russian scare had been a false alarm, it had underlined the importance of coastal defence to a nation of islands. As a result, a New Zealand navy of sorts developed, undergoing a number of incarnations in order to fit the needs of a rapidly growing country. The navy's first ship, HMS *Philomel*, was sent to the New Zealand Station by the RN in mid-1914. However, due to the outbreak of war these initial steps towards the creation of a proper navy were of little use as the RN's priorities and New Zealand's place in them changed dramatically.

Although the First World War was very much a northern hemisphere affair, the threat posed by German raiders in New Zealand waters was very real, with minefields laid by the German raider *Wolf* in early 1917 off Farewell Spit and the Three Kings Islands. The subsequent sinking of three merchant ships later in that same year led to the development of the New Zealand navy's first minesweeping flotilla. However, it wasn't only on ships at home that New Zealand men served. During the First World War a number of New Zealanders travelled to Britain to volunteer for service with the RN; one of the Admiralty's new dreadnoughts had been paid for by New Zealand and bore the country's name; and New Zealanders served on board *Philomel* when the ship was serving with the RN in the Mediterranean and Persian Gulf.

Following the First World War the New Zealand navy came into being, albeit as a branch of the RN, as ships designated for the New Zealand Station began to arrive and the training of naval men began in earnest. In the 1920s, the New Zealand naval force became known as the New Zealand Division of the Royal Navy. Between the wars the navy was called into service on a number of occasions in both a civil and offshore capacity and was involved in such emergencies as the Mau unrest in Samoa in early 1930 and the Napier earthquake a year later.

War intervened once again during the second half of the 1930s. The first inklings of another conflict of global proportions were felt with the invasion of Abyssinia by Italy in 1935. It was not until 1939, however, that Britain, and all that that term encompassed in terms of allies and Dominions, declared war on Germany. The Second World War was a busy time for the now rapidly expanding New Zealand Division. There were its own naval needs to be taken care of at home and obligations in other oceans on both sides of the equator. New Zealand ships and New Zealand men 'did their bit' in every theatre of war in both Europe and in the Pacific. Those who did not join the New Zealand Division volunteered for service with the RN

HMS *New Zealand* & the Maori Charms

In mid-1913, shortly after it was commissioned into the Royal Navy, the 'gift' battlecruiser HMS *New Zealand* – which the New Zealand Government had taken out a two million pound loan to pay for – journeyed to the home Dominion via the west coast of Africa and southern Australia. The purpose of this voyage, shortly before the outbreak of the First World War, was to 'show the flag' – a way of saying thank you to the people of New Zealand for their generosity.

The vessel visited numerous New Zealand ports in the two months that it was in New Zealand waters, maintaining a relentless schedule of ship visits, luncheons, sports days and civic receptions during its tour of both islands and both coasts. By Captain Halsey's own count he personally made more than 60 speeches in the 10 weeks the ship was on tour. In addition, a large number of gifts were presented to the captain and the ship, including a flax piupiu and perhaps a greenstone tiki, too, although references to the tiki come and go. Accompanying these particular Maori gifts was a prophecy – it could have even been a blessing – regarding the ship's fortunes in war if the two items were worn by the captain while the ship was in battle.

Interestingly, although the prophecy has been not only remembered but also carved into the annals of Royal and New Zealand naval history, whether there were one or two sacred objects, where the artefacts came from and who presented them is unrecorded. Even the port in which the ship was at anchor when the presentation was made is unrecorded; however, it seems likely, according to the *Evening Post* at the time, that Wellington was the location even though Maori taonga were gifted to Captain Halsey at virtually every port the ship visited.

Both of the ship's captains, Halsey and J. F. E. Green, are said to have worn the 'Maori charms' in battle – and the prophecy of good fortune appears to have worked. At first, the sight of Halsey with the piupiu hung around his neck and the tiki clutched in his hand startled the crew; however, as the warship passed through this battle and the next unscathed, the legend and faith placed in the 'charms' grew.

When command of the battleship passed to Captain Green, so did the artefacts, their instructions of use and the story of the prophecy. During the Battle of Jutland on 31 May 1916, as *New Zealand* went to action stations, Green draped the piupiu over his shoulders and took his place on the bridge – much, it was said, to the crew's relief. In spite of the ship being involved in some fierce actions, it came through the war virtually unscathed and casualty free. However, ultimately the ship's luck was to run out after the First World War when it was, due to fundamental design shortcomings, one of the vessels lost to the scrapyard when the post-war call for military down-scaling inevitably came a-calling.

as they had done in the Great War. The biggest change that the Second World War brought for the New Zealand navy was at first largely administrative, as, in the midst of the fighting, the Royal New Zealand Navy (RNZN) came quietly into being as an entity in its own right. It would be close to three years before hostilities ended and the brand-new New Zealand Navy could start finding its sea legs.

Any naval story is one of ships and sailors and the things they do for their country. Ships, like sailors, have a limited operational life and need to be replaced. The constant need to keep the RNZN fleet operational and fully manned is a prevailing theme from the end of the Second World War to the present day. While ships, like their crews, have come and gone over the past six decades, what has been established since the end of the war is a routine range of tasks – some clearly visible, others less so – that the navy has undertaken as part of its commitment to New Zealand and a host of strategic alliances with other nations. The evolution of the modern RNZN has been characterised by a pattern of activity – constant patrols both in home waters and in distant oceans, exercises with allied navies, serving in trouble spots around the globe (both in the form of ships and, in some instances, individuals), ceremonial duties and those in survey and research capacities. As the world and the means of fighting wars has changed, so too has the RNZN, constantly evolving to meet the needs and obligations of the country it calls home.

This book is intended above all as a celebration of the New Zealand navy and the people who serve in it. It seeks to explore the details

Piupiu gifted to Captain Halsey while in NZ and worn during HMS New Zealand*'s First World War naval battles.* 2007.1.1

HMS New Zealand *in Auckland, 1913.* ABT 0056

The piupiu was returned to Halsey and briefly journeyed home when Halsey lent it to the New Zealand Division of the Royal Navy to be displayed in the New Zealand Centennial Exhibition in Wellington in 1940. Upon his death in 1949, Halsey, by then Admiral Sir Lionel Halsey, bequeathed the piupiu to his youngest daughter, Ruth. Mrs Joan Wood, another of Halsey's daughters, recalled that: 'Lord Mountbatten tried hard to get hold of the Maori skirt when my father died, but my sister was having none of that!' Ruth Halsey's wish was for the piupiu to return to New Zealand after her death and upon that occurring, her nephew John Wood became the custodian of the piupiu facilitating its journey back to New Zealand as per his aunt's wishes. In due course, having decided that this was the taonga's rightful resting place, the piupiu was offered to the Navy Museum.

What became of the tiki, or even if such an object existed, is at this point unknown.

– whether objects, letters, oral histories or archival photographs – that contribute to the big picture in order to find the human dimension in over 100 years of naval history. For this reason *Service from the Sea is* dedicated to the unsung – those who never got the chance to tell their story themselves.

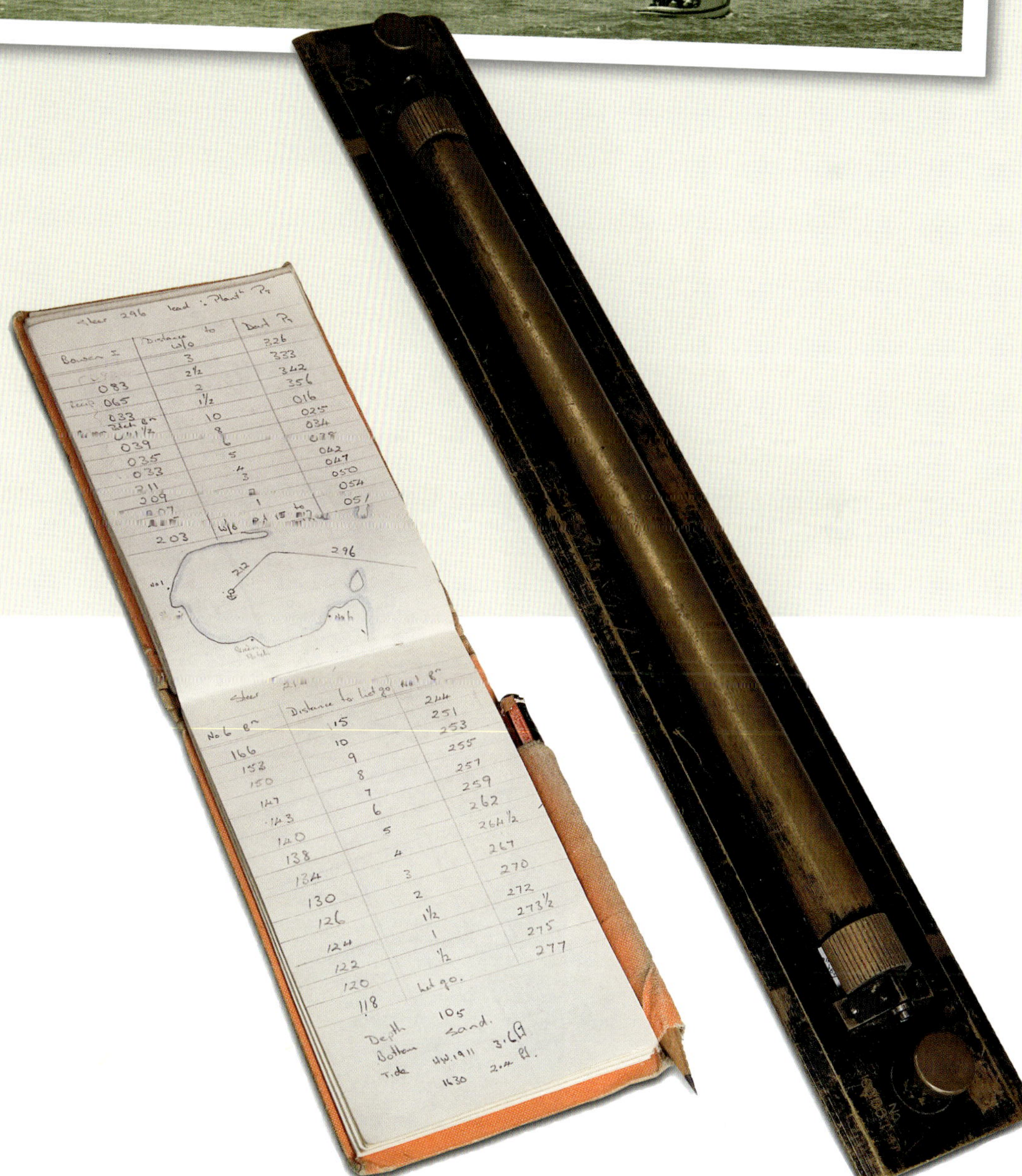

Navigating officer's notebook. DNA 0001

Parallel ruler for navigation. IBC 0026

Ditty box containing family photographs, medals and other items belonging to Acting Petty Officer T. Hutchins who joined the navy in 1933 and served in HMNZS Achilles *at the Battle of the River Plate. Ditty boxes were introduced in the navy in the 1870s. They were plain, unstained wooden boxes, issued to navy sailors to keep personal possessions in, such as photographs, letters and trinkets. They ceased to be navy issue in 1938 when adequate kit lockers were provided on ships.* CQE 0008

This octant is believed to have been used at the Battle of Trafalgar by Midshipman Jas Poad in 1805 on the Victory. IBC 0066

Silver globe on a plinth inscribed 'Wardroom Mess HMS NZ from Wardroom Officers 1913'. FT 0232

Metal 'dog tag' stamped with wearer's name and next of kin: 'John G Hilliard LT COMDR RNZN Mrs J G Hilliard 14 Cathedral Place Auckland NZ' along with a greenstone tiki. DGB 0055

The Royal New Zealand Navy Museum

During the early 1970s, as the result of an increasing number of donations by ex-naval men, it became evident that an adequate means of caring for and displaying these treasures from the past was needed.

In 1974, under the auspices of the Commodore Auckland, Commodore J. F. McKenzie, a room was made available in HMNZS *Philomel*, at the naval base at Devonport, Auckland. The 'museum' was open for two hours a week mainly for naval personnel, although groups visiting the naval base were also welcomed. From the outset, the Museum's policy was to create and maintain a permanent record of the history and development of the RNZN. Advice was sought from the Auckland War Memorial Museum on basic conservation and display techniques.

By 1981 the need for a proper museum facility, including a store to hold items not on display, was championed by the then Chief of Naval Staff, Rear Admiral K. M. Saull. A modest building on the edge of the naval base was chosen and the RNZN Museum moved to its present site in Spring Street and was officially opened on 5 May 1982. A modest extension was added to the existing building and the project came to fruition with the annex opening in December 1989. The Trust Board of the Royal New Zealand Navy Museum was established in May 1988 and the role of the Museum was described as follows: 'To be an educational and recreational facility that presents to the RNZN and the public in general, the naval influence on the history of New Zealand.'

Collection

The Navy Museum holds a unique and wide-ranging collection of objects that tell the story of New Zealand's navy. It welcomes offers of donations of naval material relevant to the operation of the RNZN's ships, including artefacts, instrumentation and ephemera. The Museum also collects more personal items that illustrate the lives of our naval personnel both at sea and ashore.

Oral History Archive

The Navy Museum Oral History Project commenced in 1991 as part of the multi-faceted 50th anniversary celebration for the Royal New Zealand Navy. Although initially conceived as a short-term project with a focus on former chiefs of naval staff, the scope of the project was extended as its value to future researchers was appreciated. Thus nearly two decades later the Archive holds approximately 250 interviews, dating from the late 1920s onwards, on every facet of naval life from the early days of the New Zealand Division to peacekeepers in Afghanistan.

Photographic Archive

In 2008, the collection of photographic ephemera archived by the RNZN Museum numbers approximately 100,000 photographs and 140,000 negatives, with 30,000 items digitised. In addition to placing the images on a database, the photographic archive carries out ongoing conservation work on both prints and negatives.

THE NEW ZEALAND STATION 1770–1914

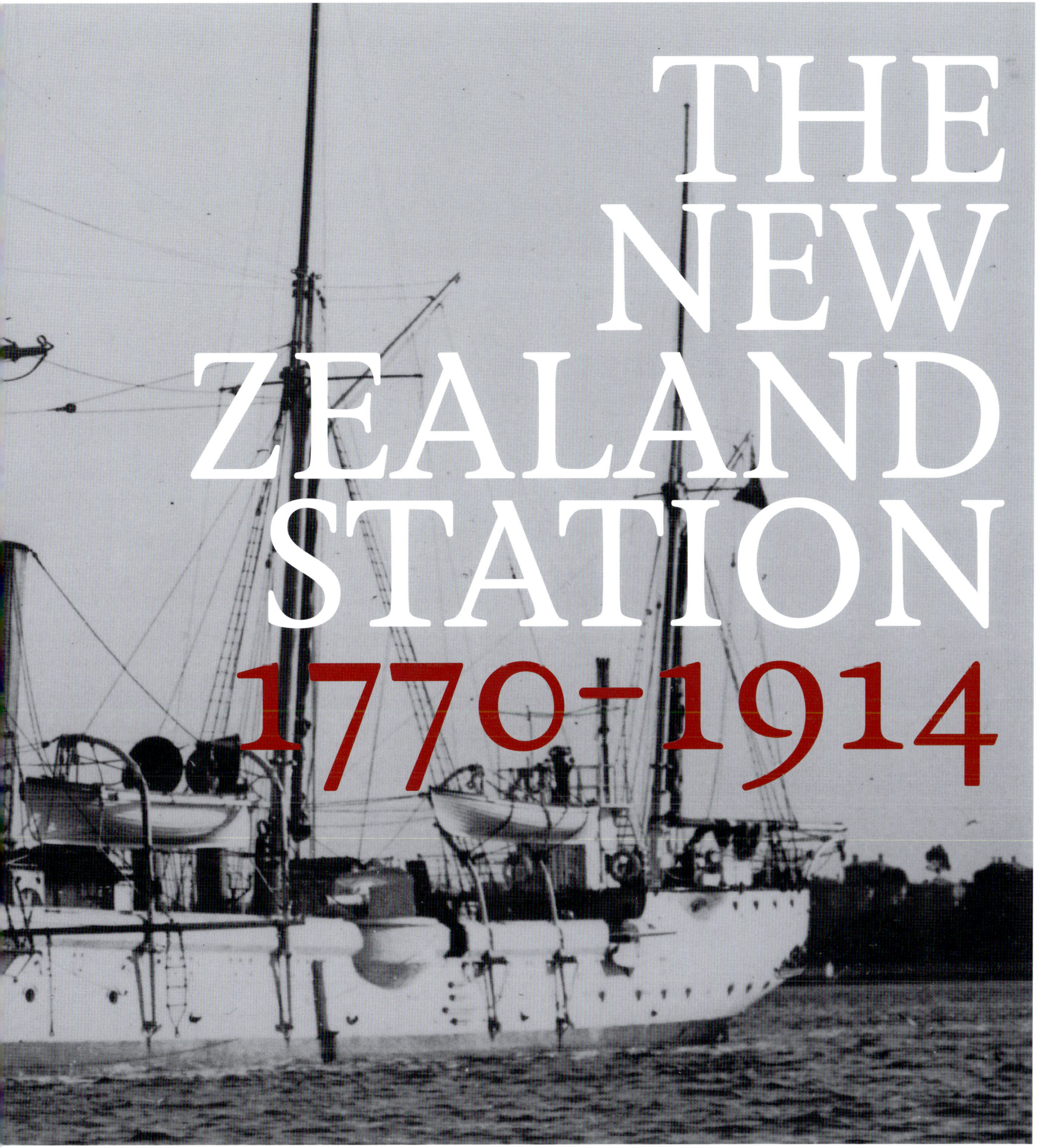

In the years following Cook's hydrographical survey of the coast of New Zealand in 1770 – presumably with the intention of ultimately taking possession of it as a British colony – the country was relatively neglected by the imperial powers. It was not until the French began to show some interest in this territory, and the increasingly lawless activities of some of its former citizens in this new land, that Britain was pressed into action.

In 1831 the French corvette *La Favorite* was spotted in New Zealand waters, causing rumours to spread that the ship's captain, Cyrille Pierre Théodore de Laplace, was intent on taking possession of 'La Nouvelle Zélande' in the name of King Louis Phillipe. However, rumours were all they were. Laplace anchored for a short period in the Bay of Islands to take care of the needs of a few sick crew members and reprovision for the remainder of his voyage around the world. Nonetheless, he is said to have compiled several survey charts of the area.

Whatever Laplace's intentions, his presence in New Zealand waters was enough to have the Colonial Office in Australia establish the post of British Resident in New Zealand. Thus in April 1833 James Busby set sail on board HMS *Imogene* from Sydney for the Bay of Islands. His mission, according to the 1966 *Encyclopaedia of New Zealand*, was: 'to exert a moral influence over the rough and ready settlement in the Bay of Islands by virtue of his powers of personal persuasion and the dignity of his vice-consul's uniform.' Neither persuasion nor Busby's impressive uniform quite achieved the desired results. Nevertheless Busby persevered. Although there was a naval presence in the Bay of Islands at this time – 14 Royal Navy ships are recorded in the area between 1833 and 1839, equating to two or three visits a year – it was hardly a daunting or constant presence.

It was in one of the inevitable lulls that, four years later in 1837, the French came calling once more – in the form of Baron Charles Philippe Hippolyte de Thierry who, as the self-proclaimed 'Sovereign Prince of New Zealand and King of Nuku Hiva, Marquesas', had decided to take possession of New Zealand. Busby was rattled enough to call a meeting of chiefs, seeking a reaffirmation of their faith in the continuing status of New Zealand as an independent state under the United Tribes of New Zealand. The colonisation bid by de Thierry was doomed to failure, perhaps due more to the gentleman in question and his hubris than any political manoeuvring by Busby.

However, with the Baron dispatched, Busby faced the much more serious problem of the

HMS Endeavour *off Young Nick's Head. Colin Wynn, acrylic on board, 1987.* FT 0905

James Cook

Captain James Cook RN (1728–79) was an English explorer, navigator and cartographer. Ultimately rising to the rank of captain in the Royal Navy, Cook was the first to chart Newfoundland before making three voyages to the Pacific Ocean during which he achieved the first European contact with the eastern coastline of Australia and the Hawaiian islands, as well as the first recorded circumnavigation of New Zealand.

Cook was born in the village of Marton in North Yorkshire on 27 October 1728, one of five children. In 1745, aged 17, he left home apprenticed to a grocer and haberdasher in the fishing village of Staithes. Eighteen months later Cook visited the port town of Whitby where he was taken on as a merchant navy apprentice in a fleet of coalers. During his apprenticeship Cook studied algebra, geometry, trigonometry, navigation and astronomy.

In 1755 Cook joined the Royal Navy, surveying and mapping much of the entrance to the Saint Lawrence River during the siege of Quebec. In 1768 he was given command of HMS *Endeavour*, a small bark that had seen service as a collier, and was instructed by the Royal Society to set sail for the Pacific in order to observe the passage of the planet Venus across the face of the sun. Cook was also, on secret orders from the Admiralty, instructed to search for the mysterious and elusive southern continent – Terra Australis Incognita – that was believed to lie in the southern waters of the Pacific.

On 26 August 1768, *Endeavour* set sail from Plymouth. Accompanying Cook were the botanist Joseph Banks, naturalist Daniel Solander, and Charles Green from the Greenwich Observatory. On 13 April 1769 *Endeavour* laid anchor in Tahiti, and the passage of Venus was duly observed. The first half of the mission completed, Cook turned his attention to the search for Terra Australis Incognita. What Cook found was not one major body of land, but two. *Endeavour* reached New Zealand shores in October 1769 and Cook spent six months off the coast compiling a chart that was remarkable in its accuracy, with only three significant errors: Stewart Island is connected to the mainland, Banks Peninsula is shown as an island, and the Waitemata Harbour is missing completely. Many of the place names bestowed by Cook, like Young Nicks Head, Queen Charlotte Sound and Cape Kidnappers, remain in use today.

Cook then sailed west, reaching the south-eastern coast of the Australian continent on 19 April 1770. On 23 April he made his first recorded contact with Aborigines, noting in his journal: 'four or five … Indians … naked and very black'. On 29 April Cook made his first landfall on the mainland at a place which he named Botany Bay. He continued northwards until *Endeavour* ran aground on the Great Barrier Reef. The ship was seriously damaged and the voyage was delayed almost seven weeks while repairs were carried out. Once repairs were complete the voyage continued and *Endeavour* arrived back in England on 12 July 1771.

Shortly after his return, Cook was once again commissioned by the Royal Society to search for the mythical Terra Australis. On his first voyage, Cook had demonstrated by circumnavigating New Zealand that it was not attached to a larger landmass to the south, and by charting almost the entire eastern coastline of Australia he had shown it to be continental in size. Nevertheless, the 'Great Southern Land' was supposed to lie still further to the south.

On the second voyage Cook commanded HMS *Resolution*, accompanied by HMS *Adventure*. Cook circumnavigated the globe at a very high southern latitude and on 17 January 1773 *Resolution* became one of the first ships to cross the Antarctic Circle. Cook almost encountered the mainland of Antarctica, but turned back north towards Tahiti to resupply his ship. He then resumed his southward course in a second fruitless attempt to find the southern continent.

Upon his return to Britain, Cook was promoted to the rank of captain, made a Fellow of the Royal Society and heaped with honours. Despite having retired from the Royal Navy, he could not be kept away from the sea. On his last voyage in 1777, Cook was once again in command of HMS *Resolution*, this time accompanied by HMS *Discovery*. The chief purpose of the voyage was to discover the famed Northwest Passage.

In 1778 Cook became the first European to visit the Hawaiian islands, which he named the Sandwich Islands. From Hawaii Cook travelled northeast to the west coast of North America and charted the coast from California all the way to the Bering Strait. Cook returned to Hawaii in 1779 and, after a series of confrontations between his men and the native Hawaiians, he was killed at Kealakekua Bay on 14 February, along with four of his marines.

exacerbating friction between the Maori population and the constantly growing number of Europeans who had started to arrive in various parts of New Zealand. The Bay of Islands, as a major port and very early mission station, was particularly volatile. Eventually the frightened pleas of the settlers – particularly when war broke out between the northern tribes – reached the ears of the Imperial Government. By 1837 the situation had escalated to such an extent that HMS *Rattlesnake*, under the command of William Hobson, was dispatched to New Zealand waters from the Royal Navy East Indies Station.

Hobson was entrusted with the task of surveying the opinions of New Zealand's residents, both Maori and settler, on a practicable means of solving the racial and cultural tensions that were arising out of their daily interactions and the settlers' need for land.

One of the many recommendations in Hobson's report was the suggestion of a treaty to establish British authority over the territory. Within three years, Hobson was to return to New Zealand as Lieutenant-Governor and Consul of New Zealand on board HMS *Herald* to take part in the signing by Maori and Europeans of the Treaty of Waitangi on 14 February 1840.

Shortly after the signing of the Treaty, Hobson, still on board *Herald* and in the company of the Reverend Henry Williams, sailed into the Waitemata Harbour seeking a suitable location for the ships of the Sydney-based RN Australian Squadron – as well as a capital for the new country. The Bay of Islands and Kororareka had outgrown their usefulness, and the northern Maori had proved to be less than friendly. The depth of the anchorage in the Waitemata Harbour, off the northeastern peninsula and below the nascent village of Devonport, made this area an obvious choice as a naval depot. (The ferry terminal now occupies the land that Hobson chose as the potential site for the establishment of a Royal Navy base.)

A signal mast was raised on what is now Windsor Reserve. It was soon joined by a weatherboard shed which served as both maintenance workshop and store, both of which were placed in the charge of a Lieutenant Snow who was also to act as signalman. Snow and his family lived in a raupo whare nearby. A magazine was erected a short time later a few hundred metres along the shoreline heading towards North Head. Dying in 1842, Hobson was never to see his navy develop much further than these few tentative steps. However, with some facilities in place, the Waitemata Harbour quickly became a regular anchorage for warships.

In 1847, Lieutenant Snow and his family were murdered, their bodies found in the burnt-out remains of their whare. The perpetrator, an escaped convict, was duly apprehended and hung at the scene of the crime. In spite of this tragedy, the increasing popularity of the Waitemata as a harbour continued and what had at first been a humble two-building affair expanded rapidly as the authorities, including the RN, responded to the growing tensions between Maori and the expanding settler population. While there had always been civil unrest in New Zealand, iwi being very factional, for the first time Maori had begun to react against the colonising power instead of one another. Hone Heke in the north was the first to boil over, rejecting British rule categorically by chopping down the flagstaff at Kororareka on four occasions before attacking the settlement itself in early 1845. It was just the beginning of

William Hobson

William Hobson (1793–1842) became the first Governor of New Zealand after a long career with the Royal Navy. During his tenure as Governor he was responsible for the drafting of the Treaty of Waitangi and its subsequent signing. While his time as Governor was not particularly illustrious from an administrative point of view, he remains a key figure in New Zealand's early post-European contact history.

Hobson was born at Waterford, Ireland, on 26 September 1793. Before the age of 10, he was sent to sea in the frigate *La Virginie* with the rank of volunteer, second class. A career at sea with the RN followed, with Hobson steadily rising through the ranks. In 1813 Hobson was appointed Lieutenant to the sloop *Peruvian*, and for the next 10 years served in the America, Channel, Mediterranean and West Indies stations. Hobson was promoted to commander in 1824, and the following year was commissioned to the sloop *Ferret*. He saw service in the West Indies, where he commanded several small vessels fighting piracy in Cuban waters. He married Eliza Elliot, the only daughter of a Scottish West Indian merchant, in Nassau in 1827 and, following Hobson's retirement, the couple set up home at Plymouth.

In 1834 Hobson was pulled out of retirement and posted to the frigate *Rattlesnake*, which was sent to the West Indies. Two years later he was detached from the West Indies Station command and posted to Australia. *Rattlesnake* arrived at Port Jackson in August 1836 and a month later was at Port Phillip, Victoria, where a new colony was being established. Hobson and his officers carried out a survey of the harbour and assisted in laying out the town of Melbourne. His work had scarcely been completed when Sir Richard Bourke, the Governor of New South Wales, received word from James Busby, the British Resident in New Zealand, of Maori unrest in the Bay of Islands. Bourke sent Hobson in the *Rattlesnake* to New Zealand under orders to protect British settlers. He was also to report on Maori–Pakeha relations.

In 1837 Hobson was ordered home and once again placed on the retired list. But continuing agitation by Maori forced the British Government to take action, with the result that in December 1838 it was decided to appoint a Governor. Hobson accepted the post and was given the power to negotiate with chiefs for cession of sovereignty of their territory. He would not be provided with a military force or be permitted to raise a militia.

Arriving in Sydney from England, Hobson sailed in HMS *Herald* for the Bay of Islands, arriving there in January 1840. With the assistance of Busby, Henry Williams and other leading members of the Church Missionary Society, he summoned the northern chiefs to meet him at Waitangi for the purpose of negotiating a treaty. After preliminary discussions and argument, the Treaty of Waitangi was signed by the northern chiefs on 6 February. Hobson intended to arrange treaty signings throughout the country for the chiefs not present at Waitangi, but on 1 March 1840 he collapsed from a paralytic stroke.

Many of the tribes had not accepted the Treaty of Waitangi and, of those that had, few appreciated what the sovereignty of New Zealand by the British Crown entailed, as the Maori and English-language versions of the Treaty contained small but crucial differences in their wording. As Hobson had no military force to support his authority, his relationship with Maori rested on a basis of mutual goodwill – a foundation which would prove inadequate to the task of brokering a mutually acceptable compromise between the settlers with their desire for land and Maori who wanted to retain their tribal lands.

However, finance would prove to be the major stumbling block of the Hobson administration. Although Hobson had been strictly warned by the Colonial Office to keep a tight control over official expenditure, little was done to curb overspending. The New Zealand Company seized the opportunity to attack the administration and pressed for Hobson to be recalled to Britain and another Governor appointed in his stead. Even at the Colonial Office there was a growing uneasiness, and on 28 February 1843 he was to be recalled to Britain. However, in fragile health from recurring bouts of yellow fever and his earlier stroke, Hobson died at Auckland on 10 September 1842.

As Governor, Hobson's greatest moment was the Treaty signing at Waitangi early in his tenure. And despite financial and administrative mismanagement, Hobson had many excellent qualities as Governor. He was a man of sociable habits and a good host, with a tremendous faculty for making friends. Deeply religious, Hobson had a well-developed sense of duty and of justice, was honest in his dealings and anxious to advance the interests of the Maori people. It was Hobson's misfortune that the weakness of his administration obscured the fundamental flaws in the policy of the Colonial Office, which was characterised by an impracticable and idealistic approach to 'the New Zealand problem'.

Portrait of Captain Hobson in gold frame. Painted by Doug Watkins in 1999 for the Heritage Hotel Apartments, Auckland, and hung in the 'Governor's Restaurant'. The artist used a period Navy Museum uniform as a model for Hobson's uniform. PAA 0036

The first New Zealand Navy

Edited extracts from: *The First New Zealand Navy; With Some Episodes of the Maori War in Connection with the British Navy* by Herbert Baillie. Printed in volume 53 of *Transactions and Proceedings of the New Zealand Institute,* 1921.

The early volumes of the *Illustrated London News* contain many illustrations of New Zealand scenes and incidents. I was particularly interested in those shown in the issue of the 30th January, 1864, among which was one of 'the gunboat *Pioneer* at anchor off Meremere, on the Waikato, reconnoitring the native position'. On looking into the subject of New Zealand's first navy I found that New Zealand had about that time quite an imposing fleet, which was manned from ships of the British Navy then on the station.

An urgent call for help had been sent to Australia, and in reply the Government of Victoria had lent its warship, the steam-sloop *Victoria* … which arrived at New Plymouth on the 3rd August, 1860. … The *Victoria* also brought a detachment of troops from Australia … [and] was engaged on the coast on various duties, including the transferring of refugees from New Plymouth to other ports.

A Naval Brigade under Captain (later Commodore) F. Beauchamp Seymour … was stationed at Waitara. … The brigade, which was in service 1860–61, was composed of men and officers from HM ships *Niger*, *Pelorus*, *Cordelia*, *Iris*, *Elk*, and the Victorian steam-sloop *Victoria*.

On the 28th March, 1860, Captain Peter Cracroft, HMS *Niger* with a force of sixty men and a 24-pounder rocket-tube, landed and captured the Maori pa at Waireka, Taranaki. … This is the action in which Seaman William Odgers won the first Victoria Cross to be awarded for service in New Zealand. He was the first man to enter the pa, and he hauled down the Maori flag[s]. He was promoted to be a warrant officer … and the Cross was presented to him on parade at Devonport, England, July, 1862.

In 1862 the Government purchased the paddle-steamer *Avon* for £2,000. This steamer … had been brought from England in sections and put together at Lyttelton in 1861. … On the 22nd November she left Lyttelton … with a crew of fifteen men from HMS *Harrier* in tow of that vessel. … The vessels arrived on the 26th November at Onehunga, where she was refitted and armoured for service on the Waikato River. She assisted in the rescue of survivors from the wreck of HMS *Orpheus* on the Manukau bar, 7th February, 1863, the men being transferred from the steamer *Wonga Wonga* which happened to be crossing the bar at the time of the disaster.

The *Avon* was towed to the Waikato Heads on the 25th July, 1863, by HMS *Eclipse*. … Thirty men were transferred from the *Eclipse* and

New Zealand Wars' 14th Regiment uniform button. CNH 0002

Pictorial dedication to William Odgers, Captain's Coxswain HMS Niger, *who was the first person to be awarded the Victoria Cross for service in New Zealand. Seaman Odgers was the first to enter the Pa at Waireka on 28 March 1860 and hauled down the Maori Flag.* PTB 0006

Carved wooden stern post from Devonport Naval Volunteers' vessel. SNA 0005

HMS Eclipse.

Commander Mayne took the *Avon* up the river to … a little below where Mercer now stands. On the 6th August Captain Sullivan … took the vessel on a reconnaissance as far as Meremere, where the Maori opened fire, which, on completion of observations, was replied to from the *Avon*'s 12-pounder Armstrong gun and a 12-pounder rocket-tube.

While the *Avon* was being fitted at Onehunga four large barges were brought overland from Auckland. These were also armoured with an iron-plate covering, and pierced for rifles and sweeps, or oars, …

In [June, 1863] a small paddle-steamer, the *Tasmanian Maid* … was purchased by the Government for £4,000. She was renamed *Sandfly* and armoured, being also armed with two 12-pounder Armstrong guns. Lieutenant Hunt … hoisted the pennant on the 23rd June, 1863, and his crew consisted of twenty-two men from the warships. … The *Sandfly* was stationed on the east coast of the North Island, her headquarters being Auckland. She took part in the blockade of the Firth of Thames and the Tauranga campaign. She captured on the 31st October the cutter *Éclair* a vessel of about 20 tons, owned by the Maori, and loaded with provisions.

The importance of having a suitable steamer for the navigation of the Waikato determined the Government to have such a vessel constructed in Sydney. … The *Pioneer* was launched from the shipyard of the Australian Steam Navigation Company, Pyrmont, Sydney, on the 16th July, 1863, having been under construction for a period of about seventeen weeks. … A report in a local paper, *The Empire* says, 'Yesterday morning there was launched from the A.S.N. Co.'s patent slip, Pyrmont, a rifle gunboat for the New Zealand Government, and intended for the service of the inland waters of the Waikato district. She is intended to carry 300 men, on a light draft of water. Her dimensions are 140 ft. in length, 20 ft. beam, 8 ft. 6 in. depth of hold, and draws only 2 ft. 6 in. of water. She will be propelled by an overhanging stern wheel, 12 ft. diameter, 7 ft. broad, driven by two engines, each 30 horse-power. She is constructed of 3/8 in. iron, which is pierced for rifles, and which will render her ball-proof. She is fitted with watertight compartments. The boilers were placed 54 ft. forward of the engines for the purpose of keeping the vessel on an even keel.' *The Empire* of the 15th September further reports, 'The officers' cabins are situated aft, and the soldiers' apartments forward; they are very large and lofty. She has a flush deck, on which are placed two cupolas, 12 ft. in diameter and 8 ft. high, each pierced for rifles and 24-pounder howitzers. The commander's station was in a turret above the engine-room, which was also shot-proof and placed aft.' … The cost of construction was £9,500. … The *Pioneer* in tow of HMS *Eclipse* left Sydney on the 22nd September, reaching Onehunga on the 3rd October, after a rough trip … On the 24th October the *Pioneer* with two companies of seamen from HMS *Curacoa* was towed by HMS *Eclipse* to the Waikato. At the same time the four armoured barges, or gunboats, were also taken to the river. … These boats were used in the different operations on the Waikato and its branches, and also in carrying stores.

On the 29th October the *Pioneer* … [landed] at Whangamarino, … the Maori position at Meremere … Shots were exchanged, but no damage was sustained by the vessel, which returned to headquarters. On the 31st October the *Pioneer* again proceeded up the river as far as Rangiriri, the Maori stronghold. A spot about six miles above Meremere was selected as a landing-place for a force of 640 men and twenty-one officers, with two 12-pounder Armstrong guns. This force was embarked on the *Pioneer* on the 1st November, and landed without opposition. During the afternoon it was found that the Maori had abandoned their position at Meremere, which was then occupied by a party of 250 seamen, under Commander Mayne (*Eclipse*), and 250 men of the 12th and 14th Regiments, under Colonel Austin, from Koheroa. This force was reinforced next day by detachments from the 12th, 14th, 18th, and 70th Regiments, amounting to 500 men.

On the 20th November General Cameron, with a force of 860 men, attacked Rangiriri. To assist in the operations an additional 300 men of the 40th Regiment were embarked on the steamers, to be landed at a selected point, so that they might make an attack on the rear of the main line of the Maori entrenchments while the main body attacked in front. … After a preliminary barrage by the Royal Artillery 12-pounders … the main body attacked the main line of entrenchments and drove the enemy to the centre redoubt, while the party of the 40th Regiment, who had been landed sufficiently near to reach their position, were able to pour a heavy fire on a body of Maori, who were driven from their position and fled

George Rowley Hill. AVA 0002

Percussion 'Pepperbox' pistol, c. 1865, from a collection assembled by George Rowley Hill (1837–1930). Hill served in the Royal Navy for ten years before joining the NZ Armed Constabulary in the early 1860s. He then joined the Torpedo Corps based in Devonport in 1886. FT 591

New Zealand War Medal, dated 1845–46, awarded to Able Seaman E. Scott. MBB 0002

Tin case with Admiralty badge embossed on front. Used to store Service Certificates when in transit between ships. GDB 0002

Figurehead of HMS Eclipse*, a Royal Navy frigate which served as part of the 'Waikato flotilla', 1863–1866, during the New Zealand Wars.* SFA 0003

towards the Waikare Lake, where a number of them were drowned. The centre redoubt, still holding out against the troops, was attacked [first] by a party of thirty-six men of the Royal Artillery, under Captain Mercer, who was mortally wounded, then by a party of ninety seamen under Commander Mayne, who was wounded. Both attempts were unsuccessful, as was another by a party of seamen … who used hand-grenades. As it was now nearly dark, the General decided to wait until daylight, when it was found that the white flag had been hoisted, and 183 Maori surrendered.

In a letter from Ngaruawahia dated the 4th December Wiremu Tamehana (William Thompson), the Maori leader, said that he had lost all his guns and powder. 'It is your side alone which is still in arms – that is to say, the steamer which is at work in the Waikato, making pas as it goes on; when they finish one, they come a little farther and make another. Now, then, let the steamer stay away; do not let it come hither. That is all.' But, as the Maori king's flag had been hoisted at Ngaruawahia in the first place, it was decided that the Queen's flag should fly there.

On the 2nd December General Cameron moved on from Rangiriri. As the outlets from Lake Waikare were not fordable, the troops … were conveyed up the river in boats manned by seamen of the Royal Navy, under Commander Phillimore. The following day the troops again moved on, and encamped abreast of the island of Taipori. Here General Cameron was delayed … until the 7th, when he moved the camp about five miles farther up the river, and met the Pioneer. Next day he went with Commodore Wiseman in the *Pioneer* to Ngaruawahia, which he found to be deserted. He immediately returned to the camp, and, after embarking 500 men of the 40th and 60th Regiments, again proceeded up the river, and landed at Ngaruawahia, where he established headquarters.

From Ngaruawahia Commodore Wiseman and a party of naval and military officers went up the Horotiu River, a distance of twelve miles, then transferred to the Koheroa and, proceeding twenty-two miles farther on (to near the site of the present town of Cambridge), located the Maori position, and returned. This incident ends the story of the British Navy on the Waikato River, though the steamers were used for some time longer on transport duty. Colonial crews were placed on board, and the Naval Brigade's operations were transferred to the Tauranga district.

Reinforcements, which had been sent from Auckland on HMS *Harrier* and *Esk* arrived at Tauranga on the 26th April [1864]. On the morning of the 27th the Maori had fired heavily on Fort Colville, but they were shelled out of their position … Captain Jenkins … took charge of the *Sandfly* which with the *Falcon* pursued the Maori who were retreating along the beach. … Both ships shelled the whares at Otomarakau. At 3 p.m. firing ceased, as the enemy had finally disappeared.

On the 29th April General Cameron made the attack on Gate Pa, with a force of 1700 of all ranks, including a Naval Brigade of four field officers, six captains, seven subalterns, thirty-six sergeants, five drummers, 371 rank and file. One hundred and fifty seamen and marines … and an equal number of the 43rd Regiment … formed the assaulting party. … The casualties of the Naval Brigade were … [in t]otal dead, 12; wounded, 29. Most of the wounded cases were classed as 'severe' or 'very severe.' For bravery in carrying Commander Hay, when wounded, off the field, Samuel Mitchell, captain of foretop, and captain's coxswain, was awarded the Victoria Cross.

The vessels [Baillie concludes] seem to have done good work, and all that was expected of them. It is to be hoped that the *Calliope* … gunboat, the schooner *Caroline*, the paddle-steamers *Avon* and *Sandfly* and the river-steamers *Pioneer*, *Koheroa* and *Rangiriri*, and the men of the British Navy who manned them, will not be forgotten in our histories.

what was to be a long and exhausting civil war between Maori and Pakeha over land issues that occurred sporadically all over the country for close to three decades. During this period of unrest, the crews of Admiralty ships provided many of the combatants involved in this struggle for the land.

As a result of the Land Wars, the nascent naval base begun by Hobson almost on the shores of the Waitemata Harbour expanded considerably in a remarkably short time. By 1864, when fighting was on the ebb, the shore facility included a barracks at Sandspit, a blacksmith's forge and a slipway. There had been some controversy involved in the building of the two-storeyed barracks block. Before such an endeavour could be attempted permission had to be obtained from the Admiralty. However, by the time the request for permission to build had arrived at the Admiralty and been discussed and duly declined, back in New Zealand it was a done deal. The barracks had already been built under the auspices of Commodore Wiseman. To say the least, the Admiralty was not entirely impressed with Wiseman's decision.

With the Maori rebellion well in hand by 1870, the citizens of New Zealand faced a new threat in the shape of the Russians. The rumour mill went into overdrive in the colony and it was widely believed that the Russians had ships in the northwest Pacific and were looking with lascivious eyes at New Zealand as a likely country to invade. Adding further fuel to the fire were various hoaxes such as the story in the *Daily Southern Cross* in February 1873 that reported that Auckland had been captured and held ransom by a force from a Russian cruiser. The story related how the *Kaskowiski* had slunk into the Waitemata Harbour – presumably under cover of darkness – and, with the aid of 'mephitic water-gas' and a 'submarine pinnace', had taken a British ship anchored there hostage. The ransom demanded of Auckland was £250,000 which, according to the feature, the town failed to provide in full. The Russians had fled with half the ransom money. The story was loaded with clues as to its fictional nature, but as always in such situations a great many people were fooled.

32-pound (6-inch) cannon ball fired by HMS Hazard *at Kororareka on 11 March 1845. Presented to the RNZN to commemorate the part played by the navy in the protection of the town during its early years of settlement.* JEB 0003

Snider Artillery Carbine .577 calibre. Used 1875–1900. JCB 0001

NZSM Badge. Submarine Miner Corps metal cap badge. T2008.2.1

ATF 0003

Again, in 1885, a report of a Russian ship attacking Wellington was, like the earlier story, pure fiction. Most interesting about these two incidents is the 12 years separating them – indicating more than a decade of preoccupation by the colony with the perceived Russian threat. Once the furore had died down over the 1873 incident, the article in the *Daily Southern Cross* highlighted the inadequacy of the New Zealand naval coastal defences – which was absolutely its intention. An invasion hadn't happened yet, but that didn't mean it couldn't. Something had to be done about New Zealand's extensive unguarded coastline.

In an expansion of coastal defences on both land and sea by the New Zealand Government, four second-class torpedo boats were purchased and the existing Naval Volunteer units, which were

AVA 0081

needed to man them, were formed into a single corps – which from June 1885 was known as the New Zealand Naval Artillery Volunteers.

In conjunction with the purchase of the 12-ton boats built by Thornycrofts, a number of coastal batteries were also constructed. By 1886 the fort on Mount Victoria in Devonport was almost complete. Three 8-inch and two 7-inch rifles and one 64-pounder artillery piece were installed on disappearing mounts. In the same year work began on the construction of a fort on Ripapa Island, in Lyttelton Harbour. It would take 10 years of using any labour available – from prison labourers to men from the permanent artillery – to construct these coastal defences.

Expansion of the dockyard and naval base on the Waitemata Harbour continued throughout this period. In mid-February 1888 Calliope Dock was ceremonially opened by HMS *Calliope* and HMS *Diamond*. So momentous was the occasion that a public holiday was declared. If the Russians or anyone else – the Japanese were also under suspicion in the years before the turn of the century – were going to invade, New Zealand was going to be ready. Although the graving dock may have been built in Stanley Bay for the Auckland Harbour Board, the implications for the burgeoning naval base in Devonport were unmistakeable. Following a period of negotiation in 1891, an area of reclaimed land at Calliope Point was offered to the Admiralty in exchange for the site at Sandspit. After the navy moved location, little development occurred until 1899 when an agreement was reached whereby the Admiralty subsidised the re-equipping of the workshops in exchange for using the Harbour Board's dock.

As the Russian threat never materialised, the anti-Russian fever that had gripped the country

Devonport Naval Submarine Miners cap ribbon. COG 0002

A crew member from the small torpedo boat flotilla that was established in 1885 in response to various invasion fears, and manned by New Zealand Naval Artillery Volunteers in the late 1800s. AVA 0106

ADA 0003

ADA 0065

Calliope Dock

The Harbour Board Dry Dock, which would become known simply as Calliope Dock, was opened on 16 February 1888 to a large and appreciative crowd. The steel corvette HMS *Calliope* led the procession into the dock, cutting the ceremonial ribbon as she arrived. HMS *Diamond* followed. Official guests included Governor Sir William Jervois; Admiral Fairfax, Commander-in-Chief of the Australasian Station; and members of the Auckland Harbour Board and City Council.

Construction on the dock began in 1884 after the work was contracted to Mr Pierce Lannigan, with the stone coming from Rangitoto Island. Like the excavation of the dock site, the stone was cut laboriously by hand. Nevertheless the dock, which was destined to be the largest in the southern hemisphere, took only a little over three years to complete. The spoil from the excavation was used in the reclamation of adjacent land that would eventually become the site of the naval base when it moved from Sandspit.

Since its construction, the dock has been lengthened to accommodate larger and larger ships and the naval base has grown up around it. During the Second World War the dockyard developed extensively, dealing with more and more work that previously had been handled in Britain. The dry dock remains in use still, over a century after it was opened with great fanfare on a summer's day in 1888.

Calliope Dock Menu. Auckland Harbour Board menu for the opening of Calliope Dock on Thursday February 16, 1888. EAE 0012

Coast Guard Artillery Pouch. Cartouche pouch worn by Devonport Coast Guard Artillery, 1890s. JGA 0014

Wellington Submarine Mining Volunteers. AVA 0011

waned, and with it the need for a flotilla of torpedo-boats and a unit of naval volunteers. The New Zealand Government had agreed to help fund the activity of Royal Navy vessels in Australasia, which was thought to be the best way of defending the New Zealand Station. This RN presence was to be an expensive endeavour, implying cost-cutting elsewhere in the New Zealand defence budget. As Grant Howard puts it so succinctly in his book *Portrait of the Royal New Zealand Navy*, 'the Naval Artillery Volunteers were doomed'. The torpedo-boats were taken out of service between 1901 and 1902, the end for the reserve coming in December 1902 when the manning of coastal artillery units was transferred to the Garrison Artillery.

Gun battery on Mt Victoria. ADC 0017

Petone Naval Artillery Volunteers. AVA 0023

However the loss of a navy in 1902 was to be short-lived and two years later the call went out for men to join the New Zealand Naval Forces. Such was the commitment to the establishment of the NZNF that a training ship was purchased, with an emphasis on general seamanship training rather than naval combat. An old gunboat, HMS *Sparrow*, was sold to the New Zealand Government in 1906 for the sum of £800. Commissioned as *Amokura* under Captain G. S. Hooper, over the next 14 years this double-rigged steam vessel trained some 527 New Zealand boys in the art of seamanship.

The area that the navy had moved to in 1880 was officially declared a naval base in 1909. The facilities expanded with this coming of age and included the construction of a set of sheerlegs – the gear used in the time before cranes to lift heavy weights on and off ships. The sheerlegs were a distinctive shoreline feature of the Waitemata Harbour until they were dismantled in 1934.

To say that Britain's attitude to New Zealand at the turn of the nineteenth century was paternalistic is something of an understatement. From a naval point of view, it is clear that New Zealand never made unreasonable demands over greater security in its own waters and a pattern was quickly established whereby whenever New Zealand made a request, the Admiralty almost always offered a compromise that was wholly advantageous to itself but which New Zealand would gratefully accept. This pattern was never to change while New Zealand's naval force remained an extension of a distinctly disinterested RN. It was not until after the Second World War that New Zealand gained naval autonomy from the mother country and began to look to its own needs rather than those of Britain.

In the early part of the twentieth century the Admiralty's hold over New Zealand's naval aspirations was so strong that when New Zealand, in response to the rapid expansion of German and French territories in the South Pacific, requested that the Royal Navy maintain a base in New Zealand, the Admiralty agreed to the deploy a number of its warships located in Australasian waters provided New Zealand and Australia pay for them. The two countries complied with this arrangement for many years despite the high rate charged by the RN for this 'navy for hire'.

The idea of a Pacific Fleet, with a unit based in New Zealand, was raised in 1909 at an Imperial Defence Conference in London. Although it was agreed to in theory, it was never to become a reality as Britain strengthened its naval capacity in home waters in response to the expansion of the defence capabilities of Imperial Germany in the northern hemisphere. Not only was the idea of a Pacific Fleet abandoned, but in the same year the New Zealand Government – 'as a gesture of patriotism and loyalty to the Crown' – offered to pay for one of the eight new battleships being built for the Royal Navy. The Dominion's commitment resulted in the passing of the New Zealand Naval Defence Act of 1909 which authorised the borrowing of £2 million with which to pay for the 18,800-ton battlecruiser. In return for this act of supreme generosity, patriotism and loyalty, New Zealand was granted naming rights when HMS *New Zealand* was commissioned for service three years later. Among its commissioning complement of 800 men were just three New Zealanders, lieutenants Alexander David Boyle and R. C. Garsia, and a midshipman, H. Anderson.

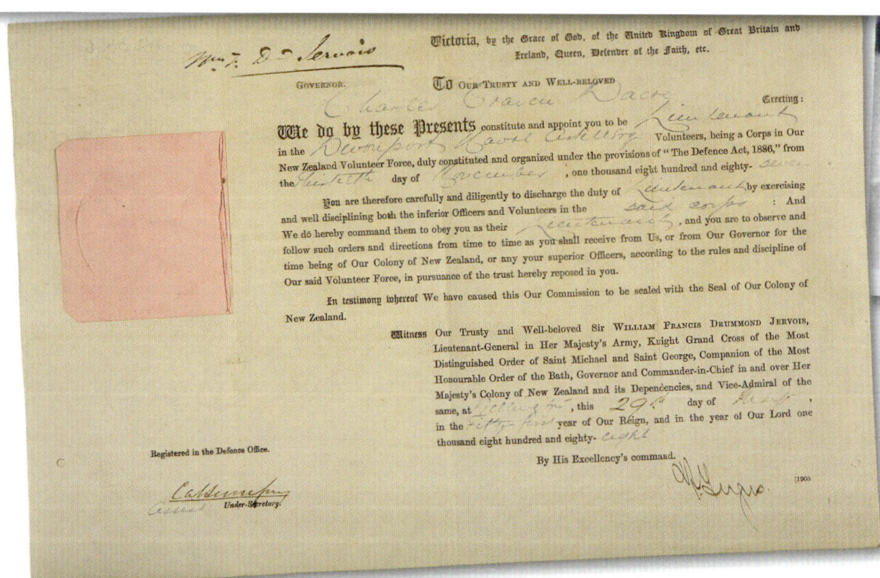

Victoria, by the Grace of God, of the United Kingdom of Great Britain and Ireland, Queen, Defender of the Faith, etc.

GOVERNOR.

To Our Trusty and Well-beloved Charles Craven Dacre Greeting:

We do by these Presents constitute and appoint you to be Lieutenant in the Devonport Naval Artillery Volunteers, being a Corps in Our New Zealand Volunteer Force, duly constituted and organized under the provisions of "The Defence Act, 1886," from the [illegible] day of [illegible], one thousand eight hundred and eighty-[illegible]

You are therefore carefully and diligently to discharge the duty of Lieutenant by exercising and well disciplining both the inferior Officers and Volunteers in the said corps : And We do hereby command them to obey you as their Lieutenant, and you are to observe and follow such orders and directions from time to time as you shall receive from Us, or from Our Governor for the time being of Our Colony of New Zealand, or any your superior Officers, according to the rules and discipline of Our said Volunteer Force, in pursuance of the trust hereby reposed in you.

In testimony whereof We have caused this Our Commission to be sealed with the Seal of Our Colony of New Zealand.

Witness Our Trusty and Well-beloved Sir William Francis Drummond Jervois, Lieutenant-General in Her Majesty's Army, Knight Grand Cross of the Most Distinguished Order of Saint Michael and Saint George, Companion of the Most Honourable Order of the Bath, Governor and Commander-in-Chief in and over Her Majesty's Colony of New Zealand and its Dependencies, and Vice-Admiral of the same, at [illegible], this 29th day of [illegible], in the [illegible] year of Our Reign, and in the year of Our Lord one thousand eight hundred and eighty-eight

By His Excellency's command.

Registered in the Defence Office.

Under-Secretary.

Naval carpentry building after fire, 1897, Devonport. ADC 0019

Commission of Lieutenant Charles Craven Dacre, 1888. DGH 0002

Robert Duke Hayward. AAA 0010

RNVR motor mechanics. ABX 0017

Volunteer Officers' Decoration presented to Lieutenant Commander Henry Parker, Devonport Naval Artillery Volunteers, 1895. The medal was awarded to commissioned Officers in the New Zealand Volunteer Forces who had completed 20 years' service. MAN 0011

Naval Brigade cap tally. COG 0001

HMS Philomel *alongside Devonport Wharf.*

AAA 0004

Amokura (1906–21)

Although *Amokura*, which was sold by the Admiralty to the New Zealand Government in 1906, was regarded as a non-military training ship, it had already seen service in South and East Africa with the Royal Navy from 1890–1900 and was on the Australia Station at the turn of the century. Originally named HMS *Sparrow*, the three-masted barquentine Goldfinch-class gunboat was laid down in September 1889 and commissioned on 13 May 1890.

As part of the ship's Australasian naval duties the *Sparrow* had regularly visited New Zealand and so was no stranger to New Zealand waters when it was purchased by the Government as a training ship for £800 in July 1906. After being sailed to New Zealand in early 1905, the ship had lain at anchor in Wellington Harbour for a year while her status as a training ship and purchase from the Admiralty could be formalised by Parliament. The steel-framed, teak-skinned gunboat was stripped of its armaments and converted for training purposes in early 1906 and was renamed *Amokura* later that year. The training ship, with an emphasis on seamanship, was transferred to the Marine Department for its day-to-day running a few months later.

Amokura received her first intake of 60 boys, all in their early teens, in March 1907. Although the ship spent the winter months in port in Wellington, well over a third of *Amokura*'s year was spent on training voyages which took it to various ports and island groups around New Zealand. It is estimated that 527 boys experienced the feel of *Amokura*'s deck beneath their feet

AAA 0021

between 1907 and 1921. As a result of this early training experience, 25 of them went on to naval service and most of the remainder joinied the merchant marine.

As sterling a service as *Amokura* was providing as a training ship, by 1919 the vessel was wearing its 30 years hard and it was decided that the ship was no longer to go to sea. In 1921 *Amokura* was paid off, having outlived her usefulness. The ship was sold in February 1922 to E. A. Jory who resold it to the Westport Coal Co. Ltd for use as a coal hulk. In 1940 *Amokura* was sold again and was towed to Kenepuru Sound in Marlborough to be used as a store hulk and jetty. As late as 1989 *Amokura*'s remains were still to be seen.

Class and type: **Three-masted barquentine Goldfinch-class gunboat**
Name: ***Amokura***
Builder: **Scott's S. B. & E. Co. Ltd, Greenock, Scotland**
Laid down: **26 September 1889**
Commissioned: **13 May 1890**
Purchased by New Zealand Government: **10 July 1906**

General characteristics
Displacement: **805 tons**
Dimensions: **50.3 x 9.5 m**
Propulsion: **1-shaft reciprocating triple expansion engine, coal, 1200 ihp**
Speed: **13 knots**
Original armament: **Guns – 6 x 4-in, 2 x 3-pdr, 3 x MGs**

In 1913, at yet another Imperial Defence Conference, the question of New Zealand developing its own naval force was again floated and once again the Admiralty rejected the concept, pressing for a continuation of the status quo of a subsidised RN force in Australasian waters. In the end, a compromise was reached whereby New Zealand would train men to become sailors and the Admiralty would provide a single training ship on which RN officers and ratings would provide a core complement of crew. Although the New Zealand Government would direct the day-to-day running of the ship, it would remain the property of the Admiralty and could be recalled for service in other waters if necessary. However, as a concession it was something of a coup. The ship sent was HMS *Philomel*, a third-class cruiser which had been commissioned for service in 1891.

The Naval Defence Act of 1913 marked the official establishment of the New Zealand Naval Forces and required young men to serve on a voluntary basis wherever they were needed – including wherever the Admiralty might need them. In addition, the Act contained a provision for the creation of a New Zealand branch of the Royal Naval Reserve. On 15 July 1914, the day *Philomel* was commissioned for service in Wellington, the possibility of New Zealand having its own navy was looking very achievable. On 4 August, less than three weeks after *Philomel* was commissioned for service and the day after it received its first intake of recruits, hostilities between Germany and Britain broke out and the establishment of a New Zealand Division of the RN, with New Zealand ships and crews, was placed on indefinite hold.

ABT 0068

HMS *New Zealand*

From 1904, Germany had greatly expanded its naval program and was rapidly building warships of all classes – a reality which lead Great Britain to rethink its own plans for naval defence. On 22 March 1909, at the height of this drive for the expansion of Admiralty capabilities, the Prime Minister of New Zealand, Sir Joseph Ward, made his offer to Britain of 'one first-class battleship and, if necessary, two,' as a gift to the Royal Navy. Unsurprisingly, the Admiralty agreed to accept New Zealand's generous offer. Although the battlecruiser was a magnificent gift, it would continue to cost New Zealand in terms of interest repayments on the £2.3 million raised in loans to pay for the ship for some 21 years after the ship itself had been scrapped.

An *Indefatigable*-class battlecruiser, HMS *New Zealand* was built by Fairfield Shipbuilding and Engineering Co. Ltd of Glasgow and was commissioned by Captain Lionel Halsey, RN, on 23 November 1912. Her original complement included three New Zealanders, lieutenants David Boyle and R. C. Garsia and Midshipman H. Anderson. Boyle would have the distinction of remaining with the ship for its entire career. There had been problems over the cruiser's naming, as another Admiralty vessel already bore the name 'New Zealand'. However, the new battlecruiser, paid for by the New Zealand

Mahogany sideboard from the Admiral's dining cabin of HMS New Zealand. *After the ship was broken up, the sideboard was shipped to New Zealand and was for many years in the Members and Spouses Lounge in Parliament Buildings, Wellington, before being passed to the Navy Museum.* SFB 0001

Launching axe in silver casket. Inscribed 'Presented to Lady Ward by the Fairfields Shipbuilding & Engineering Coy Ltd on the occasion of the Launch of Armoured Cruiser New Zealand *(C) 1 July 1911'.* GFD 0008

To
Captain Lionel Halsey R.N.
in command of
His Majesty's Battleship "New Zealand"

Sir,
On behalf of the Residents of the Grey, who one and undivided are loyal and devoted lieges of our Sovereign Lord the King, we tender you and your officers and men a whole hearted welcome to the West Coast.
As New Zealanders we glory in our connection with the mammoth of strength and power under your command and we welcome you a gallant officer and gentleman as the guardian of the honour and interests of our Dominion.
We wish you and your ship's company every prosperity and trust that H.M.S. New Zealand will ever be a factor in world peace. Should, however aggression make action necessary, we know that the noble traditions and glorious records of His Majesty's Royal Navy will be well and worthily upheld.
On behalf of our School Children we desire specially to thank you for your courtesy, kindness, and consideration.
We have the honour to remain,
Sir,
Yours very sincerely,
Mayor of Greymouth
Chairman of Greymouth Harbour Board
Chairman of Grey County Council
Chairman of Grey Board of Education

Greymouth N.Z.
June 6th 1913

Captain Halsey, 1913. ABT 0146

Scroll with a message of welcome presented to Captain Lionel Halsey and the Crew of HMS New Zealand *by the Mayor of Greymouth, 6 June 1913.* PTF 0003

public, prevailed and wrested the name from the existing RN list ship, which was subsequently renamed *Zealandia*.

After being inspected by the King, *New Zealand* sailed from Portsmouth on 8 February 1913 and arrived at Wellington on 12 April 1913. *New Zealand* and her crew were given a warm welcome in the country as the ship steamed round both islands. During her stay of more than 10 weeks in New Zealand waters, the ship was inspected by nearly half

ABT 0057

HMS New Zealand *silver tea set. Presented by the Auckland Harbour Board to HMS* New Zealand*, 1913.* FT 0369

Medallion commemorating the visit of HMS New Zealand *to New Zealand in 1913.* MDC 0017

a million people. *New Zealand* left Auckland on 25 June 1913, returning to England in November 1913. Nine months later, Britain was at war with Germany and *New Zealand* was seeing action in the North Sea. It was one of the few big British warships that took part in all three major North Sea naval actions – Heligoland Bight in August 1914, Dogger Bank in January 1915 and the Battle of Jutland in May 1916. *New Zealand* served out the remainder of the war with the battlecruiser force of the Grand Fleet.

Shortly after the end of the Great War, *New Zealand* embarked on a cruise of Britain's Dominions with Viscount Jellicoe on board to observe and report back to the Admiralty on the naval defences of Britain's Dominions. The ship was given another magnificent welcome on her second visit to New Zealand waters. After her return to England, the *New Zealand* was paid off into reserve and the warship was little more than 10 years old when it was stripped and sold to shipbreakers in December 1922 – a victim of the Washington Naval Treaty of 1922 which limited the naval capabilities of each of the treaty nations. However, the ship's 4-inch guns were sent out to New Zealand and were later used at Fort Dorset and Godley Head.

Class and type: ***Indefatigable*-class battlecruiser**
Name: **HMS *New Zealand***
Builder: **Fairfield Shipbuilding & Engineering Company Ltd, Glasgow**
Laid down: **20 June 1910**
Launched: **11 July 1911**
Commissioned: **23 November 1912**
Displacement: **18,800 tons**
Dimensions: **179.8 x 24.4 m**
Propulsion: **4-shaft turbines, coal, 44,000 ihp**
Speed: **26 knots**
Complement: **800 officers and ratings**
Armament: **Original configuration – 8 × 12-in guns, 16 × 4-in guns. Added later – 2 x 3-in AA guns, 2 x 21-in torpedo tubes submerged and 1 aircraft from 1917-19**

THE
GREAT
WAR
1914–1918

On 15 July 1914 HMS *Philomel* was commissioned, forming the nucleus of the New Zealand Division of the Royal Navy as a training cruiser, and placed under the command of Captain Percival Henry Hall-Thompson who also filled the position of Naval Adviser to New Zealand. *Philomel* was by no means a new ship when the New Zealand Division received her, having been first commissioned by the Royal Navy in November 1891.

With hostilities commencing shortly after her commission for use in the New Zealand Division, operational control of *Philomel* reverted back to the Admiralty and the recall of the two RN ships, HMS *Psyche* and *Pyramus*, which had both briefly joined *Philomel* on the New Zealand Station, was imminent.

A few days after war had officially been declared on 1 August 1914, the three vessels formed part of the escort for troopships carrying a composite force to occupy German Samoa. No resistance to the occupation was put up at Apia and *Pyramus*, *Philomel* and *Psyche* returned to New Zealand waters. Six weeks later in mid-October, *Philomel* left New Zealand with *Pyramus* as part of the escort for the New Zealand Expeditionary Force convoy bound for Egypt – and *Psyche* wasn't far behind. *Philomel* would not return to New Zealand until her oceangoing life had in effect come to an end in April 1917.

With *Pyramus*, *Psyche* and even *Philomel* now well out of New Zealand waters, things were looking rather dire for the New Zealand navy, particularly as the war was not as far away as it seemed. Although the northern hemisphere bore the brunt of hostilities, the war came to New Zealand's doorstep in June 1917 when a German raider began operating in New Zealand waters.

In November 1916 the German raider *Wolf* sailed from Kiel under orders to 'interfere with shipping in distant waters …', a task which it performed with extraordinary thoroughness. While operating off the coast of New Zealand, the *Wolf* laid 25 mines off the Three Kings and

35 off Farewell Spit. The raider then crossed the Tasman Sea and laid a further 30 mines near Gabo Island off the New South Wales coast. These minefields would ultimately cause the loss of three merchant steamers – the *Cumberland* off Gabo Island on 6 July 1917, the *Port Kembla* off Farewell Spit on 18 September 1917, and the *Wimmera* off the Three Kings on 26 June 1918.

As the New Zealand Station lacked a minesweeping force, two fishing trawlers, *Nora Niven* and *Simplon*, were quickly requisitioned by the Government and equipped for this role. A further two vessels, *Hananui II* and *Tutanekai*, were also requisitioned for minesweeping service, but the difficulty of obtaining a crew for the Marine Department cable ship and lighthouse supply steamer *Tutanekai* meant that it was not always available for operations, making *Hananui II* redundant in its intended role of accompanying *Tutanekai* and destroying any mines it found. Although *Hananui II* and *Tutanekai* played a minor role during the war, the minefield off Farewell Spit was swept a second time in the summer of 1919 by *Hananui II*. The New Zealand Railways workshops made the minesweepers four sweep kites, as none were available in the country at the time. In total,

Officers on HMS Psyche. ACJ 0531

Oak rum barrel. Used to issue daily rum ration until 1990. 1465

Copper half gill rum measure. 1465/2

HMS Pyramus *going alongside at Lyttelton probably during the cruise of the battleship HMS* New Zealand *around various ports of the home Dominion during the autumn and winter of 1913.* ACJ 1102

Mine at Great Barrier. AUO 0057

Mine Clearance Service Badge. Awarded to Signalman H. Middleton during the First World War. 863

Mine detonator horn from a First World War mine. JHB 0001

these vessels swept 17 mines off Farewell Spit and 18 in the Three Kings area – the mines unaccounted for were thought to have sunk or broken adrift. The captains of New Zealand's first minesweeping fleet were each awarded the Meritorious Service Medal for their efforts. *Philomel*, which by this time had returned to New Zealand for use as a depot ship, dusted off her cobwebs and was briefly recommissioned in 1918 as a base ship for the Farewell Spit minefield sweep. In mid-1919, three Flower-class RN sloops visited New Zealand to ensure that the minefields were clean. With the cessation of hostilities the requisitioned sweepers were returned to their owners and their commercial careers. *Nora Niven* was still operational at the outbreak of the Second World War and was once more brought back into service as a minesweeper.

New Zealand also contributed to the war effort at sea in other ways. Due to the quality of the coal from Westport's legendary mines and its superiority as a fuel for ships, much of the Westport coal output during the war years was

.303 Lee Enfield rifle used during the First World War by the grandfather of the donor (J. Baldwin). JCB 0019

.455 calibre Webley Mk V1 revolver. In use 1915–1923. JCC 0007

immediately exported for naval use – to such an extent that the domestic market had to be supplied with imported coal from Australia. In terms of naval war intelligence, New Zealand played its part in the establishment of a Naval Intelligence Centre in Wellington which reported to the Australian Commonwealth Naval Board in Melbourne. In addition, civilian radio operators were trained in naval communication procedures and kept a listening watch from New Zealand's marine radio stations which were incorporated into the Royal Navy's global radio network.

As Europe bore the brunt of fighting during the First World War, if New Zealand wished to support Great Britain in its hour of need its forces had to make the long journey to the heart of hostilities. They did so – in part, in the shape of the large contingent of New Zealanders who crewed *Philomel* and others who served in the many branches of the Royal Navy at every level.

In late October 1914, having been ordered to Singapore, *Philomel* left the New Zealand Expeditionary Force convoy to Egypt, for which it was serving as an escort vessel, off Western Australia. Along with *Pryamus*, she joined another convoy escort bound for Suez. After a refit in Malta, *Philomel* spent the next two years in the Middle East serving with the Royal Navy, first in the eastern Mediterranean and later in the Persian Gulf.

While *Philomel* was patrolling the Gulf of Alexandretta in early 1915, a landing party of two officers and 15 men was sent ashore to inspect a convoy of pack animals heading towards the settlement of Alexandretta for smuggled contraband. The landing party was ambushed, and Captain P. H. Hall-Thompson opened fire with the ship's guns to cover the retreat. As a result of this altercation with the Turks, Able Seaman J. T. Moreton, a New Zealander, in all likelihood became New Zealand's first naval casualty of the war. During the two years that *Philomel* was serving away from New Zealand waters, the ship lost six of its New Zealand crew. For the remainder of the cruiser's time with the RN, the vessel was sent to the Persian Gulf, a relatively quiet spot in terms of naval operations. Bearing in mind the ship's urgent need for an extensive refit, this was perhaps a wise decision. Captain Hall-Thompson noted that, 'owing to [the] foul condition of [the] ship's bottom', he was forced to cut the engines back to 100rpm – 'which would normally give about 13 knots but produced about 11'.

Thus, the ship languished in the Persian Gulf, far from the action. Although *Philomel* assumed a role of some importance during the campaign in Mesopotamia for a brief period in 1916, her duties were largely confined to keeping the peace and showing the Union Jack. When *Philomel* docked at Bombay in January 1917, an inspection of the ship revealed the need for extensive repairs. The boiler bearers were buckled, the main transverse bulkhead had worn thin, the plating under the boilers was in poor condition and the upper deck plating and ventilating trunks were in an advanced state of decay. After much discussion it was decided that, because of the cost involved in bringing the old ship up to date, it would be patched up for the voyage home to New Zealand – after

HMS *NEW ZEALAND* & THE NORTH SEA BATTLES

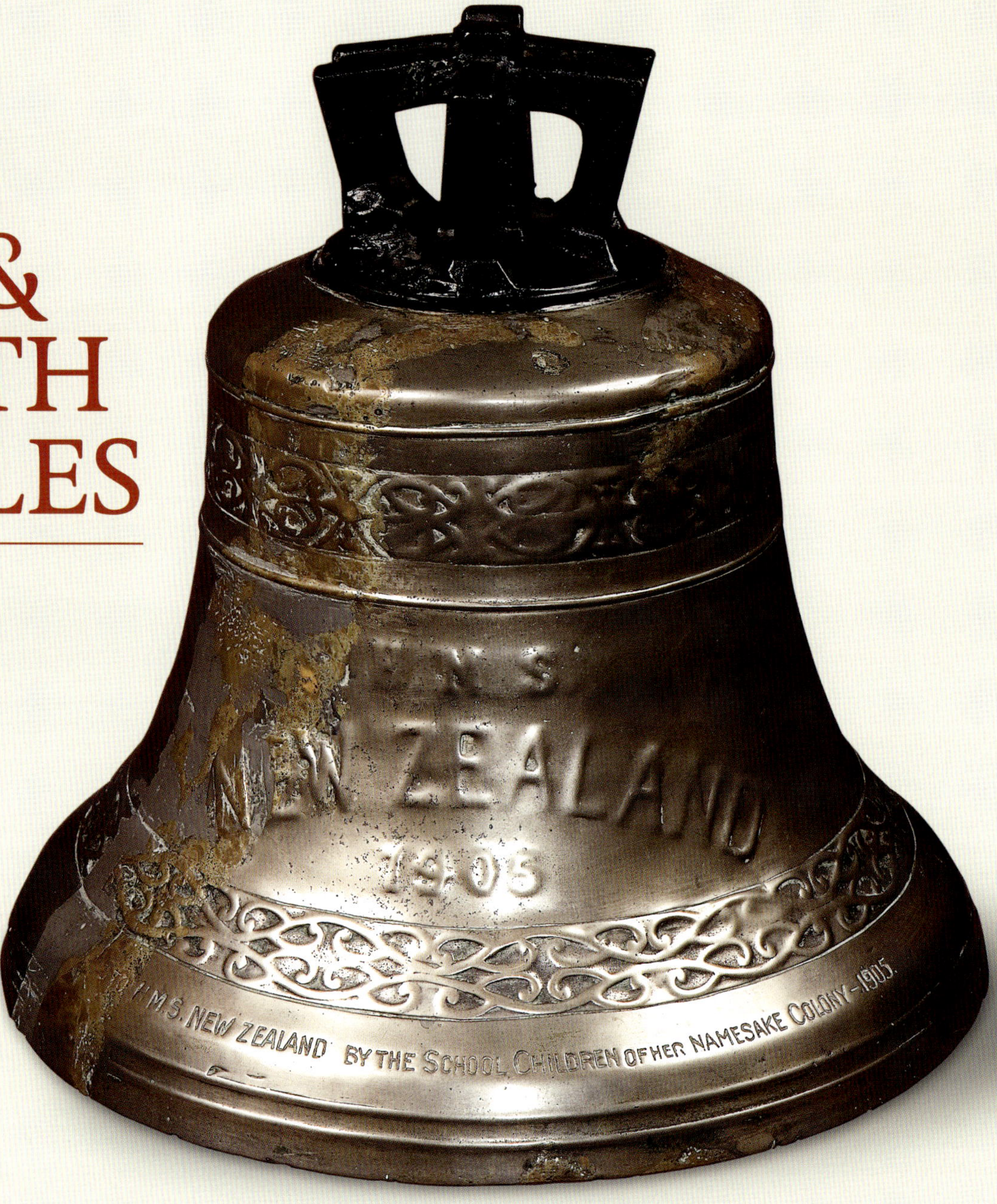

Representing the Dominion by proxy, HMS *New Zealand* was 'in the thick of it' during the three major battles conducted in the stretch of cold ocean known as the North Sea. In addition to the dreadnought and its handful of New Zealand crew, there were approximately 400 Kiwis on board various ships of the British Fleet during the engagements fought in the early part of the First World War.

Battle of the Heligoland Bight, North Sea, 28 August 1914

The Grand Fleet, as the main British battlefleet was called, sailed north on 3 August 1914, the eve of the declaration of war, and spent the very first day of the war in search of the enemy. An encounter with Admiral Friedrich von Ingenohl and his High Seas Fleet did not eventuate, as expected, on the fleet's fourth day at sea (or on any day thereafter), and the German fleet spent much of August sailing the waters of the North Sea unhindered.

On 28 August a raid was carried out on Heligoland on the north German coast to disable the port and put an end to the daily German anti-submarine patrols that were threatening submarines working out of Harwich. The British cruisers entered the Bight at dawn, engaging the German light forces that came out to meet them. However, as a result of what Matthew Wright in *Blue Water Kiwis* called 'abysmal lapses in Admiralty staff work', a state of confusion reigned as the additional British naval forces that arrived failed to identify their own ships and their positions, a situation no doubt exacerbated by the thick pall of smoke and haze created by the gunfire and smoke generated by the assembled ships.

Under the command of Captain Halsey – who appeared on the conning tower dressed in the Maori piupiu and tiki that had been gifted to the ship as good luck talismans when it had visited New Zealand two years earlier – *New Zealand* scored a torpedo hit on the cruiser SMS *Köln*. The German cruiser was sunk moments later by the guns of HMS *Lion*. In addition to *Köln*, the cruiser SMS *Ariadne* was badly damaged and on fire as it limped away from the fray. The Admiralty did not emerge scot-free, as the cruiser flagship HMS *Arethusa* sustained damage during the opening minutes of the engagement. Having made its mark, the British Fleet retreated. They had, according to the British papers, 'singed the Kaiser's moustache'.

HMS New Zealand *ship's bell. Inscribed [presented to] 'HMS New Zealand by the school children of her namesake colony – 1905'.* FT0038

HMS New Zealand *wooden battle honours boards with brass letters 'Heligoland August 1914', 'Dogger Bank 1915' and 'Jutland May 1916'. Now in St Christopher's chapel, HMNZ Naval Base, Devonport.* FT 0041-43

'Welcome to HMS New Zealand' sheet music. Song by Bert Rache with words by Margaret A. Sinclair, 1919. GGC 0004

Battle of Dogger Bank, North Sea, 23 January 1915

After learning of a German naval presence in the Dogger Bank area through intercepted intelligence in late January 1915, Vice Admiral Sir David Beatty (with five heavy ships) intercepted Vice Admiral Franz von Hipper and his command of three German battleships and an armoured cruiser at approximately 8 a.m. on 23 January. With the range between the two fleets closing, Beatty gave the order for his ships – which included HMS *New Zealand* – to open fire. *New Zealand* engaged the battlecruiser *Blücher*, crippling the German ship. The German flagship *Seydlitz* was also damaged. Realising they were outgunned, the German vessels went on the defensive and broke away.

When a British victory seemed imminent and the Admiralty ships were about to set off in pursuit, the British flagship HMS *Lion* suffered water damage to one of her engines and, losing power, fell back from the fleet. As *Lion* lagged increasingly behind, the flag signals transmitted by Beatty became indecipherable and the Royal Navy ships abandoned the chase, allowing von Hipper and his battleships to escape – the cause of much recrimination at the Admiralty in the days that followed. As Hipper disappeared at speed, attention turned to the floundering *Blücher*. Fired on at close range by the five British ships, the German cruiser stood little chance. The vessel bravely hoisted its colours a few minutes before midday and, less than an hour later, rolled over and sank, leaving its surviving crew adrift in the wintry North Sea. Although many seamen died, approximately 180 crewmen including the captain were picked up by the British ships. A zeppelin that indiscriminately bombed both the German survivors and the rescue crews hampered the rescue effort considerably.

The Battle of Jutland, 31 May–1 June 1916

With the German High Seas Fleet in command of the North Sea by early 1915 and proving to be a real menace to the Royal Navy, First Lord of the Admiralty Winston Churchill was desperate to see a turn in the tide. The long-awaited battle finally took place at the end of May 1916 after information was received that the Germans were planning an attack on Sunderland on England's northeast coat.

Four Royal Navy fleets were ordered to sea on 30 May. The next day, Vice Admiral Beatty, in command of six battlecruisers including *New Zealand* and four battleships, reached the RN rendezvous point. Von Hipper's cruisers were sighted shortly afterwards. Leaving the battleships behind, Beatty's cruisers closed in fast, opening fire on Vice Admiral von Hipper's ships when the range had closed to 15,000 yards. The Germans returned the favour, with serious consequences for the British warships. Within minutes of the action starting, HMS *Tiger* and HMS *Princess Royal* had sustained hits. Von Hipper's flagship *Lützow* engaged the British flagship *Lion*, which took a shell in the Q-turret. It was some time before the damage inflicted by the British ships on the German fleet began to show, but some of *Queen Mary*'s shells finally began to find their mark on *Seydlitz*. However, the RN ships were taking an even more severe pumelling and withdrew.

Unfortunately for the British Fleet, the German battleship *Von der Tann* had their range and remained in action when all the other guns had fallen quiet. Twenty minutes after the battle had begun, two salvos from *Von der Tann* ripped apart *Indefatigable* and sank it with all hands on board. Its sister ship, *New Zealand*, almost suffered the same fate a few minutes later when an 11-inch shell struck X-turret. Though no casualties were suffered, the damage caused was enough to put the turret out of action for 25 minutes. By this stage, the four RN battleships under the command of Rear Admiral Hugh Evans-Thomas had caught up and joined the fray. The German battleship *Seydlitz* was torpedoed and *Queen Mary* was slammed with five shells which tore the ship apart in a series of massive explosions, sinking it with incredible speed.

When the German High Seas Fleet under the command of Vice-Admiral Reinhard Scheer was spotted closing fast on the battleground, Beatty ordered his ships to turn tail. This tactical manoeuvre was intended to lead the German naval force towards Admiral Sir John Jellicoe and the waiting Grand Fleet. Again, poor communications were the undoing of the Admiralty ships and Evans-Thomas and his command of super-dreadnoughts were left to face both von Hipper's cruisers and Scheer's High Seas Fleet. Despite this setback, Beatty's ruse worked and the High Seas Fleet followed the RN ships towards the ambush set by Jellicoe's Grand Fleet which had finally arrived on the scene. A dozen hits were scored on the German ships before Scheer made the decision to withdraw and the guns fell silent. The German commander then made the unaccountable decision to turn back towards the pursuing British ships and the German ships again came under bombardment. Turning yet again, the German navy managed to escape into the mist.

Jellicoe pushed south to place the British ships in a position which the Germans would have to cross in order to return to their home ports and waited. As the day came to a close, the British cruisers spotted the German ships one last time, and *New Zealand* fired some of the last shells in the Battle of Jutland. To avoid further attack, Scheer passed behind the waiting British ships after negotiating the German minefields that had been laid in the area. Although the light British rearguard spotted the German fleet as it snuck through, and attacked it, the Germans escaped into the night.

Throughout the battle, Captain J. F. E. Green, who had taken over command of *New Zealand* from Halsey, like his predecessor wore the Maori piupiu and greenstone tiki given to the ship in 1913 with the instruction that they were to be worn by the captain whenever the ship was in action. The crew showed great faith in these taonga and there are stories of seamen looking to the bridge to check that the captain was wearing them as the cruiser steamed into action. Halsey had worn them in battle at the Heligoland Bight and at Dogger Bank and it was only right that Green should keep the tradition alive and adopt Maori dress for the Battle of Jutland. At Jutland, the third major sea battle in which the ship took part during the First World War, *New Zealand* came under heavy fire but was hit only once on her after turret and sustained no casualties.

After Jutland, the German High Seas Fleet was rarely at work in the North Sea – the British took charge of this important defensive stretch of ocean for the remainder of the war.

which it would be paid off, recommissioned with a small maintenance crew and continue operating as a stationary depot ship at Thorndon in Wellington Harbour.

Because *Philomel* was the New Zealand Division's only ship of any size, New Zealanders who wished to serve at sea during the war joined the Royal Navy and were dispersed among its various branches. Although these personnel retained a sense of national identity and pride in their origins, many wearing fern leaves on their uniforms, they were considered an integral part of the Royal Navy, virtually indistinguishable from the many thousands who served at sea during these years. Although technically Royal Navy personnel, the married men among these New Zealand 'hostilities only' seamen had their RN pay topped up to the level received by equivalent ranks of the New Zealand Expeditionary Force. During the First World War these Kiwi volunteers could be found at sea with the Grand Fleet, airborne with the Royal Naval Air Service, beneath the waves in submarines or on land providing crucial support for the first three branches of the service. In addition, a number stayed on to support the Allies during the intervention against the newly risen Bolshevik movement in Russia in 1919.

Carved pulpit with New Zealand coat of arms. Originally from HMS New Zealand, *it is now in St Christopher's Chapel, HMNZ Naval Base, Devonport.* FT 0070

Blue silk wall-hanging embroidered with the words 'Victory for the Allies' over the flags of the allied countries. Purchased in Egypt by B. D. R. Sprange at the end of the First World War. GEK 0010

AAC 0016

HMS *Philomel*

Motto: *Fide et Fortitudine* – 'By Faith and Fortitude'

Philomel was one of nine 3rd-class Pearl light cruisers built in Britain between 1888 and 1892, five of which were sent to Australia for service on the Australia station. *Philomel* was commissioned on 10 November 1891. From 1892 the ship served on the Cape of Good Hope Station, often sailing north towards East Africa. From 1897, the ship also served on the West Africa Station, taking part in the Boer War of 1899–1901. Unaccountably, the ship was paid off in March 1902 and *Philomel* languished in reserve until late 1907 when the vessel underwent an extensive refit in Ireland at Haulbowline Dock. *Philomel* was recommissioned on 1 February 1908 and in 1909 was sent to the East Indies Station in Aden. She was placed on patrol duty in the Persian Gulf until 1913 when the ship was selected by the Admiralty as a loan vessel for the New Zealand Station and was

AAC 0092

subsequently paid off by the Royal Navy. The ship was recommissioned for its new duties in October 1913 and was intended to serve as a training vessel for the nascent New Zealand Division of the RN. Sailing with her first intake of recruits on 30 July 1914, *Philomel* was immediately recalled and reverted to the Admiralty's operational control. The First World War broke out four days later, on 4 August. Initially operating out of New Zealand with two RN P-class ships, HMS *Pryamus* and HMS *Psyche*, all three warships were soon ordered to foreign waters by the Admiralty.

The war was cut short for *Philomel* in 1917 when it became evident that the vessel had long passed its best, and it returned to New Zealand to be commissioned as a stationary depot ship in Wellington Harbour from 20

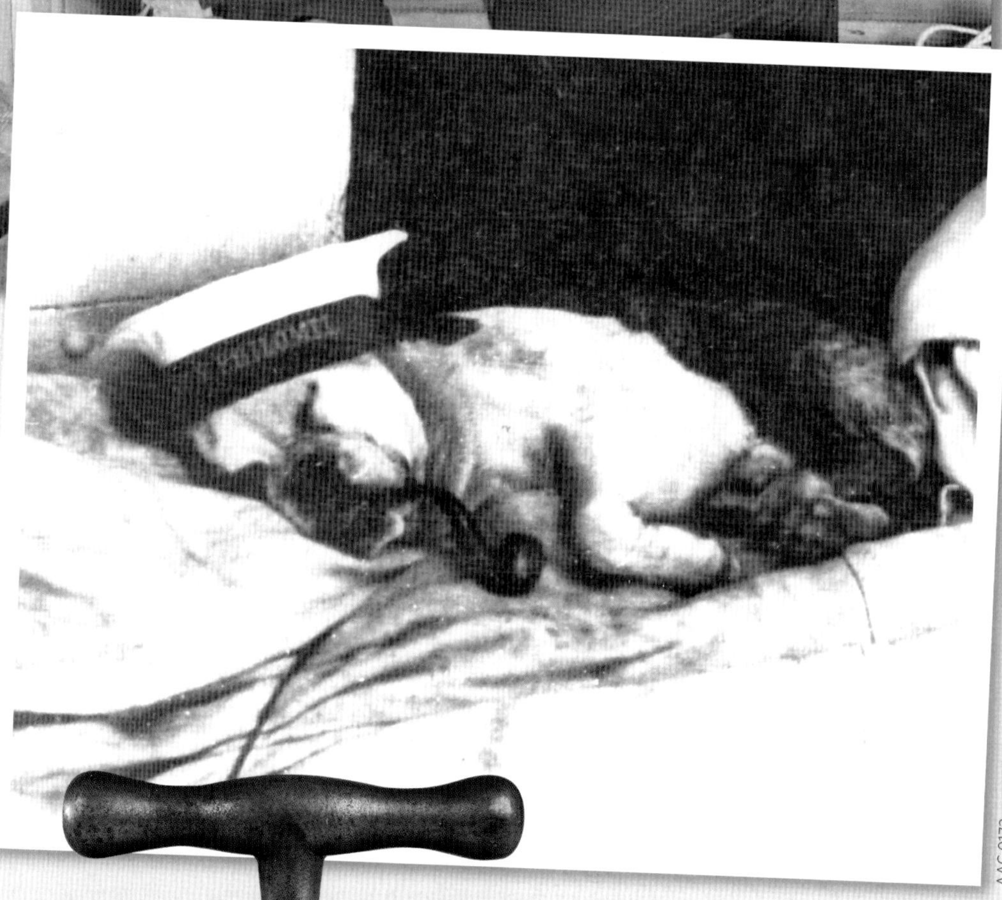

AAC 0173

Philomel *deck cleat. Brass boat or davit cleat from HMS* Philomel *1891–1946.* SDA 0003

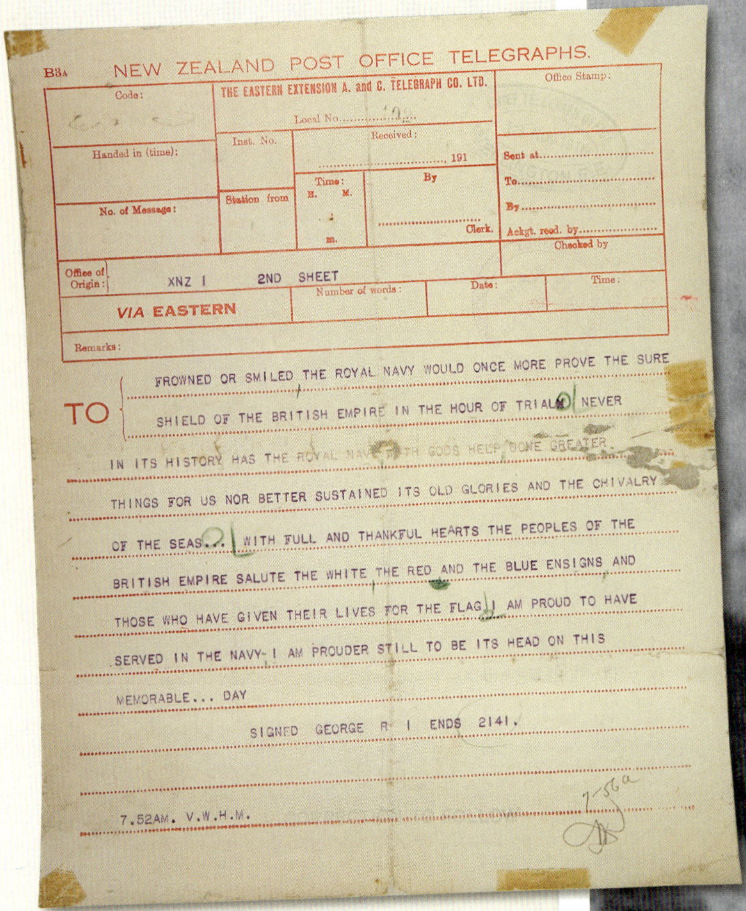

B3A NEW ZEALAND POST OFFICE TELEGRAPHS.

THE EASTERN EXTENSION A. and C. TELEGRAPH CO. LTD.

Code: | Local No. | Office Stamp: | Handed in (time): | Inst. No. | Received: ..., 191 | Sent at | To | By | No. of Message: | Station from | Time: H. M. m. | By ... Clerk. | Ackgt. recd. by | Checked by

Office of Origin: XNZ I 2ND SHEET

VIA EASTERN | Number of words: | Date: | Time:

Remarks:

TO

FROWNED OR SMILED THE ROYAL NAVY WOULD ONCE MORE PROVE THE SURE SHIELD OF THE BRITISH EMPIRE IN THE HOUR OF TRIAL. NEVER IN ITS HISTORY HAS THE ROYAL NAVY WITH GODS HELP DONE GREATER THINGS FOR US NOR BETTER SUSTAINED ITS OLD GLORIES AND THE CHIVALRY OF THE SEAS... WITH FULL AND THANKFUL HEARTS THE PEOPLES OF THE BRITISH EMPIRE SALUTE THE WHITE THE RED AND THE BLUE ENSIGNS AND THOSE WHO HAVE GIVEN THEIR LIVES FOR THE FLAG. I AM PROUD TO HAVE SERVED IN THE NAVY- I AM PROUDER STILL TO BE ITS HEAD ON THIS MEMORABLE... DAY

SIGNED GEORGE R I ENDS 2141.

7.52AM. V.W.H.M.

April 1917. The ship was briefly brought back into active service on two occasions – the first in 1918 to aid in the clearing of German-laid minefields off Cape Farwell and the Three Kings, and again in 1921 when it was moved to a new berth at the 'training jetty' at the Devonport Base, thus cementing another block in the formal establishment of the New Zealand Division that same year.

After being fitted out as a training ship, *Philomel* began a 25-year stint as a training and depot vessel, with her first intake coming aboard in May 1921. As her role as a training vessel evolved, *Philomel* underwent a number of modifications. The engine and boilers were removed to create classrooms, makeshift cabins were erected on deck as extra accommodation for recruits and armaments training was re-established. Many hundreds of recruits did their training on board the ship that gave its name to the naval base before its training role passed to HMNZS *Tamaki*, based at Motuihe Island, on 20 January 1941.

After decommissioning, *Philomel* was stripped by the navy and sold to the Strongman Shipping Co. Ltd of Coromandel on 23 December 1946 for the sum of £750. The hulk was towed to the Coromandel and run aground so that it could be completely stripped of steel, timber and the few fittings that remained. Once *Philomel*'s bones had been picked clean, the remains were towed out to the 100-fathom line, a dozen or so miles east of Cuvier Island, and sunk by means of explosive charges placed in her bow on 6 August 1946, 22 days short of a 59-year-long career.

Philomel lacked its own ship's badge until one came to light around 1926 – possibly the result of mess-deck patriotism during the First World War. When the RNZN began formalising ships' badges in the late

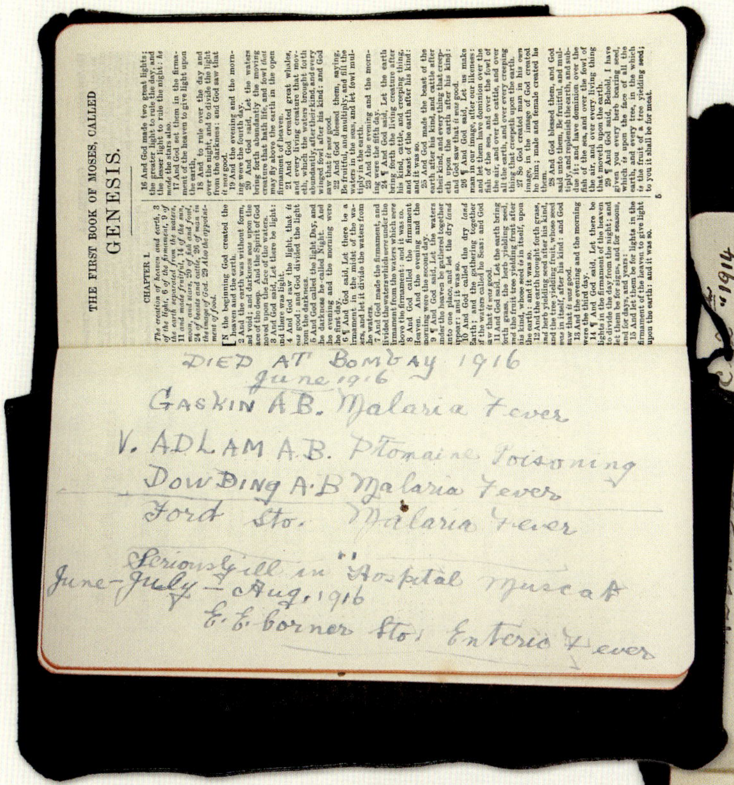

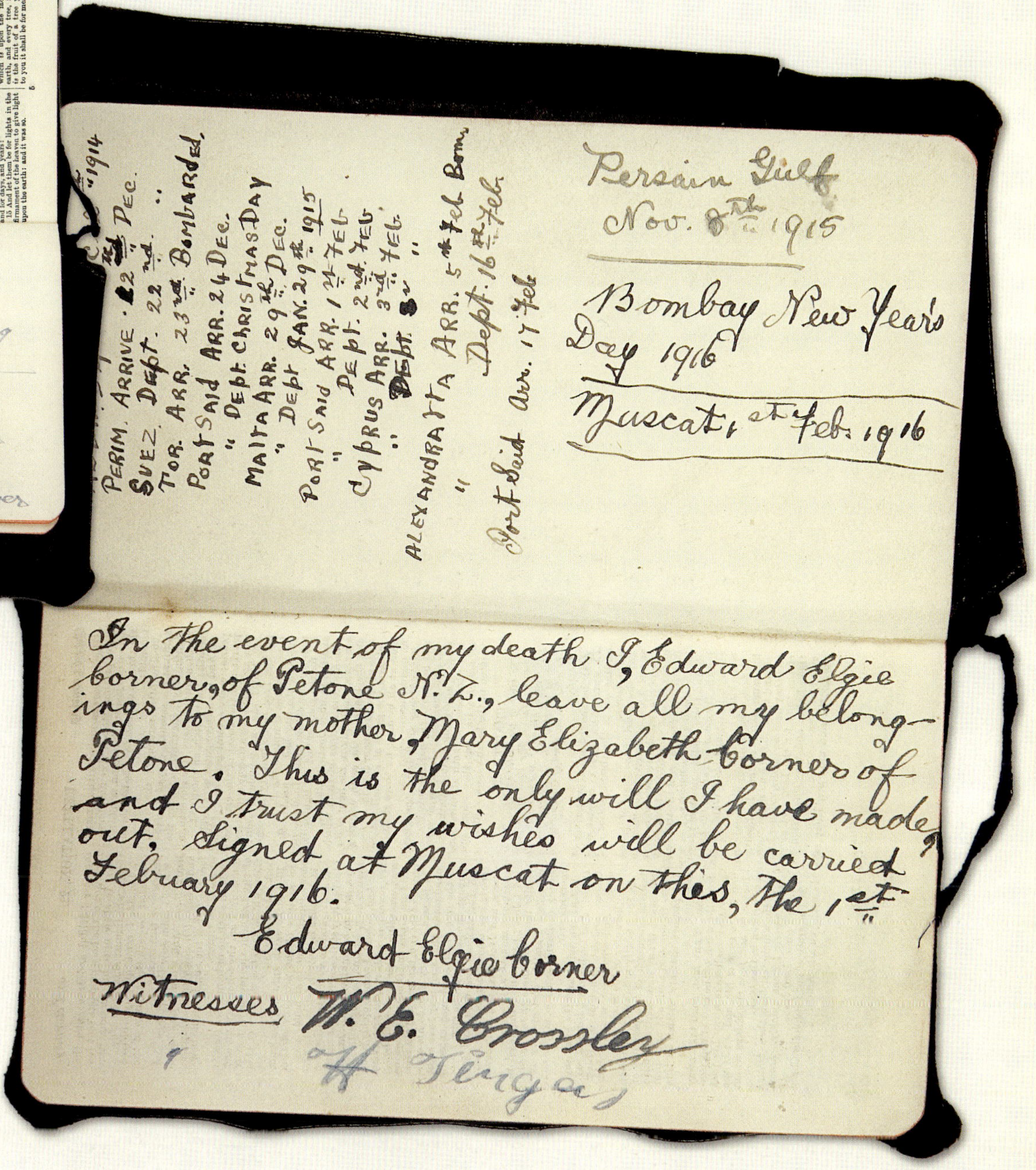

1950s, the unofficial badge that had been in use over the years was inspected by the Naval Board and the College of Heralds and deemed unsuitable. A number of alternatives were suggested, and in the end, the figure of Philomela, the unfortunate princess of Greek mythology, holding a nightingale became the official ship's badge. However, the figure of Philomela was ripe for reinvention and for a period in the mid-1960s she was sometimes depicted as a Maori wahine. Despite a push to have her officially recast as a Maori maiden, tradition prevailed.

Class and type: **Third-class Pearl light cruiser**
Name: **HMS *Philomel***
Builder: **HM Naval Dockyard, Devonport, Plymouth**
Laid down: **9 May 1889**
Launched: **28 August 1890**
Commissioned: **10 November 1891**
Commissioned New Zealand Division: **October 1913**

General characteristics
Displacement: **2575 tons standard**
Dimensions: **84.7 x 12.5 m**
Propulsion: **2-shaft reciprocating, coal, 7500 ihp**
Speed: **19 knots**
Complement: **220 officers and ratings**
Armament: **Guns – 8 x 4.7-in, 8 x 3 pdr, torpedo tubes – 2 x 14-in**

Original telegram from HM King George V issued to all ships, 11 November 1918. EGB 0004

Bill, Philomel*'s dog.* ABY 0072

Leather-bound Bible belonging to Stoker E. E. Corner, who served in HMS Philomel*. Inside the Bible is a list of dates when the ship was visiting various ports and taking part in actions as well as a list of all the men who died on HMS* Philomel *during the period 1915–1916. In the back of the bible is Corner's will.* DJA 0011

Nearly 200 New Zealanders volunteered for the Motor Boat Reserve, many of whom distinguished themselves in action. Although service in the MBR was essential if largely uneventful, a number of New Zealanders in the reserve were involved in the raids on Ostend and Zeebrugge in April and May 1918, and around a third of them were decorated for their endeavours.

A handful of New Zealanders also served in HMS *New Zealand*, the battleship that their nation had gifted to Britain as a show of support for the Empire. The ship, as Matthew Wright observes in *Blue Water Kiwis*, 'fought for the Dominion by proxy, a patriotic focus of national and imperial pride for most New Zealanders'. And the dreadnought gave the nation much to be proud of, acquitting itself magnificently in the three major battles of the North Sea: Heligoland Bight, Dogger Bank and Jutland. One of its New Zealand crew, Lieutenant Commander David Boyle from Christchurch, had the distinction of serving on board the battleship for all of its (albeit abbreviated) life, from commissioning in November 1912 to its end in a shipbreaker's yard a decade later in 1922.

Beyond the acts of gallantry, the decorations for bravery above and beyond the call of duty and the names inscribed into the pages of history were the many New Zealanders who saw out the Great War in the Royal Navy as largely unsung heroes – those who survived to return home and those who didn't make it.

The best-known of the German raiders to operate in the South Pacific was undoubtedly Count Felix von Luckner. Offered the command of captured American clipper *Pass of Bahama* (renamed *Seeadler* – sea-eagle) in late

William Edward Sanders VC, DSO 7 February 1883–14 August 1917

William Sanders was a New Zealand recipient of the Victoria Cross – the highest and most prestigious award for gallantry that can be awarded to British and Commonwealth forces – for his efforts against enemy submarines while in command of HMS *Prize*, a Q-ship. Sanders was regarded by the Admiralty as a highly experienced and intelligent sailor. Having worked on steam and sailing ships for over a decade before the outbreak of hostilities, he gained rapid promotion through the ranks of the Royal Navy and gained command of his own ship within a year of joining the Royal Naval Reserve.

The son of Edward Holman Cook Sanders, bootmaker, and Emma Jane Sanders (née Wilson), William Sanders was born in Kingsland, Auckland, on 7 February 1883. He was educated at Nelson Street and Takapuna primary schools and, on leaving school aged 15, he was placed by his parents with a Queen Street mercer – although he had long expressed an interest in the sea and wanted to make it his vocation. He lasted a year with the mercer before signing on with the steamer *Koiti* in 1899 as a cabin boy. In just 12 years he rose through the ranks while serving in both sail and steam vessels, from cabin boy to master mariner. In 1906 he joined *Aparima*, a Union Steamship Company vessel, and this was followed by the Government steamer *Hinemoa*. Before transferring to the Craig Line, Sanders spent two years on the Jagger and Mitchelson barquentine *Sonorita* operating between Australia and New Zealand.

On the outbreak of war in 1914 Sanders volunteered for the navy. When his application was rejected, he joined the troop carriers HMNZT *Willochra* and HMNZT *Tofua* which were transporting New Zealand troops to the Middle East. In less than six months Sanders had left the troopships and joined the tramp steamer *Hebbern Jan* which was heading for Britain. Arriving in Scotland 12 weeks later, Sanders promptly caught a train to London and volunteered for the Royal Navy. Commissioned as temporary sub lieutenant in the Royal Navy Reserves on 19 April 1916, Sanders was sent to HMS *Excellent* to do a three-month-long junior officers' course before being appointed in rapid succession to HMS *Sabrina*, HMS *Idaho* and HMS *Heligoland Morley* – as second in command – on 6 September 1916. Within six months, Sanders had been promoted twice – to lieutenant on 5 February 1917, and to lieutenant-commander on 25 April 1917. In addition, he was given command of HMS *Prize* – a spoils-of-war ship, as the name suggests. A three-masted merchant schooner, it had been captured from the Germans in the early day of the war. While *Prize*'s appearance as a merchant ship was retained, the vessel was equipped with concealed armaments and operated as a 'bait' ship to lure and destroy German submarines.

Less than a week after Sanders' promotion to lieutenant-commander, HMS *Prize* was on patrol south off the Irish coast at latitude 49.44 N, longitude 11.42 W, when she was sighted and engaged on 30 April by a German submarine, U-93. The vessel was commanded by Lieutenant Commander Freiherr von Spiegel, who took *Prize* for a merchant ship. After the 'panic party' from *Prize* had taken to the whaler and the ship appeared to be sinking – all part of the 'merchant ship' charade – the U-boat approached to within 80 yards of her port quarter. Although *Prize* was holed at the waterline in three places and the engine room set ablaze, Sanders held his fire till the submarine had moved in for the kill. When the submarine finally came into range, Sanders had the White Ensign hoisted and opened fire. Within a few minutes the submarine was on fire and her bows rose into the air. The U-boat disappeared from sight, and was believed to have been sunk by both the crew of the *Prize* and several of the German crew – including her captain, who had ended up in the sea when the submarine started to go down.

Sanders, who had been cool and resourceful in action, proved equally capable in directing emergency repairs to the badly damaged *Prize*, which reached Kinsale Harbour in Ireland after two days of steaming on a single auxiliary engine. Although the U-93 was justifiably claimed as sunk, her second in command had managed to regain control of the stricken U-boat and had nursed it safely home to Germany – where no doubt he gave an accurate description of their opponent and its siren song to unsuspecting submarines. For this action Sanders, was awarded the Victoria Cross.

Prize fought a further engagement by a German submarine on 12 June 1917 and Sanders added the Distinguished Service Order to his Victoria Cross. It had been a very eventful few months. However, Sanders' run of luck doing an extraordinarily dangerous job was soon to come to an end. In mid-August 1917 *Prize* was again acting as a lure in the Atlantic off the south coast of Ireland, accompanied by a well-concealed British submarine, D-6. On the day in question, 13 August, *Prize* twice sighted a German periscope and subsequently engaged U-48 directly, as the British submarine was unable to manoeuvre into position to attack with its torpedoes as arranged. *Prize* scored two hits before the submarine slipped away. However, the German submarine remained below the surface, stalking the Q-ship, waiting for its chance to torpedo it. At 1.30 a.m. the following morning, just as the escorting British submarine, D-6, had surfaced to recharge her batteries, the enemy U-boat struck, firing two torpedoes into *Prize*, destroying the ship and taking the lives of her crew and commander.

In June 1918, Sanders' father received his son's VC and DSO from the Governor-General of New Zealand at Auckland Town Hall.

First World War motor launch. ABX 0132

Motor launch spark plug. SSG 0001

Imperial German Navy ensign made from a flour bag at Motuihe Island Internment Camp by POWs from SMS Seeadler. *The ensign is believed to have been flown during the escape of the Germans, led by Count von Luckner, from Motuihe in December 1917.* SFD 0008

1916, von Luckner was responsible for sinking 86,000 tons of Allied shipping with the loss of just one life during his near-mythical 224 days at sea. Much of von Luckner's success came from his ability to pass off *Seeadler* as a merchant ship and thus catch Allied shipping off guard. While in the Atlantic, von Luckner captured three steamships and a number of sailing boats, taking many prisoners whom he released onto a French clipper – even though he knew that such an act would give away his location and compromise his activity in the Atlantic.

Von Luckner moved to the South Pacific, where merchant shipping and the much-needed supplies it provided for the German raider were scant, eventually forcing *Seeadler* to go ashore to reprovision. In late July 1917 the ship made anchor at Mopelia in the Society Islands. It had been there only a few days when a freak tidal wave smashed it against the reef, severely damaging the clipper and leaving von Luckner and his crew without a ship. Von Luckner decided to sail the ship's whaler to the Cook Islands with a group of hand-picked men in the hope of capturing a ship and sailing it back to the Society Islands to retrieve the rest of the crew. The 18-foot open whaler, which leaked even after extensive repairs, was christened *Kronprinzessin Cecile* and set sail for Atiu where the crew found nothing to their purpose. Nor was there a suitable ship to be taken at Aitutaki – and the men had the bad luck to be identified as Germans, leaving von Luckner and his crew with no choice but to set sail again. Von Luckner decided that Fiji should be their next destination and, due to remarkable seamanship and a good dose of luck, *Kronprinzessin Cecile* eventually arrived in Katafanga in the Fiji Islands.

After resting for several days, the party made its way to Wakaya where several likely looking ships awaited their perusal. A fantastic (and, as it proved, unbelievable) story was concocted by von Luckner in which the German naval men became Dutch-American sailors crossing the Atlantic on a wager. Suspicious that the strangers were in fact Germans, Sub-Inspector Hill of the Fiji police force chartered a steamer and went to Wakaya to investigate. Von Luckner and his men were on board a schooner when Hill, armed only with a single revolver, and half a dozen policemen came looking for them. By hinting that the canvas-covered objects on the charter boat's deck were guns, Hill was able to bluff the much more heavily armed German party into surrendering. Von Luckner was said to be outraged when he later learned that he had been resoundingly fooled.

The captured Germans spent a period of time in jail in Fiji before being transferred to *Tulane* for passage to New Zealand. After a brief holding period in the Devonport torpedo yard, the group was sent to Wellington where the crew was transferred to Somes Island. Von Luckner stood trial and was subsequently incarcerated on Motuihe Island in the Hauraki Gulf, very much separated from his crew still in Wellington. During the First World War Motuihe, like Somes Island, was used as an internment camp for Germans from Samoa, which had been captured very early on in the war, as well as other German nationals. While von Luckner did not lack distraction and conversation, it was not sufficient to prevent him from devising an escape plan to accompany the good deal of escape equipment that the long-term prisoners had collected.

On 13 December 1917, during a stormy night a mere three weeks after his arrival, the barracks

were set on fire, telephone communication with the mainland was terminated and von Luckner, a German officer and seven merchant navy cadets escaped in the island's motorboat *Pearl*. A search of the Hauraki Gulf turned up no sign of the Germans and it was thought that a high sea had put paid to their escape plan and that *Pearl* had foundered. However, von Luckner and his eight companions had made landfall at Red Mercury Island. Audacious to a fault, he immediately began making plans to capture two traders, *Rangi* and *Moa*, that the escapees had spotted near the island. The aim was to take both, sinking one and sailing the other to freedom. *Rangi* got away, but *Moa* was taken by the Germans, who signed on its crew as civilians who were eligible for pay during the period of their incarceration on what was now an enemy boat, and set a course for the Kermadec Islands.

Although hit by a storm that resulted in the loss of *Pearl*, which was under tow, as well as much of *Moa*'s deck cargo, *Moa* and her crew made it to their destination, arriving on 21 December 1917. The plan to leave the captured crew at the government stores cache in the Kermadecs was abandoned due to the presence of noxious volcanic gases, so a decision was made to take them to Macauley Island and transmit a radio message disclosing their location so that they could be picked up. But before this could be done the armed steamer *Iris*, which had been in hot pursuit of the Count, caught up with *Moa*. The Germans attempted to escape but flight was futile and von Luckner and his men were forced to surrender for a second time.

Arriving back in New Zealand, the Count and his comrades spent two weeks in Mt Eden jail before being dispersed to various prison camps. Von Luckner and a Lieutenant Kircheiss were sent to Fort Jervois on Ripapa Island in Lyttelton Harbour, where they proved to be popular with their captors. However, refusing to give up, von Luckner began immediately to

APO 0002

Count Felix Nikolaus Alexander Georg von Luckner 9 June 1881–13 April 1966

Count Felix von Luckner's determination to wage war without incurring casualties either on board his own ship or those of his enemies has made him a true hero and legend of the First World War. During the course of his exploits at sea between 1916 and 1917 only a single accidental death was incurred. Although very much a man of war, and although he was known as Der Seeteufel (the Sea-Devil), von Luckner believed in sinking ships and destroying cargo, not taking lives. The unfortunate fatality was Douglas Page, a seaman from the freighter *Horngarth* who died after having being scalded by steam released from a cracked pipe damaged by a shell from von Luckner's clipper SMS *Seeadler*.

Born into a noble family in Dresden, Germany, on 9 June 1881, accounts of von Luckner's early life vary tremendously – especially as the most unreliable source on von Luckner was the man himself who was, to say the least, fond of a good story. In *Blue Water Kiwis*, Matthew Wright argues that, because of his loathing for horses, he deserted the cavalry in 1895 at the age of 14 and went to sea. Other more fanciful versions of his childhood include the story of how, at the age of 13, von Luckner ran away from home to see Buffalo Bill's Wild West Show. According to his own account, he signed up, under the assumed name of 'Phylax Lüdecke', as an unpaid cabin boy on the Russian sailing ship *Niobe* travelling between Hamburg (Germany) and Australia.

Arriving at Fremantle, Western Australia, von Luckner jumped ship and claims that he spent the next five to six years pursuing an eclectic array of occupations in a remarkable range of countries. These jobs included joining the Salvation Army, assistant lighthouse keeper, kangaroo hunter, circus worker, professional boxer (due to his exceptional strength), fisherman, seaman, guard in the Mexican army for President Díaz, railway construction worker, barman and tavern keeper. According to legend, in addition to all this, he also served a short time in a Chilean jail, suffered broken legs twice, and was thrown out of hospital in Jamaica for lack of money.

Returning to Germany, von Luckner's life becomes easier to track as, at the age of 20, he entered a navigation training school. By 1908 he had joined the Hamburg-Südamerikanisch Line steamer *Petropolis*, intending to work for nine months before volunteering to serve in the Imperial Navy for a year in order to obtain a naval commission. He claimed that he had vowed not to return to his family, who had given him up for lost, except in uniform. In February 1912 he was called up by the German Imperial Navy and served in the gunboat SMS *Panther*. In the early part of the war von Luckner saw action at the Battle of Heligoland Bight, and during the Battle of Jutland he commanded a gun turret aboard the battleship *Kronprinz Wilhelm*.

Intending to revive commercial raiding, the Imperial Navy equipped the impounded three-masted windjammer *Pass of Bamaha* (1571 tons) with two 105 mm guns hidden behind hinged gunwales, several machine guns, and two carefully hidden 500 HP auxiliary engines. She was commissioned as *Seeadler* (sea eagle) and von Luckner was appointed her commander. *Seeadler* left port on 21 December 1916 and would spend the next 21 months successfully disrupting commercial shipping in the Indian and South Pacific oceans before being wrecked in the Society Islands on 24 August 1917. Setting sail in *Seeadler*'s whaler, von Luckner and some of his crew got as far as Fiji before being made prisoners of war and sent to New Zealand.

At the end of the First World War von Luckner was repatriated to Germany. He wrote a book of his adventures which became a best-seller in Germany, and Lowell Thomas' book about him spread his fame even more widely. An entertaining speaker – if something of a braggart and a relentless self-promoter – von Luckner was widely admired for his seamanship and for having fought his war with such integrity. Such was the man's charisma that many cities in the United States made him an honorary citizen.

In 1937 and 1938, he and his wife undertook a round-the-world voyage in his yacht *Seeteufel* which included ports of call in New Zealand and Australia. Although on the whole he was warmly welcomed, some viewed him as an apologist for the Nazi regime which was going from strength to strength in Germany. During the Second World War, Hitler tried to use the Count for propaganda purposes, although, as a Freemason, von Luckner belonged to a group that was abhorrent to the Nazis. He refused to renounce his membership of the Masons or the various honorary citizenships granted in the USA, and consequently suffered by having his bank account frozen. At the end of the war, the mayor of Halle, where von Luckner was living, asked him to negotiate the town's surrender to the approaching American forces. While he complied with this request, he did not return to the town after hearing that the Nazis had condemned him to death.

The Count married twice, first when he was very young to Petra Schultz, with whom he had a daughter, Inge-Maria, born in 1913, and for a second time to a Swede, Ingeborg Engeström, with whom he had no children. After the Second World War, Luckner moved to Sweden, where he lived in Malmö with Ingeborg until his death.

Von Luckner's ship Seeadler.

look for a means of escape. He later claimed that he had intended hiding in an empty tar barrel, armed with a knife, and that once the barrel was loaded with its fellows aboard the coastal schooner that picked them up and it was underway, he would spring out of the barrel and take the crew single-handedly. He would then commandeer the vessel which he would sail back to Fort Jervois and retrieve Kircheiss

ABT0080

Pelorus Jack & HMS *New Zealand*

Animal mascots were not uncommon on board ships at the turn of the century and naval vessels were no different. Shortly after the commissioning of HMS *New Zealand*, George Burton, a New Zealander living in the United Kingdom, presented the crew of the battlecruiser with a bulldog puppy. Named Pelorus Jack, the pup's arrival on board coincided with the ship's round-the-world voyage which was to include New Zealand as one of its ports of call.

The day before sailing the ship was inspected by King George V, Winston Churchill, the Admiral Prince Louis of Battenberg and Sir Joseph Ward, a former New Zealand Premier. The press were out in force for the occasion. In its issue of 5 February, the *Daily Graphic* reported that the King had addressed the ship's company including Pelorus Jack who had sat politely on a grating throughout as if listening to the royal speech.

A dog's life can be dangerous aboard a warship and the cruise was not without incident. A Certificate for Wounds and Hurts was issued on 13 February 1913, noting that Pelorus Jack, 'being then actually on His Majesties Service in hauling on the starboard after-guy of [the] main derrick was injured ... by getting his head drawn into a block, sustaining the loss of his left lower canine and the fracture of several other teeth together with various contusions and superficial injuries'. The certificate went on to note that the dog was 'sober at the time'.

During the world cruise, Pelorus Jack received a number of gifts. Among them were two sterling silver dog collars, one from the citizens of Johannesburg and the second from a group in Pretoria calling itself 'the New Zealanders of Transvaal'. These collars were intended for use on ceremonial occasions.

Pelorus Jack was entered on the ship's book as 'Puppy' on 4 February 1913, the day of his arrival on board as tradition demanded. While serving as a Puppy he attained the rank of 'superior'; however, after this first promotion his ability is noted as only 'satisfactory'. Nevertheless, Jack progressed through the ranks, attaining the rating of Leading Seadog on 1 January 1915. As Pelorus Jack had seen action while serving on HMS *New Zealand*, he was entitled to naval prize money and in addition qualified for the 1914–15 Star, the British War Medal, 1914–20, and the Victory Medal, 1914–18. Sadly, the rating in charge of the ship's mascot failed to apply for Pelorus Jack's awards.

The English bulldog who had seen more of the world than most people even now can imagine met an untimely end on 24 April 1916, after falling down the ship's forward funnel. He had lived a very full life despite being only a little over three years old at his death. Having begun life in the White Horse Inn in Hampshire, England, Pelorus Jack had gone on to 'join the navy and see the world'.

Silver dog collar presented to HMS New Zealand *for Pelorus Jack by the Pretoria Public Works Department, 6 March 1913.* FT 0071

before setting sail for the Society Islands where the remainder of his crew may or may not be still waiting for him. (The *Seeadler* crew had in fact long departed. Having seized a schooner, they had been wrecked on Easter Island and were then in internment camps in Chile.)

Daring as the plan was, it was never to be put to the test as von Luckner was transferred back to Motuihe before he could attempt to put it into action. The Count later claimed that he had delayed his escape from Fort Jervois out of respect for its commanding officer, Major Leeming, and was waiting for him to go on leave so as to not embarrass him. The truth, whatever it was, was undoubtedly more prosaic than the Count's version of it.

However, now back on Motuihe, von Luckner was to discover that his fellow prisoners were not simply sitting around waiting for the end of the war and escape was high on their agenda. How von Luckner managed to get himself included in the escape party – if in fact an escape was planned – is anyone's guess, though fast talking seems the most likely reason. According to the Count, an escape attempt was scheduled for 18 November 1918 when, armed with stolen pistols, the escape party would hide out in a cave until the heat had died down and then seize a passing ship. The supposed attempt was aborted when the armistice was signed on 11 November, just a week before it was scheduled to take place.

Section of von Luckner's wooden cell from Ripapa Island on which he wrote '109 weary days in this dreary place … we are fed up with this … and off we go …'. GLG 0005

6-lb brass cartridge case. This cartridge was fired by the cable ship Iris *across the bow of the* Moa *when Count Felix von Luckner made his escape from Motuihe Island in the scow during 1917.* JEC 0023

Von Luckner's Ripapa Island cell key. Felix von Luckner, a Lieutenant Commander of the Imperial German Navy, was captured and sent to Ripapa Island in Lyttelton Harbour after escaping from Motuihe Island. GLG 0004

BETWEEN THE WARS 1918–1939

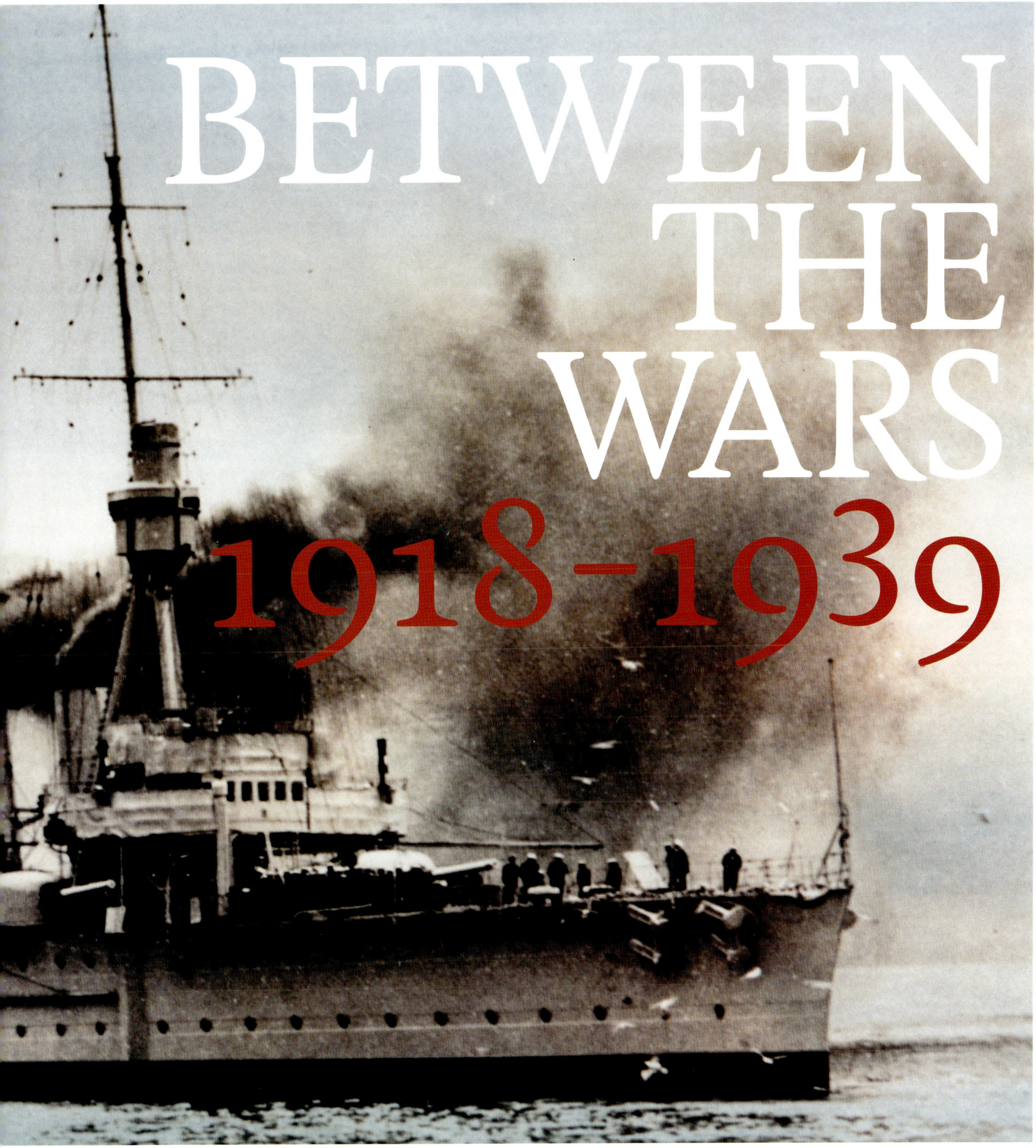

The cessation of hostilities in 1918 saw hopes of establishing a New Zealand navy in its own right once more thrown into uncertainty. The only naval ship of any size to be found in New Zealand waters in 1918 was HMS *Philomel*, now stripped of her armament and completely shut down, tied up alongside the docks in Wellington Harbour as a depot vessel.

As Matthew Wright ominously suggests in *Blue Water Kiwis*, these were 'the locust years'. To further hinder New Zealand's aspirations for its own naval force, the Admiralty revived the idea of a single Imperial Navy answerable to an Imperial Naval Authority – namely, the Admiralty. Unsurprisingly, none of the British Empire's far-flung Dominions wanted much to do with this proposal. Following the Imperial Conference of 1918, it was decided to maintain the status quo with regard to the Naval Defence Act 1913 which gave Britain control of New Zealand's naval forces in times of war. Viscount Jellicoe, the First Sea Lord, visited the Dominions shortly after the end of the war on board HMS *New Zealand*. Jellicoe reached Sydney just as peace was formally declared; he arrived in New Zealand a few weeks later where, unsurprisingly, the ship was given a tremendous welcome.

As a result of his fact-finding mission, Jellicoe proposed a fleet of eight battleships, eight battlecruisers and a variety of smaller vessels which would largely be based in Singapore – but some would be based in Australian waters and paid for by the two Dominions on either side of the Tasman Sea. The New Zealand Naval Forces would be formally recognised as a division of the Royal Navy. The New Zealand Division, as it was to be called, was eventually to consist of three light cruisers, a naval air school, six submarines and a submarine depot ship, supported by a number of smaller auxiliary vessels. Although Jellicoe considered that a naval dockyard was unnecessary, he recommended that *Philomel* be converted into a training ship.

Britain in its benevolence would consider this arrangement as contributing part of its Eastern Fleet and would provide 75 per cent of the finances, with Australia contributing 20 per cent and New Zealand taking care of the remaining 5 per cent. According to two documents in Navy Archives entitled 'Missions: Lord Jellicoe's Visit to New Zealand 1919' and 'Secret – New Zealand Naval Estimates', when considered in conjunction with the country's continuing loan repayments, this amounted to a total payment of £461,307 from 1920–21 which would gradually rise to peak in 1927–28 at £1,319,841, and then drop to a mere £1,123,434 per year after the New Zealand loan was repaid in full.

N.Z.

H.M.S. NEW ZEALAND

Know all men by these presents that our trusty and well-beloved

Alexander David Boyle.

has served as a Novice on board the good ship "New Zealand" and that this day he was duly initiated according to the mystic rites and ceremonies, and we do signify to all whom it may concern that it is our Royal Will and Pleasure to confer upon him the "FREEDOM OF THE SEAS" and to exempt him from further homage.

Given under our hand and seal at our Court on the Equator the 18th day of February One Thousand Nine Hundred and Thirteen.

NEPTUNE, Rex.

Crossing the line certificate issued to A. D. Boyle onboard HMS New Zealand, *18 February 1913.* EEC 0011

A naval tradition since the 1700s, a Crossing the Line ceremony is performed when a ship crosses the equator and results in the initiation of every 'novice' (those who have not yet crossed the equator) on board. The ritual takes place in Neptune's Royal Court with the purpose of appeasing the god of the seas. Those who have previously crossed the equator undertake a variety of roles in the ceremony, dressing up as King Neptune, Davy Jones or part of the Royal Court. Initiation may include a dunking, shaving of the head or administering a 'bitter tonic' or 'soap pill'. Once the novice had been initiated they would then be issued a certificate signed by 'Neptune Rex'.

The Crossing the Line ceremony can be interpreted as a simple initiation rite or entertainment for the ship's crew; however, it also offered sailors the opportunity to 'let off some steam'. Crossing the Line remains part of a sailor's experience at sea today.

HMS New Zealand *in Lyttelton, 1919.* ABT 0015

HMS Chatham *signalmen.* AAB 0058

Chromed 12-pounder cartridge-case dinner gong engraved with a dragon motif, used in the Warrant Officers Mess HMS Dunedin. TGX 0005

While Jellicoe's plan made good sense to the New Zealand Government, it was far from being a done deal. A straitened economy produced a marked reluctance to support the funding of a long-term and expensive build-up of the country's naval defences beyond the RN's contribution, particularly after 1929 when New Zealand was forced to suspend its loan repayments. (It was not until until the end of the Second World War in 1945 that the last payment was made on a RN warship scrapped in 1922.) So while the New Zealand Government agreed with Jellicoe's proposal in theory, in reality they settled for a single light cruiser, the commissioning of *Philomel* as a training ship and the establishment of a Naval Board. These new 'ships' were joined by RN sloops HMS *Veronica* and *Laburnum*, which were based in New Zealand waters from late 1920 and 1922 respectively. The cruiser commissioned through the agreement to the New Zealand Station was HMS *Chatham*, which arrived in the Waitemata Harbour on 26 January 1921. Its commanding officer, Captain Alan Hotman RN, was 'triple-hatted' while on service in New Zealand, being not only commanding officer of a vessel, but also Commodore Commanding, New Zealand Station and Naval Advisor to the New Zealand Government.

Shortly thereafter the New Zealand Naval Board was created by an Order in Council, with the Minister of Defence, Sir Heaton Rhodes, as chairman. In June 1921 a further Order in Council was issued, renaming the New Zealand Naval Forces as the New Zealand Division. With this important decision made and a new vessel – HMS *Chatham* – secured, all that remained was to decide where a naval training base should be established. When Auckland was chosen, it was necessary for the neglected HMS *Philomel* to be moved north. The suggestion that the ship would have to be towed was shelved when the engineer commander of *Chatham*, with a work party of artificers, managed to bring the ship back to life. Under the command of Lieutenant Commander John Walsh RN, *Philomel* made an uneventful journey north to Devonport with a skeleton crew. The ship was gutted and refitted to suit its new role as a training ship.

Developments were also underway ashore, with the creation of a parade ground and training facilities as auxiliaries to the dockyard. Now all they needed was recruits. In August 1921, 40 young men joined the New Zealand Division of the Royal Navy. One, brand-new seaman boy, George Davies-Goff, would eventually become the first Commodore, Auckland. *Chatham*, meanwhile, had embarked on her first cruise of New Zealand waters, flying the flag.

By 1924 it was felt that *Chatham* had 'done her dash' as far as the New Zealand Division was concerned. Included in the British Special Service Squadron visiting New Zealand waters was the D-class light cruiser HMS *Dunedin*, which was to replace *Chatham* in the New Zealand Division. Included in the complement of this much more modern cruiser was a detachment of Royal Marines. Soon after, the problem of logistical support arose for ships on duty in New Zealand waters – a problem solved through the transferring of the oiler, RFA *Nucula*, from the Admiralty list to the New Zealand Division, thus giving it greater flexibility both around the New Zealand coast and in the Pacific. *Dunedin*'s sister ship, HMS *Diomede*, was loaned to New Zealand a year later. *Diomede* had the unusual distinction of being originally commissioned in 1922 by Captain J. S. M. Ritchie – the first New

HMS *Veronica* & *Laburnum*

HMS *Veronica* and HMS *Laburnum* were fleet-sweeping sloops of the *Acacia* type – a division of the much larger Flower class which came into being during the First World War. The design of the over 100 ships that constitute the Flower class was based on merchant vessels and the ships were built very quickly in commercial rather than Admiralty shipyards. They varied tremendously in appearance, especially after they had been adapted for specialised roles as escorts, minesweepers and decoy warships.

After a period of service with the Royal Navy during the First World War, both *Veronica* and *Laburnum* were sent to New Zealand to operate as ships of the New Zealand Division. *Veronica* arrived in September 1920 and *Laburnum* in March 1922. Both sloops spent a fairly unremarkable decade and a half in New Zealand waters. They took part in ceremonial occasions, conducted the annual cruise of the Pacific Islands under New Zealand administration, and generally flew the flag for New Zealand and the Division. However, *Veronica* had the distinction of being tied up in Napier during the earthquake of 3 February 1931. The ship had berthed at Port Ahuriri only three hours before the earthquake struck, and the distress signals she transmitted gave the first news of the disaster. With all

ABM 0015

communications temporarily cut, the only communiqués in and out of Napier were courtesy of *Veronica*'s radio.

Leaving New Zealand in February 1934, *Veronica* returned to Britain to pay off, the sloop being sold for scrap and broken up the following year. Life as a drill and training ship for the Straits Settlement Naval Volunteer Reserve in Singapore was to be *Laburnum*'s fate – a role it retained until it was scuttled when Singapore fell to the Japanese in early 1942. The wreck was moved in 1946 to become part of a breakwater constructed of hulks until it was removed and scrapped in the late 1960s.

Class and type: **Flower class, *Acacia*-type**
Name: **HMS *Veronica***
Builder: **Dunlop, Bremner & Co. Ltd, Port Glasgow**
Laid down: **January 1915**
Launched: **27 May 1915**
Commissioned: **August 1915**
On NZ Station: **19 September 1920**
Paid off (NZ): **24 February 1934**
Displacement: **1200 tons standard**
Dimensions: **80 x 10 m**
Propulsion: **1-shaft reciprocating 4-cylinder triple expansion engine, coal, 1800 ihp**
Speed: **16.5 knots**
Complement: **104 officers and ratings**
Armament: **2 x 4-in, 4 x 3-pdr, 2 x 2-pdr MGs**

Class and type: **Flower class, *Acacia*-type**
Name: **HMS *Laburnum***
Builder: **Charles Connell & Co. Ltd, Scotstoun, Glasgow**
Laid down: **February 1915**
Launched: **10 June 1915**
Commissioned: **August 1915**
On NZ Station: **11 March 1922**
Paid off (NZ): **11 February 1935**
Displacement: **1200 tons standard**
Dimensions: **80 x 10 m**
Propulsion: **1-shaft reciprocating 4-cylinder triple expansion engine, coal, 1800 ihp**
Speed: **16.5 knots**
Complement: **104 officers and ratings**
Armament: **2 x 4-in, 4 x 3-pdr, 2 x 2-pdr MGs**

AAB 0057

HMS *Chatham*

The third battleship to bear the name *Chatham*, the cruiser was named for the English town of Chatham in Kent where the naval base of the same name and Chatham Dockyard were located. HMS *Chatham* was commissioned to the New Zealand Station in October 1920, having been first commissioned into the Royal Navy some eight years before. A *Chatham*-class light cruiser, the ship had seen service in the Mediterranean during the First World War, chiefly as part of the 2nd Light Cruiser Squadron. From 1916 to 1918, *Chatham* was the flagship of the 3rd Light Cruiser Squadron of the Grand Fleet – although due to mine damage and consequent repairs, it missed out on the Battle of Jutland. At the cessation of hostilities, *Chatham* was placed in reserve until recommissioned for service in New Zealand waters as a vessel of the New Zealand Naval Forces.

Although it was decided that the ship should be crewed predominantly by RN loan personnel, the Royal Navy was unable to provide as full a complement as they had originally envisaged and local men were offered three-year engagements. A total of 293 ratings were recruited through this manpower initiative, which formed nucleus crews for both *Chatham* and *Philomel*. RN loan ratings and New Zealand recruits filled the manning shortfalls.

On *Chatham*'s voyage to New Zealand the ship called at a number of ports in the West Indies as well as Hawaii, Samoa and Fiji. At each of the more inviting ports the odd desertion occurred, with the loss of 10 sailors in total.

Within two months of the cruiser's arrival in New Zealand on 28 February 1921, *Philomel*, which had undergone repairs on a Wellington Harbour slipway, was once again seaworthy and, after being sailed to Auckland, took over the task of training new recruits. Thus freed of training duties, *Chatham* commenced service with a cruise of New Zealand in May 1921, calling at seven ports. A Pacific Island cruise followed in July, during which a whale's tooth was gifted to Commander John Walsh during the ship's visit to Lautoka. Returning to New Zealand, *Chatham* stopped briefly on Raoul Island to take on board shipwrecked survivors of the *Colombia River*. A second New Zealand cruise followed the next year during which their Excellencies, the Governor General and Lady Jellicoe, sailed on board the ship to the Chatham Islands. In late 1922, an outbreak of cerebrospinal meningitis forced the ship to spend a month in quarantine on Motuihe Island in the Hauraki Gulf – a site which 20 years later would become the Royal New Zealand Navy training establishment.

Chatham was joined in New Zealand waters by the RN Special Service Squadron led by the battlecruisers HMS *Hood* and *Repulse* in April 1924. A regatta was held in honour of the visit, and the cutter crew of the *Chatham* won the Frobisher Cup. The event was something of a swansong for the cruiser as HMS *Dunedin* had arrived with the Special Service Squadron to take over *Chatham*'s role on the New Zealand Station. *Chatham* reverted once more to the Admiralty. After a year's service as the flagship of the 4th Light Cruiser Squadron of the East Indies Fleet, *Chatham* paid off in November 1925. The cruiser was finally sold for scrap in 1926.

The *Chatham*'s original badge design was taken from the coat of arms of that city. During 1958–59, when the Naval Board was putting together a collection of ships' badges to decorate its boardroom, the Admiralty advised that no badge had been officially registered for the ship following the First World War. However, hanging in the cafeteria of HMNZS Dockyard was a drawing of the *Chatham* badge attributed to Captain T. H. B. Shaw RN when he was Captain Superintendent of the Dockyard in 1956 and a ship's badge was devised for *Chatham* based on this design.

Class and type: **_Chatham_-class light cruiser**
Name: **HMS _Chatham_**
Builder: **HM Naval Dockyard, Chatham, Kent**
Laid down: **3 November 1911**
Launched: **19 November 1911**
Commissioned: **3 December 1912**
Paid off: **11 November 1925**

General characteristics
Displacement: **5400 tons standard**
Dimensions: **139.6 x 15 m**
Propulsion: **4-shaft geared turbines, coal, 25,000 shp**
Speed: **25.5 knots**
Complement: **475 officers and ratings**
Armament: **Original configuration – 8 x 6-in guns, 8 x 1-in guns, 1 x 3-in AA, 4 x 2-pdr MGs, 2 x 21-in torpedo tubes**

T 2008.10.1

AAD 0139

HMS *Diomede* & HMS *Dunedin*

HMS *Diomede* and HMS *Dunedin* were two of eight D-class ships ordered by the Admiralty during the latter part of the First World War, though neither were completed until after the cessation of hostilities. *Dunedin*, which was completed in December 1919, joined the British Special Service Squadron in the Indian Ocean in late 1923. The squadron visited the New Zealand Station the following year and, on 11 May 1924, *Dunedin* took over from HMS *Chatham* as the station's flagship. *Diomede*, which was commissioned in April 1922, was offered to New Zealand as a loan ship in early 1925 following early service on the China Station. The ship was refitted and commissioned at Portsmouth and arrived in Auckland on 21 January 1926.

Both vessels largely continued the same routines established by the departed *Chatham*. Following the Mau demonstrations in Apia, Samoa, *Dunedin* was stationed there for a period of two months in early 1930, and was later called from Auckland, like its

AAE 0016

sister ship *Diomede*, to provide assistance in Napier after the catastrophic earthquake of 3 February 1931. *Diomede*'s time on the New Zealand Station was cut short in October 1935 when it was required by the Admiralty for service on the East Indies Station following the Italian invasion of Abyssinia. The ship never returned to New Zealand waters as in early 1936 it was sent back to Britain, paying off in March that year. The same day, HMS *Achilles* was commissioned as a replacement for *Diomede*. A similar fate awaited *Dunedin*, which left New Zealand in early 1937 and was paid off when *Leander* was commissioned in April 1937 – like *Achilles*, destined for the New Zealand Station.

Both *Diomede* and *Dunedin* were recommissioned into the Royal Navy and saw active service in the early part of the Second World War. *Dunedin* met its end in the mid-Atlantic, northeast of Brazil, when it was torpedoed by a German submarine on 24 November 1941. *Diomede* lasted a little longer; it was removed from active service in 1943 and redesignated as a training ship early the following year. In 1946 the ship's useful life was deemed to be over and it was sold for scrap.

Class and type: **D-class**
Name: **HMS *Dunedin***
Builder: **Sir W. G. Armstrong, Whitworth & Co. Ltd, Walker-on-Tyne, Newcastle. Completed by HM Dockyard, Devonport**
Laid down: **5 November 1917**
Launched: **19 November 1918**
Commissioned: **13 September 1919**
Paid off (NZ): **30 April 1937**
Displacement: **4650 tons standard**
Dimensions: **144 x 14 m**
Propulsion: **2-shaft geared turbines, oil, 40,000 shp**
Speed: **29 knots**
Complement: **450 officers and ratings**
Armament: **6 x 6-in, 2 x 3-in, 4 x 3-pdr MGs**

Class and type: **D-class**
Name: **HMS *Diomede***
Builder: **Sir W. G. Armstrong, Whitworth & Co. Ltd, Walker-on-Tyne, Newcastle. Completed by HM Dockyard, Devonport**
Laid down: **3 June 1918**
Launched: **29 April 1919**
Commissioned: **24 April 1922**
Displacement: **4765 tons standard**
Dimensions: **144 x 14 m**
Propulsion: **2-shaft geared turbines, oil, 25,000 shp**
Speed: **29 knots**
Complement: **475 officers and ratings**
Armament: **Original configuration – 6 x 6-in, 2 x 3-in AA, 4 x 3-pdr MGs**
1929–32 – 3 x 4-in AA replaced the 3-in, 2 x 2-pdr, 10 x MGs, 12 x 21-in torpedo tubes

A watercolour of HMS Dunedin *painted on a feather.* PAJ 0003

AAK 0017

HMS *Wakakura*

The *Castle*-class trawler *Wakakura* – the first New Zealand vessel to bear that name – was purchased as a training vessel by the New Zealand Government for the newly established Auckland Division of the Volunteer Reserve in 1925 for the sum of £5000. It would be the mainstay of the Reserve and remained in service until the end of the Second World War.

Built in Canada, the vessel begun its service life with the Royal Navy in October 1917. One of 60 *Castle*-class vessels built for the Admiralty during the First World War, the minesweeper was manned by a Canadian crew and saw very little action. By 1920 the ship, then known as TR. 1, was paid off and, along with a number of other vessels, was sent to Inverness to be fitted out for resale by the Admiralty. It was, however, a further five years before the refit for the New Zealand Division was completed and the vessel began sea trials under its new name of *Wakakura* which, most appropriately, meant 'canoe school'. In June 1926 the vessel set sail for New

AAK 0027

Bosun's call on a silver chain, belonging to Leading Signalman F. Turvey who served on HMS Philomel. ISA 0004

Zealand waters and its new role as a training vessel, but for a variety of reasons failed to make its destination until January the following year. It was not until 7 May 1927 that the first intake of reservists finally trod her deck. The following year, three new Reserve Divisions were established in Wellington, Lyttelton and Christchurch and, from then until 1940, *Wakakura* spent approximately three months with each of the divisions.

When *Niagara* was sunk in June 1940 in the German-laid Hauraki Gulf minefield, *Wakakura* was pulled off its training role and transferred to minesweeping duty with the First Minesweeping Group. The vessel stayed minesweeping until April 1944, after which it was converted to dan-laying, working with the 7th Trawler Group on the last sweep on the Hauraki Gulf field. *Wakakura* was paid off in October 1945 and was moored at Herald Island until sold some 18 months later; it was used as a cargo ship until the end of 1948 when it was laid up at moor in Shoal Bay. The vessel was finally sold in 1952 and dismantled the following year.

Class and type: ***Castle*-class trawler**
Name: **HMS *Wakakura***
Builder: **The Port Arthur S. B. Co., Canada**
Laid down: **31 May 1917**
Launched: **September 1917**
Commissioned: **17 October 1917**
Paid off: **17 October 1945**

General characteristics
Displacement: **530 tons standard**
Dimensions: **40.8 x 7.2 m**
Propulsion: **single-shaft triple expansion engine, coal, 420 ihp**
Speed: **8.5–10 knots**
Complement in NZ waters: **26**
Pennant No: **T00**

Stanley Parslow

Stanley Parslow, who joined the New Zealand Division of the Royal Navy in 1928, was a seaman boy on board the D-class *Dunedin* during the aftermath of the Mau unrest in Samoa in early 1930, and the devastating earthquake in Napier the following year.

These extracts from Parslow's oral history transcript shows how the Mau movement was viewed by one seaman in particular, and probably by the rest of *Dunedin*'s crew. Although the transcript suggests that the demonstration had yet to occur, the record clearly shows that *Dunedin* arrived in Apia after the event.

Samoa, January 1930 – *Dunedin*:
Stanley Parslow: I was a young seaman then and on leave, and I was called back to the ship immediately – she was ready to sail for Samoa. Apparently ... some of the Samoans decided they wanted the country without any restraints, so they killed off two of the policemen, the New Zealand policemen [stationed there].

We went at our best speed to Samoa, and we anchored off, and these people calling themselves the Mau Mau [sic], and wearing distinctive lavalavas, which they wrapped around themselves, blue with a stripe in, went bush – the ones that had apparently done the killing included. There was a fear of a general uprising, and it had to be seen whether they had any possibility of getting other weapons – they had weapons of a type. We had heard from some of the loyal Samoans that they had them cached up in the hills somewhere, they had guns. It was decided to put shore parties ashore to see if they could get hold of these guns before the Mau Mau [sic] were able to use them. Being a seaman boy and with another chap named Chirnside, a seaman, one of my own class, we were sent to go with a shipload of troops and row them ashore and land them, you see. This particular time was night-time and they wanted to surprise the Mau Maus [sic]. They knew where they had grouped, and they knew that they definitely had caches of arms. This night-time we set out, and we had someone to steer us through the coral reefs because they were unknown to us. ... Our job was to tend the cutter and run her ashore to let the troops off, you know, and take the empty boat back to a little ship called the *Dunedin*, which belonged to the Government. ... Anyhow, we landed these troops ashore ... and then we had to return to the ship.

Another time we landed troops in daylight. I don't know what happened to Chirnside, but ...

INT: What? You picked the troops up in New Zealand before you sailed or ... ?
SP: Oh yes, they were our own men.

INT: Marines, were they?
SP: No, they were seamen, a group of seamen. I called them troops, but they were seamen.

INT: They were an armed party of sailors?
SP: They were, yes.

INT: How did they get on?
SP: Well they captured quite a number of the Mau Mau [sic]. I don't know, it could have been 15 or 20 of them, and they had to be taken back to the *Dunedin*. I think it was about two days' sailing, or something like that to the prison at Apia, which of course was the main town. These Mau Mau [sic] were taken out to *Dunedin* ... and then the seamen had to go back somewhere and [they] left Chirnside and myself to stand guard over these Mau Mau [sic] and take them back to prison in Apia. We had them up forward and roped off there and Chirnside took the first watch. And I said: 'What have we got to guard ourselves with?' And he says: 'They have given us rifles and a bayonet, but no ammunition in case we sho[o]t somebody!' I said: 'Oh well, that's all right.'

Zealand-born officer to command an RN vessel on the New Zealand Station.

Britain's desire to consolidate its defences in the Far East led to a decision to expand its presence in Singapore, pegging Singapore Harbour as its major naval base in the region. Invoking the name of Empire, British Prime Minister Stanley Baldwin urged its Dominions in the region to contribute to the establishment of the Singapore Station. New Zealand's Prime Minister, Gordon Coates, came up with three suggestions in response to Mother England's latest call for lucre and men. According to Grant Howard's book *The Navy in New Zealand*, these were:

The sum of £1 million to be paid to His Majesty's Government as a contribution towards the Singapore Base, this amount to take the form of annual payments to be spread between the present date (September 1927) and the completion of the base, estimated at seven or eight years.

A third D-class cruiser to be maintained (by New Zealand), but when it is necessary eventually to withdraw the two existing cruisers they will be replaced by two B-class cruisers.

Prior to the date when the B-class cruisers will be taken over, alterations in the equipment and plant of the New Zealand Naval Base will be required for the up-keep of B-class cruisers and these will be undertaken.

In 1927, Parliament passed an Act undertaking to support Britain's establishment of a naval base in Singapore by 54 votes to 10. The leader of the Labour Party, Harry Holland, voiced his party's disapproval: 'The Labour movement opposes it because it sees in the proposal an incentive to further warfare; and, as much as any section of the community, we desire that

AAE 0026

there should be peace throughout the world.' But New Zealand was committed. Even after the Wall Street crash of 1929 and the subsequent Great Depression which saw New Zealand gripped by enormous hardship, with government spending slashed to the bone, the payments for the building of the Singapore naval base continued.

From the earliest days of planning a New Zealand naval force, provision had been made for the establishment of a naval reserve. The Naval Defence Act of 1913 authorised the establishment of a New Zealand naval reserve, although the advent of the First World War disrupted plans and the recruiting of reserves did not get underway until late 1922. In 1925 the purchase from the Admiralty of a *Castle*-class minesweeper, for the sum of £5000, for the newly formed reserve was approved by Cabinet. The newly commissioned HMS *Wakakura*, as the ship was known on the New Zealand Division, arrived in New Zealand waters over a year later. The vessel proved to be less than a bargain as her initial purchase price had risen nearly £20,000 as the result of extensive repairs on three separate occasions during its journey from Britain to New Zealand. The ship arrived in early 1927 and was converted for its role as a training vessel at the Devonport Dockyard. The creation of the Royal Naval Volunteer Reserve (New Zealand) was a popular move, with divisions rapidly established in Auckland, Wellington, Christchurch and Dunedin. Nearly 500 men had joined the Reserve by 1929, the majority ratings who formed a peacetime minesweeping force.
The New Zealand Division's wide-ranging responsibilities between the wars included the islands of the southwest Pacific which were regularly toured by New Zealand naval vessels. Most notably, an uprising by the Mau movement in Western Samoa led to the Division mobilising on behalf of its Pacific neighbour.

In the early 1920s, Western Samoans had begun a peaceful protest campaign against New Zealand rule known as Mau – a term which translates roughly as 'strongly held opinion'. It was a mainstream, non-violent protest movement – not unlike the events at Parihaka in Taranaki over half a century before – against the mistreatment of the Samoan people by the New Zealand administration which had taken over from the German colonial regime after the First World War.

Brass knuckleduster as used in the Mau uprising in Samoa during 1930. JSA 0001

A few days after Christmas, on 28 December 1929, Mau's elected leader, High Chief Tupua Tamasese Lealofi, led his uniformed followers in a peaceful demonstration in downtown Apia. New Zealand police officers attempted to arrest one of the other leaders and when he resisted, a struggle developed between police and the Mau. The police began to fire randomly into the crowd and a Lewis machine gun, mounted in preparation for the demonstration, was used to disperse the protesters. Chief Tamasese was shot from behind and killed while trying to bring calm and order to the demonstration. Ten other Samoans died and a further 50 or so were injured by gunshot wounds and police batons on a day that would come to be known in Samoa as Black Saturday.

Although the New Zealand Division was not in Apia during the protest and subsequent massacre, *Dunedin*, with a De Havilland Moth seaplane and three members of the air force on board, was despatched to Apia in early 1930 for a period of two months, charged with the task of restoring order to the shattered island. It was the Division's first taste of active service. The Mau movement grew, remaining steadfastly non-violent, and expanded to include a highly influential women's branch. It finally gained a long-desired independence for Western Samoa in 1962.

Civil defence was, and remains, an integral part of the New Zealand navy's range of tasks. This was admirably illustrated in the case of the

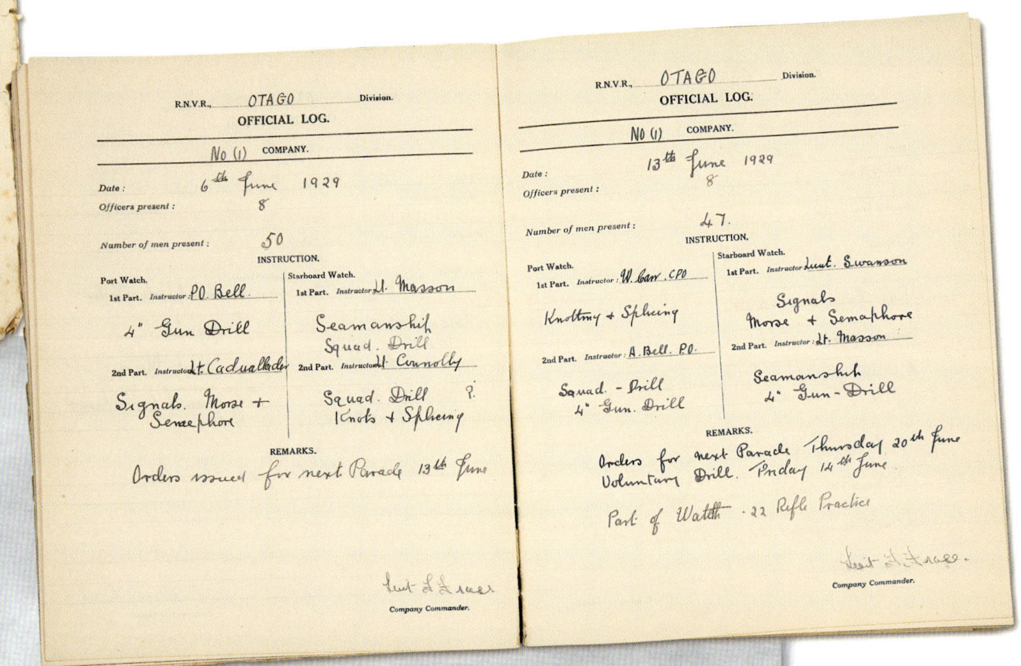
R.N.V.R. OTAGO Division.
OFFICIAL LOG.
No (1) COMPANY.
Date: 6th June 1929
Officers present: 8
Number of men present: 50
INSTRUCTION.
Port Watch.
1st Part. Instructor P.O. Bell.
4" Gun Drill
2nd Part. Instructor Lt Cadwallader
Signals. Morse + Semaphore
Starboard Watch.
1st Part. Instructor Lt. Masson
Seamanship Squad. Drill
2nd Part. Instructor Lt Connolly
Squad. Drill. Knots + Splicing
REMARKS.
Orders issued for next Parade 13th June
Company Commander.

R.N.V.R. OTAGO Division.
OFFICIAL LOG.
No (1) COMPANY.
Date: 13th June 1929
Officers present: 8
Number of men present: 47.
INSTRUCTION.
Port Watch.
1st Part. Instructor W. Carr. CPO
Knotting + Splicing
2nd Part. Instructor A. Bell. P.O.
Squad - Drill
4" Gun. Drill
Starboard Watch.
1st Part. Instructor Lieut. Swanson
Signals
Morse + Semaphore
2nd Part. Instructor Lt. Masson
Seamanship
4" Gun-Drill
REMARKS.
Orders for next Parade Thursday 20th June
Voluntary Drill. Friday 14th June.
Part of Watch .22 Rifle Practice
Company Commander.

AAE 0096

Diomede Chronicle, *dated 1 July 1932. The ship's newspaper contains daily world news and photographs of recent port visits.* BJA 0023

Log of 'A' Company Otago Division of Royal Navy Volunteer Reserves (NZ) from 26 June 1928–25 November 1930. FLD 0002

AUS 0008

AJS 0006

Napier earthquake of 3 February 1931 which destroyed much of the town, nearby Hastings and the surrounding Hawke's Bay countryside, and took the lives of 256 people. At the time, the damage was estimated to be in the region of £10 million. Nearly 30,000 people were denied the basic amenities of life, including food and water, in the weeks after the earthquake.

The soon-to-be-replaced Flower-class sloop HMS *Veronica* happened to be alongside in Napier when the tremors started and, because conventional communications had been disrupted by the devastation, it was the radio operators on board *Veronica* who communicated to the outside world that a natural disaster of major proportions had occurred and that help was desperately needed. In addition, the ship immediately landed personnel to provide both medical assistance and to augment the relief parties. The whole town centre had been virtually destroyed, including the hospital, and those building that had not collapsed caught fire, burning without check as the town's water mains had been destroyed. Within four hours of the initial communiqués from *Veronica*, the Division sent further help – 15 doctors, 11 nurses and a wide variety of supplies left from Devonport on board *Diomede* and *Dunedin*. The ships' galleys baked bread throughout the journey so that they had a supply for the survivors and relief parties when they arrived.

A temporary hospital was set up on the racecourse on the outskirts of Napier, and *Veronica* provided food and accommodation for some 200 refugees. None of the ship's officers or crew paused for rest all through that first night. By morning, *Dunedin* and *Diomede* had arrived and armed Royal Marines were put ashore to patrol the streets and guard key installations. The dead and the dying were said to have been lying in the streets. The population was in a state of profound shock owing to the magnitude of the disaster. One of the most difficult tasks carried out by the navy was the search of the hospital and nurses' home which had collapsed, burying both patients and their caregivers alive. Many of the more than 250 dead were buried in a common grave, where the funeral ceremony was conducted by the naval chaplain from *Philomel*, Reverend G. T. Robson.

Despite these efforts, the navy was not satisfied with merely getting its hands dirty and a relief fund was established to which navy men contributed a total of £530 – an average of around 10 shillings per man, more than a day's pay. The many messages of thanks for the navy's role in the relief work included one from Parliament. The owners of the *New Zealand Herald* and the *Auckland Weekly News* presented *Veronica*'s radio operators with silver cigarette cases, and the Auckland Branch of the

Reverend George Trevor Robson OBE

Included in the naval contingent that was rushed to Napier on 3 February 1931 in the wake of the earthquake was 'Padre Robbie', the gentleman charged with the care of the spiritual health of the navy between 1927 and 1948.

Born in Te Aroha in 1887, Reverend Robson was once described as 'a man of infinite patience who apparently was never in a hurry, never too busy to see any caller, yet managed to do a vast amount of work among and for the naval men and their families'. He was ordained into the Anglican Church in 1912 and worked in ministries in New Plymouth and Kohukohu in the Hokianga.

Enlisting in the army in mid-1914, just before the outbreak of the First World War, Robson was not called up until early 1917 and was sent overseas as a Territorial Service chaplain. For his work amongst the dying and injured during an engagement in France near the Forest de Normal, Robson was awarded the Military Cross 'for conspicuous gallantry and devotion to duty'.

Returning to the Far North after the war, he soon took up an appointment as vicar of Te Awamutu. Five years later, in 1927, Robson entered the New Zealand Division of the Royal Navy as Base Chaplain at *Philomel*, a position he would hold for the next 21 years.

During Padre Robbie's time as chaplain the Second World War came and went, as did ships and men, and the New Zealand Division finally separated itself from the Admiralty and became the Royal New Zealand Navy. It is written of Robson that, during his tenure at *Philomel*, he knew every man that passed through the base.

For his service in the navy, Robson was made an Officer of the Most Excellent Order of the British Empire in 1948. Even after retirement, he kept up his interest in the navy and was involved in a number of ex-navalmen's organisations as well as the Navy League.

Chaplain Robson's black embroidered preaching scarf with ribbons. 1691/5

Navy League presented a silver cup to the New Zealand Squadron which would become known as the Veronica Cup. The ship's bell, which was installed as part of the earthquake memorial on Napier's Marine Parade, and one of its nameplates were gifted to the city after *Veronica* was paid off and scrapped in mid-1935.

Not all disasters were the work of Mother Nature. The Great Depression cut deep into New Zealand society, and at one point the unemployment figures rose above 100,000 – approximately 40 per cent of the male working population. The expression 'simmering discontent' was an understatement. By 1932, the Unemployed Workers Union had 13,000 paid-up members and the Communist Party was actively represented on both the UWU and various other committees.

The catalyst came during a meeting at the Auckland Town Hall on April 14 1932 which, because of lack of room, had to exclude thousands of mostly unemployed men. Frustration at being kept out of the meeting – denied not just a voice, but an ear as well – caused the crowd to erupt in violence. Both the Division and the Reserve were despatched to help restore law and order on the streets of Auckland, at one point marching down Queen Street with fixed bayonets. The following night a crowd gathered on Karangahape Road, although violence was kept in check on this occasion. Rioting also broke out in Wellington, although to a much lesser extent, when an angry crowd of unemployed took to Lambton Quay in a rampage of window-smashing that was quickly quelled.

The general down-scaling of naval activity at home following the First World War, New Zealand's support for the expansion of the

Singapore Station and the economic depression of the early 1930s should all have slowed the development of the Devonport Dockyard and Base considerably. However, there was less development in the period from 1900 to 1920 than in the 20 years following the war when the country was gripped by considerable hardship. During the years immediately after the war, the ships *Veronica*, *Laburnum*, *Chatham*, *Dunedin*, *Diomede* and *Wakakura* had all spent time on the Division and a thriving Volunteer Reserve had developed in the mid-1920s.

As far as the Dockyard and Naval Base were concerned, by early 1932 the need for a major overhaul of the facilities at Devonport was recognised and a program of improvements was put into action. The Auckland Harbour Board undertook to modernise some of the dock equipment including the lengthening of Calliope Dock and the extension of the auxiliary jetties. Included in the renovations was the installation of light machinery, the siting of a 12,000-ton oil fuel tank on reclaimed ground in Stanley Bay and improvements to the pumping mechanism for the dry dock. As a result of these changes, the first refit of a cruiser was undertaken in 1931.

A new agreement was reached between the Auckland Harbour Board, the New Zealand Government and the Admiralty in 1936, whereby land, workshops, wharves, jetties and seabed belonging to the Auckland Harbour Board were transferred to the Crown, while ownership of the dry dock remained with the Auckland Harbour Board. The Admiralty's rights to use the dockyard facilities remained intact. These improvements, in conjunction with the construction of new workshops and storehouses and the development of specialised equipment, all carried out by the navy, enabled two cruisers, two RN sloops and number of minor war vessels – small ships – to be refitted in the late 1930s, in preparation for the outbreak of war. Although the newly modernised dockyard was capable of conducting complete surveys, refits and maintenance work, it was unfortunately not suitable for repairing major battle damage – as became evident in the case of *Leander*, after it was torpedoed by the Japanese in the Pacific in 1943.

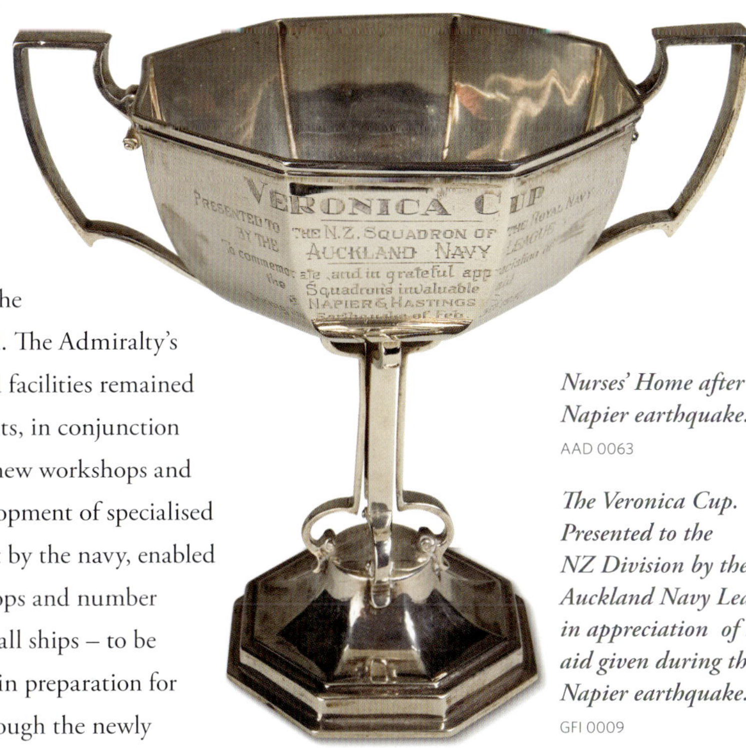

Nurses' Home after the Napier earthquake.
AAD 0063

The Veronica Cup. Presented to the NZ Division by the Auckland Navy League in appreciation of the aid given during the Napier earthquake.
GFI 0009

Ma Burrows – Mother of the Navy

Mrs Emily Burrows who had immigrated to New Zealand before the Great War earned the title Mother of the Navy due to her two decades of active work in sailor welfare. The reason for Ma's interest in the sailors was due to her only son William, who lost his life while serving on the Royal Navy vessel HMS *Irresistible* during the First World War.

Living as she was in Devonport village, 'Ma' as she became known was a regular visitor to the nearby naval base, always bringing with her treats such as fruit, lollies and flowers and an endless supply of motherly cheer. Such a regular feature was Ma at the naval base that it was said in the end everyone on the base from the Commodore to the lowliest seaman boy had made her acquaintance. In time Ma achieved a kind of quasi-military status and was awarded honorary medals for her services to her 'boys'.

Upon her death in 1933 the Mother of the Navy was awarded a full military funeral service, including the sounding of the last post, which was paid for by the sailors of the New Zealand Division of the Royal Navy. The vast number of sympathy cards that arrived upon Emily Burrows' death, indicative of the impact she had on the navy in the formative years of the New Zealand Division.

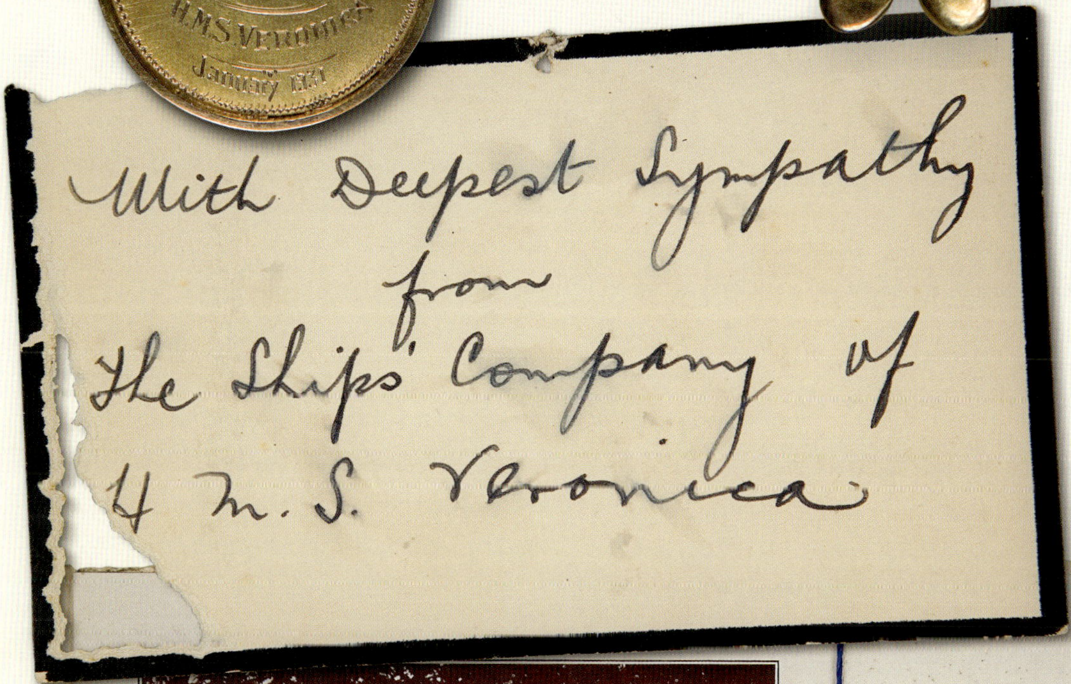

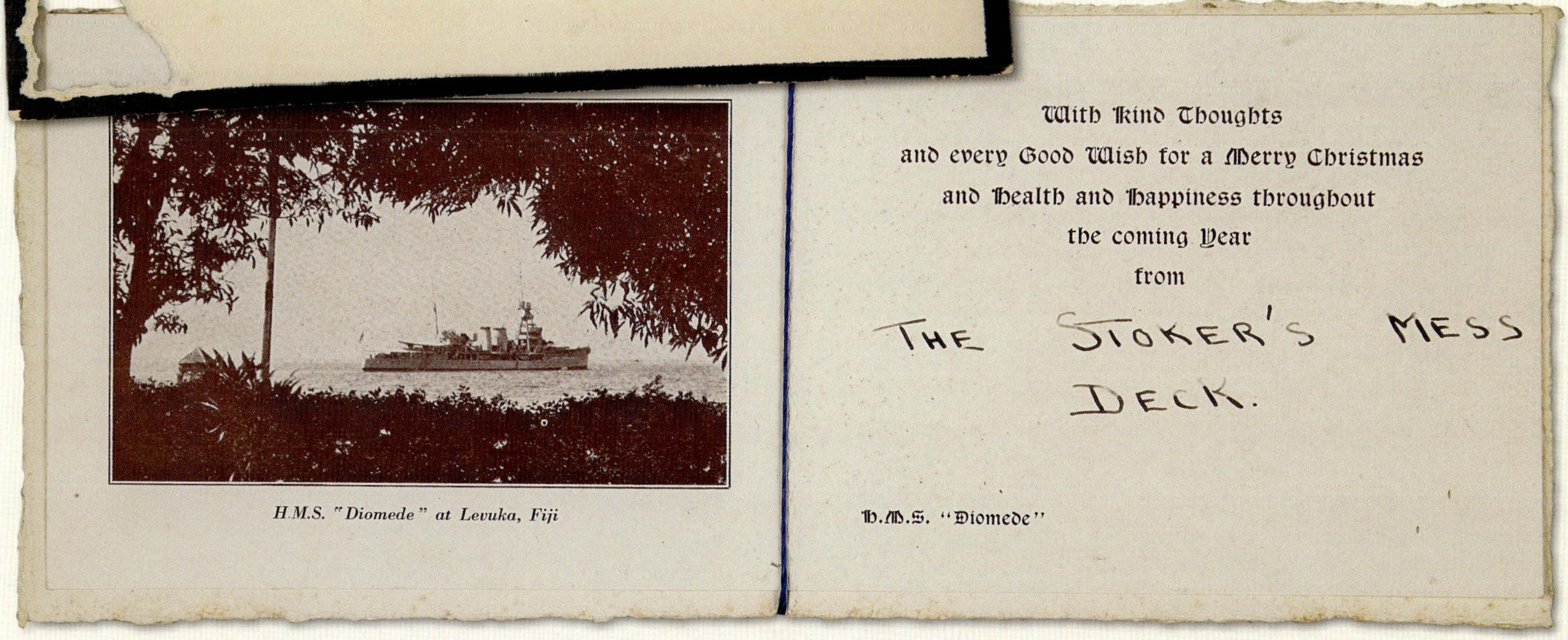

Green mantle clock presented to Ma Burrows from the crew of HMS Veronica *for her help during the years 1927–1929.* ICA 0028

Gold medallion presented to Ms Burrows for Long Service and Good Conduct by the seamen of the HMS Veronica*, January 1931.* MDE 0014

Gold bar brooch presented to Ma Burrows in 1928 by HMS Dunedin*.* MDE 0013

Sympathy card attached to flowers at Mrs [Ma] Burrows' funeral from ship's company HMS Veronica*.* EAK 0008

Christmas card to Ma Burrows from the Stoker's mess deck, HMS Diomede*.* EAB 0160

Armband issued to members of the Volunteer Reserve who were put on the street during the Auckland Riots to prevent citizens looting. CTG 8002

Wooden truncheon issued to Naval landing parties acting as sentries to prevent looting during Auckland riots, 1932. JBA 0001

Commander Charles Palmer

Charles 'Bunty' Palmer, who would go on to join the New Zealand Division of the Royal Navy in September 1939 and would be awarded the Distinguished Service Order and mentioned in despatches twice, started his naval career in 1929 when he joined the Auckland Division of the Volunteer Reserve. As a reservist he was part of the naval force that provided assistance to the police during the Queen Street riots in Auckland in 1930, an experience he recalls in the following extract from his oral history interview held in the RNZN Museum.

Charles Palmer: The riots in Queen Street. I was a rating at the time, and we were attending a parade at headquarters when a phone call came through for assistance. Our company of 60 marched to Queen Street and assisted the 18 sailors from *Philomel,* who had been rushed over to assist the police. It had the desired effect, and there was quiet at least for that night.

INT: What was the trouble, what was it about?
CP: Well, at that particular time there had been considerable unemployment, and a crowd went up Queen Street to hear a man talk. Somebody hit him on the head, there was blood. The crowd went berserk, ripped palings off local fences and started to beat up people. They went right through Queen Street from the Town Hall down like a packet of salts, smashing windows on both sides of the street and looting the shops.

INT: What year was this, Bunty?
CP: I am just trying to think.

INT: 1930 or 1931 I think, was it?
CP: Yes, I think it was. It was unbelievable. My mother and others came down with cups of tea for the sailors, because we remained on duty until well after daylight next day. Next night and the following night we fell in, all three companies at headquarters and awaited calls if required. Nothing eventuated until Saturday night when a similar occurrence almost took place in Karangahape Road. We were rushed there in buses, moving in line abreast. We endeavoured to clear the crowds but there was nothing like the smashing of windows that there was in Queen Street, although there was the odd attack. Sunday, too, we were called to the Domain for similar protection but nothing eventuated. Later on in Wellington and Christchurch similar riots occurred. In fact a man was killed in Christchurch. That was the only bloodshed.

Despite Italy's invasion of Abyssinia in 1935, an empire-building German Chancellor called Adolph Hitler making the headlines through shocking events such as the notorious Night of the Long Knives, and much of Europe in a political ferment, a war on the scale of the Great War of 1914–18 must still have seemed unimaginable in the middle of the decade. But the writing was on the wall, even in the far-flung Dominion of New Zealand.

In response to the invasion of Abyssinia, *Diomede* set sail for North Africa where the ship was made available to the Royal Navy. After 14 months in the area, the ship returned to Britain and was paid off in October 1936. The replacement ship for *Diomede* was the newly commissioned *Leander*-class cruiser HMS *Achilles*, a ship that was to become famous in the annals of New Zealand naval history. The changeover was the epitome of ease, with the *Diomede*'s total complement of crew simply walking onto their new cruiser. The intended sail for home waters in the new ship was postponed by increasing tensions in both Spain and North Africa. *Achilles* was ordered to join the RN Second Cruiser Squadron of the Home Fleet in Gibraltar in a show of Admiralty force in the Mediterranean. After three months on patrol with the Squadron, *Achilles* was released and continued its journey to New Zealand, arriving in Auckland in early spring 1937.

The New Zealand Division's fleet underwent other changes, besides the swap of *Diomede* for *Achilles*, during the build-up to the Second World War. The two Flower-class sloops *Veronica* and *Laburnum* had been replaced in the mid-1930s with *Grimsby*-class oil-burning sloops. HMS *Leith* had arrived in late 1934 and HMS *Wellington* six months later. In addition, the Admiralty sent the survey ship HMS

AAF 0030

Endeavour and *Leander* to the New Zealand Station in 1937; during its time in New Zealand waters it compiled 10 new coastal survey charts.

However, surveying and civic duties were soon to be put to one side as the decade drew to a close. War was imminent. Despite the Labour Government's public support of the League of Nations and often-voiced doubts about Imperial policy, when the crunch came Prime Minister Savage's mandate, 'When Britain is in trouble, we are in trouble', held sway. The bonds that tied New Zealand to the Mother Country were still stronger than New Zealand's own rapidly developing national identity. In reaction to Hitler's invasion of Poland on 1 September 1939, New Zealand, independently of Britain, declared war on Germany. Five days later, a dying Prime Minister Savage broadcast the following statement on the radio: 'With gratitude for the past and confidence in the future we range ourselves without fear beside Britain. Where she goes, we go; where she stands, we stand. We are only a small and a young nation, but we march with a union of hearts and souls to a common destiny.'

Six months later, it seemed that the whole world was at war and Savage was dead, succeeded by his deputy, Peter Fraser, who would steer New Zealand through the turbulent years of the Second World War.

Chrome-plated cigarette case engraved on the lid with 'A. D. K. [Kennedy] HMS ACHILLES 1940'.

GSC 0013

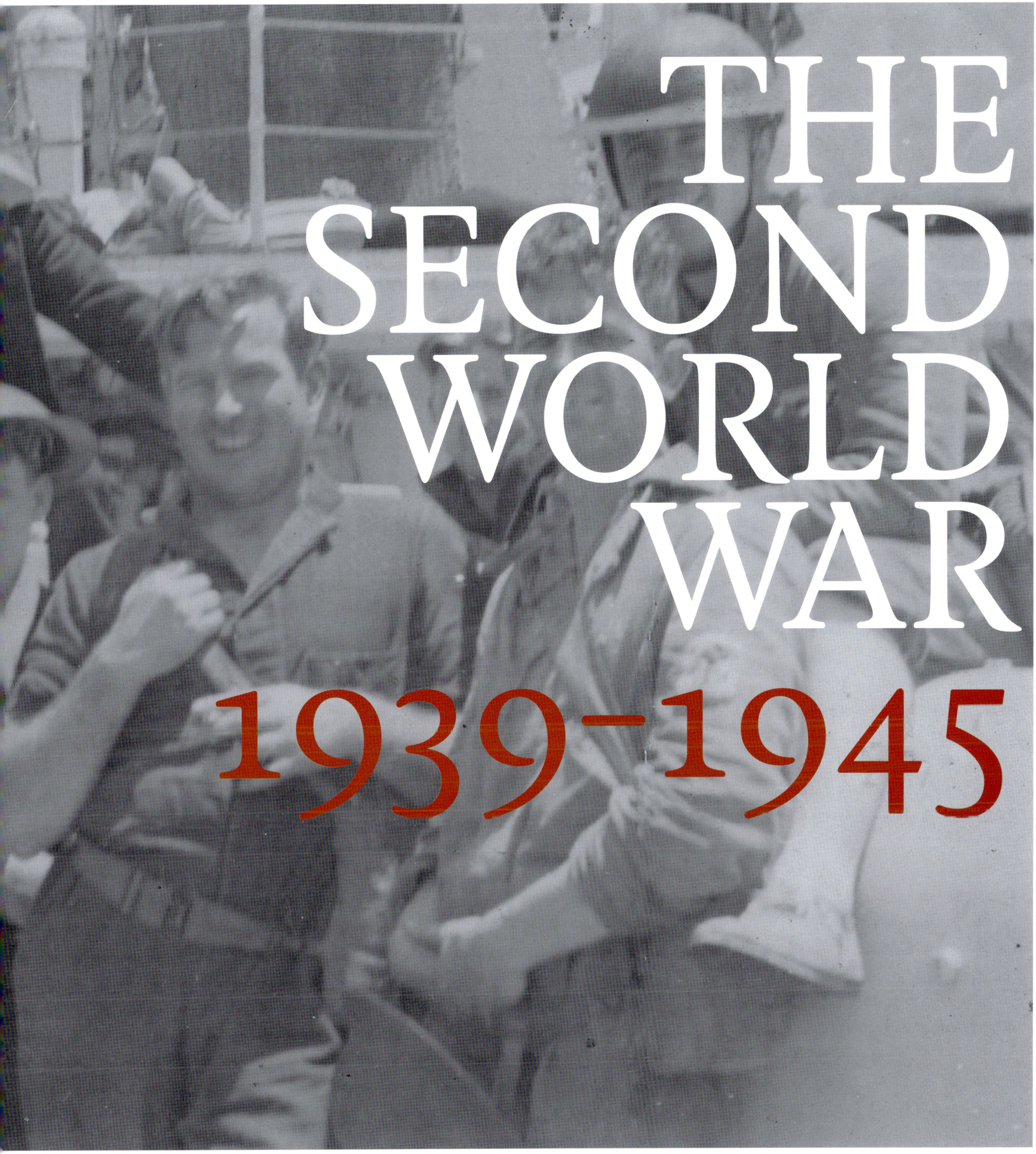

THE SECOND WORLD WAR 1939–1945

With the outbreak of war imminent, in August 1939 the British Government had taken the vessels of the New Zealand Division under its control, in accordance with the longstanding agreement between the Division and the Royal Navy that covered such circumstances as war. The sloop HMS *Wellington* was recalled from Pacific Island duty and HMS *Achilles*, HMS *Leith* and HMS *Leander* were ordered to complete full war storage. Two days before war was officially declared, *Achilles*, under the command of Captain W. E. Parry RN, was ordered to the West Indies to join the Royal Navy Fleet stationed there.

Within five hours, the ship had a full complement of crew, including two junior Naval Reserve officers poached from *Leander*, and had left HMS *Philomel* behind. *Achilles* carried a crew of 567, comprising of 536 ratings (316 of whom were from the New Zealand Division) and 26 officers, five of whom also came from the Division. The ship was well on her way across the Pacific on her journey to Balboa and Panama when a signal came through on 2 September to alter course for Valparaiso, Chile. A further signal was received 12 hours later, at 1 a.m. on 3 September 1939. Hostilities with Germany had commenced. The war had finally begun.

The ship arrived in Valparaiso to re-store and refuel in preparation for six weeks of patrolling the waters off Chile, Peru and Ecuador as a member of Force G in the company of HMS *Exeter*, HMS *Cumberland* and HMS *Ajax*. In all, eight hunting groups were formed to protect trade routes in the area, seeking out and destroying enemy raiders.

By early December 1939 it was estimated that the German raider *Admiral Graf Spee*, which had done considerable damage to a number of RN vessels, was in the River Plate area off the coast of Rio de Janeiro. Commodore Henry Harwood, who was in charge of the RN's South American Division to which Force G was affiliated, sent *Achilles*, *Ajax* and *Exeter* in search of the German ship. *Cumberland*, another of the ships in Force G, was undertaking routine maintenance in the Falkland Islands and was absent from the hunt.

BATTLE OF THE RIVER PLATE

AUG 0278

AUG 0110

At 6 a.m. on 12 December the three ships rendezvoused off the River Plate, and by midday Harwood had signalled his intention to find and attack the German 'pocket battleship', *Admiral Graf Spee*. On the morning of the 13th the ships went to dawn action stations for a practice run, after which they stood down.

Shortly after 6 a.m., the signalman on watch on board *Ajax* reported smoke on the port horizon. *Exeter* was ordered to investigate and, within minutes, *Admiral Graf Spee* was seen heading towards the three ships, on the attack. Thus on the morning of 13 December 1939, off the southwest coast of South America, in the early days of the Second World War, there commenced a mighty sea battle between the German pocket battleship *Admiral Graf Spee* and the British naval ships *Ajax* and *Exeter* and the New Zealand Division cruiser *Achilles*. In response to the German battleship's aggressive move, *Exeter* fired three salvos in quick succession that did considerable damage to the enemy before sustaining a direct hit on its own B turret. Continuous hits on *Exeter* occurred over the next 10 minutes until *Ajax* and *Achilles* managed to cross to the opposite side of the German battleship and opened fire. Despite the barrage it was receiving, the *Admiral Graf Spee* continued to return fire, landing two hits on *Achilles*, killing four and seriously wounding several men including Captain Parry.

Ajax had two of its gun turrets put out of action by shell-fire, and by this stage the damage onboard *Exeter* was so extensive that it was forced into retreat. However, the German ship, too, was beginning to falter after shells had hit its control tower, injuring Captain Hans Langsdorff. Despite this, the pocket battleship was still a formidable opponent, retaining her capacity for full speed and a full complement of armament.

With *Exeter* out of action and *Ajax* with two turrets damaged and fast running out of ammunition, Commodore Harwood decided to break off the action and take up a shadowing position. For its part, *Admiral Graf Spee* had sustained 23 hits including one on the bow which had compromised the battleship's seaworthiness and destroyed its fresh-water distillation plant. In addition, 37 of the German ship's crew had been killed, and another 57 injured including Langsdorff himself – a situation which no doubt influenced the captain's decision to enter the neutral port of Montevideo. *Admiral Graf Spee* anchored in the harbour shortly after midnight and a whole new battle, this time over the fate of the ship, began.

'This was the first time that we were firing just the same as we had been taught to fire, and all that sort of thing. We … knew there was some big bugger out there who was trying to blow us right out of the water. I suppose there was a little apprehension and that sort of thing, but I can't say that I felt any fear really, and I don't think anybody else did. [It] got the adrenalin flowing, though.'

'Our march up Queen Street was quite memorable. There were supposed to be 100,000 lining the streets that day. They gave us a big cheer. There were banners all over Queen Street and that sort of thing. Then we had a big reception at the Town Hall. We drank all the beer they had supplied. Sir Ernest Davies, head of New Zealand Breweries, likewise the Mayor of Auckland, said: "Hold on, boys." And back they came with plenty more beer. We had quite a grand day and it was very, very memorable. I was a Hamiltonian and, on my leave in Hamilton, the Council down there gave us a local reception and that sort of thing. We were big-time heroes for a short period. Then it was back to the nitty-gritty … '.

Petty Officer McKenzie – *Achilles*, A-turret

Captain Parry on the Bridge of HMS Achilles. *The injury on his right leg was sustained during the action against the German pocket battle ship the* Graf Spee *at River Plate, mid-December 1939.*
AUG 0197

'There was a lot of German sympathy, you know, in South America and a lot of Germans went there. … I had been to a football match, Paraguay versus Uruguay, and after the match I got a taxi and said: "Stop at every pub." At one of these pubs a chap had a bit of paper and he asked me to draw the ship. Well, I'm no sketch artist, but I did what the bloke had said and I had the guns sticking out all over the place. It was in Montevideo … and he was asking me all sorts of questions and evidently I was observed. The next thing I knew Captain Parry called for me, and evidently it had been reported to him and it turned out that he was a German spy.'

'[In one] of [the] lulls in firing, I stepped out onto the mess deck and they were putting the wounded on the locker tops. There was Eddie Shirley, he had a beard [and] it was all messed up and he was also wounded down the side and there were two or three other wounded, but they were looking for space for them. They were being carried down in stretchers and then put on top of these lockers. … I made my way back to the handling room and there were more boom-booms and then we continued until the next lull with humping these damn shells and putting them in the hoists. That is all I knew. You weren't afraid, you weren't scared. … You were twisting this way and that way and hunting around, that was continuous. You were too busy [even] during the lulls that were only a few minutes [long] anyway, you didn't have time to feel scared. You were busy. It wasn't until about two or three days after, when you realised what could have happened. Then you daren't say "pass the salt" across the table or you would get a punch on the nose. It was delayed reaction.'

'In Buenos Aires a lot of the German sailors were in the same drinking houses and restaurants, as we were. There was one place that I was in and there were 50/50 Germans and Brits and the sailors were exchanging ribbons. I was wearing a red badge and a German chap came up to me and wanted my badge, and he gave me his ribbon and I stupidly said, "No." Not that I [had] any [negative] feeling about their sailors … they were only doing a job like I was. I turned it down, and when I got back to New Zealand the sailors were getting as much as 50 quid for a cap ribbon – and I turned it down.'
Commander Cutts – *Achilles*, B-turret

Facts and Figures

	OFFICERS KILLED	WOUNDED	RATINGS KILLED	WOUNDED
EXETER	5	3	56	20
AJAX	-	1	7	14
ACHILLES	-	2	4	7

Battle of the River Plate
ABLE SEAMAN HUIA BEESLEY

Huia 'Harry' Beesley, who joined the New Zealand Division in 1932 as a boy seaman, was on board HMS *Achilles* during the Battle of the River Plate, seeing out the action as a member of the ship's 4-inch gun crew, a number of whom were killed or injured during the course of the engagement.

Huia Beesley: On the 12th of December we did a full 'action stations' emergency. This was what we would do should we encounter … the raider … Having heard of him last on such and such a date, he should be there [at the River Plate estuary] on the evening of the 12th. He was there on the morning of the 13th. We were called to dawn action which happens every morning … We remained closed up until daylight with full sweeps – 360-degree sweeps of the horizon to see if [any]thing was there. … About 6.10 the alarms went again and it was all go. It was the *Graf Spee*, sighted in the horizon about 14–15 miles away. The tip of her mast was the only thing to be seen. It was full action stations. … *Exeter* was despatched from line ahead. It was *Ajax, Achilles, Exeter. Exeter* was despatched out to the port and within minutes there was a flash on the horizon and … the shells started landing

INT: Well, tell me a bit about it from your personal point of view.
HB: … My action stations was on the open P1HA gun which is down on the iron deck, just below and aft the bridge. … Unfortunately, young Ian Grant who was alongside of me copped it in the chest. He died immediately. A chap called – I think his name was Marr or Marra, I have just forgotten his name – he dropped to the deck. He was shot all around the buttocks. There was no use leaving him there. We couldn't do anything as far as firing was concerned. I picked him up, threw him over my shoulders like a sack of coal to get him down to the sick bay. … Anyway, I deposited him in the sick bay and came up. We just had to stay at our action stations until such time as things ceased. It was as simple as that. We fired a couple of shots, but to no avail at all. I don't think they were to

AUG 0196

any avail at all. . . . Later on in the day of course . . . why [*Admiral Graf Spee*] turned and went in towards Montevideo I do not know. I don't think anybody will know to this day. . . . She was in the shadow of the setting sun. She was running in to the west and you could see her silhouette[ed] into the setting sun. . . . We waited [it] out . . . while all the diplomatic activity was going on. . . . The only ship that came along to give us any assistance was the *Cumberland*. She eventually came. There was a bit of alarm when she started to come over the horizon, too. We thought, hello, was it the *Prinz Eugen* or something like that? We thought it was, you know it was anybody's guess. . . . Well, eventually, I think it was a Sunday when we got news that the *Graf Spee* had sailed. Well, that was it. It was tense.

INT: Did you close up at action stations?
HB: Close up at action stations? Very much so. I might add we never had much ammunition left anyway. I think there was only about ten rounds a gun left, as I recall. She [*Admiral Graf Spee*] could have blown us right out of the water had she known. Then all of a sudden there was a mighty flash on the horizon where she [the German ship] had run herself on to the English Bank – set charges had exploded. And she exploded and boom!

The next day we cruised up close to her, dipped the flag. Yeah, we dipped the flag to what was then a burned-out hulk and then went on about our business. The war was still on and we had to carry on with our duties. Action started, action carried on and action finished.

INT: Did you go ashore after action at all?
HB: Yes, we had a weekend in Buenos Aires, and there was quite a large English element down there. We were given all sorts of welcome[s and] activities. I have forgotten exactly where it was, but there was garden parties. There was free this and free that and it was quite a weekend, you know.

There was still a few German sailors around who were waiting then to be interned, I believe. People thought there might have been fisticuffs ashore when we met up with each other, but there was nothing like that at all. These guys were Imperial Naval ones. They weren't Nazis, [they were] Imperial Naval men. On the odd occasion where we did see each other, we saluted each other and carried on.

Tray purchased in Rio de Janeiro. GEB 0004

Y-turret from Achilles *mounted on display at Devonport Naval Base.* JDC 0001

AUG 0246

Battle of the River Plate

CHIEF ELECTRICIAN ROBERT HARVEY

Robert Harvey joined the New Zealand Division of the Royal Navy as a seaman boy in 1936. He spent a little over a year training in HMS *Philomel* before being posted to HMS *Achilles* in mid-1937 and was still on board in late 1939 during the ship's part in the Battle of the River Plate, seeing out the action from his position in B turret.

Robert Harvey: At 1 a.m. on the 3rd September, our time ... war was declared. That's when we received – and I remember having – a copy of the signal. I had it for years, but have lost it now. All it said was: 'To all ships home and abroad, commence hostilities at once with Germany.' Then the time and origin of the signal and so on. We got a big thrill then, as kids, a big thrill, because ... gee ... war. It made us think.

INT: How old would you have been?
RH: Eighteen and a half. I suppose I was as brainless as the rest of them, but it didn't sink in for a while that this was serious and war could be serious. We were well away from the dangerous part anyway in our minds, and so it didn't worry us that much. Youth is a marvellous thing, you just don't worry about those sort of things at the time.

... We were in company with *Ajax* and we met *Exeter* in the morning, and then they carried out the exercise. ... They had been given orders from the Admiral (he was a Commodore at the time) of what to do in the event of meeting a raider.

... As far as the actual action itself went, we went to normal cruising action stations at that time of the morning, it might have been 5.30 or a little bit before that. ... then when it got light, they fell out action stations and closed up cruising stations.

INT: Did *Ajax* launch her aircraft at all?
RH: No, she didn't launch it until the action had actually started. She got it off when guns were firing. *Ajax*'s after-guns were firing on a forward bearing at the time – it took a bit of nerve on the part of the pilot. I think she carried two in the crew. ... The second time when we got the action alarm, the old da, da, da, da ... a frightening thing to hear. ... It was the real thing from then on and so we just got cracking and, once again, being the age I was, like many of them in the gun house ... you have got the drill that you have been taught to do and it's more or less automatic. You think that if you think too much you get frightened. The fear doesn't seem to come to the forefront. You have got a job to do and you do it. It's not until about an hour and a half later, as it was in that case, that we decided: Crikey, a shell could have come through here! ... We kept flat out, or we appeared to be. There was a little bit of a lull at times.

... I had a mental [image] of the possibility of a shell arriving and what the hell would happen. You know, if one arrives in here. Because I knew she [*Admiral Graf Spee*] had big shells – 690 lbs I think. I knew something bad would happen if they arrived in, but fortunately none did ... .

INT: What happened after this hour and a half of intense activity, and then *Graf Spee* headed off towards South America or towards Montevideo? What happened to you, were you stood down?
RH: When they had the lull in the action they allowed us to come on the upper deck, when they realised where she was going ... and we were chasing her. ... Anyway, *Achilles* was given permission to open fire and it was not far off Punta del Este, the place where they used recently for the Whitbread Race. We opened fire with five broadsides and then we turned to port and skedaddled.

... What happened as far as clearing up decks went – because there was a certain amount of damage, although very little on our ship and it was mainly structural damage. The shock of discharge of the guns always creates a bit of a havoc inside a ship. We know that things are put together and hopefully that they don't fall apart, but even chips from the deck head dropped down when they were firing broadsides, and all that had to be cleared up. A lot of woodwork fell down, particularly in the officers' area of the ship. Things that hadn't been secured.

We were clearing up after the action and really we were on a bit of a high as you can imagine – everything seemed to be going so successfully that we were mentally up in the air a little bit. Overnight, if I remember, we closed up most of the night and we were allowed to get our heads down ... but I don't ever remember getting back into the hammocks that night and nobody seemed to want to, because you were in a state of high elation.

Chrome and brass firing tubes from Achilles *during the Battle of the River Plate.* JEH 0012-17

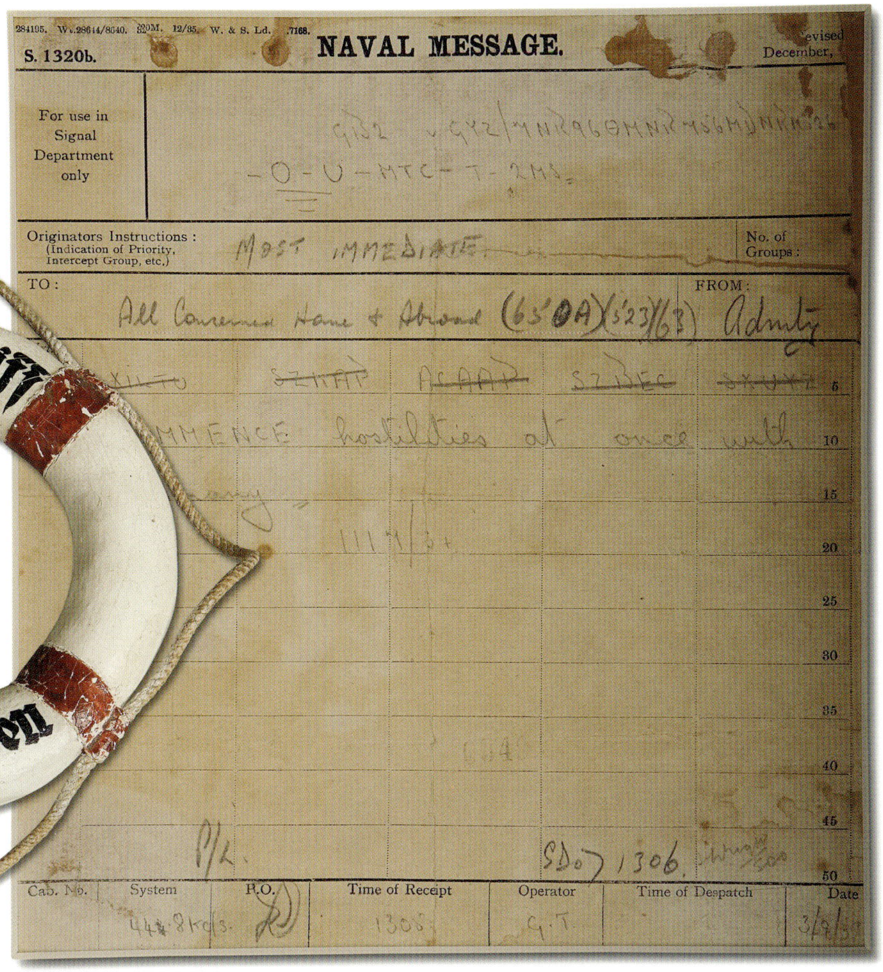
S. 1320b. NAVAL MESSAGE.

For use in Signal Department only

Originators Instructions: (Indication of Priority, Intercept Group, etc.) MOST IMMEDIATE

No. of Groups:

TO: All Concerned Home & Abroad

FROM: Admty

COMMENCE hostilities at once with Germany

Cab. No. | System | P.O. | Time of Receipt | Operator | Time of Despatch | Date

Telegram signal – Commence hostilities at once with Germany. T.2008.14.2

Souvenir life buoy obtained by Stoker McIver from a German sailor from the training ship Schlesien whilst in Kingston, Jamaica, prior to the Second World War. McIver later lost his life when HMS Neptune sunk in 1941. GEL 0002

Although the British wanted *Admiral Graf Spee* to be given a mere 24 hours' grace, the Uruguayan authorities granted the Germans four days in which to ready themselves for sail. During this four-day wait, the British cruisers patrolled the north and south line just outside the three-mile limit. The aircraft on board *Ajax* was launched on the morning of 16 December, but poor visibility limited intelligence regarding *Admiral Graf Spee*'s movements. Later, describing this four-day vigil, Captain Parry wrote:

'The next four days and nights, although uneventful, were full of anxiety. Fortunately the American Broadcasting Service kept our enemy in a blaze of publicity; but naturally we had to remain ready for immediate action for it was always possible that he might slink out unmolested. This entailed keeping all hands at their stations all night and very little sleep could be got by those of us who might be faced with a quick decision. The first twenty-four hours were perhaps the most critical, for it was not until the evening of 14 December that we were reinforced by the *Cumberland* and her welcome 8-inch guns. During this time the splendid spirit of the ship's company was most inspiring. If anyone's spirits had been inclined to droop they could not have failed to be revived by the strains of Maori music and songs, or the shouts of merriment which came from the various quarters. On the last evening the captain decided that the degree of readiness might be slightly relaxed to allow a proportion of the ship's company to sleep in their hammocks; but a few minutes later he received a unanimous request from all quarters that they would prefer to remain all night ready at their stations. Such a gesture is unforgettable.' (S. D. Waters, *The Royal New Zealand Navy: Official History of New Zealand in the Second World War*: 63)

The captain of the *Admiral Graf Spee*, Hans Langsdorff, had three options available to him: he could try and break through the British cordon outside the harbour, he could let his ship be interned, or he could scuttle *Admiral Graf Spee*. Berlin was duly notified of his predicament and placed the decision back in Langsdorff's hands, the only proviso being that the battleship not be interned by the British. On the morning of 17 December, Langsdorff made the decision to scuttle his ship, thus saving the lives of his crew. Preparations for sinking the vessels began immediately and included the arrival of boats from Buenos Aires, which had a large German population, to take off the crew.

At sunset the same day, with her battle ensigns flying on both the foremast and mainmast, *Admiral Graf Spee* weighed anchor and set sail for the mouth of the harbour where the British forces were waiting. Four miles off the coast and still in neutral waters, the ship stopped at 7:54 p.m. and the scuttling charges were detonated. The pocket battleship slowly sunk into the estuary. Her pride and most of her crew, if nothing else, were still intact.

AAF 0275

HMS *Achilles*

MOTTO: *FORTITER IN RE* – 'UNYIELDING IN ACTION'

Achilles has proved a popular name for Royal Navy ships. The *Leander*-class light cruiser which served with the Royal New Zealand Navy in the Second World War, and made a name for herself in the Battle of the River Plate, was the seventh and probably most famous to bear the name.

The seventh *Achilles*, and the one synonymous with New Zealand, was launched on 1 September 1932 by Lady Stanley, the wife of the Parliamentary Secretary to the Admiralty, and commissioned into the Royal Navy in October of the following year. Although the ship served with the New Zealand Division of the Royal Navy from late 1936, most notably in the Battle of the River Plate, it spent much of its wartime service as one of the fleet ships of the newly formed Royal New Zealand Navy in more mundane yet still vital service as a convoy escort vessel in the South Pacific, and later with the British Pacific Fleet for the attacks on Japan. *Achilles* returned to the RN in September 1946 and was purchased by India in 1948 for service in the Royal Indian Navy and renamed *Delhi*. The ship returned to New Zealand at a later date in command of the Indian navy.

AUG 0223

As the result of rekindling the relationship, when the cruiser was formally decommissioned on 30 June 1978, some of her fittings, including the Y gun turret and the director control tower, were gifted to the RNZN. Both the gun turret and control tower can be found at the harbourfront entrance of the Naval Base at Devonport. The silver bell which was presented by Lady Stanley at the ship's commissioning is also held in the Navy Museum's collection. *Achilles*' other major claim to fame is that she played herself in a film about the Battle of the River Plate.

Achilles' ship's badge, which was designed in England by a Major ffoulkes and approved on 20 July 1931, bears the helmeted head of Achilles on a red background and the motto

Fortiter in Re, meaning either 'unyielding in action' or 'bravely in action'. Variations of the badge have appeared over the years, some with a blue background, some with the classical hero Achilles' profile rendered in silver and yet others with the ship's motto set out under the head. Records show that both the (official) red and the blue backgrounds were used during the ship's service in New Zealand. Interestingly, when the Naval Board began collecting ships' badges for their boardroom, the *Achilles*' badge with its regulation red background supplied by the Dockyard was returned – with the request that it be painted blue.

Class and type: ***Leander*-class light cruiser**
Name: **HMS *Achilles***
Builder: **Cammell Laird and Company Ltd., Birkenhead, Merseyside**
Laid down: **11 June 1931**
Launched: **1 September 1932, and completed on 10 October 1933**
Commissioned: **5 October 1933**
Commissioned New Zealand Division: **31 March 1936**
Returned to Royal Navy: **September 1946**

General characteristics
Displacement: **7030 tons standard**
Dimensions: **169 x 17 m**
Propulsion: **4-shaft geared turbines, 6 boilers, 72,000 shp**
Speed: **32 knots**
Complement: **550 officers and ratings**
Armament: **Original configuration – 8 x 6-in and 4 x 4-in guns. Rearmed in 1943–44 with 6 x 6-in guns, 8 x 4-in anti-aircraft guns, 15 x 40-mm anti-aircraft guns, and 8 x 21-in torpedo-tubes in two quadruple mountings**
Pennant number: **70**

Communion set presented to the RNZN in memory of Claude Francis Webster, Chaplain RNZNVR, who served in HMNZS Leander *1941–44. Webster died on active service on HMNZS* Achilles, *November 13 1944.* ICB 0001

In Buenos Aires that night, Langsdorff wrote three letters: one to the German Minister of War, one to his wife and one to his parents. In the first he explained his actions. Included in this letter was the following statement: 'For a captain with a sense of honour, it goes without saying that his personal fate cannot be separated from that of his ship.' He then unfolded the ensign flown by *Admiral Graf Spee* during the battle, lay down on it and shot himself in the head.

Ajax, *Achilles* and *Exeter* were variously dispersed for repairs and other duties in the area and by the end of January 1940 *Achilles* set sail for New Zealand, arriving to a heroes' parade in Auckland. There was also a civic luncheon at the Auckland Town Hall, during which Captain Parry was presented with a traditional Maori cloak.

Back in Britain, Commodore Harwood was promoted to Rear Admiral and consequently made a Knight Commander of the Order of the Bath for his role in this major sea battle. Each of the captains was made a Companion of the same Order. Various awards were made to the crews of the three ships for their contribution to this important early battle of the Second World War.

For the cruiser HMS *Leander*, the start of the Second World War was not as dramatic as for its fellow cruiser *Achilles*. In August 1939 the ship was sent to Fanning Island in the central Pacific with troops on board to protect the trans-Pacific cable station there. The cables had been cut by German naval forces in 1914 during the First World War – hence the rapid response in landing a garrison there at the first inkling of war 20 years later.

Graf Spee *scuttled by her crew.* AUG 0133

Achilles *welcomed home to Auckland.* AAF 0118

Special edition of the Picture Post *on the Battle of the River Plate, including the return to London of* Ajax *and* Exeter *companies.* END 0007

After disembarking the protection force on Fanning Island, *Leander* returned to New Zealand waters for patrol duty, focusing on the search for German raiders in the uninhabited Campbell and Auckland Islands. Bad weather on the ship's first visit to the area is thought to be the reason why *Leander* failed to sight the German supply ship *Erlangen*, which was at anchor in Carnley Harbour in the Auckland Islands. According to published German accounts, *Erlangen* spent five weeks at the head of North Arm, the innermost inlet of Carnley Harbour, harvesting native timber – some 400 tons in total – to supplement her rapidly diminishing coal supply. *Leander*'s stay in New Zealand quickly came to an end. The Admiralty requested that the cruiser be transferred to its command in accordance with its prewar agreement with the Government, and in May 1940 the ship left New Zealand waters.

With *Leander* away with the Royal Navy in the Indian Ocean and *Achilles* in dry dock, though close to finishing her refit, the New Zealand Government was unsurprisingly concerned. Warships were needed to safeguard shipping. The New Zealand Naval Board's policy was to provide escorts not only for merchant ships but also for those vessels carrying Australian and New Zealand air trainees to Vancouver and, later, New Zealand troops to Fiji, in addition to vessels carrying phosphates from Nauru and Ocean Islands. A number of unsuccessful requests were made through 1940 and 1941 by the New Zealand Government for the return of *Leander* to the New Zealand Station. *Achilles* was back on duty by June 1940 with the armed merchant cruisers HMS *Monowai* and HMS *Hector* performing crucial convoy escort work. As a consequence of the demand for escort vessels, the newly repaired *Achilles* spent much of 1941 almost continuously on convoy duties. The escorting of refrigerated cargo ships, known as AP convoys,

Battle of the River Plate

'Better a thousand live young men than a thousand dead heroes.'

Captain Hans Langsdorff, *Admiral Graf Spee* – 17 December 1939

AAF 0043

AAF 0125

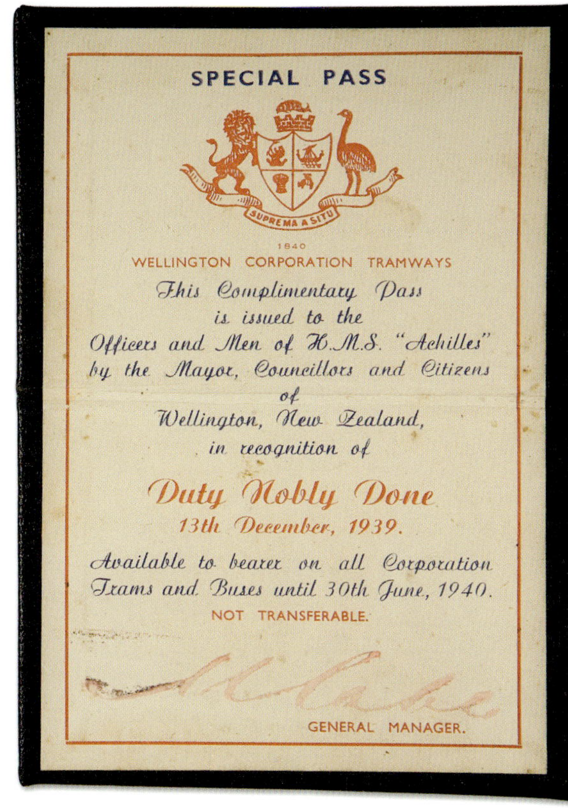

SPECIAL PASS

SUPREMA A SITU

1840

WELLINGTON CORPORATION TRAMWAYS

This Complimentary Pass is issued to the Officers and Men of H.M.S. "Achilles" by the Mayor, Councillors and Citizens of Wellington, New Zealand, in recognition of

Duty Nobly Done

13th December, 1939.

Available to bearer on all Corporation Trams and Buses until 30th June, 1940.

NOT TRANSFERABLE.

GENERAL MANAGER.

AUCKLAND METROPOLITAN AREA

This Complimentary Pass is issued to the Officers and Men of H.M.S. "ACHILLES" by the combined Metropolitan Transport Operators of AUCKLAND in recognition of DUTY NOBLY DONE 13th December, 1939

COMPLIMENTARY TRAVEL TICKET

Available to bearer on all City and Suburban TRAMS OMNIBUSES and FERRIES on any route at any time during a period of seven days after arrival of the SHIP at Auckland.

NOT TRANSFERABLE

Special passes allowing complimentary travel on trams, buses and ferries. Issued to the Officers and Men of Achilles *'in recognition of a duty nobly done' at the Battle of the River Plate.* EBB 0012 & EBB 0013

was begun by *Monowai* in late 1940, but soon afterwards the task fell mainly to *Achilles*.

Though hardly the most glamorous of tasks, especially after the excitement and glory of the Battle of the River Plate, the statistics showed that *Achilles* was by no means on holiday. Since its post-River Plate refit in the first half of 1940, the ship had clocked up an impressive 82,679 miles and averaged 24 days a month at sea. However, this meant that New Zealand waters were unprotected for extended periods of time when the Division's vessels were away on duty – although all ships in the area were continually on the lookout for German raiders. These ships would remain on this continuous round of escort duties and trooping for a little over two years until they were absorbed into the Anzac Force in early 1942.

When *Leander* left Wellington for service with the RN in May 1940, an interchange of farewell signals between the New Zealand Division ships included one from *Achilles* to *Leander* wishing her 'as good luck as we had' – to which the departing cruiser replied: 'We will do our best.' The cruiser detached from the convoy it was acompanying in the Indian Ocean, having been ordered to proceed independently to Alexandria, then the Red Sea, to join the Fourth Cruiser Squadron, East Indies Station. *Leander* arrived at Port Sudan on 4 June.

While based at the East Indies Station, *Leander* was charged with the largely monotonous task of protecting friendly shipping and escort duties across the narrow waterway between Aden and Suez. In just under five months, the

AAG 0268

AAG 0138

HMS *Leander*

MOTTO: *QUI PATITUR VINCIT* – 'WHO SUFFERS CONQUERS'

In total, the Royal Navy has had six ships that have borne the name *Leander*. The vessel linked with New Zealand naval history was the fifth in an illustrious line-up and was transferred to the New Zealand Navy in 1937, seeing service as a New Zealand Division ship in the Mediterranean and Pacific during the Second World War.

Leander was launched at Devonport on 13 July 1929 and was commissioned into the Royal Navy as HMS *Leander* on 23 July 1931, serving with the New Zealand Division from 1937 until 1941 when the New Zealand Division of the RN became the Royal New Zealand Navy. *Leander* was subsequently commissioned as HMNZS *Leander* in September 1941. In mid-July 1943 *Leander* was severely damaged when it was hit by a torpedo at Kolombangra in the Pacific. It would not be until 1945 that repairs to *Leander* were completed, and the vessel was returned to the Royal Navy. *Leander* was scrapped in 1950.

Leander's ship's badge was derived from the coat of arms of Royal Navy Admiral Sir Thomas Thompson, who was the commander of the first ship to bear the Leander name. Commissioned in 1780, the first *Leander* was a 4th rate of 50 guns which took part in the Battle of the Nile. The badge in its current form was redesigned in the 1930s when the Leander class of cruisers were being built.

Class and type: ***Leander*-class light cruiser**
Name: **HMS *Leander***
Builder: **HMNB Devonport**
Laid down: **1 August 1928**
Launched: **13 July 1929**
Commissioned: **23 July 1931**
Commissioned HMNZS *Leander*: **September 1941**
Returned to Royal Navy: **27 August 1945**

General characteristics
Displacement: **7270 tons standard**
Dimensions: **169 x 17 m**
Propulsion: **4 Parsons geared steam turbines, 6 boilers, 4 shafts, 72,000 shp**
Speed: **32.5 knots**
Range: **5730 nm at 13 knots**
Complement: **570 officers and ratings**
Armament: **Original configuration – 8 x 6-in guns, 8 x 4-in guns, 12 x 0.5-in machine guns, 8 x 21-in torpedo tubes**
Armour: **3-in magazine box, 1-in deck, 1-in turrets**
Aircraft carried: **One catapult-launched aircraft. Original type – Fairey Seafox catapult. Aircraft later replaced with Supermarine Walrus**
Pennant number: **75**

Barrel brush for rocket flare. T2008.4.1

1" line throwing pistol. JCC 0006

cruiser clocked up 30,874 miles and escorted 18 convoys. The ship's Walrus aircraft was used during this period to search, unsuccessfully, for an Italian submarine which had torpedoed and sunk the Norwegian tanker, *James Stove*, about 12 miles south of Aden. While the Walrus' reconnaissance was unsuccessful, the anti-submarine and minesweeping trawler HMS *Moonstone* spotted a periscope and dropped two depth charges, forcing the surfacing and surrender of the vessel, the Italian submarine *Galileo Galilei*. The submarine's casualties numbered 12 including the commanding officer, and a further four submariners were wounded.

A further successful attack on another Italian submarine off the southern coast of Eritrea on 27 June by *Leander*, in concert with HMS *Kandahar*, HMS *Kingston* and HMS *Shoreham*, followed soon after. Following an initial attacked by *Shoreham*, the submarine had run aground. The attack recommenced with the bombing of the vessel by *Leander*'s Walrus, which was followed by the straddling of the submarine by *Leander*'s guns. The Walrus spotted two men swimming away from the sub and two others, one of whom appeared to be dead, were seen on the beach. The submarine was *Evangelista Torricelli*, the same class as the captured *Galileo Galilei*. It was the fifth Italian submarine destroyed or captured in just eight days by the RN.

A few months later, on the afternoon of 19 October, a single aircraft dropped four bombs close astern of a steamer in a Red Sea convoy in which *Leander* was acting as escort. A further attack was made on the convoy the following morning, with no damage reported. The following day, *Leander* sighted two patches of smoke which turned out to be two enemy destroyers. When the enemy vessels failed to answer a challenge by HMS *Auckland*, another of the ships on escort duty, *Auckland* opened fire, causing the two enemy destroyers to separate and subsequently turn away at full speed, firing their after guns and torpedoes. Two torpedoes were fired in the direction of the Australian Navy escort vessel HMAS *Yarra* which managed, due to some deft manoeuvreing, to avoid being hit.

At this point *Leander* altered course, leaving the convoy in pursuit of the enemy destroyers, and opened fire at 2.45 a.m., expending in a scant six minutes a total of 129 rounds of 6-inch shell. She lost sight of the German ships after the first salvos and the search – which the destroyer HMS *Kimberley* had now joined – began in earnest. However, because of fears for the safety of the convoy *Leander* returned to her escort position. Meanwhile, *Kimberly* engaged one of the enemy destroyers near Harmil Island and, although coming under fire from both warships and a shore battery, managed to get the better of an Italian ship which was identified as *Francesco Nullo*. It was subsequently sunk by two of *Kimberly*'s torpedoes.

With the enemy destroyer taken care of, *Kimberly* turned her attention to the shore battery until she sustained a hit in her engine room. With *Kimberly* damaged, *Leander* once more disengaged from the convoy and rushed to the RN ship's aid, joining *Kimberly* a few hours later. As a result of the damage to the engine room, three shipwrights and an engine-room artificer from the New Zealand cruiser were sent to assist in the repairs. *Kimberly* was taken in tow by *Leander* at approximately 10 p.m. that evening, and both ships rejoined the convoy shortly after midday. The next day the tow of *Kimberly* was transferred to *Kingston*. Both ships left the convoy the next morning, bound for Port Sudan. The rest of the convoy's journey passed uneventfully.

Brown leather case embossed 'Drown Sorrows in Smoke'. GSC 0009

AAG 0032

During the New Zealand cruiser's five months of duty in the Red Sea area, it had clocked up an estimated 30,874 miles and escorted 18 convoys totalling 396 ships. A small Greek tanker which was torpedoed was the only vessel lost.

Leander's next mission was the demolition of a fish-canning factory and a wireless direction-finding station on the coast of Italian Somaliland in late November 1940. On 29 November the New Zealand cruiser's Walrus aircraft made two single-bomb dive attacks, the second under enemy rifle fire, on the direction-finding huts. Both were misses. *Leander* then opened fire on the factory and the Walrus dropped a stick of incendiary bombs, after which both ship and Walrus withdrew. Approximately two hours later the Walrus made a second attack on the direction-finding station, again not scoring a hit. However, aerial photographs showed extensive damage to the factory from *Leander*'s guns and it was felt that it had been put out of operation.

Soon after, having completed five months of convoy duty, the New Zealand cruiser set course for Bombay, arriving on 2 December 1940 for a much-needed stint in the dry dock for maintenance and a 25-day rest for the crew, who were primarily accommodated ashore.

Leander accompanied a further two convoys in the Red Sea, in late December and early January 1941, before setting a course for

HMNZS *Monowai*

The armed merchant cruiser *Monowai* began its life in early 1925 as the mail and passenger ship *Razmak*. It was renamed *Monowai* in late 1930 and entered passenger service between New Zealand and a variety of destinations including Australia and the United States. Named for the lake in Western Southland, the vessel was taken over by the navy on the outbreak of the Second World War and turned over to the Devonport Dockyard for conversion to an armed merchant cruiser. By August 1940 *Monowai* was on escort and patrol duty in New Zealand waters and the South Pacific, joining the Anzac Squadron in April 1942. Within a year it had become clear that armed merchant cruisers were vulnerable to submarine torpedo attack and *Monowai* was scheduled, like others of her ilk, for conversion to other duties such as trooping, for which they were better suited. However,

AAH 0020

Brass plaque inscribed 'By Virtue of Her War Service this ship has been created an Honorary Member of the Auckland RSA'. It is unique in that it is unusual for a ship to be made a member rather than individuals and may be the only ship that has been so recognised in this country. GFG 0067

when *Monowai* arrived at the Devonport Dockyard for her refit in March 1943, it was decided that the cruiser was surplus to requirements in the Pacific and was sailed to Britain where it was paid off as a Royal New Zealand Navy armed merchant vessel in June of that year.

Although her service in New Zealand waters may have come to an end, *Monowai* was converted by the British to an assault landing ship and was occupied throughout the remainder of the war transporting troops and refugees in North Africa and the Mediterranean. In addition, *Monowai* was among the ships which ferried British and Canadian commando troops to Normandy's Gold Beach on D-Day in June 1944. In just four months, the vessel made 20 round voyages between Southampton and Normandy and a further 25 to Le Havre. After the Normandy operation, *Monowai* did an extraordinary amount of steaming as it performed as a 'jack of all trades' carrying troops and refugees and repatriating prisoners of war. She saw time in port in Odessa, Italy, India and Singapore – all in just over six months. It is estimated that the vessel carried over 100,000 people in the months immediately following the end of the war.

By 1949 the ship was once again in service as a passenger liner for the Union Steam Ship Company, doing the New Zealand to Sydney run. In June 1960 *Monowai* was sold to the Far East Metal Industry and Shipping Company Ltd in Hong Kong, arriving in that port three months later, destined for scrap.

Class and type: **Armed merchant cruiser**
Name: **HMNZS *Monowai***
Builder: **Harland Wolff Ltd, Greenock, Scotland**
Laid down: **20 June 1923**
Launched: **16 October 1924**
Commissioned as *Razmak*: **26 February 1925**
Commissioned as *Monowai*: **November 1930**
Commissioned (New Zealand Division): **21 October 1939**
Paid off (New Zealand Division): **18 June 1943**

General characteristics
Displacement: **4925 tons standard**
Dimensions: **158.2 x 19.3 m**
Propulsion: **2-shaft reciprocating 4-cylinder QE with low-pressure double-reduction exhaust turbines, 14,740 bhp**
Speed: **18 knots**
Complement as AMC: **366 officers and ratings**
Armament: **Original AMC configuration – 8 x 6-in, 2 x 3-in AA, 6 x 20-mm MGs, 8 x depth charges**
Pennant number: **F59**

6-inch practice shell. JEA 0007

Colombo, the capital of Ceylon, in preparation for duty in the Indian Ocean. Although the New Zealand Government had asked for the return of *Leander* to New Zealand waters, the Admiralty requested that the cruiser remain in the Indian Ocean searching for raiders for a further three to four months until a ship became available to relieve her. The Government agreed to the request with the proviso that if Japan entered the war, or activity by raiders increased substantially in the South Pacific, the ship would be immediately returned to New Zealand waters.

While seeing out duty in the Indian Ocean on 22 February 1941, *Leander* passed down the west side of the Laccadive and Maldive Islands in search of Italian ships rumoured to be in the area. Suspicions were vindicated when a ship was spotted with a gun mounted on the forecastle and a silhouette that resembled the Italian Ramb class of fruit carriers.

The New Zealand cruiser went to action stations, ordering the vessel to hoist her colours. The unidentified ship responded by hoisting the British merchant ensign; however, when ordered to make her signal letters, she hoisted four letters not listed in British signal books. *Leander* ordered the ship to 'stop instantly'. Initially unresponsive, after a few minutes she hoisted the Italian merchant ensign and turned her guns on the New Zealand cruiser, which was now broad on the Italian ship's beam and vulnerable to machine gun fire and possibly torpedo attack. A few minutes later the Italian ship opened fire and *Leander* immediately retaliated. After firing off five salvos in one minute, the New Zealand cruiser signalled by flags: 'Do you surrender?' As at this point it was clear that a number of *Leander*'s salvos had found their mark

AAG 0173

and the crew of the Italian vessel was frantically abandoning ship, *Leander*'s boarding cutter was lowered with a view to saving the Italian ship for RN purposes. An Italian officer who was in the water hailed the boarding party and warned them not to approach the ship as she was on fire and heavily loaded with ammunition. As the fire spread aft there were two explosions and within minutes the enemy ship had sunk.

Survivors were fished out of the water and comprised the captain, 10 officers and 92 ratings, of whom one was seriously wounded and died while undergoing surgical treatment. He was buried with full naval honours at sunset. Interrogation of the Italian prisoners of war established that the ship was *Ramb I*. The prisoners were duly transferred to the RN oiler *Pearleaf*, and taken to Colombo accompanied by an armed guard.

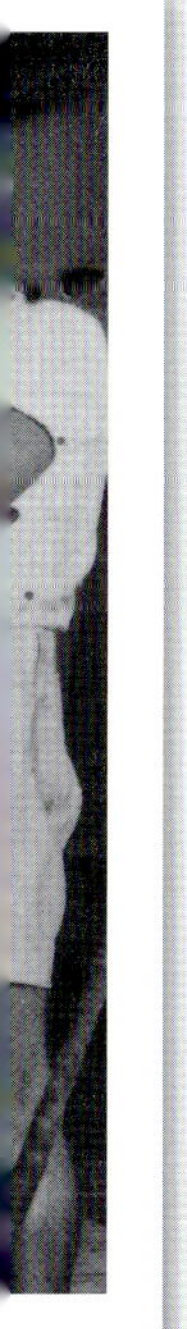

AAG 0131

In company with *Canberra*, *Leander* was then dispatched to patrol the Saya de Malha and Mauritius areas of the Indian Ocean to search for enemy raiders and supply ships. It was known from intelligence reports originating from German prisoners taken from captured enemy ships that the pocket battleship *Admiral Scheer* had been operating in the Seychelles–Saya de Malha area during February 1941, and it was possible that she or other raiders or their supply ships might be encountered at any time. Although *Admiral Scheer* had in fact left the Indian Ocean by this time, there was much lower-deck speculation on board *Leander* on the possibility of a 'second River Plate'. Thus, when on 5 March 1941 the *Canberra*'s reconnaissance aircraft sighted a pocket battleship in the vicinity, there were 'great expectations' of another mighty sea battle as *Leander* went to action stations. The enemy battleship turned out to be *Leander* itself, and was thus a false alarm.

During this period, the possibility of *Leander* being returned to the New Zealand Station was again raised by the New Zealand Government and, once again, the Admiralty's desire to retain the ship for its own purposes overrode any concerns the Government might have had, leading Prime Minister Fraser to state that the Government held no objection to the Admiralty retaining *Leander* as part of its fleet provided that, if the situation should deteriorate at home, the ship would be sent back to serve in the New Zealand Division's home waters. And so the cruiser continued to operate with the RN.

While patrolling between Mauritius and Madagascar in late March 1941, *Leander* sighted a ship carrying Vichy French markings on her bows and quarter. Because the ship resembled the German raider *Atlantis*, which had been known to disguise herself on occasion, the New Zealand cruiser went to action stations and a boarding party was prepared. As the unidentified vessel made no reply to repeated flag and lamp signals requesting her name and ordering her to stop, *Leander* fired two rounds of blank ammunition and, when these failed to produce the desired result, two 4-inch shells were fired across the stranger's bows.

At this point the ship, the French motor-vessel *Charles L. D.*, finally stopped and *Leander* sent away a boarding party. A few minutes later, despite *Leander*'s request that she not use her radio, *Charles L. D.* transmitted the words 'Vive l'Angleterre!' and then sent a coded message evidently reporting her position. *Leander* responded by sending a signal, 'Defendu Radio', repeating the request for an end to radio transmission and underlining it with a burst of machine-gun fire over the ship's masthead. The boarding party cut the falls of all the boats on board *Charles L. D.* and searched the ship,

Leander – 1941
'At the special request of First Lord of Admiralty, I have at once agreed in the circumstances to *Leander* being despatched to the Mediterranean. Help of *Leander* type of cruiser essential to support our men in Crete ...'.
23 May 1941 – Prime Minister Peter Fraser to Acting Prime Minister Walter Nash

Ratings No. 2 dress uniform and kit bag. CAN 0036 & CQC 0006

Leander in the Mediterranean – 1940–41

COMMANDER S. F. HERMANS

S. F. Hermans, who joined the New Zealand Division of the Royal Navy in 1939, was on board HMS *Leander* during the cruiser's time in the Mediterranean during 1940–41 when the ship attacked and sunk the Italian raider *Ramb I*. Hermans' action station during the battle was on the plot.

Hermans: Every time that we spotted a ship … I had to … plot the enemy ship position in relation to us so that we could get an estimate of the speed [at which it was travelling]. On this particular occasion, we started … working up … speed but getting no closer. … We gradually closed [in on] it – she was still battling along, and it took a while. We signalled her to stop, and she took no notice, so we fired a shell, one 4-inch across her bows. She then slowed down, and we closed in. I called up to Johnny Kirk and I said: 'What is she?' And he said: 'Oh, one of ours.' … As we went to open the deadlights – well, just as I opened them – I heard the Chief Yeoman through the voice pipe yelling out and he kept on saying to the captain: 'It's an Italian raider.' He said: 'Oh, you know we've got to make sure.' And we were making sure all right, we closed to well within a mile or so. And just as I opened up the deadlights I heard the Yeoman say: 'She is hauling down her flag, sir.'

At that very moment I saw flashes of gunfire coming from the forward guns. They were 5.9 or damn near 6-inch guns. Two mounted forward and two aft. The shells went hurtling over the bridge. The others went astern and fortunately missed us and, at that time, Pop Harvey, who was the gunner in charge of the 4-inch guns on that side, opened up and put a 4-inch shell right through her [the raider's] W/T office. Immediately 'Guns' swung the 6-inch round and we were so close that the shells were going clean through her and exploding some distance away on the other side. That set the ship on fire, and she eventually sank.

We were pretty lucky, because a few months later the German raider *Kormoran* sank HMAS *Sydney* in exactly the same situation. She got fooled into going into close range and was sunk, and all the ship's company [was] lost without trace.

INT: What you are saying is that the enemy vessel deluded *Leander* into getting too close and *Leander* didn't realise it was a raider until right at the last minute?

SH: Yes, absolutely correct. I don't think [the] C'n'C gave Captain Bevan much of a recommend afterwards because, there is no doubt about it, the ship was endangered. Instead of keeping its distance … I suppose that it is all right talking in hindsight … instead of keeping astern of her, we pulled in broadside on just a mile or so off.

INT: On the beam?

SH: Right on the beam, you see. They had the guns hidden with canvas screens or something, and they dropped them, and the first thing I saw when I looked through the opened scuttle was the gun flashes. [*Ramb I*] was able to get, oh, about four or five salvos away.

INT: When you had sunk the raider, did you pick up any survivors?

SH: Yes. That was awfully interesting. The 4-inch shell which went through their W/T office killed one of their ratings and badly wounded another one. They were the only casualties. We could see that the ship was on fire. We sent a boarding party across, but before they got to the *Ramb I*, an Italian officer called out: 'Don't go near there. The

Ramb I *on fire with survivors in life boats.* AAG 0116

Prisoners from Ramb I *on board* Leander. AAG 0105

Ramb I *on fire prior to sinking.* AAG 0118

Pair of steel handcuffs c. 1941. IDC 0001

Box made and used by J. Sevi to send presents home to his wife during the Second World War whilst he was on active service. ELM 0002

ammunition is on fire.' Even before they got back to our ship, they had the first explosion on board. And we were so close, that much debris was landing on our deck. The interesting thing was that the ratings came across in their lifeboats, but the officers swam across to us. They had one wounded rating with them and he died soon afterwards, and that evening he was buried at sea. The chap who was killed went down, with his ship. They were the only two casualties.

INT: What did you do with the prisoners?
SH: We took them to Addu Atoll, I think it was, where there was an oiler waiting and we fuelled from her. We were on patrol, and she was returning to Colombo soon afterwards, and so we put the prisoners on her, with a guard party on board. . . . The other interesting thing . . . among my duties onboard, was that I was included with the Captain of Marines as one of the interrogating officers. Our job was to interrogate the ratings, while the Captain and the Commander and somebody else interrogated the officers. I think, on this occasion, we were all there interrogating them and we tried to find out the movements of the *Ramb I*.

finding two scuttling charges. The boarding party was relieved by an armed guard and the captured ship set sail for Mauritius, worked by all the ship's company with the exception of the master and the first and second officers.

By the end of May 1941, *Leander* was in the Mediterranean to lend 'support to our men in Crete' who, along with British troops, were being evacuated from the area. Crete had been captured after a bitter struggle lasting from 20 May to 1 June, in which the Germans exploited their superiority in aircraft and airborne troops to overwhelm the gallant defenders. Losses to the Mediterranean Fleet in the Battle of Crete were substantial, and thus the New Zealand cruiser was a most welcome and useful addition.

By this time a dangerous situation had also developed in Syria, and signs of enemy infiltration included German aircraft making use of Syrian airfields. The situation would have serious consequences if the Germans should take complete control of Syria. To prevent this situation, it was deemed necessary for Britain and her Allies to occupy the country. A naval support fleet was established and Force 'B' sailed from Alexandria on 7 June to join British and Free French troops in the invasion of Syria. Although *Leander* had not been included in the original line-up, within a week of the fleet's departure the New Zealand cruiser sailed from Alexandria to join Force 'B', relieving *Ajax*. On 15 June an attack on Force 'B' was made by eight German bombers. Three British fighters drove off the bombers before the enemy could complete their attack, and one bomber was shot down. Although another attack was made an hour later by approximately 16 French and German aircraft, Force 'B' remained unscathed.

A week later, Force 'B' had another brief encounter with the enemy. While four destroyers carried out an anti-submarine patrol to seaward, *Naiad* and *Leander* made an inshore search, screened by destroyers. At 1.48 a.m., when the ships were approximately

Tuffnel box containing model lead ships, used for recognition training during the Second World War. 1449/1 (1)

Sikes's hydrometer used for ascertaining the strength of spirits and for determining the weight per gallon of spirits. Used mainly for rum. TKH 0006

Signal lantern. Hand-held and battery-powered portable lamp for signalling between ships. SCE 0005

10 miles north of Beirut, *Naiad* sighted two French destroyers. The enemy escaped at high speed behind a smoke screen and under covering fire from a coastal defense battery. The French destroyers were engaged by Force 'B' for 11 minutes and several hits were eventually claimed. Shortly afterwards, in early July 1941, hostilities in Syria ceased and an armistice agreement was signed at Acre.

After landing troops in Cyprus in mid-July as part of Operation Guillotine, *Leander* joined the Mediterranean Fleet for exercises. The cruiser's time with the Fleet was brief, as within days orders were finally received for her return to New Zealand. After a quick spruce-up in dock in Colombo, *Leander* set sail for home waters, arriving back in New Zealand in early September 1941 after an absence of 16 months.

In New Zealand, there was a great deal of concern and discussion over the level of threat in home waters. Compared with Europe and the northern reaches of the Pacific, the enemy presence was minimal. Nevertheless, German raiders were operating in New Zealand waters, laying mines and torpedoing ships.

As a direct result of the threat posed by raiders in South Pacific, and after much vociferous lobbying by the New Zealand Government, in early 1940 the Admiralty had temporarily allocated the armed merchant cruiser *Hector* to the New Zealand Station to coincide with *Leander*'s departure. However, within six months the Admiralty was requesting the ship's return. This was strongly opposed by the New Zealand Naval Board because of the German raider threat in New Zealand waters. Cabinet had approved the purchase of three ships with minesweeping, gunnery and torpedo-training capabilities to form the nucleus of a small home fleet. The shipbuilding contract was duly tendered out and the work went to Henry Robb Ltd, of Leith, Scotland. Although the keels of *Moa*, *Kiwi* and *Tui* were laid in March 1941, the Admiralty's own considerable shipbuilding needs had priority, and it would be a further two years before the three new vessels arrived in New Zealand.

In the interim, the New Zealand naval authorities had earmarked 15 coastal vessels for possible conversion to minesweepers. Three Auckland-based trawlers – *James Cosgrove*, *Thomas Currell* and *Humphrey* – were selected for immediate conversion by the Dockyard. In a matter of days, the three ships were fitted out and on duty. The ship's company of *James Cosgrove* consisted entirely of officers and ratings of the New Zealand Division of the RN Reserve and what remained of the Volunteer Reserve, many of whom had been absorbed into the New Zealand Division of the RN. The other two vessels were crewed by both merchant marine and naval personnel, and their respective masters were given temporary naval rank and retained command. The reservist training ship *Wakakura* was placed under the command of Lieutenant Commander A. D. Holden who became senior officer of the New Zealand Minesweeping Flotilla, which now totalled four ships.

As a result of the increased presence of German raiders in the Pacific and the southern reaches of the Indian Ocean, in a memorandum to the Minister of Defense the newly appointed Chief of the Naval Staff, Commodore W. E. Parry (of the Battle of the River Plate fame), pleaded the case for expansion of the minesweeping flotilla. He considered the current four sweepers 'totally inadequate to ensure even reasonable security from enemy mine laying activities'. Furthermore, Parry felt that a 'serious situation … may result if mine laying should be carried out by the enemy in New Zealand waters … [as] there is nothing to prevent … armed raiders laying mines off the coasts of New Zealand'.

Parry's concerns were vindicated soon after the sinking of the passenger liner *Niagara* off the Hen and Chicken Islands in June 1940 and the subsequent discovery of the minefield laid by *Orion* across the approaches to the Hauraki Gulf, underlining just how close the enemy was coming to New Zealand and the country's very real fears of an invasion. The sinking of *Niagara* shook the nation considerably and provided the impetus for the rapid conversion of a number of small coastal ships and the training ship *Wakakura* into a domestic minesweeping flotilla. Reluctance to take over local fishing and merchant vessels vanished overnight and resulted in the prompt requisitioning of the fishing trawlers *South Sea* and *Futurist* as minesweepers and the 50-ton wooden vessel *Coastguard* as a danlayer, in addition to the trawler *Nora Niven* and the harbour passenger vessel *Duchess*. These five vessels were manned by an assortment of naval crews and members of their existing crews who were to be trained and redeployed as needed.

SCE 0005

In the subsequent sweeping operation of the minefield in the Hauraki Gulf that had set all this frantic activity in motion, it was calculated that the 25th Minesweeping Flotilla swept 106 mines while a further 27 were accounted for in other ways – a total of 133 out of the 228 mines believed to have been laid. Many others were thought to have sunk or broken away from their moorings and drifted out into the open ocean. On completion of this task in late September, the Flotilla was sent a message from the Naval Board congratulating it on a 'very creditable piece of minesweeping …'. It added that 'Special credit was due to Coastguard for her part in these operations.'

The German raider *Orion* returned to New Zealand waters in mid 1940 and struck her second blow to merchant shipping with the sinking of the French steamer *Notou*, on passage from Newcastle to Noumea, and *Turakina*, attacked in the Tasman Sea. The wireless signals transmitted by *Turakina* while under attack meant that the raider's position could be more or less fixed and this knowledge was in effect responsible for chasing the enemy ship out of the southern reaches of the Pacific.

It would be a further two months before *Orion* struck once more, although this time in company with *Komet* and the supply ship *Kulmerland*. On the morning of 25 November the steamer *Holmwood*, bound for Lyttelton, was stopped by *Komet*, which was disguised as a Japanese ship. The 29 passengers and crew, including four women and two children, were taken off the ship, which was then sunk by gunfire.

AUO 0009

AUCKLAND HARBOUR

In June 1940, the German raider *Orion* laid the first row of mines across the eastern approaches to the passage between Great Mercury Island and Cuvier Island. A second barrage of mines was laid across the approaches to Cuvier Island in a zigzag which overlapped the southeast end of Great Barrier Island. A third and much longer barrage was laid across the northern approaches to the Hauraki Gulf. It extended from a point off the northern end of Great Barrier in a wide arc 10 kilometres off the Mokohinau Islands and thence in a straight line to the northwest, passing about nine kilometres beyond the Maro Tiri – Hen and Chicken – Islands to a point about seven kilometres from the mainland. All the mines were of the moored contact type. Six days elapsed before the minefield claimed its first victim, the outward-going passenger liner *Niagara*. With 136 passengers, general cargo, and a shipment of gold bullion valued at £2,500,000 on board, the ship hit a mine just off the Hen and Chicken Islands and sank.

LYTTELTON & WELLINGTON HARBOURS

Shortly after midnight of 24–25 June 1941, the German vessel *Adjutant* laid 10 mines close in across the approaches to Lyttelton Harbour. Barely 24 hours later, the same ship arrived off Pencarrow Head and laid a double row of 10 mines across the entrance to Port Nicholson. *Adjutant* then made off to the eastward at her best speed to rejoin her sister ship *Komet*. There is no record of any suspicious vessel seen in the vicinity of either port at that time. *Adjutant* was a small vessel closely resembling a minesweeper, several of which were then working between Lyttelton and Wellington, and she might well have been mistaken for one of these had she been seen in harbour at night.

Nothing was known of the minefield in Wellington Harbour laid by *Adjutant* until more than four years later, when its existence was revealed by captured German documents.

Unlike those laid by the raider *Orion* in 1940 in the Hauraki Gulf, these were a magnetic type of ground mine. As thousands of ships passed safely over the areas in which they were laid without a single reported detonation, the mines were probably defective.

In his assessment of *Adjutant*'s mine-laying operations, Rear Admiral Robert Eyssen, commanding officer of *Komet*, remarked that 'at Wellington, all the depths [at which the mines were laid] exceeded twenty metres but a large number of ships of over 10,000 tons put in there, and as this port is very favourably situated in relation to the magnetic zone … the mines, if they work at all, should, according to the data available, also detonate satisfactorily with vessels of 5000 to 7000 tons. I do not think the *Adjutant* was seen during the operation, in spite of the searchlight activity'.

Less than two days later the raiders intercepted and sank SS *Rangitane*, which was fully loaded with a cargo that included frozen meat, dairy produce and wool bound for the United Kingdom. Her crew numbered about 200 and in addition she was carrying 111 passengers, including 36 women. Unlike *Holmwood* 48 hours earlier, *Rangitane* was able to transmit both a 'suspicious ship' (QQQQ) and 'raider' message (RRRR) back to New Zealand. *Orion* and *Komet* retaliated against this show of defiance by opening fire. *Rangitane* was badly damaged in the attack: five passengers including three women were killed and a number wounded, one of whom, a woman, died on board *Orion* the next day. Two stewardesses and three engine-room hands were also killed, and five other members of the ship's crew were wounded. All the surviving passengers and crew were taken off the ship by a German boarding party, after which *Rangitane*'s sea-cocks were opened and the vessel was finished off by a torpedo from *Komet*.

The sinking of *Rangitane* and *Holmwood*, following the loss of *Niagara* and *Turakina*, set aflame rumours in New Zealand that the enemy was being supplied with inside information. These rumours intensified a few months later, in January 1941, when statements in the press by survivors of enemy attacks, who had been set ashore by the German ships operating in the Pacific, gave support to public fears. At a subsequent Commission of Inquiry, Captain H. L. Upton, master of *Rangitane*, and Captain Miller of *Holmwood* both stated that the Germans had claimed that they knew the departure times of ships from New Zealand and Australia and that they had met *Rangitane* by design and not by accident. However, these claims were not upheld by the Commission's findings which, according to S. D. Waters in *The Royal New Zealand Navy: Official History of New Zealand in the Second World War*, concluded that 'the actual successes of the raiders in the Pacific over a period of months do not appear consistent with their having had, during that period, any such information …'.

After the war, the official war diaries of *Komet* and *Orion* were made available and supported the Commission's findings that the interceptions of *Turakina*, *Holmwood* and *Rangitane* were entirely fortuitous. The law of averages meant that eventually the raiders were going to come across a likely target – it was simply a case of one's number being up. After the sinking of *Rangitane*, the German raiders left New Zealand waters intent on destroying the phosphate works, the harbour installations and the wireless station on Nauru and Ocean Islands.

Despite a doubling in size of the minesweeping flotilla in New Zealand waters in June 1940, following the sinking of *Niagara*, Commodore

A British Mk IV mine manufactured in Australia in 1942. A number of mines of this type were laid in the approaches to Auckland during the Second World War as a defensive measure to safeguard the harbour from enemy ships and submarines. The field was swept in 1944 when the threat of invasions to this country had diminished. T2008.14.2

Minesweeper cutter. Blade for cutting mine cable to allow the mine to float to the surface for disposal. SIL 0003

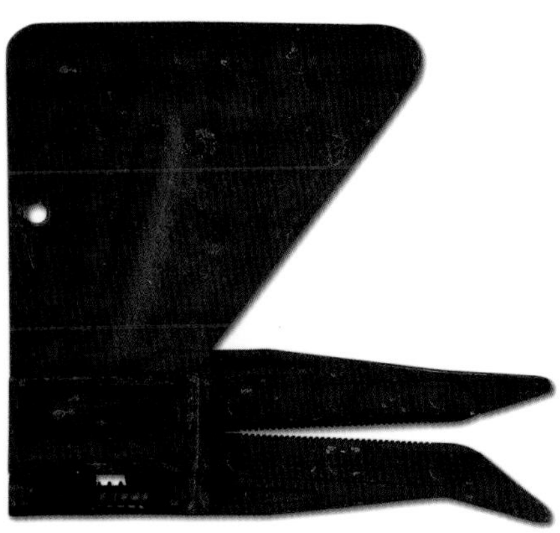

OC3-0-12

German Raiders

The German raiders that operated in the Pacific in the early stages of the Second World War were very well equipped and capable of remaining at sea for 12 months or more, with the assistance of fuel tankers and store ships and supplementing by supplies looted from captured vessels. Great use was made by the raiders of disguise. Dummy ventilators, samson posts and other deck fittings, as well as false bulwarks and deck-houses, were often set up and the ships were repainted frequently to change their appearance. Special workshops were established on board to construct this camouflage equipment and to carry out the extensive, never-ending repairs necessitated by the raiders' long periods at sea.

In general, the armament on a German raider consisted of five or six 5.9-inch guns, a number of smaller guns, and four or more underwater torpedo-tubes. The ships were fitted with the director system of fire control and elaborate wireless telegraphy plants. Most of them carried a small seaplane, and several were equipped for mine-laying. Regardless of their tactics in approaching a merchant ship, the attack was always sudden and ruthless – the primary targets were the victim's wireless room, navigating bridge and defensive gun.

The first German raider to operate in the Pacific and bring the war to the shores of New Zealand was *Orion*, a single-screw cargo steamer that had been converted by the German navy. Built at Hamburg in 1930 and originally called *Kurmark*, the 7021-ton gross register vessel was built for the Hamburg–America Line. Propelled by geared turbine engines, the raider had a maximum speed of approximately 14 knots. The ship could carry 4100 tons of oil-fuel and its armament consisted of six 5·9-inch guns, one 3-inch gun and six light anti-aircraft guns, and six torpedo-tubes in triple mountings. It also carried an Arado seaplane.

Komet, which joined *Orion* in the Pacific, was a relatively small ship of 3287 tons gross register. Built in 1937 and propelled by two oil-engines geared to a single shaft, *Komet* had a top speed of about 15 knots. *Komet* was armed with six 5·9-inch guns, nine light anti-aircraft guns, six deck and four underwater torpedo-tubes. Like *Orion*, it carried an Arado seaplane and in addition had a high-speed motor launch.

In the course of their respective cruises which together covered a period of 20 months, *Orion* and *Komet* sunk or captured 17 ships, totalling 114,118 tons. All but two of their victims were attacked in the Pacific and four were sunk by them in New Zealand waters over a period of six months. Considering the great volume of valuable shipping in a state of constant movement in the South Pacific, the total of vessels taken by the enemy raiders was relatively small. It also provided sound evidence of the protective value of evasive routeing and the escorting of merchant shipping in time of war.

Oral History

The Sinking of SS *Rangitane* – 27 November 1940: Memories of Nurse Florence Mundie

Florence Mundie, a Scottish Red Cross Nurse in her mid-40s, was on board *Rangitane*, returning to Britain, when the ship encountered the German raiders, *Orion* and *Komet*.

At 3.45 a.m. I was awakened by a loud 'boom!' I thought, Oh, there must be submarines about and we are dropping depth charges. . . . I decided to dress immediately and put on a warm woolly jumper over my nightdress and crossed to my wardrobe to get a skirt on. . . . I don't remember ever putting that skirt on, for there was a tremendous explosion which seemed to rend the ship in two, and within the next minute or so another frightful shell burst right beside me. . . . Our cabins were amidships – right under the bridge – and got the worst of the shelling. . . .

I was banged, bruised and burnt and wounded. Something hit me on the head and another thing, swift and sharp, went around my chin. I carefully put the back of my hand up and knew my chin was hanging down. At the time all this happened, another strange thing occurred which surprised me greatly. The clothing on my body, from the ground to my shoulders, sizzled like something frying and completely disappeared without a flame. There was a nasty singed smell. It was due to some kind of gas from the exploded shells. My hair singed and my face and neck were badly burnt. My eyes were painful, the eyelashes and brows having been burnt. . . .

I had only heard three shells explode and, as the young German doctor said later, there were many, many more. I don't know what could have happened. Perhaps I was stunned for a while. Later there were various bruises and cuts I could not account for. . . . The Germans seemed to think I must have been unconscious. Anyway, there I

OC 3-0-6

'*Survivors on Emirau Island*'. *Painted by Nurse Mundie, a passenger on SS* Rangitane *when it was attacked and sunk by German raiders. She was among those prisoners placed ashore on Emirau Island.* PAA 0025

OC 3-0-19

was standing at the same place and it seemed to me that everything had happened there in seven minutes. . . . The ship was so quiet. . . . There was such a dead silence that I had the feeling that everyone had gone and I had been left to go down with the ship.

On going a yard or so into the . . . [gangway] to make my escape, I discovered the other cabins had been completely blown away and the passageway as far as I could see was a red blaze of flames, quietly burning away. There appeared to be no way out. I went back into my cabin and groped about where the porthole had been, to see if there was a hole so that I might get through into the sea. The woodwork was hanging in strips. I pulled at it feebly, but could find no way out. . . . Then I became absolutely exhausted and terribly weak. . . . Then I put my hand on a pile of debris beside me and was about to lay my naked body on it. At the moment I was on the point of giving up, when my body touched the spiky wood I heard a cry for help away down in the distance. It just occurred to me to do the same, so I shouted 'Help!' But nobody came. . . . However, again I heard that cry and with all my strength I called 'Help! Help!'

A few minutes later, one of our men had come up the long passage and stood at the side of the flames. He quietly and calmly said: 'Can you walk over here?' . . . After walking to him, he took me down the passage to a cabin. The chief engineer was there. They got a little white boiler suit, which I put on ... then they covered me with blankets. I could not talk, but tried to say thank you. It was very cold. My body seemed frozen and I could not stop shaking all the time. There were several of our men busy working about, putting out fires, et cetera. They never left me alone, though. So quiet and kind they were, and the ship might have broken up [at] any minute.

At this time there were only a few left on the ship. After a while, they asked me if I felt able to go on deck. I was most anxious to go. My will was still strong, my desire to live – although my physical strength was now very low and would peter out [at] any moment if my will weakened. The outside air and light revived me immediately. I was quite aware of what was happening and was glad to get away from the smoky atmosphere of the sinking ship.

We got into number 11 lifeboat, which was full. We were not long in the sea before it was noticed that the boat was full of shrapnel holes. The men began bailing with big cans. It was a hopeless job. They worked and worked – then the order was given for so many to swim. . . . I threw the blanket off and wanted to swim, but strong arms behind me held me tight. . . . I would have drowned had I tried to swim – my condition was too weak for that. I was bleeding from my head, face and chest. Before we left the *Rangitane*'s deck, it was daylight. I looked across with my half-closed, burnt eyes and noticed two dark ships. I said to the men: 'What are these ships? Are they British?' Our men did not answer me.

HMNZS **Breeze.** ABN 0049

HMNZS Hawera *crew in Fiji, 1944.* ABN 0070

Parry requested still more vessels for conversion to sweepers. In his opinion, a mobile flotilla of at least six sweepers and a pair of sweepers at each of the main ports of Wellington, Auckland and Lyttelton was the minimum force required. In response to this request by the Chief of Naval Staff, *Matai*, *Puriri*, *Rata* and *Gale* were selected for conversion in August 1940.

In addition to the policy of requisitioning existing coastal vessels and converting them for minesweeping duties, a scheme was hatched in mid-1940 to build minesweeping trawlers in New Zealand. Cabinet approved the building of six Castle-type trawlers on 1 June and some weeks later authorised the construction of another six trawlers. As with *Kiwi*, *Moa* and *Tui*, under construction in far-off Scotland, it would be some two years and well on in the war before these ships were ready to be commissioned for service.

The New Zealand Division's minesweeping flotilla was duly named by the Admiralty the First (NZ) Minesweeping Flotilla – the 25th Minesweeping Flotilla. In April and May 1941, the converted merchant ships *Matai*, *Puriri*, *Rata* and *Gale* were commissioned as fast minesweepers. *Puriri*, however, was not to last long as a member of the 25th, falling victim to a mine approximately nine miles northeast by north from Bream Head.

On 13 May the fishing launch *Pearline* had fouled a mine while bringing her nets in and had marked it with a buoy and reported it to the naval launch *Rawea*, which was in the area. *Gale* and *Puriri*, which were at sea at the time, were sent a signal from Auckland instructing them to assist *Rawea* in destroying the mine. Due to rough seas, poor visibility, problems in locating the buoyed mine and poor communication by the senior officer on board *Gale* with *Puriri*, the task proved a difficult one. Following in the *Gale*'s wake, *Puriri* had taken a four-point bearing which placed her one and a half miles due west of the mine's reported position when, on her turn to starboard, there was a violent explosion. *Puriri* had found the elusive mine in the worst possible way. Her commanding officer, Lieutenant D. W. Blacklaws, and four ratings were killed and one officer and four ratings injured. The minesweeper sank so quickly that the five surviving officers and 21 ratings were ordered over the side, where they floated until plucked from the water by *Gale*.

The subsequent enquiry laid the blame almost entirely at the feet of the commanding officer of *Gale*. *Puriri* was replaced by *Breeze*, a sister ship to *Gale*. At the end of 1941 the 25th Minesweeping Flotilla was sent to the Pacific, chiefly the Solomon Islands, where it remained based until shortly before the end of the war.

Three composite minesweepers adapted from Castle-class vessels being built at shipyards around New Zealand, and known as LL minesweepers, were commissioned in mid-1942. These vessels were fitted with specialised electrical equipment to deal with magnetic mines. With *Kapuni* and *Hawera*, these ships formed what was known at first as the LL Minesweeping Flotilla, then from May 1945 as the 194th Auxiliary Minesweeping Group. These 'double L' sweepers spent many months of service on the New Zealand coast – although their training and equipment was not put to any practical test as no magnetic mines were ever found or suspected in New Zealand waters.

When the first of the New Zealand-built Castle-class minesweepers began coming into service in 1943, the owners of coastal vessels requisitioned in more difficult times began to press for the release of some of their ships. On 17 May, the Minister of Marine put the case for the owners

of requisitioned ships in a memorandum to the Prime Minister. He referred in particular to the difficulties being faced by the coal and timber trade, but the Prime Minister rejected his appeal on the grounds that the danger to shipping from Japanese submarines was still too great for naval defences to be reduced.

This decision was reviewed in September 1943, when the strategic situation in the Pacific was steadily improving and the need to conserve manpower was paramount. As a result, *Rata* was paid off on 11 October 1943 and the two trawlers, *Phyllis* and *Nora Niven*, in February 1944. In addition, *Futurist* was withdrawn from minesweeping duties and converted into a boom-gate vessel at Wellington. *Aroha*, the first of the new Castle-class steel-hulled minesweepers, was commissioned in May 1943, followed over the next six months by *Awatere* in June, *Hautapu* in July, *Maimai* in September and *Waipu* in November. At the end of 1943, there were 24 anti-submarine and minesweeping vessels and two danlayers in service in New Zealand waters. With the lessening of the threat in the southern reaches of the Pacific and manpower shortages looming, the final four Castle-class vessels were cancelled and work suspended on a further two.

In 1941 Prime Minister Peter Fraser was already making overtures to the United States, and the establishment of a New Zealand navy, separate from the RN, was a part of his overall thinking on his country's relationship with the United States. On 1 October 1941, some two years after the start of the war, the naval forces of New Zealand got what they had long wanted – the recognition of a New Zealand navy in its own right. The Royal New Zealand Navy Order 1941 stated that: 'The New Zealand Naval Forces shall henceforth be styled the Royal New Zealand Navy, the Royal New Zealand Naval Reserve, and the Royal New Zealand Naval Volunteer Reserve respectively.' The order added that: 'The ships belonging to the Naval Forces shall henceforth be styled His Majesty's New Zealand Ships.'

For many New Zealand men serving overseas, in various branches of the Royal Navy, this change in status was largely administrative and the full ramifications of naval independence would not truly be felt until after the war. Nevertheless, the breakaway from the Admiralty was the beginning of a new era. There would be no going back and, over the years that followed, the navy – and New Zealand as a whole – would gradually distance itself from Mother Britain as it developed its own sense of identity. The bombing of Pearl Harbour in December 1941 and the fall of Singapore soon after created a significant change in the navy's priorities at home as the war moved irrevocably into the South Pacific. Branches such as communications were fast-tracked for expansion, as was the role of civilian staff, including women, particularly in Navy Office in Wellington. The coding and cipher offices, both crucial for maintaining the navy's global communications network, underwent considerable change and post and telegraph staff were recruited to work in various locations from Pitcairn Island to the Auckland Combined Headquarters in Epsom to the wireless telegraphy station at Waiouru – which had some of the most modern transmitting equipment of the period.

In June 1943 the British War Cabinet offered two corvettes as a gift to the newly established Royal New Zealand Navy. This offer was gratefully accepted by the Government, which insisted that New Zealand would pay the cost of modifying and equipping the vessels for service in tropical waters. *Arabis* was commissioned on 22 February 1944 and sailed

HMNZS Muritai. ABN 0024

via Panama to Auckland, arriving in August. *Arbutus*, which was commissioned a few months later, followed the same route as her sister ship to Auckland. Both were sent to join the 25th Minesweeping Flotilla in the Solomon Islands. Unfortunately, *Arbutus* was severely damaged when she grounded on a reef off the Fiji Islands in October, causing considerable damage to her propeller and approximately 25 feet of her bottom. After being repaired at the Dockyard, which took some time as replacement parts had to come from Britain, *Arbutus* was lent to the British Pacific Fleet in February 1945 as her services were no longer required in the Solomon Islands. The corvette was fitted out as a radar servicing and repair ship in Australia and subsequently did duty in the Fleet Train during the invasion of mainland Japan.

In May 1944, *Hawera* and *Kapuni* were stripped of their LL minesweeping equipment and fitted out for service as supply ships for the Western Pacific. They left Auckland for Suva in June the same year. *Waiho*, the eighth and last of the new steel minesweepers, was commissioned in June 1944. She joined the 97th Minesweeping Group at Auckland, replacing *Muritai* which became a tender to HMNZS *Tamaki* for the sea-training of new entrants.

On 16 May 1944 a start was made on sweeping the defensive minefield laid in March 1942 across the main channel in the Hauraki Gulf. This major task, known as Operation PM, was carried out by several boats from the 7th Trawler Group (including *Sanda*), and assisted by *Muritai*, *Kaiwaka* and *Coastguard*, and three motor launches used to sink the mines. *Kaiwaka* and *Coastguard* worked alone for the first six days to make sufficient clearance for the other ships to

Minesweeping New Zealand – 1940

CHIEF PETTY OFFICER IVAN BROWN

Ivan Brown was a founding member of the Otago Division of the Volunteer Reserve, joining in 1928. He was called up in 1940 and spent most of the war in New Zealand on board various minesweepers. He was the coxswain of *Puriri* when it was sunk by a mine in the German-laid Hauraki Gulf field.

Ivan Brown: Then from the South Seas I went to – it had to be *Puriri*, I think. That's right – the *Puriri*. . . . She was a twin-diesel cargo vessel that belonged to the Northern Steamship Company, taken over by the navy. Up in Devonport they took the foremast out, and put a gun on there, and fitted her with sweeping gear. I was actually in base at the time. I was being used to break in other coxswains for the smaller trawlers, like *Humphrey* and [*Thomas*] *Currell*, and all of those.

INT: On-the-job training for the guys?
IB: Yes, training the coxswain to take over, and at the same time standing by as *Puriri* was being fitted out.

Now, while she was being fitted out, the raider appeared and sank one of the *Rangi* boats. There was a quick draft. *Puriri* could be steamed up, she was diesel, she could be got underway quick. There was a truckload of blankets chucked aboard and some food, and I was sent over, and there was a mixed crew of T124s and RNVRs, and we got aboard her and away we went. We were supposed to go and see if we could find any survivors. . . . Anyway we didn't see anything, we just turned around and went back and finished the refit. She was commissioned, I have an idea – that would be somewhere about May. Oh, that's right, 19th April to 23rd May – she was only in commission a month.

We were on our first sweep – in those days we swept in relays from Tiritiri up to Whangarei, and

Survivors of the Puriri. ABN 0002

then on right up. As you know, towing sweeps is only about a 3-knot job. And we arrived at Whangarei with the *Gale* ... We got word that a fisherman had pulled a mine out, up in his nets, out of Whangarei [Harbour]. He had obviously been where he shouldn't have been, and he dragged it for a while, and then he cut it loose. He said it was floating on the surface when he cut it loose ... We were ordered out the next morning to find this. *Gale* was the senior ship. We went out to the area and posted all sort of extra lookouts and whatnot, and we steamed up and down and up and down. John Rhind was our number one. We met him and we were to go and draw the rum for the day ...

Anyway, we went down below, and we brought up the rum ... and ... I stepped over the lintel into the mess and that's when she hit the mine. ... It blew the bottom of the forward hold – it must have landed right on the forward hold. She was ballasted – they had put in 12 x 2 framing, it was full of rock. ... The rock went up in the air. ... I stepped out onto the afterdeck and down was coming the rocks, so I went back under cover. By this time she was going. The two stewards were – this was of course just after 11 – preparing the wardroom for the officers' meal. The front of the superstructure was completely demolished by the rock, and those two stewards were killed. The second engineer was sitting in his cabin, in the same row of offices. He was blown backwards out through the door into the hall. The skipper was on the wing bridge with a signalman. The signalman went over the back of the bridge and landed in the lifeboat, and the skipper went over the side. We never saw him again.

The lad that went over the back had the presence of mind to throw out what lifebelts were there, because she was going fast by this time. There was one chap, an AB, he was in the paint locker, which was right aft. The lid flew over and locked him in. He got out, and I have never seen a chap do such a dive. I hadn't left the ship by then. I saw him – he flashed past me and left the deck, and he went over the guard rail, straight over the side, beautiful dive. He told me afterwards, he said: 'The rivets were actually popping out in the hull.'

INT: Really, what sort of a mine was this – a contact mine?

IB: It was a moored mine, the old-fashioned sort. It must have sunk down again a certain amount during the night, because we landed right on top of it. I decided it was time for me to leave, and I threw off my heavy jersey and I slid down the side of her until my heels touched the belting, then I dived off there. When I came up she was standing on her end, and two chaps were going up the guard rails. One of them was the only active service rating aboard, a Chief Petty Officer ERA Trevor Martin from Auckland – 'Pincher' Martin. And the other one was the second engineer, and they just floated off as she went down.

All the bridge area ... that suddenly collapsed and blew the air whistle and down she went [in] a minute and a half. Alan Bell managed to get a snap of her from a distance. ... Well they [*Gale*] were about a mile and a half or more ahead of us. They came back and lowered a boat and picked us up. Then along came one of the cruisers – she was returning, I am not sure which, it was *Diomede* I think – she was returning to base, and she sent over a boat. They transferred most of our people onto her. I didn't go because I had casualties on the *Gale* – some of them were badly knocked about, and I opted to stay with them to see that they got to hospital. I didn't go on the cruiser. ...

I still maintain that we should have retired from the area and put out sweeps. If we had put out sweeps, the *Gale* would have caught the mine in her sweep, because we were following directly behind her. ... No, so anyway, that was the story of the good ship *Puriri* – [it had] only been commissioned a month.

manoeuvre. The other vessels then joined in and, despite delays caused by bad weather, a total of 394 mines were located by the end of June.

In March 1945, *Sanda*, *Scarba*, *Killegray* and *Inchkeith* from the 7th Trawler Group, with *Waipu*, *Wakakura*, *Kaiwaka* and *Coastguard* as danlayers, then began Operation NA – the final clearance of the German minefield laid very early in the war by *Orion* in the approaches to the Hauraki Gulf. Although this field had already been swept, a number of mines remained unaccounted for. The minesweepers spent eight days sweeping off Great Barrier Island, but no mines were found. From 8 April, the sweepers searched most of the area extending north and west of the Hen and Chicken Islands and the mainland. Once again no mines were found, and on 21 May a temporary halt was called to sweeping.

Two months later, a signal was received from the British Naval Officer-in-Charge at Wilhelmshaven, Germany, giving the number of mines – 228 – laid by *Orion* five years before and their approximate positions. This invaluable information was supplemented by a copy of the German raider's track chart. Acting on this precise information, the sweepers carried out a further search of the northern area; however, when operations ceased three months later in mid-October 1945, no further mines had been found. The last sweep of the Cuvier Island area, which was to be the final task for *Arabis*, *Arbutus* and *Kiwi*, which had all returned from the Solomon Islands in 1944, and the three danlayers, started on 7 March and was completed in early June 1946. Again no mines were found. The total number of mines accounted for from the end of September 1941, when the field was first swept, to mid-1946 was 133, leaving slightly fewer than 100 unaccounted for, if full credence is given to *Orion*'s track chart. After nearly five years of buffeting and corrosion, it was thought that the remainder had either sunk or drifted far away into the Pacific.

The minesweeping flotillas, built up during six years of war, were rapidly dispersed after Victory Japan Day. Beginning with just four vessels in 1939, the minesweepers had attained their maximum strength four years later when there were 26 in commission and two in reserve. They were charged with maintaining swept channels in the approaches to New Zealand's main harbours, as well as anti-submarine patrols and escorts – long, continuous tasks involving little glory. Most of the minesweepers were dual-purpose vessels, equipped for anti-submarine duties as well as minesweeping. However, only *Kiwi*, *Tui* and *Moa*, at work in the Solomon Islands on anti-submarine patrol, ever engaged in action with the underwater enemy.

Hinau *Castle-class minesweeper.* ABN 0051

HMNZS Scarba *officers.* ABL 0024

AAJ 0003

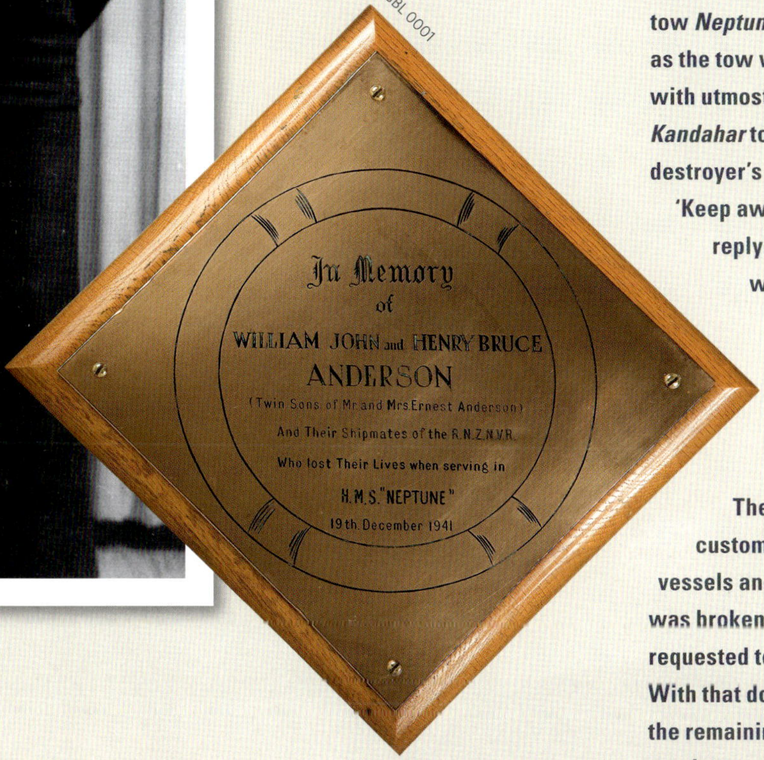

GBL 0001

HMS *Neptune* – December 1941

It was a stormy morning in the Mediterranean, just a few days before Christmas when the Royal Navy *Leander*-class cruiser HMS *Neptune* struck a mine and was sunk. More than 750 men, of which 150 (two officers and 148 ratings) were New Zealanders, lost their lives. Though not officially a New Zealand ship *Neptune*'s sinking and the subsequent loss of life brought death and grief home to New Zealand.

In July 1941, *Neptune* spent six months undertaking a number of roles, including intercepting enemy convoys and providing support for their own ships. Air reconnaissance from Malta on 18 December 1941 revealed that an Italian battleship force which had caused some concern to a fuel-oil convoy to Malta a few days earlier was cruising in an area about midway between Malta and Benghazi. Three cruisers including *Neptune* and four destroyers sailed from Malta at high speed that evening to try to intercept. The Royal Navy force was approximately 20 miles off Tripoli when *Neptune*, which was leading, hit a minefield a little after one in the morning. Its silhouette against the flash of that initial explosion the first indication of the danger in which the force suddenly found itself. *Aurora*, which was next astern, was hit less than a minute later and, still going at full speed, *Neptune* hit another mine which wrecked her propellers and steering gear and brought her to a standstill. A minute or so later a third mine made contact and exploded. The cruiser listed, but remained floating, albeit in a minefield. Because Tripoli was only a little over 30 kilometres away, it was imperative that the crippled ships should get as far from the enemy coast as possible before the enemy realised they were there and could exploit the opportunity. The commander of one of the destroyers, *Kandahar*, wanted to go to *Neptune*'s aid but was told to lay off until the cruiser had drifted clear of the minefield. Preparations to tow *Neptune* were made by *Penelope*. However, as the tow vessel was cautiously edging its way with utmost care towards its injured compatriot, *Kandahar* too struck a mine which removed the destroyer's stern. *Neptune*, flashed to *Penelope*: 'Keep away'. *Penelope*, complied reluctantly, replying: 'Regret I must keep clear.' There were still hopes that it might be possible to rescue the crews of the two ships adrift in a minefield; however, a few hours later *Neptune* hit a fourth mine, rolling over and sinking within five minutes. The risk was deemed too great for the customary pick-up of survivors by the other vessels and subsequently the wireless silence was broken and a submarine or flying boat was requested to search for survivors in the water. With that done, and dawn very much imminent, the remaining ships left the possible *Neptune* survivors and the crew of *Kandahar* to their respective fates.

When the *Neptune* had struck the fourth mine, the order had been given to abandon ship, however as the ship sank so quickly the majority of the crew went down with the cruiser. Those that did manage to get off lost their lives trying to swim to the crippled *Kandahar*. There was only one survivor, Leading Seaman John Walton, an English rating. He had been one of only 16 men left afloat on a single raft when daylight came. This handful of survivors included a single New Zealand rating, Able Seaman J. B. Quinn from Wellington. One by one the survivors succumbed and this may well have been Walton's fate had he not been picked up by an Italian destroyer on Christmas Eve and taken prisoner of war.

WRENS

'Wrens are playing a fundamental part in many spheres of naval activity and have applied themselves to the work that they are efficiently carrying out with zeal and enthusiasm. ... By their bearing and loyalty and sincere dedication to duty they have proved that they take a pride in themselves, in their uniform, in their ship and in the Service. ... I am very proud of the Wrens.' Commodore Sir Atwell Lake, Chief of Naval Staff *WRNZNS Magazine* (Issue 1, November 1943)

APD 0044

APD 0015

Second World War Wrens' felt hat. CEC 0020

'They [the rats at Hinemoa Street] became so bothersome that we obtained a fox terrier called Rua. The boys on the mess decks set large wire traps at night, then in the morning took Rua out into the street with the trapped rats and let them go one by one. Rua never missed one of them.' Wren Midge Lee

APD 0103

EVD 0028

Chief Petty Officer Wren Joan Matthews

Joan Matthews joined the Women's Royal Naval Service in July 1942, the fourth Wren to be recruited. After six months of basic training in the shore establishment HMNZS *Philomel*, she was posted to the shore establishment HMNZS *Cook* in Wellington, where she worked as a driver. Matthews was for a time driver for the Chief of Naval Staff, Commodore Sir Atwell Lake. She developed eyesight problems and worked as a clerk in the Regulating Office at the Hinemoa Street Depot in Wellington until early 1944, when she spent a short period in the shore establishment HMNZS *Tasman* in Lyttelton. In mid-1944, Matthews returned to *Cook* and the Regulating Office. In May 1945 she moved to Auckland and worked in the *Philomel* drafting office.

In 1946 she travelled to the United Kingdom to be part of the Victory Parade celebrating the end of the war. On her return to New Zealand in September 1946 she left the service. However, Matthews rejoined the Royal New Zealand Navy in 1947, shortly after the naval mutiny, staying on for less than a year. She retired from the Wrens in 1948, having attained the rank of Chief Petty Officer Wren.

ERE 0005

'Then there was Miss Herrick's onions. She had some fixed ideas about diet. Always brought her own lunch and it always contained an onion. I've no doubt that her insistence on good wholesome food helped her live to a great age. But the smell of onion each day ... !'
WRNS 3 Suzanne Walker – Writer
Navy Office, circa 1942–43

DLA 0215

Fourth Officer Barbara Macky

Fourth Officer Barbara Macky joined the Women's Royal Naval Service (New Zealand) in 1942. She worked in signals at the Combined Headquarters in Epsom, Auckland, in the Merchant Shipping Office: Navy Operations, Wellington, and the Fleet mail office back in Auckland, and was briefly employed in the Captain's office before becoming ill. Macky retired to shore at her own request and was discharged in January 1946.

Barbara Macky: A lot of the signallers were sent to Waiouru [Irirangi]. They were frozen in their boiler-suits and they got permission to wear trousers ... but there was never any question of the girls on the [Commodore's] barge not wearing trousers. It was the only possible rig for sailors ... I don't think it was a question of like or dislike. It was what you had to wear, because you had to be able to bend over, climb up ... whatever ... and still be reasonably dressed. ... It was a very smart uniform. ... I was signalling and we wore our dress uniform all the time. I did do the [signalling] course, but I was never called upon to do semaphore. . . . That photograph of me holding an Aldis lamp, that is the one and only time I ever held an Aldis lamp in my whole naval career as a signalman. . . . We had to learn to march. We had sessions on naval etiquette, who to salute and what you do and don't do.

INT: What did your job at Auckland Combined Headquarters actually involve?
BM: Well, we had a battery of telephones – the old sort that have one handle, and they have silver bells across the top. Each of those was connected with a coastal observation point – like to the island or around the coast, lighthouses or whatever. They would ring in on a regular basis with sightings of ships that had passed through their sector at whatever time. We took that information and handed it through to these various officers. They went upstairs to the operations room and plotted the ships' progress.

We used to receive coded messages from ships and cipher messages from ships and they all went to Wellington to be decoded. The messages to Wellington went on a Creed machine. It was what the Post Office used to use in those days when we all used telegrams. Toll calls were so expensive and usually the sound was difficult, so they all went by Creed, and at the far end the message came out typed in a strip and glued onto a piece of paper. At the sender's end, the typewriter side of it, your copy comes out like a Braille strip . . . with little holes. An experienced reader . . . could take the strip and just read: 'We are proceeding to Wellington at so many knots . . .', and so on. I never got anywhere near that [proficient]. Because I could type, I could send the Creed messages. The typex ones were confined to officers, but because I could type and had worked my way up a bit, I could send those to Wellington too. But we never deciphered them. It doesn't sound like a day's work, but it kept us busy.

INT: Did you have parades quite regularly? Was it to boost morale?
BM: There was a lot going on to boost the patriotic spirit. . . . Anything that would give it a boost – a bit of military band music and stuff. I can remember the first one we were in, I remember being told: 'If you so much as glance to one side or the other, bang goes your leave for the next 10 years!'

INT: The Patriotic Fund, what was that?
BM: . . . We had concerts and parades and anything anybody could think of, and the money went into sending parcels to men overseas. They used to contain knitted socks, balaclavas and scarves, most of which ended up in Egypt of course. A fruit cake and sweets. Like a Red Cross parcel, but they were provided by the Patriotic Fund.

INT: [What was Auckland] . . . like during World War II?
BM: There were dances. Once the Americans came, they set up rest and recreation places. There was one at the White Heron in Parnell, one at Glen Innes. I think there was a camp at Papakura. . . . That was really our [total] recreation [during] the war. . . . Your pleasures had to be simple. But we didn't know any better and so we were quite happy. . . . We used to go to dances in long frocks on the tram and you had to come home at 11 p.m., because that was the last tram.

Superintendent of Wrens M. V. Morten

Mary Morten joined the Women's Royal New Zealand Navy Service in early 1942, as part of the second intake. She came from a background of service in the Girl Guide movement, where she had gained considerable experience in catering and supervising groups of young women. Initially, Morten was posted to Wellington and served at Worser Bay in the harbour control organisation that was located there.

In late 1942, Morten moved to Auckland, like many of her fellows, and joined the staff of the new wardroom in HMNZS *Philomel* as a caterer and steward. She was quickly promoted and within a year was a Petty Officer Wren in charge of quartering. Morton lived for a time in Elizabeth House and then in the barracks at the top of Victoria Road, Devonport, where she witnessed a fire that broke out in the recreation room. She was promoted once more in 1944 to Fourth Officer and, by the time she was discharged from the Royal New Zealand Navy in 1946, had attained the rank of Third Officer.

Morten rejoined the Wrens in 1949 and was instrumental in re-establishing the branch at Elizabeth House. She became Superintendent of Wrens in 1955 for a period of two years before retiring from the service.

Post-war Wrens Officer Uniform. T 2008.9.1

THE SECOND WORLD WAR: KIWIS ABROAD

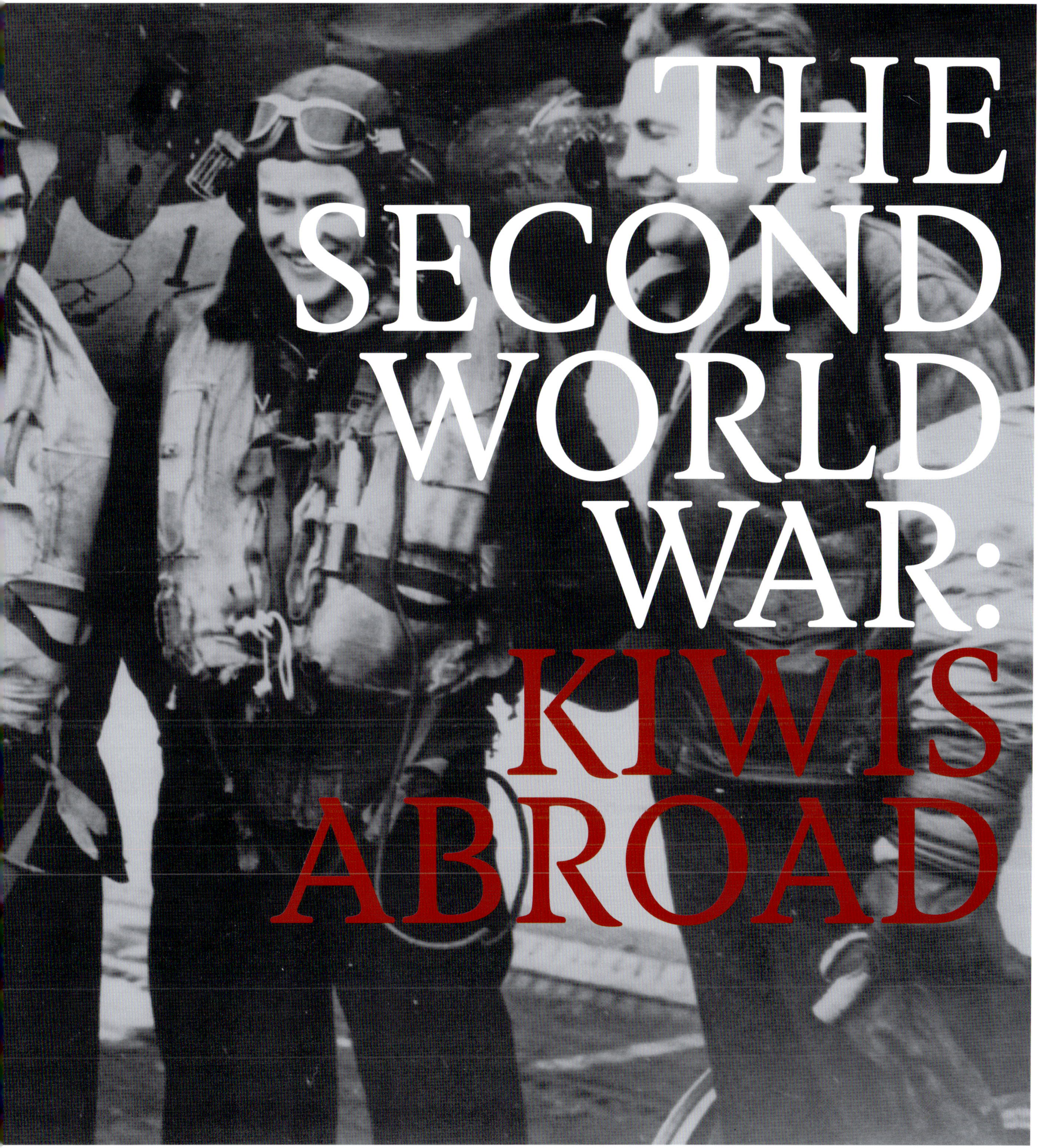

In September 1939, when war was declared, the naval authorities were well aware that a large number of New Zealanders were keen to join the navy. However, the requirements of the New Zealand Division of the Royal Navy were such that many men who would have been ideal candidates for naval service due to their civilian experience were lost to the air force and army, simply because they were surplus to demand.

Signalling lantern with filters. Used at night for communicating between ships in convoy. SCE 0002

Up until the outbreak of war, New Zealand ratings made up just over half the complements of the two cruisers, HMS *Leander* and HMS *Achilles*, and HMS *Philomel*, the base ship and training establishment. The remainder were Royal Navy men on loan to the New Zealand Division. As these 'loan men' were needed back in Britain, it was decided to replace as many men as possible on the three ships with New Zealanders.

While the New Zealand Division might not have had a need for all these navally inclined men, the Admiralty certainly did and requested four groups in particular from New Zealand: trained naval reserves surplus to domestic requirements; trained civil air pilots for service in the Fleet Air Arm; yachtsmen or ex-merchant marine officers suitable for Royal Naval Volunteer Reserve (RNVR) commissions; and telegraphists, signalmen, artificers, scientists and skilled electrical workmen.

However, as the need for manpower increased, the New Zealand Division found itself in the previously unimaginable position of competing with the other services and, within a few months of the outbreak of war, Navy Office began several recruiting schemes to meet not only the needs of the New Zealand naval forces but those of the Admiralty as well.

As far as the Royal Navy's requirements were concerned, it was announced in the national newspapers that the New Zealand Government would arrange for the selection and medical examination of men and that those selected would be given free transport to Britain and 'guaranteed at least the same treatment in respect of pay, allowances and pensions as if they had enlisted in the appropriate rank in the New Zealand forces'. Applications from young men between the ages of 18 and 25, qualified to hold technical ratings as engine-room artificers, electrical artificers, shipwrights, joiners, blacksmiths, plumbers, painters, telegraphists and signalmen, were subsequently called for from Navy Office. A few weeks later in November 1939, the Naval Secretary was able to report to the Minister of Defence that 367 applications had been received, from which 68 'possibles' had been provisionally selected.

In early 1940 the Admiralty asked whether 10 experienced yachtsmen could be supplied from New Zealand to serve in the RN in Malaya. The call for yachtsmen elicited more than 250 responses and selection committees were set up to interview applicants. The 10 Scheme 'Y' men were duly chosen and sailed from Auckland on 29 April 1940 for Singapore. However, it was not to end there. In September a further 12 yachtsmen were requested, and another dozen in February 1941. However, as successful as the scheme may have been from the Admiralty's perspective it was not practicable for New Zealand to send 12 experienced yachtsmen to the Singapore Station every four months. Of the 32 Scheme 'Y' officers who saw service on the Station, 14 died and seven were taken as Japanese prisoners of war.

Two further recruiting schemes – 'A' and 'B' – were put in place by the Admiralty in May 1940 in Australia and Canada as well as New Zealand. Under Scheme 'A', the call went out for men aged between 30 and 40 holding yachtmasters' certificates, or having equivalent experience that would qualify them for direct commissions in the Royal Naval Volunteer Reserve. On arrival in England, these potential officers would complete officer training at HMS *King Alfred*, undergo a mandatory three months' sea-time and, if successful, be promoted as lieutenants RNVR.

Scheme 'B' sought men who showed officer potential. Candidates had to be between the ages of 20 and 30, with preference given to those between 20 and 25. Sea experience was considered useful, but not essential. A standard of education was required at least up to the level of 'school certificate' or the corresponding Dominion examination, with a knowledge of mathematics. On arrival in England, candidates would undergo preliminary training as ordinary seamen after which they were required to complete three to six months of mandatory sea-time on the lower deck. At the end of that time they would be sent for officer training and, if successful, they would be granted temporary commissions in the Royal Naval Volunteer Reserve. If not accepted for a commission, they would continue to serve as 'hostilities only' ratings for the duration of the war.

Advertisements calling for suitable applicants were taken out in the national newspapers and an interviewing board of two retired RN officers was appointed. When applications for Scheme 'B' closed at the end of June 1940, 1039 men had applied, of whom 608 were eligible and 592 were interviewed. However, just 150 were finally accepted. In May 1941 recruiting for Scheme 'B' was reopened, at the rate of 25 a month. The quota of 150 was filled by December 1941. During the five years from August 1940, 46 class groups totalling approximately 1100 New Zealand Scheme 'B' ratings were sent to Britain for training, of whom 690 were commissioned as officers.

In June 1940, Scheme 'F' for naval airmen came into play. Suitable recruits were sent to HMS *St. Vincent*, a training establishment in England, for initial naval training, after which they were selected to undergo training as either

Stamps used for proof-marking armament stores. JFG 0001

pilots or observers. All those who successfully passed these courses were to be granted temporary commissions in the Air Branch of the Royal Naval Volunteer Reserve. Those not qualifying were to be offered transfer to air gunner or some other technical rating and be eligible for commissioned rank under normal naval conditions. Pay and allowances would be at Royal Navy rates, but the New Zealand Government would supplement them by paying the difference between the RN and the higher New Zealand rates.

Although the Scheme 'F' ratings travelled to Britain in civilian clothes, they were recorded as naval personnel in the ship's passenger list. They were instructed not to conceal their naval status if taken by the enemy – an order which became particularly relevant when *Rangitane*, with a draft of 18 Fleet Air Arm recruits on board, was sunk by the German raiders *Orion* and *Komet* on 27 November 1940 and her passengers and crew taken prisoner. Between July 1940 and June 1945, 1066 Scheme 'F' recruits were drafted overseas. Approximately 600 New Zealanders served as first-line pilots and observers in the Fleet Air Arm.

With so many keen to 'do their bit', the recruitment of men from New Zealand to serve in Royal Navy ships and shore establishments during the Second World War presented few problems. With few exceptions and despite the fairly rigorous selection process, the New Zealand Government and Navy Office were able to meet the RN's quotas with relative ease. In all, approximately 7000 New Zealand men, most 'hostilities only', served with the Royal Navy during the Second World War. In September 1944, when the total strength of the Royal New Zealand Navy was 10,635, a total of 4901 men were serving overseas under the auspices of the RN – without any loss of their 'Kiwi' identity.

Many New Zealand Reserve officers from the RN officer training establishment HMS *King Alfred* chose service in Coastal Forces after receiving their commissions. Small ship flotillas operated off the coasts of England – and to a lesser degree Scotland – as well as from bases in the Mediterranean, West and South Africa, the West Indies, Iceland, and the Indian Ocean. These little ships fought in countless actions and were used as minelayers, minesweepers, anti-submarine escort vessels and smoke-layers. They also performed a wide range of duties in combined operations – as headquarters ships, navigational leaders, flank patrols and ferries for raiding parties and secret agents. Approximately 1560 coastal craft – harbour-defence launches, motor torpedo boats, motor gunboats and motor minesweepers – were built during the war. At the peak period in 1944, some 3000 officers and 22,000 ratings were serving in Coastal Forces.

In July 1940, 14 officers of the prewar RNZNVR, including Lieutenant P. Phipps, Commander R. Newman, Lieutenant C. G. Palmer and Lieutenant J. Lennox King, were appointed to 10 minesweeping and anti-submarine vessels – forming the 24th M/S A/S and the 25th M/S A/S. At this point the Battle of Britain was at its zenith, and the enemy was inflicting considerable damage on Britain's harbours, both at home and abroad. In addition to the constant danger of minefields, the English Channel convoys frequently had to run a gauntlet of gunfire from the heavy German batteries mounted on the French coast.

Second World War gunner in full action dress, wearing a steel helmet and anitflash hood and gloves. JGC 0027, 081/2/3 & T2008.5.1

As senior officer of the 50th Minelaying Flotilla based out of HMS *Beehive*, Felixstowe, Lieutenant M. C. Waylen took part in the first minelaying operation of foreign ports by motor launches based in England. After completing 24 'lays', Waylen was awarded the DSC – as was Lieutenant Walter Drake who eventually became senior officer of the 51st Minelaying Flotilla, which was also based out of *Beehive* and which took part in 34 successful minelaying operations in enemy waters in the North Sea.

One of the 'aces' of Coastal Forces, and a good friend of Walter Drake's – both men had worked as juniors in the same branch of the Bank of New Zealand in Wellington – was a young New Zealander called G. J. 'Jim' MacDonald who ultimately was awarded a DSO, DSC and two bars. MacDonald joined the RNZNVR in 1938 and as an able seaman served briefly as a DEMS gunner in the Pacific. At the end of 1940 he went to England and, after attending HMS *King Alfred*, the officer-training school, MacDonald became first lieutenant in MTB31. He gained his DSC for his part in an action in the English Channel on the night of 3–4 March 1942 when MTB31 was attacked by three German E-boats and caught fire forward and in the engine-room. Although the order to abandon ship was given, MacDonald remained with the boat fighting the fires and jettisoning depth-charges and the remaining torpedo to lighten her – actions that helped considerably in salvaging the boat when assistance arrived.

One of life's consummate over-achievers, MacDonald was awarded a bar to his DSC in July 1943 as senior officer of the 21st Motor Torpedo Boat (MTB) Flotilla. The citation mentioned no fewer than nine actions in four months in which he had taken a leading part.

APE 0116

Lieutenant Jim MacDonald

'Lieutenant MacDonald is a likeable and fearless young New Zealander who has always been outstanding in action. ... Cool and level-headed, he has the knack of making quick decisions and inspiring his flotilla-mates with a fine confidence; the result being that they follow him into action with the sure knowledge that they are on top of the job. This attitude of mind is half the battle in these short, fierce Coastal Forces actions. ... His leadership, cool courage and unflagging keenness to get at the enemy after 4½ years of war are an inspiration, not only to his flotilla officers and men, but to us all.' Captain, Coastal Forces (S. D. Waters, *The Royal New Zealand Navy: Official History of New Zealand in the Second World War*: 491)

Torpedo sight – the invention of Lt MacDonald used to calculate torpedo speed and direction to engage enemy shipping from motor torpedo boats. Prior to this invention launching torpedo from a boat was a very hit-and-miss affair. When the Admiralty saw the results that MacDonald was achieving they ordered them made and fitted to all MTBs. SIJ 0001

Submariners Stoker Philip Le Gros, Lieutenant Con Thode and Stoker Bruce Bennett. Le Gros and Bennett both served on the RN submarine HMS Torbay *and Thode has the distinction of being the only RNZNVR officer to command a submarine – the HMS* Scythian. ADB 0001

MacDonald was the youngest officer in the RN to command a MTB flotilla. A second bar to his DSC was awarded in July 1944 for his 'brilliant initiative' as leader of the 21st MTB Flotilla in two actions and seven successful minelaying expeditions. In one action when his own boat was sunk, he simply transferred to another and continued the attack.

MacDonald was awarded the DSO in September 1944. The citation stated that great courage and skill were shown on the night of 4–5 July 1944 when three attacks were made on a heavily escorted enemy transport until it was forced to take refuge in port. On turning homeward at dawn, the MTB flotilla met a convoy of six ships and, under intense gunfire, sank two by torpedoes and damaged two others by gunfire. One citation noted that: 'It is not mere chance that casualties under … [MacDonald's] leadership are small. … Experience, skill and true courage are great assets.'

MacDonald was not the only New Zealander serving on MTBs to be decorated. On 12 May 1944, when four MTBs were engaged in an action with three escort trawlers at the western entrance to Cherbourg Harbour, the Oerlikon magazine on MTB454 caught fire. A serious explosion was prevented by the quick actions of yet another New Zealander, the boat's first lieutenant, Sub Lieutenant Guy Natusch from Hawke's Bay, who threw the ammunition overboard. He was awarded a DSC for his efforts.

Although the decorations awarded to Coastal Forces went mainly to the senior officer in command, this was not always the case. Able Seaman A. Horsefall, a gunner in MGB13, was awarded the DSM for service in action in an attack on a German raider escorted by four torpedo boats, eight minesweepers, and 10 or more E-boats.

From 1942, many New Zealanders served in Coastal Forces based in the Mediterranean, taking part in the landings along the coasts of North Africa, Sicily, Italy and southern France. Commander R. Newman, who started out in the 24th Minesweeping and Anti-submarine Flotilla, was sent to Alexandria in early 1943 to take over as senior officer of the 2nd Minesweeping Flotilla. He was promoted captain of the flotilla in June 1943. During that year the flotilla swept minefields in Libyan harbours, off Malta, along the south coast and round the heel of Italy, and up the Adriatic coast as far north as Ancona.

For more than 12 months from the end of 1943, support to Crete and other occupied islands was provided by the landing of agents, arms and supplies from coastal craft. Lieutenant R. A. Logan, in command of ML355 based at Tobruk, was awarded the DSC for making 11 trips to Crete, landing approximately 60 agents and evacuating some 100 persons – in addition to unloading an average of one ton of supplies on each journey. When the German evacuation of the Aegean islands and Greece began in September 1944, Coastal Forces flotillas swept the heavily mined approaches to the many harbours; a number of New Zealanders were mentioned in despatches for their courage during these operations.

Approximately 200 New Zealanders served in submarines during the war. While many of them were ratings, a fair number of officers commissioned under Scheme 'B' volunteered for the branch as first lieutenants and navigators. One, Lieutenant Commander Con Thode, earned the honour of taking command of a submarine. These submarines, their crews and depot ships saw service in a variety of locations including the coast of Norway, the Mediterranean, North Africa and the Far East following the Japanese invasion.

Stoker Petty Officer Philip 'Froggy' Le Gros served in submarines for more than four years. Much of that time was spent in the Mediterranean in *Torbay*, which would sink

20 enemy supply ships. Le Gros joined the submarine branch in March 1941 at the start of *Torbay*'s commission under the legendary Commander A. C. Miers VC, DSO, RN. Amongst *Torbay*'s many impressive feats was the evacuation from Crete of 130 British soldiers, including 50 New Zealanders and Australians in August 1941; the landing on the Libyan coast of 40 commandos charged with attacking Rommel's headquarters in November 1941; and trailing four enemy troopships complete with escorts into Corfu Harbour in March 1942.

In the latter action, the submarine waited at the mouth of the harbour until nightfall to surface and charge her batteries then at daybreak entered the harbour, torpedoing and sinking two supply ships. The enemy retaliated by hunting the submarine around the harbour with a destroyer, dropping approximately 40 depth charges, none of which connected. After 17 hours in the harbour, *Torbay* made her escape through the long narrow channel that fed into it. Commander Miers was awarded the Victoria Cross and a further 23 awards were made to members of the crew. Le Gros was mentioned in despatches.

In July 1944 Thode, the only RNZNVR officer to command a submarine during the war, was appointed to the command of the newly commissioned *Scythian*. After trials and working up, *Scythian* was posted to Trincomalee in Ceylon from where, between February 1945 and the end of the war, she sank 12 vessels by gunfire on her first three patrols in the Strait of Malacca.

A few New Zealanders also saw service in midget submarines, known as X-craft. Lieutenant H. P. Westmacott was in command of X24, which in September 1944 was charged with destroying a large floating dock at Bergen in Norway. X24 was towed from the Shetland Islands to Norwegian waters by the submarine *Sceptre* and, after slipping the tow and passing through some 30 miles of fiords, arrived at its target. Two delayed-action charges were placed under the dock, causing severe damage and breaking it in two. X24 escaped undetected to rejoin the waiting *Sceptre*. Westmacott received a DSO for this operation to add to his DSC.

Lieutenant W. J. Lanyon 'Kiwi' Smith also saw considerable service in midget submarines. He was First Lieutenant of XE3 when the submarine was part of Operation Struggle, a series of attacks by the 14th Submarine Flotilla against enemy ships in the Singapore area. On 31 July 1945 XE3 was engaged in limpet-mining *Takao*, a Japanese heavy cruiser, in Johore Strait, Singapore, when it became jammed under the ship. The diver of XE3 squeezed through the hatch, which could not be fully opened, and secured six limpet mines in pairs under the ship's keel. It took Smith, whose job was to surface and dive the midget submarine, more than an hour to free it from its position under the Japanese destroyer and return to the waiting *Stygian*, which was acting as a depot submarine for the midget.

Convoys to North Russia were among the most hazardous of the many sea operations carried out during the Second World War. In addition to the constant danger of submarine and air attack was the ever-present spectre of the mighty German warships. Added to the risk of attack were the diabolical conditions that the convoys faced in the Arctic Ocean. From 1942 the convoys were run mainly during the winter months, when the long hours of darkness reduced the risk of air attack. Bitter Arctic gales and winter snowstorms inflicted sometimes quite serious damage on the ships. Between August 1941 and May 1945, more than 40 convoys totalling 792 ships were sailed outward and 739 returned. Sixty-two ships were sunk on outward passages and 28 on the return journey, with a loss of 829 lives.

ACJ 0660

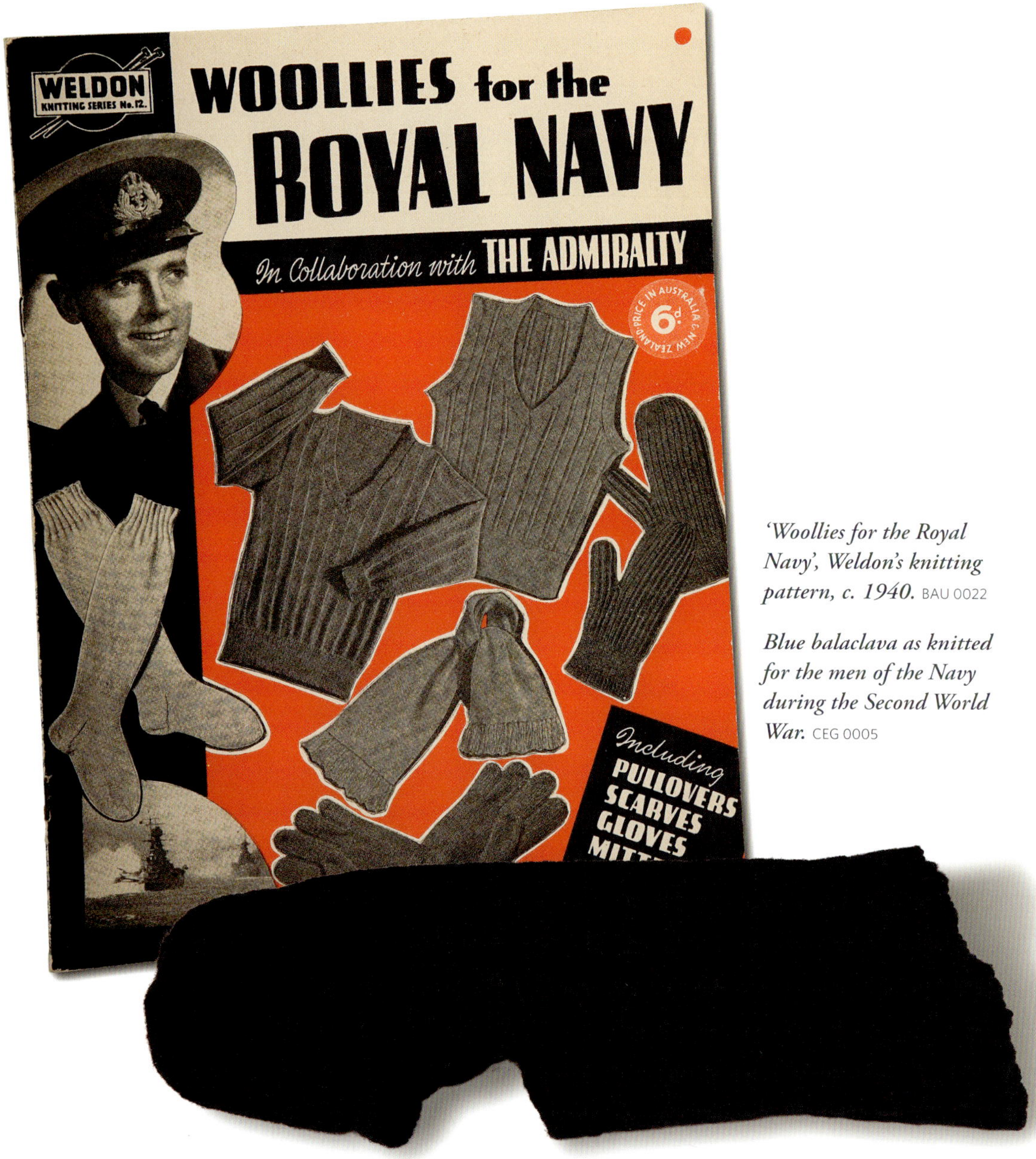

'Woollies for the Royal Navy', Weldon's knitting pattern, c. 1940. BAU 0022

Blue balaclava as knitted for the men of the Navy during the Second World War. CEG 0005

The successful defence of convoy JW 51B against heavy odds is one of the legends of the Russian convoys. On 22 December 1942, 14 merchant ships and their escort vessels sailed from Loch Ewe, Wester Ross, Scotland. There were New Zealanders, some of them veterans of the Arctic passage, in several of the escort ships. Three German destroyers were sighted at 8.30 a.m. on New Year's Eve when the convoy was about 220 miles northwest from Kola Inlet near Murmansk. An hour later, the German heavy cruiser *Admiral Hipper* appeared out of the gloom. The convoy was screened with smoke and two of the escort vessels detached to engage *Admiral Hipper* which, although hit several times, returned fire on HMS *Onslow*, hitting the RN ship three times in rapid succession and causing it to catch fire. The fires aboard *Onslow* were successfully fought by parties organised and led by New Zealander Lieutenant Lewis King, who was consequently awarded the DSC for his actions.

Hundreds of New Zealand officers and ratings saw service on RN vessels during the Battle of the Atlantic. Their ships took part in many battles with packs of the dreaded German U-boats in the grim months of 1941–42 and in the successful counter-offensive that destroyed nearly 500 U-boats in the following two years, turning the balance of the war in favour of Britain and her allies.

Lieutenant S. G. Jervis was awarded the DSC for his skilful work as anti-submarine control officer in holding contact with the U-boats in May 1943 when HMS *Oribi* took part in one of the grimmest convoy actions in the Battle of the Atlantic. A convoy of 42 ships was attacked for several days by a large pack of U-boats which sank 13 of the ships. Five enemy submarines were sunk by the escort vessels, including one by ramming by *Oribi* and a sixth by a Canadian aircraft. This action is regarded as a turning point in the Battle of the Atlantic, as it marked the end of large-scale attacks by U-boats and Britain's victory in the fight for the Atlantic.

Petty Officer A. Wood from New Zealand, who had seen action on board HMS *Achilles* during the Battle of the River Plate, was serving in *Woodpecker*, one of the vessels of the famous Second Escort Group that, on one patrol in early 1944, sunk six U-boats in 10 days – three within 17 hours. Wood was awarded the British Empire Medal 'for outstanding courage, enterprise and devotion to duty'. Lieutenant Commander L. P. Bourke was also involved in the destruction of a number of U-boats in the Atlantic and duly decorated. In January 1944, he was making his first convoy escort as commanding officer of the frigate HMS *Bayntun* when a U-boat was detected by radar. After a long hunt and three depth-charge attacks, the submarine was finally sunk and Bourke was awarded the DSC. A year later, while still on board *Bayntun* which, with the other ships of the Tenth Escort Group was patrolling off the Shetland Islands, the escort group sank three U-boats within two weeks and Bourke added a bar to his DSC.

Outstanding among the many New Zealanders involved in the invasion of Normandy – D-Day – on 6 June 1944 was Lieutenant Denis Glover, who after the war would become one of New Zealand's most distinguished poets and publishers. He was in command of the landing craft LCI(S) 516. After landing part of a commando force at Ouistreham, he skilfully extricated his vessel from beach obstructions, drawing alongside another landing craft which was sinking and taking on board approximately 200 soldiers in a vessel designed to carry 100. Returning to Ouistreham, Glover landed all the men successfully before going to the rescue of another sinking landing craft and taking off her crew. Over the days of the Normandy offensive, Glover work tirelessly and was subsequently awarded the DSC.

Lieutenant N. S. Prebble, who was also in command of a landing craft, landed a number of Black Watch and Gordon Highlanders near Courselles. His cool and skilful handling of his ship successfully got his 203 soldiers ashore. Sub Lieutenant B. L. Twomey was in charge of an LCM (landing craft, mechanised) which he took within close range of enemy machine-gun nests and for two hours provided a smoke screen to cover other landing craft going in to the beaches. The LCM was under heavy fire the whole time and Twomey's vessel was hit repeatedly. He was awarded the DSC for his part in the operation.

New Zealanders were also on board RN ships when Japan began its invasion of the Far East in early 1942.

Two days before the surrender of Singapore in February 1942, a plan to evacuate approximately 3000 nominated persons was put into effect. Many of the New Zealand ratings who had been based in the Singapore Station sailed on 10 February and reached Batavia safely. Those who left just three days later were not so lucky, as their ships were sunk by the Japanese and many were killed or taken prisoner.

In accordance with the evacuation plan, Motor Launch 310, commanded by New Zealander Lieutenant H. J. Bull, left Singapore with Rear-Admiral E. J. Spooner and Air Vice-Marshal C. W. H. Pulford, five staff officers and 26 other ranks on board. The launch was attacked by aircraft and a destroyer two days later near Bangka Strait and, after sustaining damage, was beached on nearby Tjibea Island. Soon after the Japanese boarded the launch, wrecked its machinery and ordered the crew ashore. A native canoe was made seaworthy and Bull, with two ratings and two natives, paddled for seven days to reach Merak in Java, where arrangements were made to send help to those remaining on the island. Bull was awarded the DSC and fellow New Zealander, Able Seaman L. B. Hill, the DSM for courage and devotion to duty. However, help arrived too late and

HMNZ Transports badge. Worn by personnel on troopships to denote that they were on active service and not eligible for service in the Army. The blue enamel background to the inscription indicates that the badge was that of an officer. MDD 0055

Souvenir booklet issued in conjunction with 'Salute the Sailor Week', September 3–9, 1944, in support of the Victory Loan Campaign. GEP 0024

19 officers and ratings, including two New Zealanders, either died on Tjibea Island or were taken prisoner by the Japanese.

Lieutenant E. N. Derbidge of Christchurch was on board *Li Wo*, which sailed from Singapore on 13 February. The boat had a single 4-inch gun (with only 13 rounds) and two machine guns as her armament for the evacuation voyage. She had survived several air attacks when, nearing Bangka Island, the crew sighted an enemy convoy escorted by a heavy cruiser and destroyers. As escape was impossible, *Li Wo*

APE 0020

'The flotilla made a grand sight, steaming down to the open sea, threading its way in line ahead through the massed transports, crowded with men and vehicles that lay at anchor in the land-locked roadstead. The Commandos on deck looked around at the unfamiliar scene, at the waters they had exercised in so often. They were cheerful but restrained. For many it would be the last sight of England.' Denis Glover

D-DAY 6 JUNE 1944

On 6 June 1944, 24 hours after it had been initially planned to commence, approximately 6000 warships and 200 aircraft squadrons crossed the English Channel en masse for the Normandy coast. This massive assault on German-occupied France would mark a crucial turning point in the Second World War.

The naval component of the invasion was code-named Operation Neptune and had been on the planning table from as early as 1940, undergoing endless fine tuning and, after the American entry into the war, the need to factor the United States' massive military power into the equation.

Vice-Admiral Sir Bertram Ramsey was given the task of overseeing the planning of the naval contribution to this attempt by the Allies to regain ground in Europe. The Royal Navy was charged with sending out minesweepers to clear the beach approaches and undertaking the gargantuan task of landing thousands of ground troops on French soil under the bombardment that would take place between the many German shore batteries and the Admiralty's cruisers, battleships and destroyers. In short, the navy's task was to ensure 'the safe and timely arrival of the assault forces at their beaches, the cover of their landings and subsequently the support and maintenance and the rapid build-up of our forces ashore'.

After extensive reconnaissance, it was decided that the most suitable location on the French coast for the RN to land troops was an 80-kilometre stretch between the rivers Orne and Vire. Difficulties with the area chosen included the distance from the embarkation ports and the lack of a suitable port on this short stretch of French coastline.

In the weeks leading up to the invasion, a combined sea-going force consisting of vessels and personnel from the RN, the Commonwealth, the American and various Allied European navies was assembled in British ports. Fleet Air Arm squadrons were called upon to join with the Royal Air Force to provide air cover for the invading armada. Having landed their troops on the Normandy beaches, the navy continued to operate between the English and French coasts in a constant round of bringing in reinforcements and supplies.

With the constant stream of sea traffic and lack of a suitable port in the designated assault area, two artificial harbours complete with workable piers were prefabricated in Britain and towed in pieces across the channel to France. However, only one was completed, due to bad weather. These 'Mulberries' were large enough to facilitate the off-loading of army vehicles in addition to reinforcements and supplies. Far from being the work of a single day ('D-Day'), this activity was to continue for months. The invasion of Normandy was a sustained and highly successful operation that enabled the combined Allied forces to move a great deal closer to winning the war in Europe.

White ensign flown on D-Day from LCT (landing craft tank) 933 and later autographed by the crew who took part in the operation. SFC 0029

Ear defenders and morphine issued onboard HMS Emerald *for Normandy landing bombardment force, June 1944.* CMM 0001 / IMA 0018

Pocket watch issued to R. G. Black for D-Day landings whilst serving in LCM 601. ICA 0032

attacked a transport which she set on fire and rammed, but was herself sunk and most of her crew were drowned. Ten survivors were picked up by the Japanese and made prisoners, but a few, including Derbidge, escaped by clinging to a badly damaged lifeboat. Derbidge and some of the other survivors landed on Bangka Island. A fortnight later, they were attacked by local bandits and Derbidge and three of his companions were wounded and left without food. Eventually, they were captured by the Japanese and Derbidge died while en route to a prisoner of war camp.

From early 1942, as a result of the Japanese occupation of the Far East, the New Zealand presence in the region was largely confined to Japanese prisoner of war camps. It would not be until early 1945, when the British Pacific Fleet moved into the region, that New Zealanders were once again represented on RN warships and the aircraft of the Fleet Air Arm.

Approximately 1000 New Zealanders volunteered for the Fleet Air Arm of the RNZNVR, 738 of whom achieved a commissioned rank. New Zealand naval airmen served in every one of the 50-odd aircraft carriers commissioned by the Royal Navy during the war and on all Royal Navy air stations, including those in the West Indies. In total, 152 Kiwi navy flyers were killed and many more wounded. The decorations received by New Zealand airmen during the war included one DSO, 39 DSCs and two bars, one DFC, three MBEs, 48 mentions in despatches, and two letters of commendation.

Serving in the many squadrons of the Fleet Air Arm, which with the Royal Air Force shared the defence of Malta, were a number of New Zealanders. Sub Lieutenant J. A. Cramp of 830 Squadron led a force of four Albacores from Malta in a strike on two Italian cruisers and five destroyers, hitting one of the cruisers in the attack. For this action, he was awarded the DSC for 'gallantry in circumstances of extreme hazard'. For his part in more than 20 operations from Malta involving torpedo and dive-bombing attacks on enemy shipping up to June 1942, Sub Lieutenant J. C. Morrison of 828 Squadron was also awarded a DSC.

The Malta convoy of August 1942, in which nine out of 14 merchant ships and four escort vessels were lost, was covered as far as the narrows of the Skerki Channel (between Sicily and Tunisia) by aircraft which, in one action, took on more than twice their own number. New Zealanders who performed meritoriously during this action included Lieutenant F. A. J. Pennington of 809 Squadron who showed 'great dash and initiative in combats with superior numbers of enemy fighters and bombers'. Furthermore, 'though his aircraft was hit early in the action and the air gunner wounded, he carried out further patrols and helped to account for four enemy aircraft'. For his courage, Pennington received a DSC.

New Zealand airmen were also involved in the North African campaigns. Lieutenant P. Fell, RNVR, one of the first New Zealanders to join the Fleet Air Arm in 1939, flew with 806

.303 calibre water-cooled Vickers Armstrong machine gun on tripod. JDA 0002 *(Tripod on loan from Army Museum, Waiouru.* 1995.390/2*)*

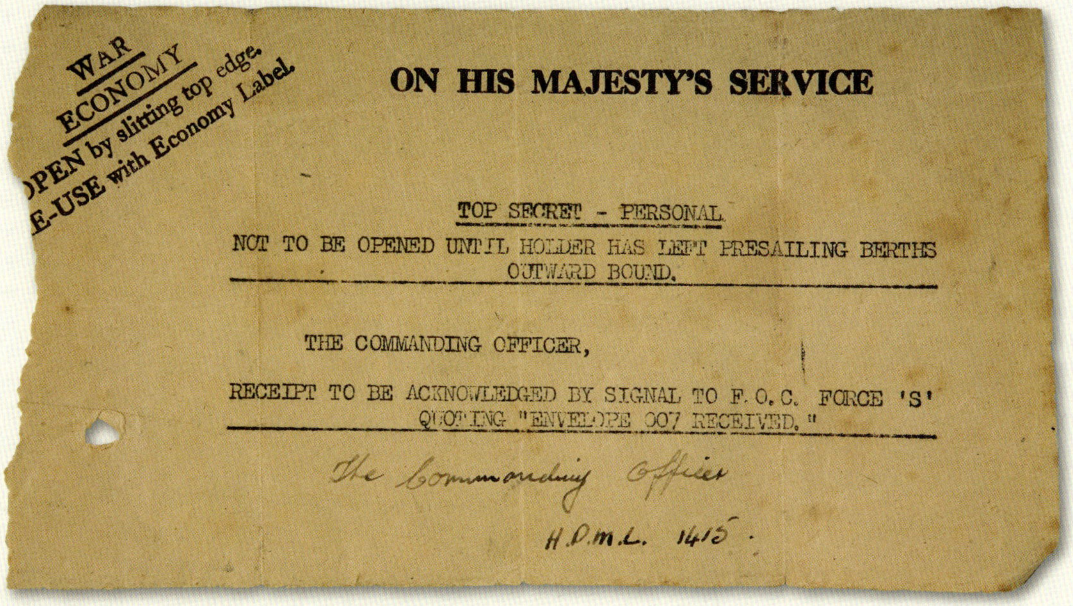

WAR ECONOMY
PEN by slitting top edge.
E-USE with Economy Label.

ON HIS MAJESTY'S SERVICE

TOP SECRET - PERSONAL
NOT TO BE OPENED UNTIL HOLDER HAS LEFT PRESAILING BERTHS OUTWARD BOUND.

THE COMMANDING OFFICER,

RECEIPT TO BE ACKNOWLEDGED BY SIGNAL TO F.O.C. FORCE 'S' QUOTING "ENVELOPE 007 RECEIVED."

The Commanding Officer
H.D.M.L. 1415.

Envelope marked 'Top Secret – Personal. Not to be opened until holder has left presailing berths outward bound'. Package contained D-Day Orders. ELM 0001

D-DAY LANDINGS

ABLE SEAMAN G. C. FORRESTER

Gordon Forrester joined the New Zealand Division of the Royal Navy Volunteer Reserve in 1938. He saw out the early part of the war on New Zealand Division ships before being sent to Britain. While serving with the Royal Navy, on board the destroyer HMS *Offa*, Forrestor did time on Russian convoy duty and was involved in the D-Day landings.

Gordon Forrester: . . . D-Day, with hundreds and hundreds of other ships taking part in the D-Day landing. We went out from Portsmouth and assembled out in the Channel and there were ships as far as the eye could see. At one stage along came the *Achilles* . . . apparently she went down to cover *Plymouth* because she had a fire aboard while she was being refitted and wasn't quite ready. . . . That caused me a bit of consternation because I had to put up with a bit of flack from the English fellows. 'Oh the *Achilles* . . . she's not rejoining us, she's getting out of the way.'

. . . We stayed out there with all the other ships and, come night-time, the convoy or the invasion force had assembled and away we went. . . . Now our task at that stage – we were at the starboard head of the invasion force, and we sailed in that position right up the coastline of France, which is Cherbourg. It was amazing, the rocket ships had gone ahead and they were clearing the beaches, and other ships were assembling down near [the] bombardment and the coastline was alive with fire. Fireworks, shells bursting, rockets, et cetera. It was very hard to describe. It was just like a big fireworks display. Like rockets going up and exploding and all that.

As we came up towards the shore, we turned around and came back out to cover the flank of the invasion force and, as the ships were passing us by, I looked up and there was the *Monowai*. I was so proud and I let everybody around me know it. It was a New Zealand ship in the invasion force, and with that we carried on. We came right out and covered . . . the back of the invasion force lines. . . . It's hard to describe how many ships were there, and how many landing craft. How many warships. It was incredible. The sky was alive with aeroplanes and Dakotas towing gliders – which was the paratroopers being landed and dropped in France. At one stage we came across a ditched Dakota with the pilot hanging on, and so we picked him up and he stayed aboard us for quite some time – and was very pleased to get off in the finish to get a bit of peace, because our guns never stopped firing.

We . . . then covered for the invasion force E-boats – whatever came our way . . . we took on. The actual bombardment of France, we never took part in that.

At one stage, during a lull, we were further along the coast, a bit down from Cherbourg, so everything was quiet and so the skipper thought he would pop in and have a look close to the shore – and the next thing we know, we got 11-inch shells exploding in our wake. There was one shore battery that hadn't been taken out. Of course it was full speed ahead and I tell you what – you look astern to see 11-inch shells falling in your wake and exploding [and] you are thinking, By cripes, go ship, go! And we did, full speed ahead, and got out of that. We signalled . . . that there was a shore base that had a go at us, and of course we stood off out and watched the shell landing on this particular gun. They took it out just like that. But we were very lucky. One 11-inch shell would write a destroyer off. . . .

So we didn't go back in for another look until Cherbourg had actually fallen, and we went in alongside and they let us go ashore and gave us a few francs. . . . [Cherbourg] was all rubble. You can imagine the streets, all rubble and that. And the Yanks and their trucks tried to run us down. . . . Thought it was a great joke making us jump out of the way. I can always say [that] I went ashore in France even though I didn't see much, just a flattened Cherbourg.

At one stage during the invasion, four battleships came, and they virtually anchored off the coast of Cherbourg and they bombarded it with their 15- and 16-inch guns, and that went on for hours. I started watching them from the upper deck and I thought, All I am seeing is guns firing and going ashore – and so I just lay down on the iron deck and went to sleep. Exhausted.

ACJ 0776

ROYAL NAVY FLEET AIR ARM – *TIRPITZ*, 1944

LIEUTENANT A. W. DIREEN

Bill Direen joined the Fleet Air Arm of the Royal Navy under the auspices of Scheme 'F' in mid-1941. In early 1944, he was part of the complement of a group of newly formed squadrons flying off the carrier HMS *Victorious*. Their most famous mission was Operation Tungsten, the bombing of the German battleship *Tirpitz* in Kaa Fiord, near Alten Fiord, on 3 April.

Bill Direen: . . . and in my diary I see we were up in the morning at 2.30 a.m. and we took off at 5.15 a.m., and by 6 a.m. we were over *Tirpitz*. . . . She was in Kaa Fiord, which is right at the bottom of Alten Fiord, right at the north-most point of Norway. She was hiding out there. She was getting ready to go to sea, to go out and do trials in Alten Fiord, which was a bit bigger than Kaa Fiord. We weren't over the target very long, fortunately . . . I think it [was] said it was all over in about a minute.

INT: It was very successful, wasn't it?
BD: Quite successful.

INT: Bill – 1836 Squadron, you were what?
BD: We were top cover. There was no enemy opposition from aircraft and so we weren't involved in any fighting. We were well over. There was a bit of shrapnel getting up to that height and on the way out, and there was also an artillery ship, ack-ack ship, but no damage was done. The airfields were snowbound, which I think accounted for the fact there weren't any enemy aircraft and also the element of surprise. They wouldn't have had time to get to us, any rate. It was a complete surprise as far as the *Tirpitz* was concerned.

INT: When the second wave came over, the smoke pots had been activated?
BD: They were pretty well obscured by smoke pots. They [the squadron] dropped some more bombs through the smoke, but I don't know whether they hit anything on that occasion.

INT: There were hits on that first wave, weren't there?
BD: Yes, I think there were something like five or six hits. One or two of them could have really done more damage if they had released the bombs a little higher, to build up their velocity. They were 1600-lb armour-piercing bombs and they had the capability of getting through the armour plate. These bombs did penetrate the upper armoured deck, but did not damage the vital lower armoured deck – so she stayed afloat.

INT: That ship had remarkable armour plate, running through one or two decks down.
BD: I think so. David Woodward's book *The Tirpitz* says there were 15 hits, some with 500-lb bombs [and] others [that] had punctured the upper armoured deck and [were] bursting below. . . .

Returning from the operation itself, I think they only lost one aircraft – I think a Barracuda or something, which was ditched. I wrote off my aircraft just through faulty landing, going far too fast. I suppose in retrospect . . . the batsman should have waved me off. But anyway, there was a lot of pressure on landing quickly, so the ship didn't have to spend too much time in the wind. I came in too fast and missed all the wires and went into the first barrier. Luckily, that barrier chopped off one of my undercarriage legs and threw me into the second one, and then I came to a halt smartly down below the island. Luckily, I was pulled up, because the broken undercarriage ploughed into the deck and brought me up pretty smartly, or otherwise I would have run forward into a lot of aircraft up front who were waiting to go down into the hangar – and so I was very fortunate in that respect. The aircraft was a complete right-off – it went over the side later.

Squadron in the Western Desert and was one of the first pilots to fly fighters from Takoradi, on Ghana's Gold Coast, across Africa to Egypt. In addition, he was a 'founder' member of 1839 Squadron that flew off the fleet carrier HMS *Indomitable* and, with *Illustrious* in May 1942, took part in Operation Ironclad, the capture of Diego Suarez in Madagascar.

From 1942, the Air Arm had a considerable defensive role protecting the Russian and Atlantic convoys which were subject to constant attack from the air as well as the sea. Fleet Air Arm protection for convoys was provided by merchant aircraft carriers, or MAC ships, 19 of which were commissioned during 1942–43. The MAC ships were either bulk grain carriers or oil tankers and, although fitted with flight decks, retained their mercantile status despite their dual role. Thus, in addition to their merchant navy crews, they carried 10 Fleet Air Arm officers, a naval surgeon and 20 naval ratings to service the aircraft. Many of them were New Zealanders. In February 1944, while on convoy duty in the North Atlantic, Lieutenant E. S. Erikson, a New Zealand pilot on HMS *Biter*, in company with another aircraft, attacked a large four-engined bomber which was shot down in flames by Erikson. Both pilots landed back on their carrier under difficult conditions and Erikson subsequently received the DSC.

In the North Sea, the Fleet Air Arm was employed in the attacks on the German battleship *Tirpitz*, anchored in Alten Fiord, Norway, where she had been damaged by midget submarines in September 1943. By early 1944, there were indications that she had undergone extensive repairs and was set to sail once more. In response, Operation Tungsten, an attack on *Tirpitz* by carrier-borne aircraft, was formulated. From 3 April 1944, over the course of five months, the carrier forces whose aircrews included approximately 60 New Zealanders made a number of separate attacks on the German battleship. During the first, eight certain and five probable hits were made on *Tirpitz*, which was burning fiercely when the last bombers left her.

The New Zealand airmen from *Indefatigable*, *Formidable* and *Furious* were once again in the thick of things during the second attack on *Tirpitz* on 17 July 1944. In the last week of August, aircraft from the same carriers made another four attacks on the German battleship. Four certain and four probable hits and two near misses were reported. Although these Fleet Air Arm strikes did not achieve a decisive result, they set the pattern for the subsequent attacks by the Royal Air Force which finally disposed of *Tirpitz*. The German battleship's end came in the RAF's third attack on 12 November 1944 when, badly damaged and on fire, the ship capsized and sank at Tromsö.

More than 60 New Zealanders served with Fleet Air Arm squadrons during the Allied landings at Salerno in Italy in September 1943. A total of ten air combats were fought from the carriers over approximately two and a half days before the enemy airfields were captured and put into operation by Allied forces. Lieutenant Commander F. A. J. Pennington gained a bar to his DSC for his 'outstanding leadership' in sorties from his ship and later from a captured airfield. The six pilots of his squadron completed 51 sorties without damage to their aircraft.
New Zealanders also served in the naval air squadrons that were among the approximately 6500 combat aircraft that played an integral part in the invasion of Normandy. From D-Day onward they gave close cover to convoys on the cross-Channel routes and in the assault areas, laid smoke screens, and spotted for naval bombardments. Lieutenant L. J. Rapson, who made nine successful night attacks on enemy light craft, was awarded the Distinguished Flying Cross for his 'skill and keenness during a long and arduous period of duty with his squadron'.

After the Japanese entered the Second World War, New Zealand Fleet Air Arm personnel were involved in many actions in the Far East and the Western Pacific.

The British Pacific Fleet struck its first blows in January 1945 when it carried out three successful attacks on oil refineries in Sumatra which were supplying about three-quarters of the aircraft fuel used by the Japanese. During the first strike – Operation Lentil – considerable damage was done to the refinery targeted. Two New Zealand pilots were mentioned in despatches for their part in this operation. Sub Lieutenant K. A. McLennan was the leader of a flight which shot down three Japanese fighters and shared in the destruction of a fourth. McLennan himself shot down one and shared a second. Sub Lieutenant H. A. Rhodes of 1834 Squadron shot down an enemy fighter and would almost certainly have accounted for another if he had not stuck to his task of giving top cover for the bombers. The second attack – Operation Meridian – took place on 24 January when 47 Avengers, 10 Fireflies, and 48 fighters attacked and badly damaged the refinery at Palembang, the largest and most important in the Far East. The strike force was intercepted some miles short of the refinery and met considerable fighter opposition and anti-aircraft fire.

Another task assigned to the British Pacific Fleet was the neutralisation of enemy airfields in the Sakishima Gunto near Formosa (Taiwan).

POW Sumatra

'The Jap officer walked in. He spoke to me first, held a pistol at my temple and asked me what was wrong with me and I told him. I thought, This is it, good-bye Mum and Dad. Nothing happened. I opened my eyes and he [the officer] was doing the same to the next guy. And he did it to everybody and finally before he walked out, he said: "You are prisoners of war from now on." I suppose in some ways we were lucky, but that was mental torture. We were lucky.'

Laurence Charles Hurndell

Laurence Hurndell was just 19 years old, that day in Sumatra early in 1942 when he had a gun held to his head and was told that he was a prisoner of Emperor Hirohito. It would be almost three years before he would be a free man once more.

Born in September 1922, Hurndell joined the NZ Division of RN in May 1941 and, after a few months of basic training, sailed to Singapore in the spring of that year for further training at the RN Naval Base there. After his arrival in Singapore, he was drafted to *Grasshopper,* a minefield patrol vessel which kept an eye on the harbour, and was, after the Japanese bombed Pearl Harbour, standing by with *Dragonfly* to take off survivors from the city.

Hurndell still has vivid memories of the night – 13 February 1942 – that Singapore fell: '. . . it was terrible, the fire. Singapore at night was just a red fire. We were . . . I suppose, about five or six miles out, and we could see the dive bombers just machine-gunning and dive-bombing around the city. There was no air opposition at all and it was just chaotic. The fires were burning and all the oil tanks were burning, and Singapore was a massive glow at night. . . . The Japanese by that time were just down the road, about half a mile away.'

***Dragonfly* and *Grasshopper,* loaded to the gunnels with evacuees, faced air bombardment off the coast of Sumatra by 127 Japanese planes. *Dragonfly* sank quickly and *Grasshopper* was severely damaged, with many deaths and injuries on board. Hurndell himself was badly wounded in the hip and groin area by shrapnel and unable to walk. When *Dragonfly* was heroically beached on an island by its captain, Hurndell had to be bodily thrown into the water. The survivors were machine-gunned by the Japanese as they came ashore.**

The prisoners, both military and civilian, were held on Singkep off the coat of Sumatra, where there was a Dutch tin mine and a rudimentary native hospital where Hurndell and the other wounded were treated. Hurndell's wound became infected and required surgery to remove the shrapnel and infected tissue. Eventually the POWs were sent north to the capital of Sumatra, Medan, where a large camp had been established in the requisitioned Dutch army barracks.

Life in the camp at Medan was extraordinarily harsh. Hunger, disease and forced labour took many lives long before their time. The prisoners subsisted on fish, rice, vegetables, tapioca and the odd snake and were regularly tortured for stealing food. For two years, the POWs including Hurndell were set to work loading ships in the Medan port, building a racecourse and carving land for grazing cattle out of the jungle. News of the war and the outside world filtered into the camp via a single crystal radio set which the Japanese knew existed but, despite repeated efforts, never found.

In early 1944, 1500 detainees including Hurndell trekked for a week through the jungle, travelling north to supplement Chinese and Indonesian labour building a railway line. The Acheh railway traversed 200 miles of mountainous, jungle-clad country, from the coast to a coalmine in the hills. Hurndell recalls the building of a viaduct without a single nail. Ironically, the Acheh job was completed a week after the end of the war. Upon the return of the labour gang to the camp at Medan, it quickly became apparent that 'something was up'. Within days the Japanese had deserted the camp, silently in the night.

On 16 September 1945, after an arduous three years as a prisoner of the Japanese, Hurndell, one of the 'lucky' ones, was repatriated to New Zealand.

Many New Zealand officers of the Fleet Air Arm took part in the 12 operations against the Sakishima airfields in March 1945. In a sweep over Ishigaki airfield, Lieutenant A. B. MacRae, leader of 1839 Squadron, was severely wounded in his right thigh but continued to attack. When he arrived back over the squadron's carrier, *Indomitable*, MacRae found that he could not lower the undercarriage of his damaged fighter and so was forced to make a crash-landing, which he did in copybook style. He was awarded the DSO for his efforts.

The carrier aircraft flew 574 sorties in total and all the enemy airfields in the Sakishima island group, as well as barracks, wireless and radar stations, were attacked, as were several coastal ships. A signal from Admiral Nimitz of the United States Navy congratulated Task Force 57 on its 'illustrious' showing, to which reply was made that the enemy would be pursued 'indomitably, indefatigably and victoriously' – alluding to the names of three of the carriers that had taken part in the strike. On this occasion, in addition to MacRae, Lieutenant J. A. Parli of 1833 Squadron showed 'outstanding leadership, determination and skill in pressing home strafing attacks on airfields in the Sakishima group in the face of anti-aircraft fire'.

Approximately 100 New Zealand pilots of the Fleet Air Arm were serving in the carriers HMS *Formidable*, HMS *Victorious*, HMS *Indefatigable* and HMS *Implacable* when they took part in the 'Ramrod' attacks on Japan in July and August of 1945. There were also many New Zealand radar ratings in the other ships of the British Pacific Fleet. Sub Lieutenant H. A. Rhodes, a fighter pilot of 1836 Squadron, fought in six 'Ramrods' and was awarded a bar to his DSC. He showed 'coolness and superb airmanship' in landing his badly damaged Corsair safely on his carrier after returning with invaluable photographs of the damage inflicted on a Japanese carrier. A mention in despatches was awarded to Sub Lieutenant Derek Morten of 1841 Squadron who had already been awarded the DSC for his part in the air strikes on *Tirpitz* the year before.

The American and British task forces attacked Honshu in early August 1945 and for two days carrier aircraft operated at full force, covering a territory that ranged from Yokohama to the northeast end of the island, bombing airfields, shipping, railways and industrial areas. Japanese kamikaze attacks began in early August, approximately a month after the combined fleets invaded Japanese home waters. With the dropping of two atomic bombs on Nagasaki and Hiroshima, the war came to an abrupt halt with the Japanese surrender.

New Zealand naval prisoners of war were interned in both German and Japanese camps. Those who were taken by the Japanese during the war in the Pacific suffered far more than their German-held counterparts, who were held under conditions laid down by the Geneva Convention in registered camps. After Victory in Europe was declared, the New Zealand POWs in German camps were freed by Allied forces and repatriated, mainly to England and then home.

As the Allied forces in the Far East began advancing into territories previously occupied by the Japanese, prisoner of war camps were discovered whose inmates included a number of New Zealand naval men who had been captured in the fighting following the fall of Singapore. These men, who were generally in very poor health, were repatriated home, sometimes via Australia, for demobilisation. After the successful occupation of mainland Japan, camps were also discovered there, and among those freed by the Allied invasion forces were two New Zealanders released from a camp at Ofuna, about eight miles from Yokosuka in the Yokohama area.

They were Lieutenant Donald Cameron of 1834 Squadron, whose aircraft had been shot down over the Sakishima Gunto on 9 May 1945, and Chief Petty Officer Telegraphist H. E. G. Newman of HMS *Exeter*, which was sunk in the Battle of the Java Sea on 1 March 1942. Both were suffering from the effects of ill-treatment, mainly in the form of malnutrition. They were later to describe Ofuna as a 'nasty little hell-hole'. Also in the camp when it was liberated were three ratings from British ships sunk in the Java Sea and 99 American airmen.

This was Lieutenant Cameron's second time in a prisoner-of-war camp. As a Seafire pilot of 880 Squadron, HMS *Stalker*, during the landing operations in Salerno, Italy, in September 1943, his engine failed and he made a forced landing on a beach. He was taken prisoner by the Germans, but escaped five days later while being transferred from one camp to another. After an arduous and perilous walk of more than two weeks, including crossing the slopes of Mount Vesuvius, he remained in hiding with Italian civilians for some time. He was found by a Royal Marines commando when Naples was captured. For his 'enterprise and devotion to duty', Cameron was awarded a mention in despatches.

Sewing kit or 'housewife' as issued to all servicemen. New recruits were told: 'If the Navy had wanted you to have a wife they would have issued you with one!' CMC 0002

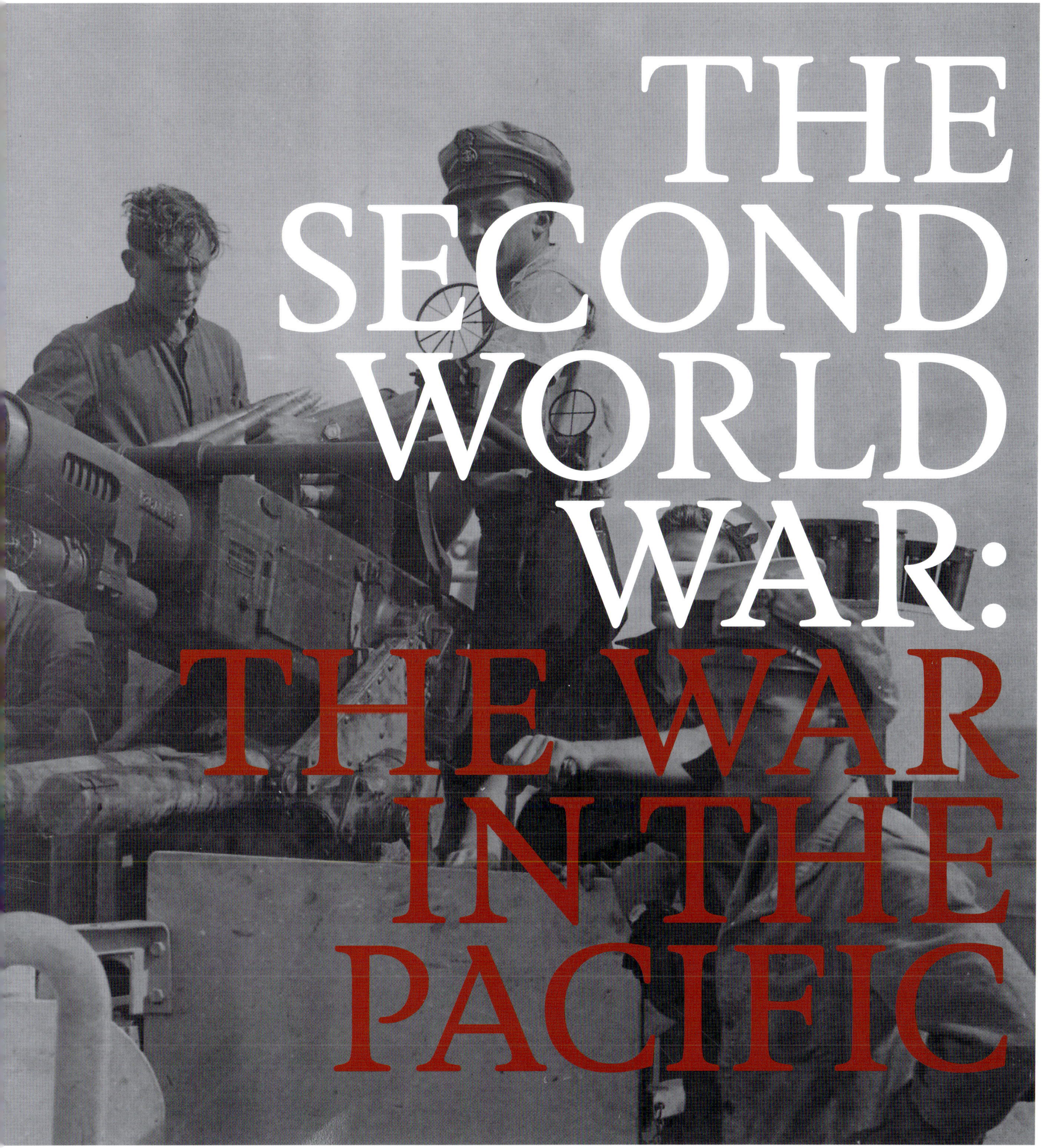
THE SECOND WORLD WAR:
THE WAR IN THE PACIFIC

In June 1940 Japan demanded that Britain close the Burma Road and the Hong Kong frontier and withdraw its garrison from Shanghai. After much negotiation, the British Government agreed to suspend traffic along the road for three months on the understanding that Japan would move toward a just and equitable settlement with China. However, in September 1940 Japan entered into a treaty with Germany and Italy, who recognised the 'leadership of Japan in the establishment of a New Order in Greater East Asia'.

At the heart of the treaty was an understanding that each would assist the others if attacked by the United States. The Burma Road reopened in October 1940 and a few months later economic sanctions against Japan were put into effect. Meanwhile, Japan stepped up preparations for war.

On the morning of 7 December 1941, in a scant two hours the Japanese completely crippled the United States Pacific Fleet for six months in their attack on Pearl Harbour. A day later Singapore was attacked, prompting the War Cabinet to agree that HMNZS *Achilles* should be sent as soon as possible to join the Eastern Fleet which was 'desperately short' of cruisers. In addition HMNZS *Leander*, newly returned to New Zealand waters from the Mediterranean and North Africa, and HMNZS *Monowai* were sent to join the Fleet in operations in the Pacific.

Only days after the fall of Singapore, the Japanese struck throughout the Far East, targeting Malaya, Siam, Hong Kong, Manila and Singapore. Japanese forces also occupied Guam, Tarawa, Makin and Wake Island by late December 1941, and Hong Kong surrendered on Christmas Day. By the end of that month, all the outlying islands north of the equator and west of the 180th meridian were occupied by the Japanese. In the early part of 1942 the Dutch East Indies, Borneo, Lae and Salamaua on the mainland of New Guinea, New Britain and New Ireland, Burma and Singapore fell in quick succession. The last city surrendered on 15 February, the same day on which Palembang, the great oil centre in Sumatra, was captured. The occupation of Java was not far behind.

In an incredibly short time the Japanese were in control of a vast area of the western Pacific. And in less than six months they had come within striking distance of Australia and New Zealand, the latter country being only too well aware of the inadequacy of its harbour defences if the Japanese decided to invade. Adding fuel to this potential bonfire was the first Japanese air attack on Darwin in February 1942.

Silk handkerchief. Trinkets like these were sent home to families from servicemen abroad. GEK 0009

The occupation of Rabaul on the island of New Britain by the Japanese in early 1942 had increased the threat to Port Moresby and New Caledonia, leading to the rapid establishment of a contiguous 'Anzac Area' in the South Pacific which included New Zealand and Australia. The Anzac Area naval force was under the strategic direction of the Commander-in-Chief United States Fleet.

Later in 1942 the original Anzac Area was disestablished and redesignated the South-West Pacific. The naval stakeholders also changed with the name, and the RNZN moved out of the area in order to consolidate its activities in the southeast Pacific with the United States Navy. This was especially important as, by March 1942, the Japanese had reached the Solomon Islands and by early July had consolidated their position with the landing of marines at Lunge and the building of an airfield.

Leander, the first New Zealand ship to take an active part in the Guadalcanal campaign, joined Task Force 64 in mid-1942 and worked mainly as an escort vessel for US troopships before being sent to Espiritu Santo to join the American Task Group 16.6 in November. A few days after joining the American ships, a crack was found in the hull plating in one of its fuel tanks and *Leander* was returned to Auckland for repairs and a refit which was not completed till early March 1943.

With the departure of *Leander* from the Pacific, the task of escort duties was transferred to *Achilles* which, as a member of Task Force 67 in late December 1942, was escorting troop transports into Guadalcanal.

Less than a week into the new year, Task Force 67 was heading east of Guadalcanal when it was attacked by 10 fighter planes and 15 bombers at approximately 9 a.m. on 5 January 1942. Half an hour later, 11 of the aircraft had capitulated to the ships' guns; however, a second squadron, initially thought to be Allied aircraft, burst through the clouds and attacked the task force vessels again. Three aircraft attacked the American ship *Honolulu* and a fourth focused on *Achilles*. A bomb hit the New Zealand cruiser's X-turret, manned by Royal Marines, with devastating consequences – the explosion blew the right side of the turret overboard and split the roof in two. Eleven men were killed outright, another two subsequently died of their wounds, and a further eight were wounded. Damage to the cruiser was minimal, as the gun turret took the brunt of the blast.

After being patched up in harbour at Espiritu Santo, *Achilles* sailed for England via Auckland in early 1943, arriving at Portsmouth on 22 March for a major refit. The ship's Royal Navy officers and ratings were discharged and many of her New Zealand ratings were sent to various shore establishments to do courses in gunnery, torpedoes, communications and radar. Nearly two years would pass before *Achilles* returned to New Zealand.

In February 1943 a second, successful, attempt to requisition *Monowai* for the Royal Navy was made by the British Ministry of War. The New Zealand Naval Board agreed to release the ship, which sailed from Auckland for the United Kingdom, arriving at Liverpool where she was paid off from the Royal New Zealand Navy on 18 June. *Leander* returned to active service at the beginning of March 1943 after an extensive refit. After arriving in Espiritu Santo, the New Zealand cruiser spent the next three months at sea with American task forces or on convoy escort duty. In mid-June she returned to Espiritu Santo and reported for duty with Task Force 18, which was to help in the combined forces' operations to clear the Japanese from their strongholds in New Georgia – where the Guadalcanal-based Japanese invasion forces had retreated six months before. The Americans faced more than six weeks of Japanese resistance in the dense tropical jungle and the campaign was punctuated by several fierce naval actions in Kula Gulf.

In early July *Leander* was called upon to replace the American ship *Helena*, which had been sunk off Kolombangara. On 13 July, shortly after midnight, the New Zealand cruiser, in company with American naval vessels, was heading towards Visuvisu Point, New Georgia,

DLA 0132

THE FALL OF SINGAPORE ABLE SEAMAN S. E. COVENEY

Stanley Coveney joined the Royal Navy Volunteer Reserve in mid-1938. He did his basic training at HMNZ *Philomel* before joining the newly refurbished HMS *Monowai*. Coveney was then drafted to HMS *Sultan* in Singapore. Shortly after he arrived, in early 1942, the Japanese took the city, leading to his part in the evacuation on board the ship *Ping Wo*.

INT: How did you get this draft to Singapore – how did that come about?

Stanley Coveney: Well we all volunteered to go to UK, and so we just put our names down ... and eventually they said the draft was to go . . . on leave prior to going to – they didn't say where – so we went to Wellington eventually . . . to Navy Office. Navy Office said the China [Station] draft was to fall in on the right, and nobody moved. [We thought,] We are not going to Singapore, we are going to UK. Well, we didn't move, so they got the papers and they read out all the names [of those going to the China Station, which included me].

INT: How many were there?

SC: About 13. . . . All ABs. . . . Some were in telegraphy and all that stuff. It was rather funny, we refused to go. 'We are not going to Singapore because we had volunteered to go to the UK.' It didn't make any difference. [Navy Office said:] 'Get in the line and get in there.' We went on the *Maekserkit* – she was a Dutch merchantman, just an ordinary merchantman, and we manned a couple of guns for them. They said to us: 'Don't worry, pay the bill when we get there. It will be all right.' It was a purser. He didn't know that we didn't have any money.

INT: They expected you to pay for your voyage?

SB: Not for the voyage, for the food. . . . They said: 'Pay when it comes time to leave.' And when it came time we had no money. Oh, gosh.

INT: This is for all the booze?

SC: This is for the booze. . . . They looked after us like kings.

INT: Had the war with the Japanese started by the time you got there?

SC: Yes, the first shells and bombs had been dropped. . . .

INT: You were drafted to *Sultan* – what was *Sultan*?

SC: It's the barracks. . . . Keppel Harbour is there and further down that way is *Sultan*. . . . It had room for married couples, and the English used to spend two and a half years [there] in pukka-sahib style.

INT: Is this where the big shipyard is, around in the Jahore Strait?

SC: Yes, where the floating dock was.

INT: What did you have to do?

SC: Well, there was big oil tanks, Shell [Oil], down where the oil was kept, and I had to march around there with a blimmin' rifle. I don't know really what I was supposed to do.

INT: There was no sign of you being drafted to a ship or anything like that?

SC: No. I decided when I saw what was happening that something was radically wrong, but I was going to do what I was told and it was just as well I did. A PO was in charge of us and he said: 'Look lads . . . I'm going down the road to try and get into town. I will come back.' But he didn't, and so I hooked up with some Pommy guys and . . . got taken to a hotel, The Ranges.

INT: Raffles?

SC: No, we weren't allowed in there. The Ranges was a flash hotel anyway, and that's where they lined everybody up and allocated people where to go to, to try and get on the big ships. 'Just do your best, see what you can do.' Well, it was a shambles . . . but they had to make up their mind in a hurry, because all of a sudden the Japs came flooding down. Anyway, they lined us up and I am sure it was [at] The Ranges Hotel. Lined us all up and allocated us to available ships. . . . The one I was on was number 13. ... the *Ping Wo*. ... Navy [were] the only ones that made a real effort to do something. The rest were just wandering around. . . . I went and got down to Keppel Harbour to try and get these guys aboard. I felt sorry for them – they were . . . blown up as they went outside. We nearly got blown up, it sure was a near miss. . . .

[*Ping Wo*] had 4-inch guns up front and she had a big well deck forward and a big one aft. Coal-burning . . . so we all started to shovel coal. . . . We filled her right up, closed the hatches . . . and said: 'Right, better get a shovel on.' I don't know whether we went through Sunda or what straits we went through – we copped a few bombs coming down, but not a lot . . . they didn't seem to want to hit us somehow. The one [ship] in front got sunk and the one in the back got sunk – we carried on and that's how it went. We were hiding during the day, and in the night-time we drove on again. . . . When an aeroplane [went overhead] or when a noise or anything [was heard] . . . we lay flat down on the deck and waited for it to go away. There was nothing to fire but a 4-inch gun.

. . . They tried to get as much edible goods as they could when we left Singapore, but . . . there wasn't a hell of a lot [to eat]. Because I remember when we came to Fremantle, the first people on board were the Salvation Army, and what did they have [but] grapes! I have never forgotten it. Beautiful big fat ones.

Two brass vases. The maker of the vases, K. B. Fraser, was killed when Leander *was torpedoed in the Solomons off Kolombangara Island, 13 July 1943.* GHE 0001

Framed picture of HMS Leander *made from cigarette paper.* PAJ 0013

when six ships, about 26 miles distant, were reported steaming southeast at 30 knots. Rear Admiral Walden L. Ainsworth, who was in command, ordered the destroyers to attack with torpedoes and the cruisers to bring all their main guns to bear. The Japanese cruiser *Jintsu* turned on her searchlights, giving the task force a literally brilliant target, and the Allied vessels blew the enemy ship out of the water.

During the next 10 minutes the destroyers discharged 56 torpedoes, including four fired by *Leander*. In retaliation, the Japanese ships discharged 29 torpedoes. These were well on their way when Ainsworth passed a signal to his ships to make a turn of 180 degrees to port in unison. However, this order was not received by *Leander* and was also missed by all the rear American destroyers bar one. The situation was complicated by the dense smoke from the guns which almost caused *Leander* to collide with *Honolulu*. Although disaster was averted, shortly afterwards the New Zealand cruiser was struck portside by a 'tin fish', despite taking evasive manoeuvres. The torpedo blew a huge, jagged hole in her port side amidships and exploded into No. 1 boiler-room, which was all but destroyed by the blast. All those in the vicinity were killed.

The hole left by the explosion was approximately 20 feet in depth from the lower deck level and 30 feet in length and caused severe distortion to the ship's armour and shell plating, extending more than 50 feet fore and aft. There was also extensive cracking to the ship's side and in the lower deck where the torpedo had exploded. Several men were swept overboard by the powerful wash following the explosion and a further seven were blown over the side. The cruiser took an immediate list of 10 degrees to port and the ship was plunged into complete darkness. The extensive damage to the electrical installation caused an almost complete shutdown of communications and a total breakdown of all gunnery fire-control and radio equipment. Throughout the long day that followed, the crew of *Leander* laboured without rest to save their ship. Their success has since been deemed one of the great damage control exercises in the history of the Royal New Zealand Navy. Working in almost total darkness and up to their waists in oil and water, a damage control party shored up bulkheads and hatches and plugged various holes and cracks. The forward boiler-room, main switchboard room, forward dynamo room, low-power room and the transmitting station were completely flooded. Five fuel-oil tanks were wrecked and the auxiliary machinery, and steam, water and fuel-oil pipe systems had sustained major damage.

Miraculously, the ship was still capable of steaming at slow speed on the two outer engines and *Leander* set a course for Tulagi Harbour. The engineers and stokers worked tirelessly in the heat and semi-darkness to keep the ship afloat and get her safely back to shore 200 miles away. *Leander* arrived in Tulagi harbour on 13 July, just after dark. The ship's company

HMNZS Leander *torpedoed in the Solomons, 1943.* AAA 0022

Leander *burial at sea.* AAG 0025

Brass tally plate from a machine onboard HMNZS Leander, *damaged in the battle of Kolombangara, 13 July 1943.* STA 0008

Souvenir programme – The Kiwi Concert Party presents 'The Road Show'. EEB 0038

assembled and the chaplain read prayers for the dead and of thanksgiving for the safety of the ship. The captain, standing by the capstan, read out the names of the dead and missing. After a week in harbour being made seaworthy, *Leander* headed for home. On 1 November 1943 a memorial tablet was unveiled in the chapel at *Philomel* to commemorate the 33 men who had been killed in action or had died on *Leander* since September.

Although temporary repairs to the hull and machinery were carried out in Devonport Dockyard, the job was beyond its scope and, after being made fit to sail, the New Zealand cruiser proceeded to Boston, Massachusetts, for a complete refit and the much-needed modernisation of armament and other equipment. *Leander* was paid off five months after her arrival in Boston. Most of the crew were sent to Britain to do courses on board the newly commissioned American-built RN frigate HMS *Tyler*.

From the end of 1941 to mid-1945 the ships of the 25th Minesweeping Flotilla, which had spent most of 1941 minesweeping harbour entrances at New Zealand's three main ports, saw continuous service in the South Pacific.

Although individual ships came and went as maintenance and improvements were carried

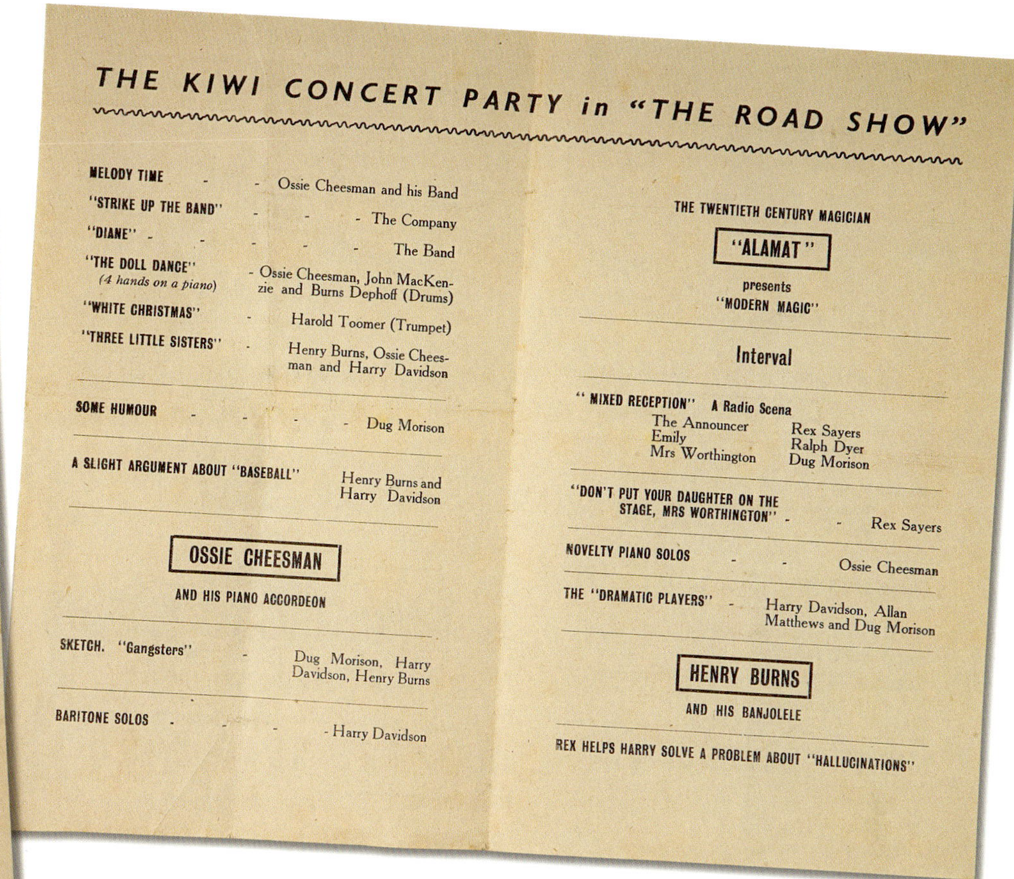

out, the Flotilla itself remained a constant presence in the area for three and a half years. The 25th MSF undertook various tasks in the Pacific including anti-submarine patrols and escort duty for the increasing number of troop transports and supply ships, especially those working out of Suva. Because of its central location, Norfolk Island was developed as a base for anti-submarine patrols from early 1942. At the end of October 1942, the New Zealand Naval Board offered the 25th Minesweeping Flotilla for service wherever it might be required in the Pacific to COMSOPAC (Commander South Pacific), which promptly accepted. The Flotilla, which then consisted of *Matai*, *Kiwi*, *Moa* and *Tui*, was sent to the Guadalcanal–Tulagi area to do anti-submarine and escort duties, beginning two and a half years of service in the eastern waters of the South Pacific.

By this stage of the war in the Pacific, with *Leander* and *Achilles* out of action, the minesweepers were the RNZN's sole representatives in the southeastern reaches of the Pacific. In fact, the RNZN had almost run out of ships: *Achilles* and *Leander* were in major refit, *Kiwi* was under repair after ramming a submarine, and *Monowai* had been taken over by the RN and was seeing duty in the Atlantic. The next two months, however, passed uneventfully enough for the 25th Minesweeping Flotilla. This was not to last.

Shortly after midday on 7 April a warning was received from coastwatchers of an imminent air attack: 67 bombers covered by 110 Zero fighters were flying southward. *Matai*, *Tui* and *Gale*, which were on anti-submarine escort duty off Cape Esperance, changed course immediately and headed at full speed towards Tulagi. The air attack came at approximately 3 p.m. when the Japanese bombers attacked the ships in Tulagi Harbour. *Moa* was hit by a 500-pound bomb which drove through her commanding officer's cabin and exploded below. Listing badly, she sank bow-first about four minutes later. Five ratings were killed. A further 15 of the crew including her commanding officer, Lieutenant Commander Peter Phipps, were injured. The quick actions of Leading Signalman J. L. W. Salter and Ordinary Telegraphist W. G. T. Bright saved the life of Signalman F. Thomas, who was severely wounded and lying unconscious on the bridge, by fitting him with a life-jacket and, as *Moa* sank, floating him off the bridge. Both Salter and Bright were awarded the British Empire Medal for their actions. *Moa* was replaced on Pacific duty by *Breeze*.

Minesweeping in the Pacific

‘[The] alert and courageous actions of the crews of these gallant little ships merit the highest praise ...’.

Admiral William Halsey (Grant Howard, Portrait of the Royal New Zealand Navy: 72)

The monotony of continuous anti-submarine patrols was relieved somewhat in August 1943, when *Tui* took part in the destruction of a Japanese submarine. Shortly after two o’clock on the afternoon of the 19th, the Asdic operator on board *Tui* reported a contact. The convoy it was escorting was ordered to alter course and commence zigzagging at full speed. Although the anti-submarine control officer did not confirm the identity of the contact, the Asdic operator was insistent that it was a submarine. *Tui* made three runs over the contact’s position, dropping four depth-charges.

By this stage, American seaplanes had arrived to assisted in the hunt. *Tui* carried out an Asdic sweep but did not regain contact, so abandoned the search to rejoin the convoy. Ten minutes later one of the seaplanes alighted close alongside *Tui*, the pilot reporting that he had seen what he took to be bubbles and suggesting that she making ‘one more run’. *Tui* complied, but again no Asdic contact was made and the New Zealand sweeper set course to rejoin the convoy once more. Shortly afterwards, what appeared to be brown smoke floats – indicating the possibility of a submarine on the surface – were seen on the horizon. An hour later, on approach, what looked like the conning tower of a submarine was sighted. *Tui* opened fire with her 4-inch gun and, as the range closed, managed to score two hits. She ceased fire after 20 rounds, and three American aircraft then attacked with depth charges. The submarine was seen to up-end and sink. *Tui* picked up six Japanese ratings, the only survivors of the submarine’s complement of more than 90 officers and ratings. Interrogation of the prisoners revealed that the submarine was the I-17. It was the 17th Japanese submarine destroyed in the South Pacific since January 1942.

Although the Solomon Islands campaign was almost at an end, there was no rest for the 25th Minesweeping Flotilla. Throughout the remainder of 1943 the sweepers were continuously employed on either anti-submarine patrols or escorting American supply ships to the Treasury Islands, where preparations were being made for the assault on the main Japanese base at Rabaul on East New Britain. The 25th Minesweeping Flotilla, and the New Zealand crews of the Fairmile motor launches, had a particularly good reputation with the Americans, who admired the efficient manner in which they carried out their endless round of duties.

On 14 January 1944 Admiral William Halsey, Commander South Pacific Area, suggested to the New Zealand Naval Board that the New Zealand Fairmile motor launches, which were no longer essential in New Zealand waters, should be employed in the Solomon Islands, thus relieving American destroyers and patrol vessels for duty elsewhere. This was approved by War Cabinet less than a fortnight later. The 12 Fairmiles were refitted for tropical service and designated the 80th and 81st Motor Launch Flotillas. The 80th Flotilla consisted of MLs 401 to 406, and the 81st Flotilla of MLs 400 and 407 to 411. They arrived in the Solomon Islands in March 1944. In less than 18 months, the 12 Fairmiles logged a total of 380,000 miles.

The unlucky craft in the Motor Launch Flotillas was ML400. On 27 April 1944, while on escort duty, she was damaged by an explosion and fire in her engine-room which caused her to drift onto a reef and sustain further damage to her hull and underwater fittings. Although ML400 was back in service by the end of the year, her run of bad luck was not yet over. On the night of 29 January 1945, while at anchor in Guadalcanal, the American ship *Serpens* was blown to pieces in a violent explosion while loading explosives. Chunks of steel weighing up to 40 pounds and other debris fell onto the deck of ML400 which was anchored nearby, causing extensive damage. The Fairmile was able to proceed under her own power to the Russell Islands to undergo repairs.

ABG 0084

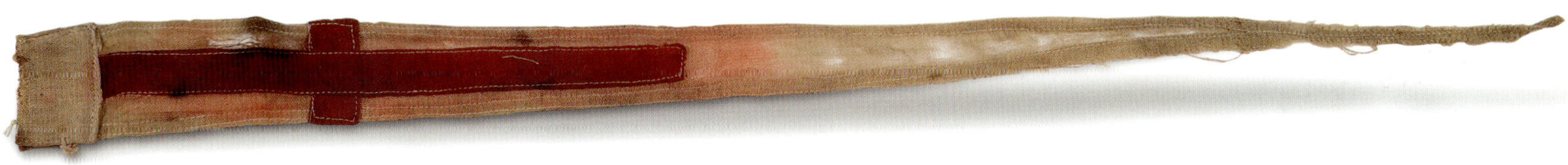

Lamp used at night attached to a halyard and hoisted up mast to indicate that vessel is engaged in minesweeping operations. SLE 0002

Commissioning pennant from the Motor Launch 409, one of the motor launch flotilla. SFI 0022

By the end of 1944 the tide of war was flowing strongly against Japan, and the Solomons had became ostensibly peaceful as Japanese resources were channelled in other directions – especially in waters closer to mainland Japan where a massive Allied invasion fleet was assembling.

In July 1943 the High Commissioner for New Zealand in London, the Rt. Hon. W. J. Jordan, raised the possibility of replacing *Achilles*, which had been seriously damaged in an explosion while undergoing refit and rearming in Portsmouth – adding approximately eight months to her initial completion date of September 1943 and stranding the crew without a ship. From New Zealand's point of view, the situation became still more pressing when *Leander* was torpedoed and badly damaged in action in the Solomon Islands in July 1943 and required extensive repairs in a dry dock in the United States. Essentially, the RNZN had two crews and no ships. Jordan suggested that HMS *Gambia*, a *Fiji*-class light cruiser, could fill the gap left by *Achilles* and that the *Leander* crew could man *Achilles* at a later date once the cruiser had completed its refit.

Although the Admiralty agreed to *Achilles'* company recommissioning *Gambia* from the RN, it required that the cruiser join the Eastern Fleet in the Atlantic and Mediterranean and, for future operations, in the Indian Ocean under

Leander*'s gun crew resting after Kolombangara battle.* AAG 0161

the control of the RN. The Admiralty had no objection to the crew of *Leander* sailing from the United States to Britain to man *Achilles* when that ship was ready to sail, nor its return to the RNZN. New Zealand, however, was to bear financial responsibility for at least part of the cost of her extensive refit and repairs.

Gambia was commissioned at Liverpool on 22 September 1943, having undergone an extensive refit which included additions to the anti-aircraft armament and the installing of elaborate radar equipment. A few of the officers and three-quarters of the ratings were New Zealanders. After a week of steaming and gunnery trials, the ship arrived at Scapa Flow on 20 October and was attached to the First Cruiser Squadron, Home Fleet. The first task assigned to *Gambia* was to take part in the interception of enemy blockade runners on passage to and from the Bay of Biscay. This task was short-lived and, three weeks later, *Gambia* returned to Plymouth for a month before joining the British Eastern Fleet. She arrived at Trincomalee on 19 February 1944, where she joined the Far Eastern Fleet Ceylon and was placed back on enemy blockade-running patrols.

At the beginning of 1944, preparations were made by the Admiralty to send a British fleet to the Pacific to take an active part in operations against the Japanese. Although Admiral Ernest King, Commander-in-Chief United States Fleet and Chief of Naval Operations, had always regarded the war in the Pacific as entirely an American affair, in January 1944 he suggested that the proposed British force be aggressively employed against the Japanese forces in the Indian Ocean. This was agreed, and preparations to establish a British Pacific Fleet with its main base at Sydney went forward during 1944. The British Pacific Fleet was a truly Imperial naval force and included substantial components from the Dominions. New Zealand was represented by the cruisers *Gambia* and *Achilles* and the corvette *Arbutus*, Australia by several destroyers and a force of 16 minesweepers, and Canada by the cruiser *Uganda*.

During April 1944, *Gambia* took part in Operation Diplomat. The Eastern Fleet was requested by the United States to carry out an attack on the Japanese forces around Singapore as a diversion for an American attack on a Japanese base at Sabang, a small island northwest of Sumatra, and to keep the Japanese occupied while the American seaborne assault on Hollandia and Aitape, on the north coast of Dutch New Guinea, was developing. In addition to the ships of the Eastern Fleet, British submarines were stationed in the Strait of Malacca to co-operate with these forces. *Gambia* took no active part in this attack.

Meanwhile, 100 miles from Sabang the American air attack was launched and was apparently a complete surprise to the enemy. As the Commander-in-Chief succinctly put it, the Japanese were 'caught with their kimonos up'. Further attacks on Japanese-held positions in the Far East in which *Gambia*, with the Fourth Cruiser Squadron, was involved included Operations Transom and Crimson. The latter brought *Gambia* into direct action against the Japanese for the first time, the ship taking part in the bombardment of the Japanese naval base at Sabang on 21 June.

In October 1944 the newly refitted *Achilles* joined the Fourth Cruiser Squadron, Eastern Fleet, in which *Gambia* was then serving.

The two New Zealand crews exchanged ships, as many of the *Achilles* ratings were due for leave and joined *Gambia*'s complement for the cruiser's first foray into New Zealand waters. Shortly thereafter *Gambia* sailed for New Zealand, arriving at Wellington on 24 November to a tremendous welcome. In addition to being inspected by various VIPs, more than 20,000 people visited the ship during the single weekend it spent in Wellington Harbour. Similar public interest was shown in Auckland, Dunedin and Lyttelton.

The Eastern Fleet was reassigned to what became known as the British Pacific Fleet for the combined forces assault on mainland Japan. There had been considerable opposition by the Americans to any role for the RN in the Pacific, including the expulsion of Japan from its occupied territories in the Far East and the eventual large-scale invasion of the Japanese mainland. However, the American forces finally agreed to an RN-led fleet operating in the area, with the proviso that they supplied themselves. The British Pacific Fleet came under the command of Admiral Sir Bruce Fraser. Fresh from its visit to New Zealand, *Gambia* joined *Achilles* and the rest of the Fleet on 17 February 1945. The month before, the British Pacific Fleet had carried out three successful attacks on oil refineries in Sumatra, badly damaging the Pladjoe refinery at Palembang and the Soengai Gerong refinery on the opposite side of the river from Pladjoe. Approximately 60 New Zealand pilots of the Fleet Air Arm were serving in the carriers which took part in these operations.

After the capture of Iwo Jima in early 1945, intensification of the air attacks on Japan called for a land base with an airfield nearer than any yet seized in the Allied push north. The obvious choice was the Sakishima Gunto group of islands off Okinawa. They had numerous airfields within fighter and medium-bomber range of Japan and good harbours. The assault on and occupation of Okinawa – the outcome of many months of sustained attack – was the greatest and most difficult combined operation of the Pacific war. The joint expeditionary force consisted of 1213 ships, 564 carrier-based aircraft and 451,870 troops from three marine and four army divisions. In this impressive line-up, the Royal New Zealand Navy was modestly represented by *Gambia*, *Achilles* and *Arbutus*, approximately 100 Fleet Air Arm officers, and sailors serving in Royal Navy ships.

Pair of Japanese naval uniform slippers made from fabric with fibre soles. CCI 0002

Japanese naval dagger. Surrendered to Lieutenant Commander Davis-Goff who was officer in charge of the Landing Party at Yokosuka Naval Base on 20 August 1945 by Commander Yuzo Tanno IJN. JRD 0001

AAF 0156

ACHILLES – X-TURRET

Warrant Officer R. W. Kirkwood

Ronald Kirkwood joined the New Zealand Division of the Royal Navy as a stoker in 1932. After service on HMS *Dunedin*, he was sent on exchange to the United Kingdom in 1936. In early 1939 Kirkwood returned to New Zealand on HMS *Achilles* and was on board the cruiser when X-turret was bombed by a Japanese aircraft.

Ronald Kirkwood: Then we joined up with Admiral Halsey in Chicago. We became part of a squadron with the Americans, the forerunner of their fleet. Halsey was in command.

INT: That was known as an Anzac Squadron?
RK: Yes. Anzac Squadron, yes. We convoyed troops to Noumea and Vila. There was an old sailing ship in Vila and as every ship counted, we were directed to salvage it. There was a bit of an estuary there – it was moored or anchored on the mud. One evening when the tide was high, we put a line on it and gave a fair bit of throttle to the engines and dragged it off. The *Westralia* was one of the ships we operated with there. When we joined up in the New Hebrides [with the rest of the Anzac Force], we covered the landing of troops on Guadalcanal – that was when the aircraft came down from Munda and bombed us.

I was on the fo'c'sle that morning and I had completed the morning watch so the mess man could clean out the mess, and I went up topsides with a book and a lifejacket and was lying back in the sun reading when I looked up and saw three or four planes overhead and thought, Don't worry, they are Americans, and joyfully went back to reading. We were only doing about four knots, the Yanks were picking up a seaplane on the mat astern of one of their cruisers, and we were just keeping station – and then there was a bit of a flurry and excitement, and someone said: 'They're not ours, they're bloody Japs!'

I looked up and you could see two red balls of fire coming towards us. ... You could see the bullets striking the water – this was on the port side of the fo'c'sle. Some way or other, I don't know whether they were ordered to, but we opened fire with an Oerlikon. Someone put the helm over and we slowly turned away to starboard as they let go their bombs and machine-gunned the quarter deck. The only casualty was a young seaman boy. Honeyfield was his name. He was just cut in half.

INT: You were on the upper deck all this time, up front?
RK: Well, as it happened, yes. Before I could man my action station, which was in the forward air compressor compartment. ... I hid behind a piece of rope, the only shelter, just near A-turret.

INT: The ship really didn't go to action stations until the bullets started to fly?
RK: That's right, and [it] never really went into action stations – it was all over [before it began]. Then it was all quiet, and casualty reports were coming back about those 13 unlucky guys, mostly Marines, [who were killed]. We were quite unprepared for it.

Achilles *X-turret bomb damage.* AAF 0156

This ceremonial life ring was used at the gangway of Achilles *during the Second World War until 1943 when the ship was bombed with the resultant loss of X-turret. A member of the guns crew in X-turret went below to clear a jam on the hoist at Guadalcanal. Whilst he was down below, the turret took a direct hit above. In his own words: 'I removed the life ring when we got back to Auckland and took it home as a keepsake – I figured they owed me that much'.* SGB 0009

INT: The bomb hit X-turret, didn't it?
RK: X – the Marines' turret.

INT: The Marines killed were those in the turret?
RK: Yes, and they killed a few others. . . . I always remember the Sergeant of Marines telling me there wasn't a real war on, and he was fed up with it. They found his head in a scupper. It was just chopped off. Pretty ghastly. They made a dummy turret and we continued for a while before coming back to Auckland.

INT: There was no structural damage to the rest of the ship?
RK: No. We went alongside an American ship and they cleared up things and cut things away, and we were operational with this plywood turret.

INT: After the bomb hit *Achilles*, where did you go to get repaired?
RK: To Lever Bros Island. We went into Santos. There was a repair ship there and the Americans did some work on the turret. The *Pensacola*, a cruiser, was in there. They [had] suffered some pretty heavy damage. It was a lovely spot we used to go ashore on picnic parties, and get rid of our energy climbing and swimming in the rivers and what have you. It was fairly monotonous, really . . . up there. It was just bad luck that we got hit, just bad luck.

ACHILLES – X-TURRET

ROYAL MARINE SEARGEANT A. F. EDWARDSON

Englishman Alfred Edwardson joined the Royal Navy as a Royal Marine in late 1935. In December 1938 he volunteered for the New Zealand Division and was transferred to HMS *Achilles*, which was also joining the New Zealand Station. Edwardson was on board the cruiser for both the Battle of River Plate in late 1939 and later, in January 1943, when the X-turret on *Achilles* was destroyed by a bomb dropped from a Japanese aircraft, with the loss of 14 lives, mainly Marines.

Alfred Edwardson: A Japanese plane had the audacity to drop a bomb on X-turret . . . [while *Achilles* was] in the South Pacific with the Fleet. It hit the Marines' turret. . . . It ruined the turret. . . . I was in the turret and I was the breech worker of the left-hand gun. I was one of the first in the turret and I thought this was an air raid, and I got an air raid shell off the ready-use rack on the side of the turret. I bent down and put it on the floor of the turret by the breech and, when I came to, I was in the gun-well! I was protected by the breech of the gun, because the bomb hit the right-hand gun. The heaviest part of the metal where that bomb hit was the truncheons, the balance part of the gun.

I was bending down and it burnt the shirt off my back and the skin off my back, and it was very painful. . . . I was in the sickbay for a few days. Looking back, it cleared up very quickly. . . . The first night was very painful and the doctor gave me a shot of morphine. I remember him saying: 'Oh, he's feeling sorry for himself.' I suffered because of my ears. Then again, I could have been dead.

The first task assigned to the British Pacific Fleet during this operation was to neutralise the enemy airfields in the Sakishima Gunto group. At dawn on 26 March fighter aircraft were flown off the carriers to attack the airfields on Ishigaki and Miyako. The strikes on the island airfields were repeated next day, when coastal shipping was also attacked. Fighting around Okinawa continued into April, with the Japanese throwing everything they had at the Allied naval force including the infamous kamikazes.

The enemy chose 1 April, the day on which the American forces made their landing on Okinawa, to make their first kamikaze attack. Ten minutes after the carriers had flown off their first fighter strike, enemy aircraft was detected by radar. Poor visibility gave an initial advantage to the Japanese, who split up their formation more than 40 miles from the fleet. All the ships were firing hard and had considerable difficulty in distinguishing the enemy from their own aircraft, which were in close pursuit of the Japanese aircraft. A few minutes into the action a kamikaze bomber dived on HMS *Indefatigable* and exploded on board, killing 14 and wounding 16. Later another dived on HMS *Victorious*, which made a successful evasive manoeuvre causing the aircraft to spin harmlessly into the sea. The written orders to the pilot were blown on board *Victorious* and, when translated, were found to indicate prioritised targets for the suicide bombers.

During the period from 6 April to 22 June, 10 major kamikaze attacks were made on American ships. In all, there were 896 enemy air attacks and approximately 4000 Japanese aircraft were destroyed, of which 1900 were kamikaze aircraft. The Japanese also defended from the sea with its navy. In early April, the battleship *Yamato*, light cruiser *Yahagi* and eight destroyers were reported by two United

Gambia *crew with captured Japanese flag.* AAI 0157

Barometer stamped 'Yokosuka Naval Base Tokio Bay 30 August 1945' around the rim. Believed to have been on a Japanese destroyer in Tokyo Bay during the surrender of Japan. Given to Lt Cdr Davis-Goff who was the officer in command of the landing party and was being escorted around the ship by a Japanese Officer at the time. SIK 0001

States submarines emerging from the Inland Sea through Bungo Strait. They were found next morning by Allied reconnaissance aircraft. One of the Japanese destroyers was sunk shortly after noon as Allied aircraft attacked. For approximately two hours the Japanese ships manoeuvreed drastically at maximum speed while aircraft showered the fleet with bombs and torpedoes. A further four destroyers and the battleship were sunk.

Shortly before daybreak on 13 April, four Japanese aircraft made an unsuccessful attack on the British Pacific Fleet. For the New Zealand cruiser *Gambia*, the attack was memorable because the ship accidentally shot down and killed the pilot of an Allied aircraft which failed to get clear of the fleet during the heavy firing.

After days of intensive bombardment by ships and aircraft, the amphibious assault on Okinawa began. Landings in great force were made on the southwestern beaches and, within 48 hours of the first landing, American troops had reached the east coast and isolated the southern end of the island. From 23 March. assembled carrier forces operated continuously for two and a half months in the Okinawa area, giving direct cover and support to the amphibious forces. This was the longest sustained operation by aircraft-carriers during the entire war.

When the British Pacific Fleet arrived in San Pedro Bay, Leyte, Philippines, on the afternoon of 23 April 1945, it had completed 31 days at sea in the course of operations against Okinawa. During that period it had been refuelled and stored six times by the ships of the Fleet Train, which had enabled it to continue to operate uninterrupted. This was the longest period that a modern British naval force of this size had been maintained at sea. While the Fleet was at anchor in San Pedro Bay, the possibility of its taking part in an operation against Borneo was considered. However, it was decided that air strikes against the Sakishima Gunto were to be continued and the Fleet returned to Sakishima in early May.

When the British Pacific Fleet arrived in the flying-off area near Okinawa at daybreak on 4 May 1945, Japanese aircraft activity was detected by radar. One small group approached the fleet and the combat air patrol shot down one Japanese fighter, the others escaping into the clouds. Since bomber strikes from the four British carriers had left the airfields on Ishigaki and Miyako – the Fleet's designated area – decimated, the aircraft and their carriers stood off and the battleships and cruisers, with six of the 14 available destroyers, left to bombard the enemy airfields on Miyako Island. *Swiftsure* and *Gambia* attacked the Nobara airfield, with *Gambia* firing 230 rounds from her 6-inch guns.

While the battleships and cruisers were away, the carriers were plagued by kamikaze suicide bombers. An estimated 16–20 aircraft attacked on 4 May, some acting as decoys so that, when

Allied aircraft engaged one group, the rest made for the ships. At 11.30 a.m., a kamikaze crashed onto the flight deck of *Formidable* and started a large fire. One Corsair and 10 Avengers were damaged beyond repair and a hole 10 feet by 2 feet was blown in the armoured flight deck. Minutes after the *Formidable* had been hit, a number of attempts were made on *Indomitable* but the carrier escaped undamaged.

The airfields on Miyako and Ishigaki were bombed again the following day. As a result of the previous day's assault by the destroyers, no anti-aircraft fire was encountered over Miyako. During the afternoon another kamikaze attack was made on the carriers and two aircraft hit *Victorious* in quick succession, the first blowing a hole in the flight deck, putting a 4.5-inch gun out of action and damaging the motor of the lift. Yet another suicide bomber appeared moments later, seemingly intent on *Gambia*, but it turned sharply and dived onto the after-deck park of *Formidable*. A huge explosion and fire marked the second hit on the carrier in as many days. Attacks on the Miyako and Ishigaki airfields were repeated on 12–13 May, with the 10th operation taking place on 16 May, when three bomber strikes were made on Miyako and two on Ishigaki. Back from New Zealand, *Achilles* joined the British Pacific Fleet on 22 May and took her place in company with *Gambia* in the Fourth Cruiser Squadron. Task Force 57 carried out its twelfth and final series of attacks on the Sakishima Gunto airfields on 24–25 May.

The determined resistance of the defenders of Okinawa was not finally overcome till 21 June. The fight had lasted nearly three months, during which time continuous assistance to the United States troops was given by the supporting ships and their aircraft. During the whole period of operations against the Sakishima Gunto, 4852 aircraft sorties were flown and 875 tons of bombs and rocket projectiles discharged. Approximately 100 Japanese aircraft were destroyed and more than 70 damaged. In May alone, *Gambia* steamed 10,684 miles. The Allies now had a base from which to launch the assault on mainland Japan.

On 28 June, following a refit, *Gambia* rejoined the British Pacific Fleet for the attack on the last bastion of Japanese resistance – Japan itself – in which the Fleet would be flying air strikes against mainland targets from its carriers. The Fleet, redesignated Task Force 37 by the Americans, sailed the same day. The role of *Gambia* and *Achilles* in the invasion was to provide protection for the carriers against kamikaze attacks. HMNZS *Arbutus* meanwhile was with the Fleet Train, doing sterling work on radio and radar repair and servicing duties for the invasion force as it attacked Japan day after day. In one period of three days, *Arbutus* went alongside approximately 40 ships in the performance of her duty.

For 81 years no hostile warship had fired a gun at the shores of Japan – a record that ended on 14 July 1945, when the Allied invasion force began the first of a series of devastating bombardments against mainland Japan. On the morning of 17 July, squadron after squadron of aircraft flew off the Allied carriers and attacked airfields, railways and other targets in the Tokyo area. That night, industrial plants along the coast northeast of Tokyo were bombarded from the sea by the assembled fleets. More than 1500 tons of shells were fired by the ships in less than an hour. A week later, on 24 July, the New Zealand airmen on the British carriers took part in a great strike on naval bases, shipping and other targets in the Inland Sea with the objective of destroying the remnants of the Japanese Fleet lying in and around Kure.

AAI 0064

HMNZS Moa. ABJ 0211

HMNZS *Moa*, *Kiwi* and *Tui*

In February 1939 it was decided to build three vessels as minesweeping, gunnery, and torpedo training ships. Henry Robb Ltd., of Leith, Scotland, tendered for the building of the vessels and was given approval on 26 September. However, because of pressure to complete Admiralty work in the shipyard, the keels of the ships were not laid until 22 March 1940.

The names *Moa*, *Kiwi*, and *Tui* were approved by the Naval Board in April 1940, but due to many delays during building, the three vessels did not arrive in New Zealand until 1942.

In December 1942, the four ships of the 25th Minesweeping Flotilla, HMNZS *Kiwi*, *Tui*, *Moa* and *Matai* were deployed to the Solomons. While on patrol off Guadalcanal, in January 1943, *Kiwi* and *Moa* were engaged in action against the Japanese submarine *I-1*. Forced to surface after depth-charges were dropped on her, the submarine was engaged by gunfire from the two ships. Following action that lasted more than an hour, *Kiwi* rammed the submarine three times before *I-1* struck a reef and was wrecked.

On 7 April 1943, *Moa* was sunk at Tulagi by a 500-lb bomb; five ratings were killed and 15 others were injured, including the commanding officer.

In August 1943, *Tui* dropped four depth-charges on a Japanese submarine, *I-17*, off New Caledonia. American seaplanes joined the hunt for *I-17*, also dropping depth-charges and it was quickly sunk.

Brass scuttle removed from the wreck of the Moa. *The scuttle is from the wardroom and the glass shattered when the ship was sunk in Tulagi Harbour by Japanese bombers in 1943.* SHB 0003

Class and type: *Bird*-class cruiser
Name: HMNZS *Moa*, *Kiwi* and *Tui*
Builder: Henry Robb Ltd, Scotland
Laid down: 22 March 1940
Launched: *Moa* – 15 May 1941; *Kiwi* – 7 July 1941; *Tui* – 26 August 1941
Commissioned: *Moa* – 12 August 1941; *Kiwi* – 20 October 1941; *Tui* – 26 November 1941
Decommissioned: *Moa* – sunk 7 April 1943; *Kiwi* – 20 December 1956; *Tui* – 22 December 1967
Pennant No: *Moa* – T233; *Kiwi* – T102; *Tui* – T234

General characteristics
Displacement: 600 tons standard
Dimensions: 51 x 9.1 x m
Propulsion: steam, reciprocating 1100 hp
Speed: 13 knots
Complement: 35 officers and ratings
Armament: Guns – 1 x 20-mm, 1 x 4-in, 5 light anti-aircraft; minesweeping equipment

MINESWEEPERS IN THE SOLOMON ISLANDS, 1942–45

CHIEF PETTY OFFICER M. SMITH

McGregor Smith joined the New Zealand Division of the Royal Navy in 1939 and was on board *Matai* when the minesweeper was in service in the Solomon Islands.

McGregor Smith: The *Matai* was the old Government lighthouse ship . . . and she was fitted up with a 4-inch gun forward and a couple of Lewis guns – that's all we had. When we got up to Christmas Island, Noumea, we were fitted with pompoms, Oerlikons, four Oerlikons as well, and she was [now an] anti-submarine [vessel]. She was the flagship of what they called the 25th MS. . . . Her skipper was a fellow called Holden, RNR, a hell of a nice chap. . . . We went up to Noumea first early in 1942, just before the Japs had taken over, 1942. The Japs had moved onto Guadalcanal at that stage, and we were operating a screen in Noumea, an anti-submarine screen. Then we moved up to Guadalcanal, about October/November 1942 it must have been, if my memory serves me right, and we acted as screen off . . . Tulagi – off the beachhead where they were landing troops and so forth. I was there when the Japanese came down, and we had a last flutter.

. . . My job was a leading sick berth attendant. I was the only [SBA for] . . . the four ships, and I used to go around and try and educate some of the cooks and stewards on the other ships – a little bit about first aid. Of course, the *Matai*, the *Tui* and *Moa*. The *Moa* and *Kiwi* sunk that submarine. I will never forget [that] day. Gordon Holden was really livid over that because we were alongside in Tulagi, and they got out and got the sort of joy of that [successful action], you see.

Then the day that *Moa* was sunk, that's the last big bluster . . . from the Japanese. They came over in a great flight of planes, and we took off like startled gazelles, anchoring out of Tulagi. We managed to get under a cliff . . . but the *Moa* fought [the attack as] she was alongside an oiler. In those days we probably didn't know a devil of a lot about fear as such. . . . No one was actually scared at all.

ABJ 0025

CONTACT!

On the night of 29–30 January 1943 *Kiwi* and *Moa* were patrolling off Kamimbo Bay when a 'contact' was made with a submarine. *Kiwi* altered course to close on the submarine in order to attack, while *Moa* maintained Asdic contact so as to direct *Kiwi* where to drop her depth charges. After *Kiwi* had dropped a 'pattern' of six depth charges, the phosphorescent outline of the submarine could be clearly seen. A further six depth charges forced the submarine to surface. The two minesweepers attacked and the submarine retaliated, opening fire with its 5-inch gun. As *Kiwi* rammed the submarine, holing it, *Moa* fired a succession of star shells and silenced the enemy's gun. A glancing blow by *Kiwi* was achieved in a second ramming. Not content with the damage done thus far and keeping up a relentless attack with its guns at close range, *Kiwi* went in to ram the submarine for a third time. The force of the impact threw a number of Japanese into the sea and *Kiwi* had to work her engines hard astern to break clear; as she did so, oil was seen to be pouring from the submarine.

The action had now lasted for nearly an hour. *Kiwi*'s 4-inch gun was too hot to use, the three ramming attempts had caused considerable damage and her Asdic gear was out of action. Unbelievably, the submarine was not only still afloat but able to keep her diesel engines going and attempted to escape. The chase was on through the night. Star shells and a searchlight were used to keep the enemy vessel in view. The submarine eventually struck a submerged coral reef where it was protected by its own shore artillery which opened fire on the New Zealand minesweepers. By daybreak, the battered forepart of the submarine was projecting an estimated 40 to 50 feet – approximately one sixth of its total length – out of the water, at a 45 degree angle.

Kiwi *in dry dock, 1943.* ABJ 0017

Bow of the sunken submarine I-1. ABJ 0090

Small tin with Japanese characters and the Rising Sun on the front with three ampoules possibly containing morphine. Item recovered from Japanese submarine I-1. IZA 0010

The 5.5-inch forward gun taken from the Japanese submarine I-1*, sunk by HMNZS* Moa *and* Kiwi*. It was salvaged in 1969 and transferred to RNZNAD Kauri Point, where it was found to still be loaded.* JDB 0006

The *I-1*, as it was later identified, was a formidable opponent for a pair of minesweepers. The submarine measured 320 feet in length and had an impressive armament and service record, having seen war service in the Aleutian Islands area, the Indian Ocean and the South Pacific.

As a result of ramming the submarine, *Kiwi* was sent to Auckland for repairs and replaced by *Tui*. Shortly before three o'clock on the morning of 31 January, just one day after the successful attack on the *I-1*, *Tui* and *Moa* spotted four Japanese landing craft which opened fire as the sweepers closed in to investigate. *Moa* engaged at close range and was hit, several of its crew being wounded, but nevertheless managed to silence one of the landing craft. *Tui* engaged the remaining three barges with her 4-inch gun and sank one with a direct hit. The remaining two craft went into rapid retreat. Steward Ernest Barton, on loan from the Royal Navy, was awarded the DSM for attending, while wounded, other injured members of the *Moa* crew.

AAI 0026

HMNZS *Gambia*

HMNZS *Gambia* was first commissioned by the Royal Navy in February 1942 and served in the Eastern Fleet before returning to Britain for a refit, which included the removal of its two aircraft and upgrading of its radar and communications capabilities.

In September 1943, as both *Achilles* and *Leander* were out of service, the newly modernised *Fiji*-class cruiser was commissioned for service with the Royal New Zealand Navy under Captain William-Powlett DSC RN. However, the ship was destined not to see New Zealand shores until the end of November 1944. It was put to work first as an anti-blockade runner in the Atlantic and in January 1944 was sent to join the Eastern Fleet once more. *Gambia* joined the 4th Cruiser Squadron in Ceylon in mid-February, as part of the build-up in preparation for operations against the Japanese in the Indian Ocean and Dutch East Indies. However, before the Eastern Fleet was redesignated the British Pacific Fleet, the cruiser managed to get away home to New Zealand for a period of three months, where it underwent a refit and visited a number of ports. It was joined for exercises in New Zealand waters by part of the Fleet, including *Achilles*, in early February before sailing to take part in the last act of the Second World War.

During the invasion of Japanese-held territories, *Gambia* was one of the anti-aircraft screen vessels protecting the aircraft carriers – although in the final strikes against mainland Japan, she used her guns to bombard a steelworks at Kamaishi on Honshu Island. At the precise time that a signal was being received on the ship stating that the war was over, *Gambia* was engaged with a Japanese aircraft and her shots have the distinction of being the last fired in the Second World War.

Japanese Naval Ensign captured by the landing party from HMNZS Gambia *at Yokosuka Naval Base on 17 August 1945.* SFD 0011

Gambia stayed on in Japan and represented the RNZN at the signing of the surrender by Japan on 2 September 1945. A month later the ship left the occupation force in Japan and sailed for New Zealand, undergoing a refit and being recommissioned with a steaming party in February 1946 for the first stage of its journey back to the United Kingdom. The RNZN crew left the ship in Sydney and hundreds of RN loan men joined the ship to take her home. In addition to the 1000 or so men on board was approximately £5 million of gold bullion which the ship had collected in Melbourne on its way out into the Indian Ocean. Travelling via the Suez Canal, *Gambia* arrived at Plymouth on 29 March 1946. The cruiser was paid off by the RNZN in mid-1946 and commissioned back into the RN. *Gambia* served for a further 14 years with the RN and was finally decommissioned in 1960.

The *Gambia* badge depicts the Arms of the former British colony of Gambia on the west coast of Africa, after which the ship was named. It was devised just as the Admiralty made the wartime decision that all new ships' badges would have a circular rather than pentagonal surround – although there are unofficial postwar examples of the badge with the incorrect shape. The badge with its circular surround was approved on 1 March 1943, six months before the cruiser was commissioned by the Royal New Zealand Navy.

Class and type: **Fiji-class cruiser**
Name: **HMNZS *Gambia***
Builder: **Swan Hunter & Wigham Richardson Ltd, Wallsend-on-Tyne**
Laid down: **24 July 1939**
Launched: **30 November 1940**
Commissioned: **21 February 1942**
Commissioned New Zealand Division: **22 September 1943**
Pennant No: **C48**

General characteristics
Displacement: **10,830 tons standard**
Dimensions: **169 x 18.9 m**
Propulsion: **4-shaft geared turbines, 72,500 shp**
Speed: **32 knots**
Complement: **920 officers and ratings**
Armament: **Guns – 12 x 6-in, 8 x 4-in. Torpedo tubes – 6 x 21-in**

On 26 July, an ultimatum calling on the Government of Japan to 'proclaim now the unconditional surrender of all the Japanese armed forces' was issued by the Allies. The events of the next two weeks were to convince the Japanese Government and people that surrender was their only option. Following the call for surrender, day after day thousands of aircraft from the Allied carriers and island bases bombed Japan's airfields, harbours, railways and industrial plants. On 2 August, 6630 tons of bombs were dropped on four industrial cities in Honshu and the oil refineries at Kawasaki. Three days later, nearly 5000 tons of bombs were showered on four other 'nominated' cities. On 9 August *Gambia* was part of a small force that helped the American navy bombard a coastal steelworks at Kamaishi in a 67-minute attack.

However, these hugely destructive air attacks were utterly eclipsed by the dropping of the first atomic bomb at 8.15 a.m. on 6 August 1945 on the city of Hiroshima. The entire epicentre of approximately four square miles was completely devastated in an instant. Fires sprang up simultaneously over the wide flat area in the centre of the city and a great 'fire storm' developed within an hour of the explosion. Of the estimated population of 225,000, more than 60,000 were killed outright or died soon afterwards and 69,000 were injured. More than 60,000 buildings were destroyed or damaged beyond repair. Less than three hours after Hiroshima had been flattened, a second atomic bomb was released over Nagasaki. One and a half square miles of the city was completely destroyed and, of the estimated population of 200,000, more than 39,000 were killed and 25,000 injured.

Nine days later, at 11.23 a.m. on 15 August, the Second World War was officially over.

Signal to cease hostilities against Japan. This refers to the last action of the war with the shooting down of a Japanese aircraft on 15 August 1945 by Gambia *off the coast of Japan. Added to the signal is: 'Judy 33 shot down over fleet while signal was flying. C. T. F.'s instructions not obeyed'.* FSC 0041

Pennant. Final Victory, Tokyo, September 2 1945, HMNZS Gambia. 48

Certificate attesting that the named serviceman served aboard HMNZS Gambia *during final operations against Japan, 1945.* PTJ 0008

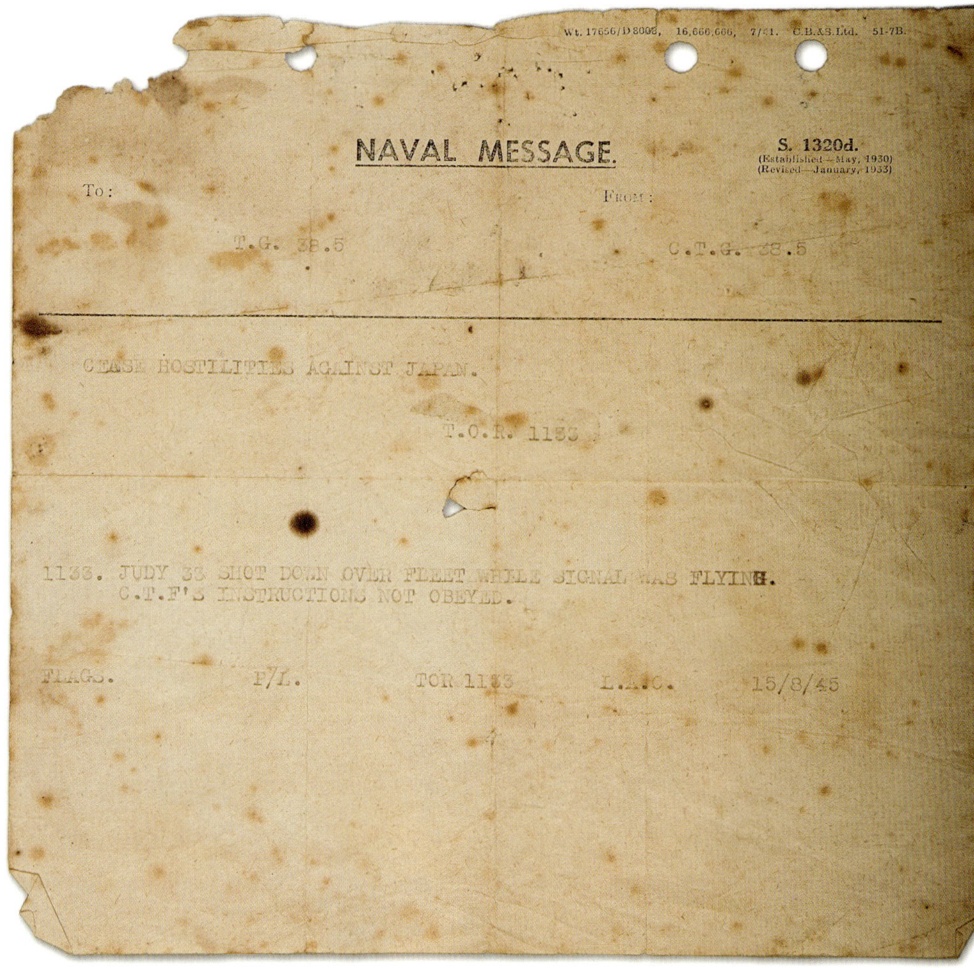

NAVAL MESSAGE. S. 1320d.

To: T.G. 38.5 From: C.T.G. 38.5

CEASE HOSTILITIES AGAINST JAPAN.

T.O.R. 1133

1133. JUDY 33 SHOT DOWN OVER FLEET WHILE SIGNAL WAS FLYING. C.T.F'S INSTRUCTIONS NOT OBEYED.

FLAGS. P/L. TOR 1133 15/8/45

This is to certify that

Chief Petty Officer C. Frew, N.Z. 968,

was a member of the Ship's Company of

H.M.N.Z.S. "GAMBIA"

during the operations of the British Pacific Fleet and U.S. Third Fleet against Japan, March—September 1945. H.M.N.Z.S. "GAMBIA" fired the last shot against the Japanese Homeland at Kamaishi on 9th August 1945: and had the distinction of representing New Zealand at the formal Surrender of the Japanese Empire in Tokyo Bay on 2nd September 1945.

C.M. Jacob.
Commander, Royal Navy

Ralph Edwards
Captain, Royal Navy

Gambia was accorded the honour of representing the Royal New Zealand Navy in the naval occupation of Japan. On 20 August the New Zealand cruiser disembarked a detachment of her Royal Marines and two platoons of New Zealand seamen under the command of Lieutenant Commander G. R. Davis-Goff of Marlborough, in preparation for the landing at the naval base of Yokosuka at the entrance to Tokyo Bay. Davis-Goff went ashore with the New Zealand platoon and organised a search of the dockyard, that proved to be largely deserted. Commander Yuzo Tanno, officer-in-charge of naval stores, was found in the administration offices with 10 junior officers and 40 guides and interpreters. All were wearing white armbands and were very polite and anxious to help. Tanno handed over a large bunch of keys and the plans of the dockyard. During the afternoon, the White Ensign

GAMBIA WITH THE BRITISH PACIFIC FLEET, 1945

COMMODORE B. E. TURNER

B. E. Turner joined the Royal Navy Volunteer Reserve in 1933. His naval career, which spanned 33 years and many ships and shore establishments, included a stint on board HMS *Gambia* during the New Zealand cruiser's time with the British Pacific Fleet when the mainland of Japan and its islands were under attack by a combined Allied force.

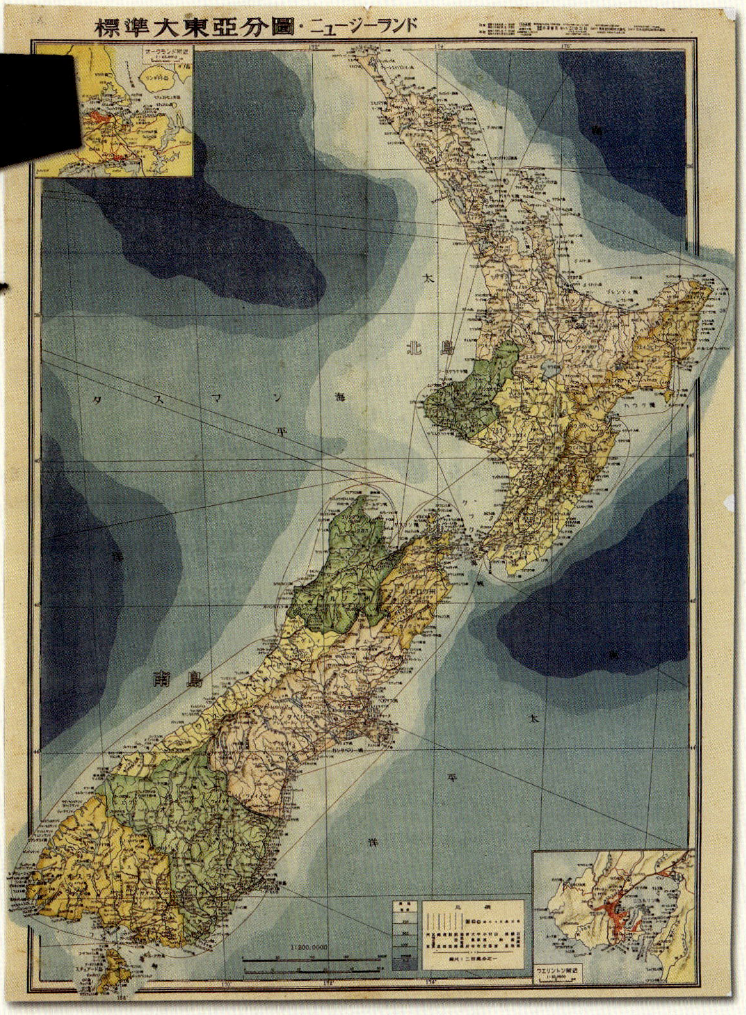

Japanese cap ribbon from the Second World War.
COF 0064

Chart of New Zealand written in Japanese recovered from the Naval Base in Yokohama in 1945.
PMC 0136

B. E. Turner: I was appointed to the *Gambia*, *Gambia* having left the Eastern Fleet and come out to New Zealand. Some of the officer complement changed and I was appointed to *Gambia*.

INT: And how many – what was the sort of proportion of New Zealanders to RN personnel in *Gambia* at that time?
BT: It would be very roughly half. John Washbourne of course was RN at that time – he was in *Gambia*. I should say it would be roughly half.

INT: And what role was she employed on whilst you were in her?
BT: We joined the British Pacific Fleet and she was essentially part of the cruiser force . . . defending the aircraft carrier[s], and aircraft carrier force, and *Gambia* was one of the cruisers.

INT: What was her specialist role? Did she have a specialist role? Was she anti-aircraft or . . . ?
BT: No, she wasn't anti-aircraft so much. But of course she became anti-aircraft because there was no surface threat, really, at that time. But there was a very strong air threat, with the kamikaze.

INT: Did she do any shore bombardments, or anything like that?
BT: Yes, we were part of the force which I think carried out the last bombardment of the war, on the Japanese mainland. I'm trying to think about the – in the early part we were interdicting Yaku Shima, which is in the Kyushu Group, during the American invasion of Okinawa. The Japanese were flying in reinforcements from the south from the Philippines and Taiwan and they came through Yaku Shima – we would interdict. We'd go in for two days, mainly air strikes. I don't think that we ever conducted any surface bombardments, and certainly *Gambia* didn't.

We had one period at that time where we had an epidemic of mumps in the ship, and it took quite a few, quite a strong percentage, of our crew out of action. So *Gambia* was – we were made the pivot ship. You understand, there were four aircraft carriers and *Gambia* was in the centre, and we, everybody kept station on us – but of course, because the aircraft carriers had a different turning circle, while we maintained our central position we also adjusted to keep the proper station, distance between the carriers.

INT: And where were you? Where was the ship when the atom bomb was dropped?
BT: It was somewhere off the coast of Japan. I am just trying to think which fleet it was . . . it must have been the third fleet. Anyway, it was Halsey in command. Halsey and [Admiral Raymond A.] Spruance used to alternate.

INT: Were you aware that the bomb was going to be dropped, or not?
BT: We weren't aware that it was going to be dropped. We only heard when it had been dropped.

The Japanese surrender. AUD 0119

Admiral Phippps (seated on right) at the Japanese Surrender AUD 0122

Gambia *in Tokyo Bay.* AAI 0021

and the New Zealand ensign were hoisted at company headquarters in the dockyard.

The entry of the great Allied armada into Sagami Wan Bay (from where the approaches to Tokyo Bay lie through the narrow Uraga Strait), on 27 August in brilliant sunshine, was a spectacular demonstration of the maritime power that had helped bring Japan to its knees. The combined fleets numbered some 400 ships, including 14 battleships, 24 aircraft carriers, 22 cruisers, 105 destroyers, 24 frigates and about 200 vessels of the fleet trains – tankers, supply ships, minesweepers, tugs and hospital ships. Overhead, more than 1200 aircraft were flown off the carriers while bombers and fighters from Okinawa and Iwo Jima patrolled over the mainland of Japan. All the fighting ships were flying battle ensigns and their crews were poised in readiness for instant action in the event of any treacherous action by the enemy – despite the white flags flying above the coastal defence batteries.

The formal surrender of Japan to the Allies was made on board USS *Missouri* on the morning of Sunday, 2 September 1945. Lieutenant J. D. Allingham of *Gambia* was ADC to Air Vice-Marshal Leonard Isitt RNZAF and accompanied him on board *Missouri* for the surrender ceremony. Over the next two weeks, the commanders of more than 5,500,000 troops of the Imperial Japanese Army on the mainland of Asia and in the Pacific surrendered unconditionally. The formal surrender of the Japanese in the South Pacific took place on 6 September on board aircraft carrier HMS *Glory*, anchored in St George's Channel about 28 miles from Rabaul, New Britain. However, Allied Forces were still accepting statements of surrender from Japanese-occupied territories like Nauru and Ocean Islands some weeks later. The British Pacific Fleet entered Hong Kong on 30 August, and the formal surrender of the formerly occupied British colony took place on 16 September. The official surrender of all Japanese forces in South-East Asia was signed at Singapore on the 12th.

After the Japanese surrender, one of the most urgent tasks confronting the Allied forces was the discovery, recovery and repatriation of many thousands of prisoners of war and civilian internees. *Gambia* worked with an American task group evacuating prisoners of war at Wakayama. When *Gambia* returned to Tokyo Bay on 20 September, the cruiser was relived from J Force duties by *Achilles*. *Gambia* set sail for New Zealand on 11 October, arriving at Auckland on the 30th. She was not to stay long in Auckland and left with an RNZN steaming party on 12 February, stopping briefly in Sydney where the steaming party disembarked and large drafts of Royal Navy ratings came on board, bringing the total of crew and passengers up to approximately 1000 officers and men bound for England. The cruiser arrived at Spithead on 27 March and was recommissioned back into the Royal Navy on 1 July 1946.

Achilles, meanwhile, stayed on in Japanese waters and spent nearly four months on patrol, making cruises to Nagasaki, Sasebo, Kagoshima and Nagoya. The monotony of patrol duty was broken by three weeks of leave in Hong Kong, following which *Achilles* sailed for home, arriving in Auckland in March 1946. After undergoing a refit, she left Auckland in late May to complete a farewell cruise round New Zealand. The depth of pride felt by New Zealanders in *Achilles*' war record was demonstrated by the thousands who visited her during this last cruise in New Zealand waters. *Achilles* sailed from Auckland for England in July and arrived at Sheerness on 10 September 1946. She was paid off a week later, having completed more than 10 years' service in the Royal New Zealand Navy. After a complete refit, *Achilles* was renamed *Delhi* and commissioned for service in the Royal Indian Navy, to which she was sold.

Admiral Phipps's cap. CEA 0020

'Welcome Home' flag used by families to welcome troops and ships home after war. This flag was hung outside the family home upon a sailor's return to New Zealand in October 1946 after continuous war service abroad with the Royal Navy since October 1941. GFB 0004

SHAKING OFF THE SHACKLES 1945–1965

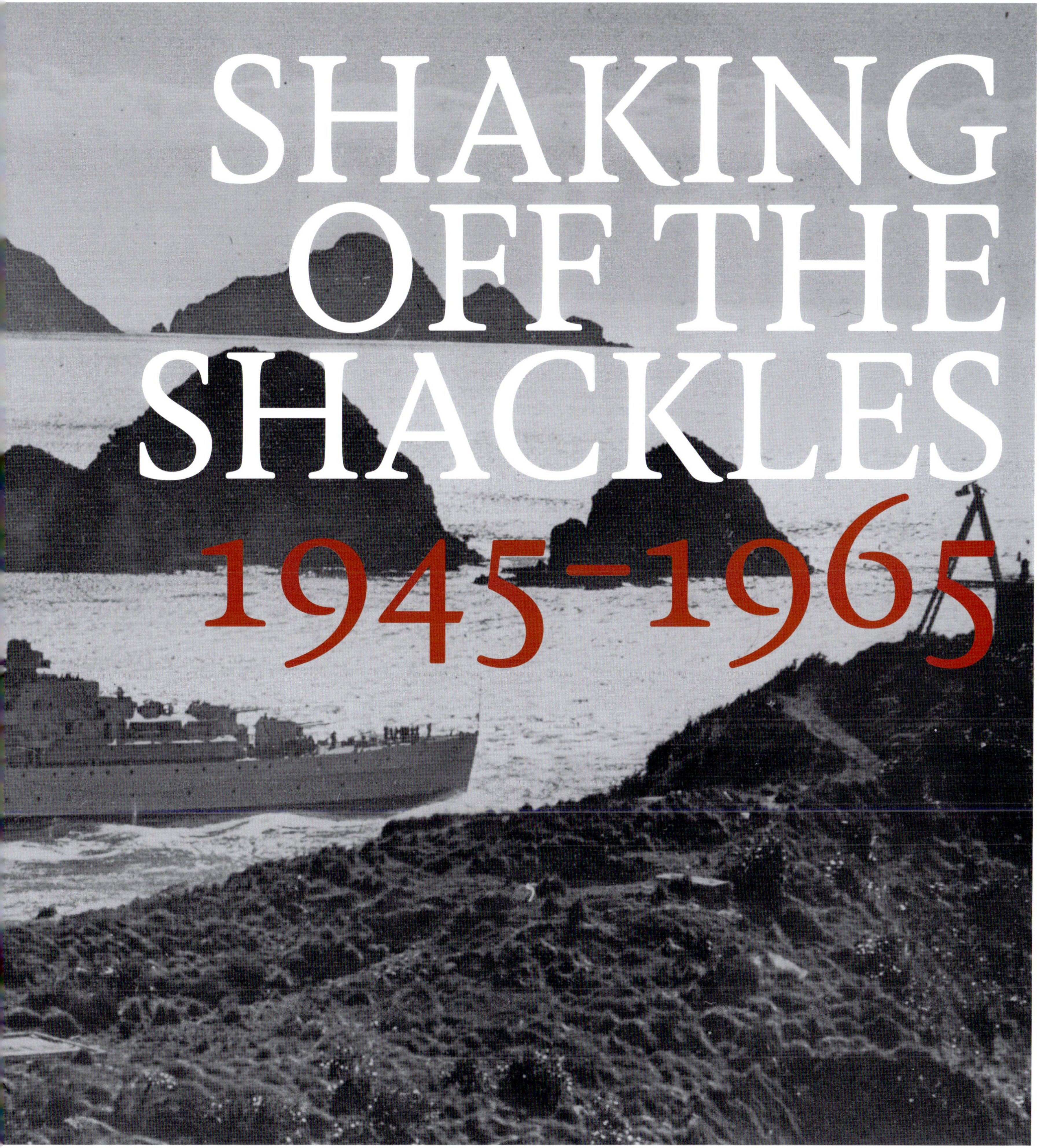

It was not until after the Second World War that the nascent Royal New Zealand Navy had the opportunity to shape its own destiny. Despite strengthening relations with the United States in the postwar period, New Zealand was still in many ways a Dominion nation. Shaking off the shackles of pro-Imperial sentiment was to be a long, slow process both for the country and its navy.

GFB 0002

The new navy's first major challenge was the lengthy task of demobilising both those who had served in New Zealand ships and the thousands who had seen war service with the Royal Navy overseas and who were now returning home in their droves. Despite the best efforts of the many Wrens who stayed on long after the armistice had been signed, the process still took more than a year to complete – after which the RNZN thanked the women's naval service for its contribution and waved it goodbye in December 1946.

Following demoblisation, the navy's priorities turned to recruiting and developing the fleet in order to fulfill its obligations both in home waters and over the commitments made under the Canberra Pact with Australia to the southern region of the Pacific that had been agreed in January 1944, before the end of the war. Included in the broad area that New Zealand and Australia considered as their own waters were a number of island nations. Some were seen as vital to the maritime strategic defences of the two Pact nations while others, like Niue and the Cook Islands, were regarded as dependencies of (in this case) New Zealand. Included in the Pacific Basin security equation was the acknowledgement that the United States, with its northwestern Pacific coastline, would remain a friendly power and take care of its own piece of the Pacific as far south as Hawaii and Samoa. This huge area is made up almost entirely of ocean – a vast expanse of blue that, in order to be adequately patrolled, would require the RNZN to invest in both ships and the men to crew them.

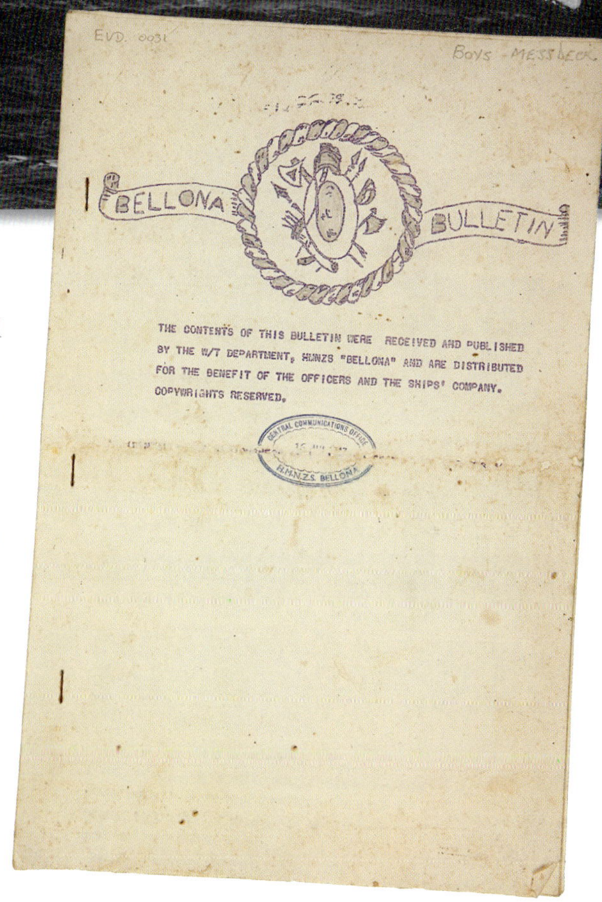
EVD 0031

BOYS MESSDECK

BELLONA BULLETIN

THE CONTENTS OF THIS BULLETIN WERE RECEIVED AND PUBLISHED BY THE W/T DEPARTMENT, HMNZS "BELLONA" AND ARE DISTRIBUTED FOR THE BENEFIT OF THE OFFICERS AND THE SHIPS' COMPANY. COPYRIGHTS RESERVED.

In terms of ships, numbers had been greatly reduced after the war. HMNZS *Gambia* and HMNZS *Achilles* had reverted to the Royal Navy in February and September 1946 respectively, and many of the minesweepers had been paid off and sent to their various fates. With only the corvettes HMNZS *Arabis* and *Arbutus* remaining to represent New Zealand's naval ambitions, it was clear that the RNZN needed to do a fair amount of 'ship-building' in order to establish itself as a credible blue-water navy.

In 1946, two former Royal Navy cruisers were commissioned into the RNZN as HMNZS *Black Prince* and *Bellona*. As the result of a domestic manpower shortage, the New Zealand Naval Board had agreed to take *Black Prince* on the condition that a skeleton crew of RN officers and ratings came with it. The combined crews of the recently decommissioned *Gambia* and *Achilles* provided the complement for *Bellona*. The RN loan personnel would stay on in New Zealand for terms of between three and six years to serve in both RNZN ships and in shore establishments. These RN loaners became an intrinsic part of the New Zealand navy in the early years as the service found its feet, offering experience and leadership in addition to making up vital numbers.

At home, recruiting for the new navy started almost immediately. Some, who had seen out the war in various circumstances, would make excellent officers and others, mainly fresh-faced rating recruits, provided new blood. What the RNZN lacked was a solid proportion of senior rates and petty officers – those serving between the decks – many of whom had been lost to their previous occupations with demobilisation.

The manpower shortage was exacerbated in 1947 when 200 lower-deck men went on strike in a dispute over disparities between naval pay rates and those of the other services and whether the promised readjustment of pay scales would be retrospective. On April 1, in reaction to rumours that no such adjustment would take place, a

Whenever a warship visited Hong Kong, a group of girls would be employed as the ship's 'side party'. They would wash, chip and paint the ship's sides in exchange for food and any unwanted items. Ah Moy's party was contracted by all RNZN ships visiting Hong Kong. GFB 0002

Complete copy of the Bellona Bulletin, *16 July 1947. Published and distributed onboard HMNZS* Bellona. EVD 0031

Lieutenant Commander C. V. Harris

Charles Harris joined the New Zealand Division of the Royal Navy in 1933 as a stoker. He was Master at Arms at HMNZS *Philomel* during the mutiny in 1947.

Charles Harris: On the 1st of April 1946 the Government announced an increase in pay for naval personnel, and nothing further was heard for months. The rumblings started on the mess decks, and through my mess man and other sources I was able to establish that there was considerable dissatisfaction with the Government over their indecision to do something about it.

I informed the Captain, Peter Phipps. Each day, each week, I was in his office keeping [him] up-to-date with what was going on. Now the year was 1947 . . . things were really getting bad. . . . I . . . knew that my staff and I would be the ones to bear the ultimate brunt of any action by the lower deck. The ships' company finally mutinied. They claimed they went on strike. Instead of falling in with both watches after lunch they congregated in the troops' canteen. Jack Cameron said that he would see them, but Peter Phipps said: 'No, I don't want to aggravate the situation. No officers will be involved – let the Master at Arms deal with the situation.'

I went to the canteen – practically all lower rates were there. As I entered the main lounge, there was a lot of yelling and screaming: 'Throw him out' [and] 'Chuck him through the bloody windows', and other complimentary remarks. The bloke who was at that point addressing the mob restrained them, and he said to them: 'Now let's hear what the bugger has got to say and then chuck him out.'

As near as I can remember, this is what I said: 'First, I want you to understand that I am more mad about this than you are. I get more pay than you, and I am losing more money over this Government's bloody inefficiency than you are, and I am definitely on your side with your complaint over not getting this rise in pay that has been promised. Now I haven't come over here to give you the heavy jaunty stuff, but what I am prepared to do is to put my career on the line for you and represent your case for you. I am doing this only if you do it my way. Turn to now and leave it to me. If we don't get an answer from the Government in 24 hours, okay, it's over to you, but remember it's the Government that's at fault, not the navy. Now, what about it?'

I had them, and they were prepared to agree. I made the fatal mistake then of leaving them, instead of letting them leave first. I found out afterwards that, as I walked out, the ringleaders were up again, on the stage: 'Don't believe that bastard – remember he's a bloody jaunty.' They then left and they marched through the dockyard to *Black Prince*, where the majority of her C & M party joined them, and they returned via the dockyard caisson, and they were heading towards the main gate between the huts and the barrack buildings. As they came to the parade ground, just before walking through, between the huts ... we were all standing on the parade, on the quarter deck as it were, waiting to see what happened.

Captain Pugh, who was an RN captain, who was then Captain Superintendent of the Dockyard – no, I believe he was NOCA, I'm not sure, but he was the senior officer . . . Captain Pugh stood in the centre of the roadway in front of these people who were walking towards him, and he yelled at the men walking towards him: 'Stop! You are guilty of mutiny!' It was as though Captain Pugh was not even there – the front rank of ratings didn't put a hand on Pugh or even push him, they just walked into him, not even seeming to look at him. He was knocked aside, his hat fell off, and he was cast aside as a much-dishevelled man. He waved at me, and I was standing alongside the Captain . . . Commander Phipps, and he [Pugh] said: 'Master at Arms, arrest those men.' Peter Phipps looked at him and said: 'Don't be a bloody fool.'

I returned to my office and . . . called the sentry . . . [on] the phone and gave him the order to open the gate without reference to any superior. At Peter Phipps' instruction, I then went to the main gate and I talked to the so-called strikers, who were then outside the gate and they had stopped there. They said . . . : 'We'll be back here at the gate at ten o'clock tomorrow morning, and if any further developments come through, then you can let us know.' And then they dispersed.

During the next few days we had to establish who had gone, to make up watch bills for essential work to be carried out by the chief and POs who, to all intents and purposes, had stood firm. . . . [All] the routine work and the general traditional business of the navy went into limbo. Everybody was bitter about the Labour Government, from the Naval Board right through to the most lowly rate. . . . The navy and the personnel were not to blame for that incident. . . . There were several meetings after that . . . when the Captain [Phipps] addressed the group and . . . Findlay the MP for, I think, North Shore at that time, was present. . . . Peter Phipps received a signal from Navy Office and that signal, as far as I can make out, stated that: 'They were to be given the option, there and then, of either returning to their place of duty forthwith or take the consequences.'

Bombardment level fitted gun mounting to give accuracy of firing. Used in Loch-class frigates in Korea. IDW 0002

Uniform of Rear Admiral L. G. Carr – tail coat with Rear Admiral sleeve lace and flag officers buttons. CAA 0022

contingent of disgruntled matelots walked off ship. They gathered in *Philomel*'s canteen to voice their grievances to the Master at Arms, C. V. Harris, who tried unsuccessfully to urge them back to work. The men then proceeded to the parade ground where they were confronted and challenged as 'mutineers' by RN loan officer Captain Pugh – again to no effect.

The next day the strikers gathered and walked en masse to *Philomel*'s gates, where they were addressed by senior base officer, Commander Peter Phipps and a Member of Parliament. They were told that their pay rates would not be retrospective and were instructed to return to ship by 10 a.m. on 3 April and face their punishment or elect to be discharged. Twenty-nine sailors walked back through *Philomel*'s gates but 180 voted with their feet, effectively dismissing themselves from the service.

A few weeks later, approximately 100 of the crew of *Bellona*, which was in Australian waters at the time, indicated that they would not be returning from their weekend leave ashore until a number of their grievances about pay and conditions were discussed. Although the men were instructed to return, 54 failed to report back to ship on the set date of 29 April. By late July, all but eight ratings had either returned to ship or been arrested by police under warrants issued by the naval authorities. Various punishments were meted out to the matelots, most of which hit them – ironically enough – in the pocket. This was not lost on the media which ensured the issue was kept alive for many months after the strike had been quashed.

This sudden loss of 200-odd sailors was part of the reason that the executive officer of *Philomel*, Commander Peter Phipps, championed the re-establishment of a women's naval service, which he had previously praised for its wartime accomplishments. Acting swiftly in the wake of the mutiny, during Easter weekend of 1947 Phipps telephoned Lorelle Corbin, a former Wren third officer, to enquire whether she was interested in helping re-establish the Wrens.

Within a week of this conversation, the Women's Royal New Zealand Naval Service was back in business. Although initially the numbers of women in the navy were minimal, by 1949 an Act of Parliament ensured that the women's service would become a permanent part of the

LOCH-CLASS FRIGATES:

HMNZS *Hawea, Kaniere, Pukaki, Rotoiti, Taupo* and *Tutira*

Initially commissioned into the RN, these six Loch-class frigates were built in the mid-1940s and saw duty as anti-submarine escorts in the mid-Atlantic, North Sea and in the Far East in the final months of the war.

New Zealand purchased the frigates in 1947, and the ships that would become known as HMNZS *Taupo*, *Pukaki*, *Kaniere* and *Hawea* were refitted and had their armament modified for RNZN requirements in a number of RN dockyards over the previous year. *Pukaki* and *Taupo* were the first to be commissioned into the RNZN on 13 September 1948, followed by *Kaniere* and *Hawea* over the following two and a half weeks. *Tutira* and *Rotoiti* would take a little longer, and were commissioned in April and June 1949.

With *Bellona* as flagship, the frigates worked in both New Zealand and Australian waters, in the Pacific on 'showing the flag' and royal cruises, running supplies to the weather stations on Campbell and Raoul Islands, and undertaking training exercises and ceremonial duties. Overseas, too, the RNZN frigates flew the New Zealand flag. In 1950 *Taupo* and *Hawea* joined the Mediterranean Fleet at Malta, and all the Loch-class ships would see active duty during the Korean War. *Tutira* and *Taupo* were paid off into reserve by the end of the war in Korea in 1953.

Pukaki, *Rotoiti* and *Hawea* subsequently spent time in the Southern Ocean as weather pickets at latitude 60 degrees south, in support of Operation Deep Freeze. In early 1957 *Pukaki* and *Rotoiti* were both on hand as weather ships at Christmas Island for the hydrogen bomb tests known as Operation Grapple. *Hawea* was paid off at that time and *Kaniere*, which had been acting as a training vessel, followed in 1960. *Rotoiti* and *Pukaki* still had some life left in them and saw duty on the Far East Station in the early 1960s. By this time, *Otago* and *Taranaki* were in service and *Rotoiti* became a training ship, finally paying off in August 1965, a few months after *Pukaki*.

Class and type: **Loch-class frigates**
Name: **HMNZS *Hawea*, *Kaniere*, *Pukaki*, *Rotoiti*, *Taupo* and *Tutira***
Builder: ***Hawea* and *Kaniere* - Smith's Dock Co. Ltd, Southbank-on-Tees; *Pukaki* and *Rotoiti* - Henry Robb Ltd, Scotland; *Taupo* and *Tutira* - Swan, Hunter & Wigham Richardson Ltd, River Tyne**
Laid down: **July–December 1943**
Launched: **January–July 1944**
Commissioned RN: **August 1944–February 1945**
Commissioned RNZN: **September 1948–April 1949**
Paid off (RNZN): ***Tutira* - 31 August 1951; *Taupo* - 26 January 1953; *Hawea* - 15 February 1957; *Kaniere* - 22 December 1960; *Pukaki* - 24 May 1965; *Rotoiti* - 6 August 1965**

General characteristics
Displacement: **1435 tons standard**
Dimensions: **93 x 11.8 m**
Propulsion: **2-shaft reciprocating 4-cylinder turbine engine, oil, 5500 ihp**
Speed: **19.5 knots**
Complement RNZN: **114 officers and ratings**
Armament as delivered: **1 x 102-mm HA MkIII, 4 x 2-pdr pompoms, 2 x 20-mm MGs, 2 x triple Squid a/s mortars**

HMNZS Kaniere. AAQ 0018

Pewter tankard with Operation Grapple badge on the front. Given to all members of the ship's company who participated in the H Bomb tests at Christmas Island 1957–58. TKK 0006

HMNZS Rotoiti *pennant.* GEH 0065

HNMZS Hawea *N.Z.K. Force sign marking the ends of Hawea's service in Korea.* PAJ 0010

Squid anti-submarine mortar mounting. This type of mounting was fitted to Loch-class Frigates. This particular mounting was never fitted to a ship but was set up in HMNZS Toroa *the RNZNVR HQ in Dunedin to enable volunteers to practise loading drills.*

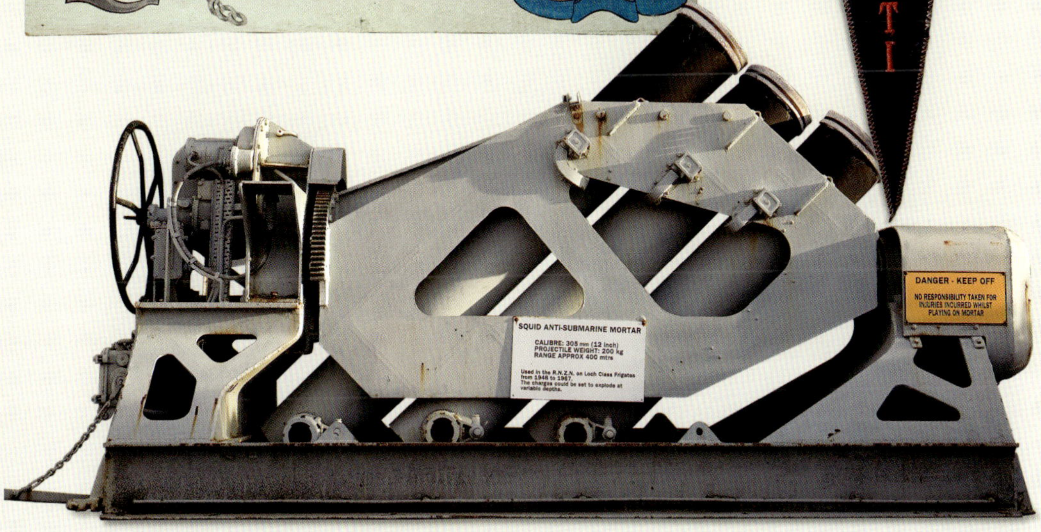

HMNZS *Endeavour*

There have been a total of five naval vessels, both RN and RNZN, working in New Zealand waters since the late eighteenth century that have borne the name *Endeavour*. This particular ship, an Antarctic supply ship, was the third. The vessel, a wooden-hulled netlayer, was built by the American Car & Foundry Co. Inc, USA, and commissioned into the RN as HMS *Pretext* in August 1944, under a lend-lease arrangement. The ship did not serve long with the RN, returning to the United States the following year. It was sold to the Falkland Islands Government and converted for use as a supply, research and survey ship under the name *John Biscoe*. The conversion included 76-mm thick greenheart sheathing and reinforcement of the bow.

In June 1956, the vessel was sold to the New Zealand Government, once again under the name *Pretext*, for £20,000. Refitting was carried out by John I. Thornycroft & Co. Ltd, and the ship commissioned into the RNZN as *Endeavour* two months later. *Endeavour* headed south as transportation for the New Zealand component of the Commonwealth Trans-Antarctic Expedition for the 1956–57 season on the ice. Another four seasons doing the runs to and from Scott Base in McMurdo Sound followed before the conditions began to tell and *Endeavour* began showing the strain on her wooden hull. In addition to summers of Antarctic voyages, the RNZN kept *Endeavour* busy in a variety of other roles including oceanographic research, supply runs to the meteorological stations on Raoul and Campbell Islands and the Pacific islands, and transporting and dumping ammunition from all three armed services.

Sold to the Shaw Steam Ship Co. Ltd in June 1962, *Endeavour* was renamed *Arctic Endeavour* and was used for many years as a sealing ship in Arctic waters. While laid up in Catalina, Newfoundland, the ship sank in November 1982 at its moorings.

Class and type: ***Ailanthus*-class netlayer**
Name: **HMNZS *Endeavour***
Builder: **American Car & Foundry Co. Inc, USA**
Laid down: **1 May 1943**
Launched: **23 May 1944**
Commissioned as HMS *Pretext*: **5 August 1944**
Commissioned as HMNZS *Endeavour*: **15 August 1956**
Paid off RNZN: **November 1961**

General characteristics
Displacement: **1275 tons standard**
Dimensions: **59.3 x 10.6 m**
Propulsion: **1-shaft GM diesel-electric, 1200 bhp**
Speed: **13 knots**
Complement RNZN: **34 plus 18 civilians**
Armament RNZN: **Unarmed**

Blue silk cushion cover. Badge of HMNZS Endeavour *hand embroided in wool. Made to order in Jamaica during a stopover on the delivery voyage 1956.* GEK 0005

RNZN. However, they were certainly not on a equal footing. Women in the New Zealand navy were still some years off achieving equality and the chance to go to sea. Still, in the immediately postwar years there was plenty for them to do at *Philomel* where the women, in the main, were located. Although many of these early Wrens found themselves performing domestic duties as cooks and stewards and serving in an administrative capacity, the establishment of the WRNZNS must have opened up whole new worlds for women who, only a generation before, would have considered a career in the navy unthinkable.

Despite a severe manning shortage, 'shipbuilding' by the RNZN continued at pace after the commissioning of *Bellona* and *Black Prince* in 1946. By the end of 1948 the Government had purchased six former Second World War Loch-class frigates from the United Kingdom. While in service with the RN, these frigates had borne the names of Scottish lochs. In keeping with this theme, after recommissioning the vessels were given the names of New Zealand lakes, becoming HMNZS *Taupo*, *Kaniere*, *Pukaki*, *Hawea*, *Rotoiti* and *Tutira*.

In addition to redeploying the crews from the paid-off corvettes *Arabis* and *Arbutus*, the RNZN recruited 330 RN ratings – with an emphasis on the seniority that was so desperately needed – and put them aboard the frigates for the long steam to New Zealand. These loan ratings, like those who had come out with *Black Prince* a few years earlier, stayed on in New Zealand for terms of between three and five years.

The first four ships arrived in Auckland in January 1949, the two remaining vessels joining them in August the following year. In late 1949 the River-class frigate *Lachlan* also joined the fleet as a loan ship. A former Australian naval vessel that was at that time in reserve, *Lachlan* had been fitted out as a specialist survey craft and was urgently required to complete the task of updating New Zealand's navigational charts – an undertaking that had been started by the RN survey ship HMS *Endeavour* shortly before the outbreak of hostilities in 1939. With the securing of *Lachlan* for what was thought to be a three-year loan period, the RNZN Hydrographic Branch was officially formed.

Steel helmet with Naval Officers' cap badge painted on front. Worn by Cdr W. Minchell O.B.E. as Inspector of Naval Ordanance RNZN 1948–74. JGC0001

The WRNZNS was not the only branch of the navy to be revitalised after a period of hiatus. Admittedly, the Volunteer Reserve had been in abeyance for far longer, having ceased to exist after the outbreak of war in 1939 when many of its number volunteered for service both at home and abroad. In 1948 the Naval Volunteer Reserve was re-established, and the former minesweeper *Tui* was drafted into Reserve training ship duties in February that year. Each of the divisions, in the four main centres of Auckland (*Ngapona*), Wellington (*Olphert*), Christchurch (*Pegasus*) and Dunedin (*Toroa*), began recruiting again towards the end of 1949. At around the same time, the Government passed the Military Training Poll Act 1949 which allowed young men to complete their compulsory military service with the Naval Reserve. This in itself must have gone a tremendous way towards swelling the Reserve's numbers and demonstrating that it was once again an intrinsic part of the country's naval forces.

By 1950 the numbers of personnel were steadily rising, the proportion of RN loan officers was dropping dramatically, and the RNZN was assembling a not unimpressive fleet for such a young navy in such a small country – enabling it to fulfill its maritime obligations in home waters, in the Pacific as part of its administrative and defensive alliance commitments, and further afield, if that possibility should arise. This latter eventuality arose soon enough, in June 1950, when civil war broke out in South Korea.

During the final days of the Second World War, the Soviet Union had advanced through the territories occupied by Japan and on to the Korean Peninsula. Stopped while still in the north of the country, the Soviet forces had helped set up a communist government in North Korea. Following the war, tensions escalated between the north and South Korea, which aspired to a democratic system supported by the United States and, in late June 1950, the Cold

North Korean flag given to Able Seaman Bill Heenan by a 15-year-old Korean boy who took it from a North Korean soldier after the boy had cut his throat. Heenan was coxswain of the motor boat carrying out an evacuation. SFH 0003

HMNZS Pukaki *engine room.*
AAO 0067

War in South-East Asia came to a head when North Korea invaded the south. The United Nations Security Council (UNSC) responded to the invasion of South Korea by the Soviet Union by sending aid to the assisted south. A call went out for member nations to help, and New Zealand and 16 other countries agreed to contribute to the proposed multinational defence force to operate in the region.

Little more than a week after war had broken out in Korea, on 25 June, the frigates *Pukaki* and *Tutira* were on their way to join the United Nations combined naval forces, beginning what would be a three-year commitment to the UNSC off the Korean coast. The two frigates arrived in Sasebo, Japan, on 1 August and soon after, travelling in a supply convoy, joined the multinational naval force operating in Korean waters,

HMNZS **Pukaki.** AAO 0023

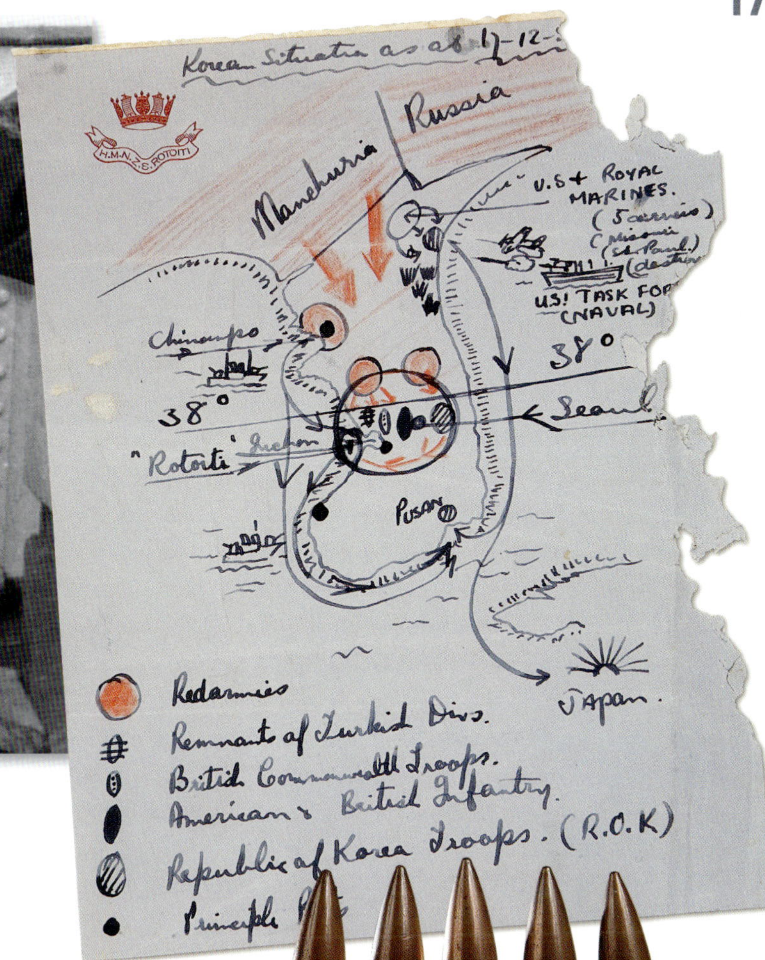

keeping supply lines to Pusan open and serving on anti-submarine patrols. By September 1950 the Chinese had answered the call for help by North Korean leader Kim Il-Sung, and Chinese forces had reached as far south as Seoul by early January 1951.

While *Pukaki* and *Tutira* had an abbreviated tour of approximately six months, the RNZN frigates that followed in their wake had considerably longer deployments, most spending a year in Korean waters. For the New Zealand naval vessels, their days were largely taken up with routine coastal patrols. Although Korean War duty was relatively uneventful, some of the New Zealand ships and crews definitely had their moments – especially *Rotoiti*, which left Auckland bound for Korea for the first time in October 1950. Having relieved *Pukaki*, the New Zealand frigate was placed on merchant ship escort duties in the waters off Inchon. Because the ship, most unusually, had a shore party of regular naval men who had been especially trained by the Royal Marines, *Rotoiti* undertook a number of beach landing raids using matelots instead of the more usual commando force of Royal Marines who had historically performed this task on naval ships.

Two such sorties were undertaken at Chinampo (modern Nampo, North Korea) in order to disable enemy gun positions. The first of these was at Song-Ni when, under cover of a bombardment provided by *Rotoiti*'s guns, the naval landing party managed to take the enemy gun position with relative ease in a flanking attack. The assault group, which included two able seaman, Norman Scoles and Jim Button, scaled a cliff and shot a Korean soldier who had been about to throw a hand grenade. Scoles and Button disarmed the position and took the remaining two soldiers prisoner. While escorting the two North Korean prisoners to the waiting boats on the shore, Button and Scoles came under attack, but *Rotoiti*'s guns soon silenced any opposition. The whole operation, from landing the assault party to leaving the area, had taken less than an hour.

North Korean prisoners on board HMNZS Rotoiti. AAR 0006

Original ink sketch entitled 'Korean Situation as at 17-12' (1951), showing deployment of forces. Drawn by N. Peach on HMNZS Rotoiti. PCE 0068

A clip of five cartridges with a North Korean soldier's cap badge attached to front. GLG 0001

LEADING SEAMAN N. J. SCOLES

Norman Scoles joined the Royal New Zealand Navy in 1945 as a seaman boy. In late 1949, Scoles was posted to the frigate HMNZS *Rotoiti* and was on board when it joined the United Nations Fleet at the outbreak of hostilities between North and South Korea. During his time on board *Rotoiti* in Korea, Scoles was a member of a landing party that captured two Korean soldiers and he went on to lead a night raiding party. Despite the tragic death of Bob Marchioni under enemy fire, this latter action resulted in Scoles being awarded the Distinguished Service Medal.

Norman Scoles: [In] July or sometime like that . . . Ted Collier, who was the Leading Signalman, he spotted movement ashore. It looked like they were getting set up to rig up a gun to harass coastal junks and sampans. . . . I was sent for, to the bridge, and Turner said, Did I reckon we could go and have a look see what it was, and blow it up if necessary? So we got our landing party together, and we were at deck level, going down in the boat, and Turner spoke to Lieutenant Webber and he said: 'You had better go with them.' So he came with us. In all the history books et cetera, it says that the unit was under Webber's command, which was far from the truth really. He had never done any of this work with us or anything – it just happened that he was the gunnery officer on the ship.

Jim Button, who was an AB, and I went along the beach and we went up around the top of this area where we were going to have a look. As we got nearly to the top of the cliff, I heard gravel rattle – a noise that [indicated] somebody was moving about. The next thing, there was a fellow about 10 yards away, and he jumped up, and he was doing a rate of knots going in the other direction. So he was disposed of – which wasn't a very nice thing. His two mates were hiding in a foxhole, which also I read in one of these books – possibly the *History of Korea* by McGibbon, where these two fellows were behind us and they looked like Mexican bandits – but they weren't, they were in a slit trench in front of us, their eyes were popping out. And they each had Russian-made grenades and they were about to let us have them. So I put a few shots in over their heads and they came out with their hands up, and we took them down the cliff onto the beach, stripped them in case of any knives or sneaky weapons, and followed them along the beach in their footsteps in case the place had been mined.

Getting up the hill to get over to where our boat was, we started receiving a bit of attention – quite frightening, really, climbing that steep hill. The lead was thumping into the hill, and actually picked up one of the captured rifles on the bloke's shoulder and ricocheted away from him, luckily – or otherwise it would have gone in his ear.
So we got them back and we kept them in the wheelhouse. Some people say that we put them in the tiller flat under a cell sentry et cetera, but those fellows were treated with respect. They had showers, and rice was their main diet. We had them for about a week or 10 days. . . .

Turner told me to escort these two fellows in the motor cutter over to the *Ceylon*. We went to the *Ceylon* and a young, very pusser sort of a chap, he told us to lay off and not to come near their gangway, and what was our business? So I told him, that we had two Korean prisoners and I had been told to bring them over. So he went away and got instructions from some superior, and came back and told us to go around a point of an island, which was about three miles away. There was an American undercover base there. So that is where those prisoners finished up.

. . . That led to a night raid later on, where *Ceylon* provided these marines. They weren't marine commandos as such . . . they were marines off the *Ceylon*. . . . As soon as we landed, Bob Marchioni and I, we went up the hill to make sure there was no one in . . . [the] slip trenches who could come in behind us. . . . Coming back down the hill, the moon came over the top and there was somebody with glasses on and I thought, Oh, that's strange! So I kept sliding along on my stomach type of thing, and I heard this voice: 'God damn, the moon's come up. That's going to ruin things.' It was the first time that I knew there were two American officers who had come ashore with the *Ceylon* boat.

At that time, things were going smoothly until one of these marines . . . was perhaps a bit 'bomb-happy' would be the term – he had been all through this before during the war and he was out of control. He was standing to attention, yelling out his number and his name and his duties to run the message from the front detachment back to the officer in charge. So that was a big decision there I had to make in a hell of a hurry. The boats' crew grabbed him and held him in the boat, while we went away to have a look to see what was going on.

. . . Bob Marchioni and Buster Dunn . . . and myself, we were the arrowhead of the attack party and we had three marines with us. We went up over the top and we had Brens either side of us, back quite a way. *Ceylon*, which was a Pommy cruiser, she went up the coast further and she was putting on a star shell display to attract the attention – if there was anyone in this area they would all be looking, and that was exactly what was going on. There were eight or 10 of these fellows standing there, pointing at what was like a fireworks display for them. It looked as though we were going to have an easy job to go in there. There

.303 Bren Mk1 LMG (light machine gun) and accessories. JCE 0011

were six of us. We probably would have got one man each, or something like that.

. . . Somebody made a noise, just a twig or something or like that – we were challenged and there was only one thing to do, and that was to bite the dust. . . . It was a gloomy, dark night – the moon was there, but not brilliant. There was stubble, I remember that. Your face straight into this stubble and it was sticking in your face, your nose and whatnot. At that stage Bob Marchioni probably thought he was doing the right thing – he disobeyed my order, and he came to his knees to throw a grenade and he was more or less cut in half by machine gun fire.

Something had to be done then in a hell of a hurry. The history books state that I came to my feet and charged these people with a grenade – which was the last thing that I would have thought of doing. I managed to get a grenade out of my shirt and I threw it in a barroom sort of throw, and that bought a lot of silence. It got the lot, and I sprayed with my Lanchester to make sure. It was a matter of withdraw, and those three marines and Buster Dunn went back along the top. I went over the cliff with Bob. I lost my knife, lost his Lanchester and my own Lanchester. . . . There was some kelp being washed up on the beach, so I dragged him out there and we lay under the kelp while I assessed things.

It was at this stage I see these three figures coming along the beach and I thought, Hell, who is it? We had a code – if you were one of the *Ceylon* party, you called: 'Rotoiti?' And the answer was: 'Ceylon.' Or vice versa. . . . [T]hankfully the word came back: 'Ceylon.' So I thought, Right, we're out of here. I asked these fellows to give me a hand to get Bob to take him back to give him a decent burial at sea, and they flatly refused to even help me. They said: 'We don't take dead men with us. He's a hindrance. Leave him there.' I said: 'No, I'm not leaving him here.' They wouldn't even give me a hand to get him across my shoulders properly. So I carried him for near enough quarter of a mile or maybe more. We had to go around the point where there was rocks and whatnot. I was pretty well shot, probably with excitement and exhaustion. He [Marchioni] was about the same weight as me. There looked like a bit of a shelter, and I don't know whether it was above or below high water or not – and I thought, We'll tuck him there and pick him up next morning. But that wasn't to be.

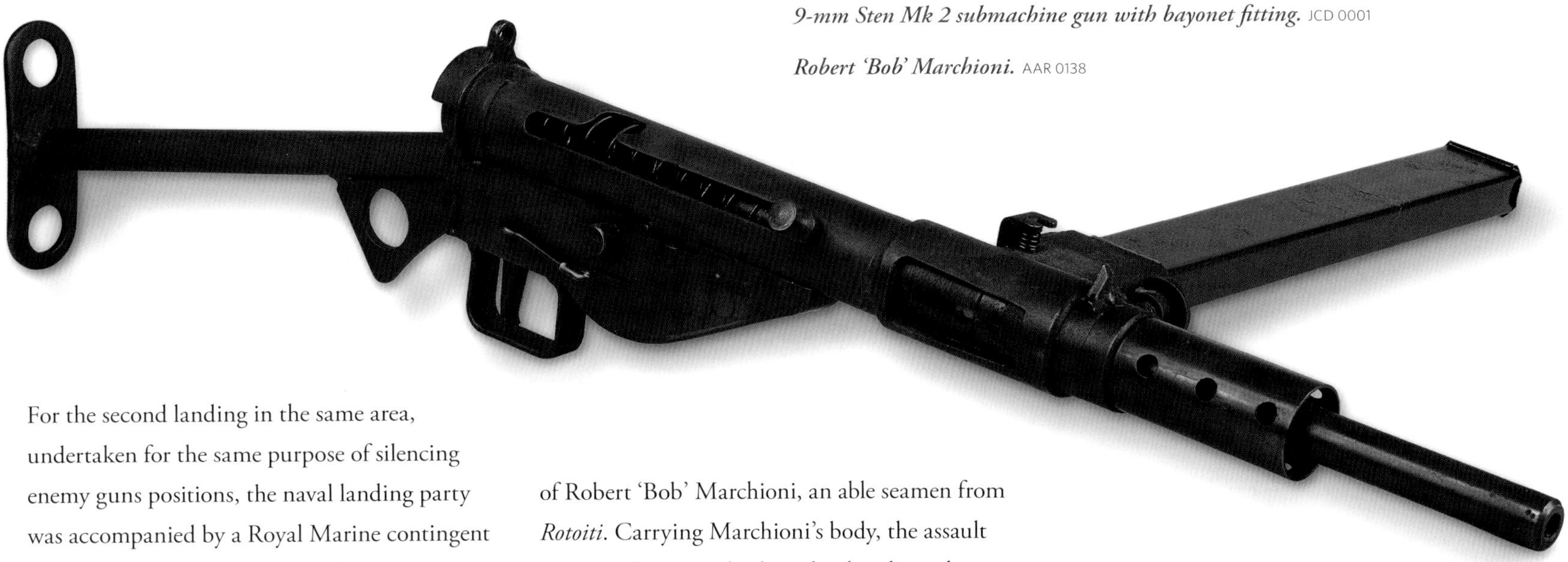

9-mm Sten Mk 2 submachine gun with bayonet fitting. JCD 0001

Robert 'Bob' Marchioni. AAR 0138

For the second landing in the same area, undertaken for the same purpose of silencing enemy guns positions, the naval landing party was accompanied by a Royal Marine contingent from another ship operating in the area. As the element of surprise was paramount, on this ocassion *Rotoiti* did not provide a bombardment of gunfire cover, but instead idled out of shore battery range, in full view of the enemy gun positions. Once landed the assault party, which once again included Scoles and Button, moved towards the enemy gun position. Unfortunately the New Zealand sailors and Royal Marines were spotted by the North Koreans and came under heavy machine gun fire, resulting in the death of Robert 'Bob' Marchioni, an able seamen from *Rotoiti*. Carrying Marchioni's body, the assault party made its way back to the shoreline where the landing boats awaited their return.

Button and Scoles were awarded Distinguished Service Medals for their role in the action and the commanding officer of the ship, Commander Brian Turner, and the commanding officer of the assault party, Lieutenant R. S. Webber, a RN loan officer, received Distinguished Service Crosses. Marchioni was posthumously mentioned in despatches and forever inscribed in naval history with the unenviable honour of being the first RNZN sailor to be killed in action during the Korean War.

Armistice talks, which would prove to be protracted, began in mid-1951. *Rotoiti* was relieved in October 1951, almost a year to the day after the frigate had left New Zealand, by HMNZS *Taupo*, and began the journey home. However, the excitement was not quite over yet for *Rotoiti*.

Late one evening, shortly after starting the journey home and while en route to Hong Kong, the New Zealand frigate intercepted a distress signal from the British merchant ship *Hupeh* near the Yangtze River. The emergency involved an attack by armed pirates – not an unusual occurence in these waters. Twenty-eight of them had boarded the British ship, turned off the navigation lights and, one would imagine, were making dire threats to all and sundry. *Rotoiti* found *Hupeh* easily enough on its radar and, to confirm the merchantman's identity by illumination and no doubt to 'put the frighteners' on the Chinese pirates on board, the naval vessel let loose with a volley of 4-inch star shell. It certainly did the trick and, with a naval vessel now close by, the captain of the British merchant ship suddenly had the upper hand. Now very much on the back foot, the 28 pirates who were effectively stranded aboard *Hupeh* – their own vessel had vanished when *Rotoiti* had steamed into view – requested only that they be landed on the nearby shore. Their wish was granted and, once divested of its unwanted passengers, *Hupeh* and *Rotoiti* continued with their respective journeys. In *Rotoiti*'s case, this included port calls in Hong Kong, North Borneo and Brisbane before reaching home.

Taupo had only been on Korean War duty for approximately five months before it, too, tasted

HMNZS Taupo. *Ammunitioning ship in the snow, North Korea.* AAS 0070

Black and white print of the New Zealand frigate HMNZS Taupo *beating off an attempted Communist invasion of Yang Do Island, Korea, in the early hours of 18 February 1952.* PAI 0222

action. On the night of 19 and 20 February 1951, information had been received through the intelligence services that an enemy invasion of Yang-Do, an island friendly to the UN, was imminent. Sure enough, as *Taupo* closed on the island, 15 enemy sampans, full to the gunnels with troops from the mainland, were well on their way to their target. The New Zealand frigate was sent in to attack the enemy invasion force, with two American navy vessels, USS *Shelton* and *Endicott*, taking cover positions. Ten of the sampans were quickly sunk but, when *Taupo* moved closer inshore to chase the remainder, the enemy shore batteries entered the fray. One shell punctured the frigate's engine room and others fell alarmingly close to the ship, causing *Taupo* to go into rapid retreat. However, *Taupo* had done enough to thwart the invasion and the North Koreans abandoned the attempt. Although the invasion of Yang-Do was certainly a high point for *Taupo* during the ship's Korean War service, during the remaining six months of the ship's year-long tour she was kept busy on patrol work and in the all-important task of disrupting the North Koreans' communication network.

New Zealand's naval commitment to the war in Korea involved the six RNZN frigates in a total of eight separate tours to the region, with *Rotoiti* and *Hawea* each making two tours over the three-year duration of the conflict.

In the early 1950s, the RNZN not only had to contend with its fleet commitments to the UNSC naval force in Korea, but also with trouble in home waters. On 13 February 1951 the Watersiders' Union, having reached the end of its patience over demands for a 15 per cent pay rise, went on strike. During the legendary 151-day standoff that followed, the Government activated the 1932 Public Safety and Conservation Act which made it illegal, among other things, to give money or even food to the families of striking workers.

Wooden carving of a sailor pushing a skip of coal. Presented by the State Coal Mines to the RNZN in recognition of their assistance in the 1951 strike. FT 230

Chromed bell inscribed 'HMNZS HAWEA'. A replica of the ship's bell was cast and presented to the RSA in Westport in commemoration of the 1951 strike. SBC 0016

COMMANDER C. R. VENNEL

Christopher 'Kit' Vennel joined the RNZN in 1946 as a naval cadet destined for the Royal Navy. He returned to New Zealand as a sub lieutenant in 1950 and was posted as the Secretary to the Captain of *Philomel*, who also held the rank of Naval Officer in Charge Auckland. Vennel was based at *Philomel* in 1951 when the watersiders and other unions went out on strike over pay and conditions.

Kit Vennel: Not only were the watersiders on strike of course, but the coalminers and also the seamen in the merchant trade. The merchant navy officers were still working. The navy – apart from having people working on the wharves and in the mines – were also manning the coastal shipping at lower deck level. It was a very big task indeed, and the time came when we ran out of sailors and stokers to send and began to send people like me, sub lieutenants . . . and other officers who could be spared.

I had this rather delightful experience of a few weeks serving in a ship called the *Perry*, which was a converted schooner and whose role was transporting explosives from ships at the powder grounds around the coast to mainly the coalmining ports – Westport, for instance. That was my 'before the mast' time in the merchant navy. We fed like fighting cocks – the scale of victuals was excellent, the pay was excellent. Unfortunately, one didn't actually get the pay – we continued to receive our naval pay, but the shipping companies had to pay in what they would have paid us into what became a naval welfare fund. It has since paid for things like the *Philomel* swimming pool . . .

INT: You acted as the crew, although you were . . .?
KV: That's right, yes. I think my status was deck boy. One did tricks at the wheel unsupervised, and things like that. We took our turns as cook – I was a dab hand at making macaroni cheese in those days by following the instructions on the packet. The lads became fed up with my macaroni cheese – the time came when they threw it overboard.

INT: What was the feeling – you know, was there any sort of feeling in society that you were scabs breaking a strike, that sort of thing?
KV: I don't think in society at large. Certainly among those affected – the strikers didn't approve of us at all. I think popular feeling was against the strikers, particularly the waterside workers for whom there was very little sympathy. They seemed to have the most wonderful racket going in terms of not working very hard and getting high pay. They tell a different tale, and now it's one of those classics of our social history and is viewed rather differently.

Once the watersiders went out, the Seamen's Union joined them in a show of solidarity, meaning that not only was no one left to handle goods at the wharfside, but shipboard crews also dropped dramatically in number. The merchant navy elected not to strike and formed skeleton crews that were rapidly augmented with regular navy men on board merchant ships. The armed forces were extensively deployed on the wharves and ships to lessen the impact of the strike.

However, not all New Zealanders were intimidated by the blackening of the strikers as communist agitators. In towns like Greymouth, which was fiercely pro-union, antipathy was shown towards 'scab' labourers working ashore, the handful of navy ships that called at the port, and naval men on board commercial vessels. Labour provided by the armed forces, at no cost to the owners of the wharves, mines and shipping companies, succeeded in undermining the strikers' struggle to have their demands met. *Lachlan* and *Taupo* were sent to the West Coast, where their crews helped shift 30,000 tons of stored coal, worked in the mines and loaded 114,000 tons of coal onto colliers waiting at Westport and Greymouth.

With the navy involved in the day-to-day running of New Zealand's commercial fleet and wharves, the steady stream of mainly agricultural exports to the United Kingdom continued much as usual, as the strike carried on into the winter. Meals for the Auckland substitute wharf workers were prepared in the galley at *Philomel* and brought by boat across the harbour. Wrens staffed the wharfside dining facilities, dishing out meals and cleaning up after the men had finished eating. A daily ration of beer was also provided to the workers.

In Wellington, much the same arrangements were put in place as at the Auckland wharves. In addition, the cruiser HMNZS *Bellona* was tied up alongside – as both a military presence to deter troublemakers and as an accommodation vessel for the approximately 500 men who worked the neighbouring wharf.

Meanwhile, the navy did not neglect its more traditional roles. By 1951 new charts covering Cook Strait, Wellington Harbour, Bluff Harbour, Patterson Inlet, and an area from Cape Saunders through Foveaux Strait to Centre Island had been completed by the survey ship *Lachlan*. Nicknamed the 'Ghost of the Coast', it became a common sight on the New Zealand coastline. The vessel also surveyed the harbour at Suva during this period and carried out survey work at Christmas and Malden Islands during the mid-1950s for the British, in preparation for the hydrogen bomb tests there. In 1963, *Lachlan* was transferred outright to the RNZN when it was bought from Australia for £16,000.

Closer to home, the navy was involved with casualties, although not among their own ranks. At 10 p.m. on Christmas Eve 1953, 151 people were killed in what would become known as the Tangiwai Disaster. The rail and road bridges over the Whangaehu River in the North Island's Central Plateau region were destroyed by a lahar shortly before the train from Wellington to Auckland was due to cross them. Depite an attempt to flag down the train when the washout was discovered, the locomotive and five carriages – approximately half the train with its 285 passengers – plunged into the river.

Although most of the staff of HMNZS *Irirangi* near Waiouru were on Christmas leave, 35 men and five officers were on deck to help when news broke of the disaster in their own backyard. The naval rescue party rigged a rope ladder across the river to facilitate the search for victims. Another party from *Irirangi* set up a relief post in the Waiouru Railway Station which included a public address system, tea and sandwiches and, later, clothing and money for the survivors. In the days that followed, the navy also joined in the unenviable task of searching for bodies and assisting the families of the victims who travelled to Waiouru to identify their loved ones. In the present day, the blue-water ships of the RNZN spend a good proportion of their time away from home waters in either deployments or on routine duties. This pattern was established after the Second World War when, in addition to the United Nations Security Council commitments during the Korean War (1950–53), the New Zealand navy was showing the flag, albeit in a small way, in other parts of the world. There was the almost continual round of voyages in the southern Pacific to various island nation dependencies, like Nuie, administered by the New Zealand Government; duties and exercises with other navies including the American and British fleets; and voyages to the United Kingdom to pay off old vessels and commission their replacements, and simply to show the flag.

While the RNZN was finding its sea legs both at home and abroad (in Korea), there was the ongoing task of maintaining and updating the fleet. When the frigate *Kaniere* was put into reserve in November 1951, the Second World War minesweepers *Tui* and *Kiwi* were recommissioned as training vessels for both RNZN and Naval Volunteer Reserve sailors. Shortly afterwards, the Australian Government gifted the RNZN a further four minesweepers. On commissioning into the RNZN, *Echuca*, *Inverell*, *Stawell* and *Kiama* retained their original names (of Australian towns), ensuring

NAVY DIVERS

The diving branch of the Royal New Zealand Navy was formed in the early-'50s and a New Zealand built tug that had initially been designated for service with the United States Navy during the Second World War, was converted for use as a diving tender. The vessel and the nascent dive team worked largely in a salvage capacity, including conducting the underwater survey on the run aground Wahine in 1968 and on the Manapouri dam project in the late-'60s. The tender was decommissioned as a dive vessel in 1978, taking up training duties thereafter.

Specialist dive facilities were fitted out in one of inshore patrol craft that were being built in Whangarei, and that vessel was commissioned into the RNZN as HMNZS *Manawanui* in 1979. Working in the same, though somewhat expanded, capacity as its predecessor the vessel and the dive team worked on a myriad of tasks in both New Zealand and offshore, including the Pacific, and in the case of the divers in the Antarctic. Survey work of interest carried out on civilian vessels by navy divers during this ship's tenure included the examination of the sabotaged Greenpeace vessel *Rainbow Warrior* in 1985 and the investigative dives on the sunk Soviet passenger liner *Mikhail Lermentov* in the Marlborough Sounds in early-1986 shortly before being recommissioned HMNZS *Kahu* and commencing a training role in 1988.

The third vessel to bear the name Manawanui and still in current operation is a purpose built civilian dive ship that the RNZN acquired from the North Sea oil fields in 1988. The vessel arrived fitted out with a diving bell, a recompression chamber, the ability to hold a fixed point at sea and onboard facilities for approximately a dozen divers all of which greatly expanded the range of work taken on by the navy divers in both a military and civilian capacity.

Additional advances to naval diving include the opening of the Slark Hyperbaric Unit, which is attached to the RNZN Hospital, in 1990. Named after a retired RNZN Surgeon Commodore Tony Slark, a pioneer in diving medicine research, the SHU has trained doctors and nurses in hyperbaric medicine since its inception. The chamber which can treat up to six seated divers simultaneously, or two prone, with an accompanying diving attendant, is one of the busiest hyperbaric recompression units in the southern hemisphere.

Navy divers on the Wahine.

On 13 December 2006 the Commander William Smith Building, the new headquarters for the RNZN Operational Diving Team, Diving School and the Maritime Operations Evaluation Team at the Devonport Naval Base was officially opened by the eponymous Commander William James Lanyon 'Kiwi' Smith, DSO, OBE. Smith who was the first lieutenant (second in command) of the midget submarine XE3 which made a successful limpet mine attack on the Japanese heavy cruiser *Takao* in Johor Straits Singapore, on 31 July 1945.

Although military diving is the primary focus of the modern day navy diver, the dive school qualifies its divers in all facets of the profession. The first stage of training covers seabed and ships' hull searches; maintenance relating to military diving and shipborne underwater husbandry tasks. Upon completion of this stage potential divers then move on to stage two of their training which take approximately 21 weeks. This course covers compressed air diving to 50 metres; mixed gas diving to 54 metres; surface supply diving to 50 metres; attack swimming using 100 per cent oxygen on a re-breather set; advanced first aid course; heavy trade and four wheel drive licence course; underwater photography and video; mine counter measure searches and tasks; beach mine clearance; and above and underwater demolition and explosives training.

In addition to its own personnel, the RNZN trains all New Zealand army, police and customs divers. Military dive training support is also supplied to Singapore, Malaysia, Fiji, Tonga and Samoa.

The Operational Diving Team badge is based on a tekoteko, the carved figure that decorates the ridge pole at the peak of a wharenui roof. Held above the tekoteko's head is a sea mine indicating the figure's military and sea-going context. The team's motto is: Whakamaaia, Whakakaha, Whakapono – Courage, Strength, Loyalty.

Siebe Gorman diving suit and equipment. This was the primary gear for divers in the Royal New Zealand Navy until the early 1960s. The suit is made from three layers of rubberised twill reinforced on the knees and elbows. The helmet, made of copper and brass, weighs 20 kg. The boots are made from leather and wood with lead soles attached. The total weight of the suit is 84 kg. The depth limitation of the diving suit is 55 m; at any greater depth the CO_2 build-up in the helmet became dangerous. IDB 0003

Brass-bodied diving compass. IDB 0001

Non-magnetic divers' knife complete with brass scabbard. IBD 0006

Gin pennant. Used at HMNZS Irirangi *by the officers. The gin pennant is flown when the wardroom wishes to host passing officers for a drink on a social occasion.* SFJ 0134

LEADING COOK T. W. ABBOT

After an early career as a baker and a policeman, Thomas Abbot joined the Royal New Zealand Navy in 1951. By 1953, Abbott was posted to the naval wireless and telegraph station HMNZS *Irirangi* and, on Christmas Day 1953, was with the first naval group on the scene of the Tangiwai train disaster in the central North Island where 151 lives were lost when a railway bridge was washed out by a lahar. Due to his police experience, he assisted with the process of body identification in the days following the disaster.

Thomas Abbot: I remember it was early evening, it wasn't too late in the evening – I got roused out of bed . . . there was a sick berth tiffy, a steward, a ship's company cook and myself, [we] were all taken . . . down to the Tangiwai River, which is just past the military camp. There had been a train accident, that's all we knew. We must have been the first [there] after the post office employee, Mr Ellis, who tried to stop that train. When we got there, we saw the bridge was all on a kilter – the road bridge, that was – we saw there was no rail bridge, and I think it was Ted Thorne who organised a rope across . . . and we crossed over. I remember the water being very high. ... It was black, you couldn't see much at all. . . . There was a great big gap in the bridge and you could see the railway engine on the north bank lying flat on its side. . . . There were still two or three carriages still perched on the edge on the south-side approach . . .

INT: What happened to the passengers that didn't get into the water? Were they still sitting there when you arrived?

TA: I didn't know that they were still sitting there, because it was so dark . . . and I don't think Ted Thorne knew either. Nobody had an idea what had happened, except that there was no bridge there and the road bridge was tilted over. . . . We went back to the camp and the next morning up we go again, a naval contingent. . . . The first day we did patrols down the river . . . and we were looking for bodies. . . . We looked for bodies, that was the first day, and the second day things were getting a bit more organised. At the skipper's house stayed the Prime Minister, Sid Holland, and the Opposition Leader, Walter Nash . . . I used to cook breakfast for them in the morning – they would have just singlets on.

. . . After about two days I was roped in by the police to help at the military camp, having had police experience . . . Our function was to meet the public as a PR type of thing. . . . I have a lot of respect for certain police personnel, because we started with absolutely nothing. In fact, Constable Barker and I only had scraps of paper with details of birthmarks, tattoos, rings or property, about people. We would try and match between . . . description[s provided by people] that would come in off the street. . . . We still didn't know what had happened – the crater lake breaking away, and so on.

... When the bodies came in, the men were put to the left, laid out on this great big floor, and the women were laid to the right. They were kept separate that way and each one was numbered. I think there were something like 145 bodies that we had. At the bottom end of the river going into the Tasman, down near the Wanganui bridge, there was a police contingent with grappling hooks – boats as well – picking up any bodies that drifted down as far as that. ... They had two coroners functioning and they had seven undertakers. The bodies were being preserved in formaldehyde. And something unusual about the bodies that I saw – the silt seemed to have penetrated underneath the skin. ...

I remember a woman came in from Napier, her daughter had been on this train – she described what she was like, with her rings and so on. We matched it up from the bits of paper that we had, and I called over a padre. We had people from the Sallies, Church of Christ, our Anglican padre from the camp – you name it, they were there. ... The idea of course was that [we] would introduce [her] to a detective or a constable, and they would go and view the body [first]. Then the constable or the detective would take note of who the person was and the padre would take the woman down for a cup of tea, and then later there would be the formal identification in front of a coroner. ... There was a co-ordinator there to arrange for the bod[ies] to be transported back to the[ir] home

HMNZS Kaniere *at Sydney, 1949.* AAQ 0054

Transmitting valve said to have been used at Irirangi *during the Second World War.* SIO 0003

town[s] in … railway wagon[s]. They were parked at Waiouru siding and they had big white crosses – they must have been six foot tall, on the side, and that's how they got back …

INT: All the relatives had to come up to Waiouru to do identification?

TA: Yes, I would say yes. I wasn't too involved with that but, yes, that would be what would have to happen. … The railway people were very good … they opened their homes to these people, took them in for accommodation and fed them and so on. The army, of course, were moving then towards feeding people. We did three weeks on that.

INT: Did the relatives actually have to be brought into this great big hall with all these bodies around?

TA: Yes, that's right.

INT: It would have been pretty emotional … ?

TA: Oh, it was. … That's right, yes – but of course once you got over that initial shock of the catastrophe, you went about doing your business without any trauma. … But it was marvellous how it sort of knitted in together like a jigsaw puzzle when we had nothing – short of marking the numbers on the floor as the bodies came in.

that the Australian connection would continue to be acknowledged. These four *Bathurst*-class minesweepers were of Second World War vintage and had been in the Royal Australian Navy reserve. However, after being refitted and modernised at the Devonport Dockyard, they were a welcome addition to the RNZN fleet.

In addition, the *Dido*-class cruiser *Black Prince* was bought out of reserve in 1953 in order to take a RNZN contingent to the United Kingdom as the Dominion's naval representative at the coronation of Queen Elizabeth II. The cruiser took part in the Coronation Naval Review at Spithead later that year.

During her return voyage to New Zealand, *Black Prince* was in the Mediterranean when a series of earthquakes devastated the Ionian Islands, killing approximately 600 and injuring a further 10,000. The New Zealand ship came to the aid of Cephalonia Island, which had sustained massive damage, basing itself at the island's major town of Argostoli. Its contribution to the multinational relief effort was the restoration of Argostoli's power supply by a party of experts from the ship, ably led by a Naval Volunteer officer, Commander Eric

Single shot, line-throwing rifle. JTB 0005

HMNZS Kiama. ACW 0035

HMNZS Black Prince *crew help clean up after the Argostoli Earthquake, western Greece, 1953.* AAM 0005

'China Joe' Stevens, who was on board as one of the Reserve representatives for the Coronation celebrations. The restoration of the power supply was an especially proud moment for the ship, because an American relief party had apparently declared the town's power station beyond repair.

With the spectre of an ever-aging fleet in mind, in the mid-1950s a completely modernised cruiser, *Royalist*, was acquired from the Royal Navy. Although still a 'secondhand' ship, the *Dido*-class cruiser had been completely refitted and extensively modernised, and boasted a state-of-the-art gunnery fire control system. Six of these refitted cruisers were planned to be produced in total, four of which the RN intending keeping for its own fleet while the remaining two would go to the New Zealand navy as replacements for *Bellona* and *Black Prince*.

Royalist was the first of the New Zealand ships out of dry dock, and *Bellona* was brought out of reserve and commissioned under the command of Captain Peter Phipps in order to take a New Zealand crew to the United Kingdom for the commissioning of the new cruiser in April 1956. Once *Bellona* arrived there, the ship paid off and *Royalist* was commissioned into the RNZN, with *Bellona*'s crew simply transferring from the old cruiser to the new. The second of the proposed *Dido*-class cruisers never eventuated, as the modernisation scheme was abandoned before all six ships had undergone their refit.

With the commissioning of *Royalist*, the New Zealand Navy once again came into company with the RN in the northern hemisphere. *Royalist*'s working up and sea trails – a very necessary part of breaking a ship in – were performed in the Mediterranean in company with the RN Mediterranean Fleet.

The New Zealand cruiser was carrying out sea trails when the President of Egypt, Gamel Abdel Nassar, took national control of the Suez Canal Company with the intention of using the money gained from shipping tolls to fund the Aswan Dam project. A number of other countries with a vested interest in the Suez Canal – a crucial stretch of water connecting the Mediterranean to the Indian Ocean – objected vociferously.

On October 29, Israel invaded the Sinai Peninsula. Two days later, British and French aircraft attacked Egyptian airfields. The RN Mediterranean Fleet, with which *Royalist* was exercising, went on high alert and it appeared that the New Zealand cruiser might see some action. However, the New Zealand Government decided that Suez was not its fight and *Royalist* quietly left the region, arriving at Auckland on 20 December 1956.

HMNZS *Bellona*. AAL 0167

HMNZS *Royalist*. AAN 0008

IMPROVED *DIDO*-CLASS CRUISERS:

HMNZS *Black Prince*, *Bellona* and *Royalist*

Originally built for the Royal Navy during the Second World War, all three frigates saw active service in a variety of theatres in the latter half of the war. In 1946, shortly after the end of the war, *Black Prince*, which had been paid off by the RN, was recommissioned into the RNZN as one of the replacement ships for HMNZS *Gambia* and *Achilles*. *Bellona*, which was commissioned into the RNZN on 1 October 1946, following a refit at Chatham Dockyard, arrived in New Zealand waters on 15 December 1946 and was designated flagship of the RNZN Fleet. It would be close to a decade before the third of the *Dido* cruisers, the slightly more modern *Royalist*, was commissioned into the RNZN. *Black Prince* was taken out of reserve in early 1953 to take part in the Coronation Naval Review at Spithead, England.

Black Prince and *Bellona* were quickly established in a routine that would characterise the RNZN Fleet in future years. There were Pacific Island and royal tours, exercises with other navies, and roles in civil emergencies like the 1951 waterfront strike. Both *Bellona* and *Black Prince* sailed to the UK, *Bellona* for a 1952 NATO excercise and *Black Prince* for the Coronation in 1953. *Bellona* was placed in reserve in February 1953 and remained in commission as a headquarters ship for the Reserve Fleet and as accommodation when ships were being refitted. When *Bellona* was paid off in 1956, *Black Prince* was entered into reserve, taking over *Bellona*'s Reserve Fleet duties; she was finally payed off on 28 November 1960.

On her arrival in New Zealand in late 1956, *Royalist* was immediately slotted into the by now regular routine of training, exercises and showing the flag both at home and in international waters. However, the frigate, commissioned into the RN in late 1943, was definitely showing its age and spent only a decade in the RNZN Fleet before its decommissioning in July 1966.

Class and type: **Improved *Dido*-class cruisers**
Name: **HMNZS *Black Prince*, *Bellona* and *Royalist***
Builder: ***Black Prince* – Harland & Wolff, Belfast; *Bellona* – Fairfield Shipbuilding & Engineering Co. Ltd, Glasgow; *Royalist* – Scotts' Shipbuilding & Engineering Co. Ltd, Scotland**
Laid down: **November 1939–March 1940**
Launched: **January–July 1944**
Commissioned RN: **September–November 1943**
Commissioned RNZN: ***Black Prince* – 1 June 1946; *Bellona* – 1 October 1946; *Royalist* – 17 April 1956**
Paid off (RNZN): ***Bellona* – 17 March 1956; *Black Prince* – 28 November 1960; *Royalist* – 4 July 1966**

General characteristics
Displacement: **5900 tons standard**
Dimensions: **156.1 x 15.4 m**
Propulsion: **4-shaft SR geared steam turbines, 62,000 shp**
Speed: **31 knots**
Complement RNZN: **550 officers and ratings**
Armament as delivered: **8 x 133-mm guns, 2-pdr pom pom, 40-mm Bofors AA**

Living conditions on HMNZS Royalist*, 1958.*

Souvenir ship's magazine marking HMNZS Royalist*'s last day at sea.* EVD 0032

HMNZS Royalist Far East commission pennant. 48

There were changes, too, in the fleet at home during the mid-1950s. In 1955 *Stawell* replaced *Tui* as the Naval Volunteer Reserve training vessel. The Solomon Islands veteran acquired yet another naval life, stripped of her armament, as a oceanographic research vessel. The navy's newfound commitment to research during this period resulted in the Government buying the research ship *John Biscoe* – which had reverted to its earlier name of *Pretext* shortly before commissioning into the Royal New Zealand Navy as HMNZS *Endeavour*.

The purchase of *Endeavour* was no doubt driven by the RNZN's need to have an appropriate vessel to carry out the latest task with which it had been charged – supporting the New Zealand party taking part in the Commonwealth Trans-Antarctic Expedition. The vessel cost £20,000 and was refitted for this specific purpose at Thornycrofts' Southampton yard in the United Kingdom. *Pretext* was recommissioned into the New Zealand navy as *Endeavour* on 15 August 1956. Two months later, the ship was in New Zealand waters and ready to work the coming summer season on the ice. As the last real frontier left on earth, from the 1950s Antarctica was to become the site of multinational rivalry.

Although naval vessels had made forays into Antarctic waters as long ago as Cook's voyages in search of the mythical land of Terra Australis Incognita – and Robert Scott Falcon, who perished in 1912 on his second trip to the ice, was a Royal Navy captain – it would not be until the 1950s that serious attempts were made to 'discover' this vast frozen continent. The initial push into these largely uncharted waters came from the United States and it was the US navy that led what would very quickly become a multinational commitment to Antarctica.

In 1955, the American naval operation known as Deep Freeze I, the first of its kind, had but a single New Zealand naval representative, Lieutenant Commander W. L. J. Smith, who was charged with finding a possible site for a New Zealand scientific base.

The following year Smith returned to Antarctica, this time as first lieutenant of the newly commissioned HMNZS *Endeavour*. As part of the Commonwealth Trans-Antarctic Expedition, *Endeavour* carried New Zealand personnel, including team leader Edmund Hillary, and equipment to McMurdo Sound, the chosen site of the proposed Scott Base. Some of *Endeavour*'s naval personnel were part of the team that erected the first huts at the new base that was officially opened on 20 January 1957. The British venture took the form of an extensive multi year program which culminated during the 1957–58 summer season in the first motorised crossing of the ice by a team lead by Vivian Fuchs.

The following summer, and for the two that followed, *Endeavour* played a major role in the logistical support of the largely New Zealand Ross Sea party of the Trans-Antarctic Expedition, and a New Zealand presence was irrevocably established at McMurdo Sound. As *Endeavour* was not fitted out with specialised icebreaking reinforcement to her hull, the ship had to be assisted through the shifting pack ice by American navy icebreakers which formed part of the United States contribution to the International Geophysical Year.

This type of work, in such extreme conditions, quickly took its toll on *Endeavour*, and by 1960 the ship was experiencing sheathing and caulking problems, the wooden hull no longer able to stand up to the rigours of Antarctic conditions. *Endeavour* made her last journey back from the ice to New Zealand in late February 1962. In the spring of the same year the new *Endeavour*, which had extensive ice-strengthening built into her steel hull and bows, was commissioned into the RNZN on a five-year loan from the United States Navy. This arrangement would be renewed for a second term in 1967.

Taking up its namesake predecessor's role, the new RNZN vessel set sail for McMurdo Sound for the first time on 10 December 1962 on the first of two voyages the ship would undertake to the ice and back that summer. *Endeavour* would continue to make these voyages south for a further eight summers, providing support in a variety of forms.

Although the RNZN frigates were not equipped to penetrate as far south as McMurdo, they did operate as crucial weather pickets and rescue ships at latitude 60 degrees south, the halfway point between Scott Base and New Zealand.

String vest issued to crew members of Endeavour I *(c. 1958) as part of their cold weather clothing.* CLC 0001

Set of 6 glasses from the Penguin Club (the USN Senior Rates Club), Antarctica. GEM 0001

REAR ADMIRAL D. B. DOMETT

Douglas Domett joined the Royal New Zealand Navy as a special-entry cadet in mid-1950. In August 1957 he was serving in HMNZS *Endeavour* during the ship's second season on the ice, providing support for the Commonwealth Trans-Antarctic Expedition. His interview gives a taste of a season on the ice with the RNZN in the mid-1950s.

Douglas Domett: The only landfall that you really make between New Zealand and McMurdo [Sound] is a little island called Scott Island, which really is just a big rock. That is also where you tend to meet the first of the pack ice. In fact, we spent about a day and a half going through the pack ice in very thick fog and navigating through it very slowly. We never actually saw Scott Island, although I managed to convince the captain that that blip on the radar was in fact Scott Island, and was the only landfall that we had before we altered course. After we cleared the pack ice, we would break out into open water. It was still a day and a half or two days to go to the entrance of McMurdo Sound. We ran on for about 12 hours to make sure that we had got through the pack, and then we altered course to the southwest towards McMurdo.

INT: Navigation would be pretty tricky down there in those days?

DD: There were no charts. In fact, once we were down there and we had offloaded all the stuff for Scott Base, we did quite a lot of navigational soundings with the first lieutenant, who was a surveyor, of course. We put up stations ashore and started to chart McMurdo Sound.

INT: Gyros go silly, don't they? Compasses certainly do.

DD: Yes, the magnetic compass does and even the gyro. … The gyro, yes – it used to wander quite a bit. Once you are in the ice, into the pack ice – we were only going roughly in the right direction because you had to go through the leads in the pack ice. The *Endeavour* … wasn't designed to leave harbour. … They … put some steel around the bow and another sheathing of greenheart around the vessel itself. … It wasn't designed really to go to sea in any sort of rough weather, and it certainly wasn't designed to spend any time in the ice, because all the outlets from the heads and galley all came out at water-level. After we had been down there a while and we were waiting for Sir Vivian Fuchs to complete his trans-Antarctic crossing, the sea was starting to freeze. We had to put the boat down and go around and chip the ice off the waterline so that the outlets from the heads and galley could drain over the side.

When we first arrived into the pack ice at the entrance to McMurdo, we slowly nosed our way through that for a day or so. The American icebreaker … had actually broken through the solid ice in McMurdo to within about 10 miles of the American base. Scott Base is just over the hill and around the point. We secured at the end of the channel that the icebreakers had broken in. They escorted us through once we got into the heavy stuff. We were still about 15 miles from Scott Base. As we were going through the pack ice, I used to spend my watch on top of the foremast with a little canvas dodger and a sound-powered telephone down to the bridge. I was looking for a break in the pack ice and the leads, so we would just navigate through, pushing the ice aside. There was no way that the *Endeavour* could break its way through – it was just nudging the ice aside and looking for open leads.

We got down there and we started to offload. Fergusson tractors had gone down the year before, when they originally built Scott Base. They would come out with a couple of sledges and, whenever they appeared, everybody would be on deck and, having loaded them, the sledges would take off. As I recall, it took them two or three hours to get back to McMurdo, to Scott Base, and they would offload. They would be back about every six to seven hours, and we would offload more supplies and away they would go again. It didn't matter what time, because by that stage it was daylight 24 hours a day.

When we got down there it was interesting, because the sun was up all the time – you didn't feel as though you wanted to actually go to sleep. A lot of us, as I recall, stayed awake for the first couple of days. The scenery was magnificent, so there was plenty to see and do. The scientists would come over from Scott Base to discuss our programme. Slowly we adjusted and went to sleep at the usual sort of time, and up the next morning. There was, at that stage, a lot of press and media interest in the Vivian Fuchs/Ed Hillary crossing. Hillary wanted to get to the Pole before Fuchs did, and all that sort of thing. Hillary's job, in fact, was to depot-lay for Vivian Fuchs who was driving across in his snowcats, which would need fuel replenishments at the depots. My understanding was that the Americans said to Ed Hillary: 'If you get to the Pole, after you put that last depot in, we'll bring you out.' Ed wasn't quite sure that, if he did that, that he could get all the way back to Scott Base again. My recollection was that the Americans said: 'Well, you have a go and lay that base and go onto the South Pole – then we will fly in and pick you up and bring you out.' Which is in fact what happened.

Then, of course, as Fuchs came through, they started to pick up the depots. Ed Hillary and the team went out and they met him, and I was fortunate enough to be at Scott Base when they arrived. After cleaning up, we had a dinner with them that night. The telegram from the Queen was read out, saying that ... Vivian Fuchs had been knighted after his crossing. It was a very moving evening.

We went to Scott's hut at Cape Evans, and we also went to Shackleton's hut at Cape Royds. When we went to Scott's hut, it was packed full of ice – it was solid. The windows had been blown in, and no one had been in there for a long time. It was the one that Scott used before he set off for the South Pole, never to come back. We started to dig this hut out – one of the officers and three or four guys. We took it in turns to dig, with pickaxes and shovels. We finally dug it out and we got down to the table, which was still set. There was an open jar of marmalade. I think the last people that were in there was about 1913, and this was 1958. There was an open jar of marmalade on the table and, although it was something like 40 years old, we ate it. ...

We had sleeping bags and used a primus to cook our own meals. We actually opened tins of cocoa and stuff that had been left down there, and cooked our own meals out of some of the supplies that were at least 40 years old. We did back-load a lot of old equipment out of there. The little funny old tractor, which is in the museum in Christchurch now, we brought back. There were still skeletons of the dogs that they shot before they left. There were skeletons of the horses that had also been shot. The chippy on board ... boarded up all the windows to make the hut weatherproof. We also re-felted the roof. That was in '58. I went down there again in the early '80s ... '83 or '84, I think – and went to have a look at the place that we had cleared out that many years before. There is a typewritten page, framed with a glass covering, saying [that] it was originally cleared out by the officers and the ship's company of *Endeavour*, and it lists the names, including mine ... of the guys that actually cleared the hut out originally.

... We went out to various islands off the entrance to McMurdo, to conduct scientific programmes. We also had Dr Falla, an ornithologist, on board. We were looking at various birds and recording the history of them and their eating habits. They asked if we could bring back and observe an Emperor penguin. We actually captured one of these Emperor penguins, and used the wing of the bridge, which was enclosed, and had the Emperor penguin up there for a few days. We couldn't catch very many fish that we thought the Emperor penguin would like, but we were trying to feed it mash and other things – but it wasn't all that interested. Neither was it very interested in the herrings and tomato sauce that Leading Cook Scoble thought it might like. Eventually, we put it back into its own element. In the meantime the scientists had measured it and got all the information that they could externally from it, and so we finally let her go.

We also went to Cape Royds, where Shackleton's hut was located. There was a big ... penguin rookery near there. It also was one of the areas in McMurdo Sound where, just inland from there, there was an outlet from Mt Erebus, which is an active volcano. There was very little snow around there during the summer and the hut was in quite good repair. We did do some more work on it, and spent some time observing the little Adelie penguins in their rookery.

We then waited until Sir Vivian arrived .... The ice was still breaking when we picked him up. We backloaded two snowcats, which we put on the foredeck, one each side of the cargo hatch. We came back with Fuchs' party on board, Ed Hillary and most of his party, and a lot of their gear, so the ship was pretty full. By this stage it was getting cold – I think it was about 30 degrees below. ... We sailed that night into a gale, and *Endeavour* used to roll! ... We were rolling more than 45 degrees one way. We had a total roll of over 90 degrees. In fact when it rolled one way, you could put your foot on a bulkhead and you were more upright than when you were standing on the deck – that's how bad it was.

1-lb tin of Fry's pure concentrated cocoa, removed from Scott's Hut at Cape Evans. SXG 0009

Ice saw used for cutting blocks of ice in Antarctica. The ice could then be loaded on the ship and used for fresh water. T2008.8.1

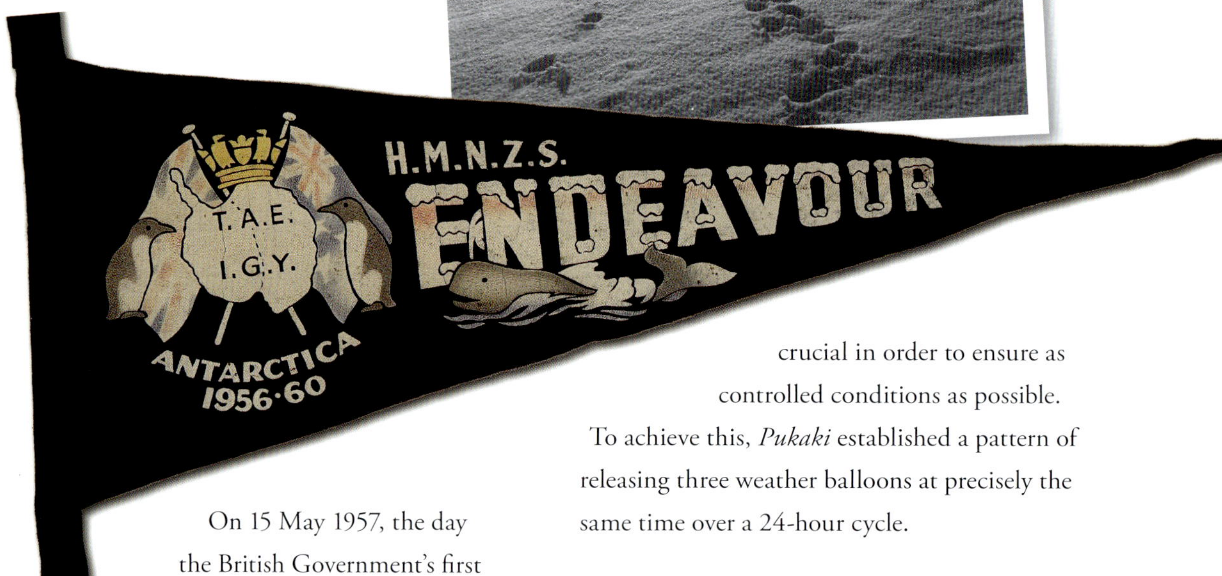

A black pennant printed with 'HMNZS Endeavour, *Antartica 1956–60'.* GEH 0027

While these duties were mostly undertaken by American navy escort destroyers, from 1961 to 1965 *Pukaki* and *Rotoiti* undertook '60 Degrees South' duties. These patrols generally lasted just under a fortnight and the conditions, which included heavy seas, snowstorms and stray icebergs, were hard on ships as well as men.

By the mid-1950s the four remaining Loch-class vessels – *Taupo* and *Tutira* had already been paid off – were showing their lack of modernity. Too slow for modern warfare, they would have to be replaced sooner rather than later. The RNZN looked once more to the United Kingdom as it started the lengthy process of gradually replacing the remaining frigates. Orders for two brand-new anti-submarine frigates were placed with two separate shipbuilders, Thornycrofts and J. Samuel White, in 1957. However, the Loch-class ships still had some life in them – which was just as well, as it took a further eight years before the last two Lochs, *Rotoiti* and *Pukaki*, were finally paid off in 1965.

On 15 May 1957, the day the British Government's first hydrogen bomb test was carried out in the Christmas Island area, the RNZN was represented by the two remaining Loch-class vessels which were there in a supporting role. *Pukaki* had arrived in the test area almost a month before the first detonation to act as a weather ship, and had a weather hut that had been made by the dockyard and placed on the frigate's quarterdeck. Because weather conditions greatly affected the tests, regular monitoring was crucial in order to ensure as controlled conditions as possible. To achieve this, *Pukaki* established a pattern of releasing three weather balloons at precisely the same time over a 24-hour cycle.

On 1 April *Pukaki* was joined by *Rotoiti*. On the day of the first test detonation, *Pukaki* was a scant 45 miles away from the bomb's epicentre, its entire crew above and below decks clad in protective clothing – despite the consensus at the time that the tests were absolutely safe. After the first test, *Pukaki* ventured to within six miles of surface zero. A further two tests followed, which *Rotoiti* and *Pukaki* observed from the outer fringes of the test site. With the

Christmas Island Christmas card.
EAB 0032

three tests completed, both ships headed home for New Zealand, *Pukaki* having been on duty for some 126 days.

Following the end of the Korean War in 1953, the RNZN maintained a major presence in the Royal Navy's Far Eastern Fleet, operating out of the Singapore Station. *Kaniere*, *Pukaki* and *Rotoiti* all saw time with the Commonwealth Strategic Reserve, as the Fleet had become known. While on duty with the Commonwealth Reserve, both *Pukaki* and *Royalist* played a very minor role during the Malayan Emergency which ultimately saw Malaya gain its independence in 1957. The New Zealand frigates were involved in ship-to-shore bombardments of Communist-held positions along the Malayan coast.

After Malaya joined Singapore, Sarawak and British North Borneo to form Malaysia in 1963, neighbouring Indonesia, citing fears for its own independence, engaged in hostilities against Malaysia. In early 1965 New Zealand sent a contingent of RNZN men to commission and crew two Ton-class minesweepers that were in reserve on the Singapore Station. This contribution to the Commonwealth Strategic Reserve was very much a scaling down of commitment when compared to the two frigates New Zealand had had on station only 10 years before during the Malayan Emergency.

Witnessing the Christmas Island nuclear tests from HMNZS Pukaki. AAO 0027

Weighted nylon mesh bag fitted with heavy zip and lock. Used for getting rid of classified documents by throwing overboard in case of take-over by the enemy. ISF 0001

Flag of Captain Inshore Flotilla (Far East) which was comprised of minesweepers from the RN, RNZN, RAN Units depicted. Top left: 6th MCM Squadron (Blackfoot) RN. Top right: 11th MCM Squadron RNZN. Bottom left: 16th MCM Squadron R.A.N. Bottom right: 11th M C M Squadron R.N. Centre: HMS Manxman, *MCM Parent ship.* SFL 0003

Operation Deep Freeze blazer pocket. Given to J. Rees who was transferred from HMNZS Rotoiti *to USS* Hissen *at position 60 degrees south, for an appendicitis operation.* CRF 0009

Blazer badge: Santon 11th Minesweeping Squadron, Malaya Borneo 1965. CRF 0042

The minesweepers were recommissioned into the New Zealand navy for the duration of the crisis as HMNZS *Santon* and *Hickleton*. In addition to the regular naval men who the RNZN provided as crew for the minesweepers were a number of naval reserve officers.

Hickleton and *Stanton* were based predominantly in Malaysian waters in the Singapore, Malacca Straits and Sarawak regions on anti-infiltration patrols. By 1966, however, as a result of internal conflict in Indonesia, its interest in pursuing hostilities against Malaysia waned and peace was declared in 1966, resulting in the withdrawal of Commonwealth Strategic Reserve ships from the area.

The two custom-built Rothesay frigates, redesignated as Otago-class ships once commissioned into the RNZN as HMNZS *Otago* and *Taranaki*, took a long time to build and finally arrived in New Zealand in 1960 and 1961 respectively. As Grant Howard puts it in *Portrait of the Royal New Zealand Navy*, *Otago* was 'the first of a new breed, bristl[ing] with … innovation'. In terms of its warfare capabilities, *Otago* had an enclosed bridge and below-decks operations room in addition to extensive armament and state-of-the-art sonar and medium-range radar. The crew's needs were not overlooked either, as the ship was fully air-conditioned in addition to more prosaic innovations such as cafeteria-style messing from a single galley. For a mere £4.5 million, the RNZN finally had a warship that had been built with the possibility of nuclear warfare very much in mind.

A funnel fitted with a 'T' bar handle and a galvanised bucket used for washing sailors' clothes. GLC 0001

Otago *at Pearl Harbour, 1966.*

Waikato *launching.* AAX 0816

However, ship purchases were not to end with the acquisition of *Otago* and her sister ship *Taranaki*. In 1962 the Naval Board called for tenders to build a third frigate. The Belfast firm of Harland and Wolff Ltd had the winning bid, beginning work on what was to be HMNZS *Waikato* in early January 1964. Developed from the Whitby and Rothesay classes, the new Leander-class frigate had, in addition to its many innovations, a helicopter with torpedo capabilities and a Seacat anti-aircraft missile system. There would, however, be a two and a

HMNZS Otago *in Cook Strait.*

Painting on silk. Acquired in Hong Kong in 1967. PAJ 0006

ROTHESAY & WHITBY-CLASS FRIGATES:

HMNZS *Otago, Taranaki & Blackpool*

Although *Otago*, *Taranaki* and *Blackpool* would become known as Otago-class vessels in New Zealand, they were in fact built as Rothesay and Whitby-class frigates (*Blackpool* falling into the latter class).

In February 1957, New Zealand ordered two new frigates through the RN as replacements for the ageing Loch classes. These two ships would become *Otago* and *Taranaki*. The third frigate, *Blackpool*, was initially commissioned into the RN, followed by a temporary commission into the RNZN five years later as a loan vessel to fill the gap between the demise of *Royalist* and the commissioning of *Canterbury*. Upon completion, *Otago* and *Taranaki* were commissioned into the RNZN in 1960 and 1961 respectively. In 1973 *Otago* accompanied a civilian peace flotilla to Mururoa to protest against France's use of the Pacific for atmospheric nuclear testing. With the creation of the 200-mile exclusive economic around New Zealand in 1978, *Taranaki* was recommissioned in early 1979 as a fisheries patrol vessel.

Although *Blackpool* spent only five years in the RNZN, the other two frigates remained in the RNZN fleet until they came to the end of their economically viable lives in the early 1980s.

Class and type: **Rothesay and Whitby-class frigates**
Name: **HMNZS *Otago*, *Taranaki* and *Blackpool***
Builder: ***Otago* – John I. Thornycroft & Co. Ltd, Southampton; *Taranaki* – J. Samuel White & Co. Ltd, Isle of Wight; *Blackpool* – Harland & Wolff Ltd, Belfast**
Laid down: ***Otago* – 5 September 1957; *Taranaki* – 27 June 1958; *Blackpool* – 20 December 1954**
Launched: ***Otago* – 11 December 1958; *Taranaki* – 19 August 1959; *Blackpool* – 14 February 1957**
Commissioned RNZN: ***Otago* – 2 June 1960; *Taranaki* – 28 March 1961; *Blackpool* – 16 June 1966**
Paid off/decommissioned RNZN: ***Otago* – 7 November 1983; *Taranaki* – 18 June 1982; *Blackpool* – June 1971**

General characteristics
Displacement: **2144 tonnes standard**
Dimensions: **112.8 x 12.5 m**
Propulsion: **2-shaft double-reduction geared steam turbine engine, 30,430 shp**
Speed: **30 knots**
Complement RNZN: **220–240 officers and ratings**
Armament: ***Otago* and *Taranaki* – Guns: 2 x 115-mm, 1 x 40-mm. Tubes: 12 x 533-mm AS torpedo tubes (later replaced by 6 x 324-mm), 2 x 3-barrelled DC mortars. Missiles: 1 x quadruple Seacat launcher. *Blackpool* – As above, minus Seacat**

Station pointer used for horizontal sextant angle plotting in the survey ship HMNZS Lachlan. IBC 0030

Red swimsuit with naval crown and RNZN on front. T2008.15.1

half year wait before *Waikato* would be ready for commissioning.

Since any navy is more than the sum of its blue-water capabilities, during this period a small flotilla of 16 motor launches was formed to meet the day-to-day needs of the RNZN. The MLs, as they were called, were used in a great variety of roles including as liberty boats servicing the training establishment HMNZS *Tamaki* on Motuihe Island, as fishery patrol vessels, and for training and hydrographic purposes. It was also during this period that the tradition of naming small ships, rather than identifying them by pennant numbers, was instigated. Those vessels on fisheries duties were given the te reo Maori names of various fish and the survey boats bore those of native birds, again in te reo Maori. By such small means did these vessels come to share in a distinctively New Zealand naval identity.

As the RNZN became more and more established, its needs ashore changed. In 1963 the shore training establishment HMNZS *Tamaki* on Motuihe Island was transferred to the mainland, sharing the land and buildings at Fort Cautley, Narrowneck, on Auckland's North Shore with the army. After the army moved to its new headquarters, the RNZN took over the whole site for its trainees.

The Devonport Dockyard, too, had continued to innovate, constantly extending the capabilities of the shipyard. In the early 1960s it was able to complete the fitting out of *Otago* and *Taranaki*, installing the frigates' Seacat launchers and missile guidance systems.

On 1 November 1965, as a result of salt-water contamination causing extensive damage to the boilers' evaporators – 'condenseritis' in matelot-speak – *Royalist*, under the command of Captain Joffre Vallant, broke down in the Solomon Islands area. Repairs were done at sea to enable the cruiser to get home. Because of major leaks in the condensers, a complete overhaul of the ship's 300 valves and 700 condenser tubes was required. A week – and many hundreds of man-hours – later, the engines were turning over slowly and, with a few days' additional repairs, the ship was capable of being nursed along at a top speed of eight knots – approximately a quarter of her normal running capacity. *Royalist* was accompanied for most of the voyage back to Auckland by the survey vessel HMNZS *Lachlan*. As the cruiser was due to be paid off in the coming year, it was decided that there was little point in repairing the engines and the ship was returned to the RN for disposal in 1967.

Wooden propellor from pilotless target aircraft shot down by Royalist off Subic Bay, Philippines in 1965. GAB 0001

AAN 0144

CAPTAIN T. M. O'BRIEN

Terence O'Brien joined the Royal New Zealand Navy as a cadet midshipman in 1955. In 1965, O'Brien was on HMNZS *Royalist* as an engine-room watchkeeper during the frigate's infamous breakdown in the Coral Sea.

Terence O'Brien: I recall very vividly what happened right from the very first minute. I was engineer Officer of the Watch. We were steaming on the after-unit – in the forward unit the boiler room was shut down, being stripped for a boiler wash. I had just wandered off on my rounds and was returning to the after engine room and had stopped by the office ... when I got a call up from the Chief of the Watch ... to say the salinometers had gone off the clock. I raced down below to try and figure out what was going on. I subsequently discovered the degree of contamination was so great that there was just no way of isolating it all. ... I raced off, found the Commander E[ngineering], told him what was happening, got down below, and by this time we had shut down. I guess at that stage the damage had been done.

It was subsequently established that the tube plates on both main condensers had warped back and exposed the condensers to sea water. ... The machinery plant was very old and had not been modernised in any way whatsoever. ...

I don't think I have ever worked so hard again in my life .... We literally just worked and worked, took salt tablets, drank water, oatmeal and water, oatmeal and water and salt and limers. There was just no time other than to flash up a boiler, steam it at low power, low pressure, distil the steam coming off, shut down the boiler, let it cool down as much as you could afford, open the doors, get in there, clean it out, fill it up with slightly less contaminated water and start steaming again. At the same time, replacing packing in every valve and almost every joint, certainly in B boiler room.

The sight of B boiler room at day two, when we got every person we could lay our hands on to pack valves, was hilarious. I mean, it was like suddenly the monkey cage at the Auckland Zoo had got liberated – there were people all over, from top to bottom, swinging on spanners, stuffing in packing material and shouting and abusing each other. Those are the people actually who probably deserve the most credit for getting the ship back. There were weapon mechanics, there were electricians. ... They weren't people who normally worked in machinery spaces, but they worked their guts out ...

I don't think its easy for people to understand today just what conditions we were living under in that ship at that time. We were in a steel box with 6-inch plates of steel around it, we had no air conditioning, we had no proper ventilation. Most of the ventilation had to be shut down. We had no fresh water for washing. As an engineer officer, I was privileged in that I got one bucket of brackish water a day, in which I started off by cleaning my teeth, washing my face ... washed my underwear and finally washed my socks, and that's all we had. Cooking was generally out of the question. I think it was on the third day ... I had a glorious feed of boiled beans, and they had been cooked in the after-galley using army field ration individual stoves.

I can remember the tug coming from Brisbane, we actually placed great store on that tug. I can recall early one morning ... [w]e were having a quick cup of tea before we went down below again, and we saw this tug on the horizon. ... It was so small. She only towed us for a few hours or so, it was a pointless exercise. ... *Lachlan* arrived ... and tried to lie alongside us – that was scary, that really was scary. This says a lot, certainly for *Lachlan*, how well she was built, because she stood the pounding she got from *Royalist*. ... They brought up a lot of the boiler-cleaning gear, they parted with some fresh water and I think we passed some fuel. We were very grateful for the help.

I think one of the most impressive things, though, was when the RNZAF Sunderland came out and dropped us mail – that was at a time when we really didn't know whether we were going to make it home or not. We were drifting down on, I think it was Palmerston Reef, and there was a real risk that we would end up on that reef. As it was, I think the *Carlock*, the tug from Brisbane, managed to get to us in time and managed to draw us away from the drift line to that reef and we avoided it. ... At the end of the day the real measure of our success was that we steamed her home. We actually got her home.

TH

A
OROUGHLY
MODERN
NAVY
1966–2005

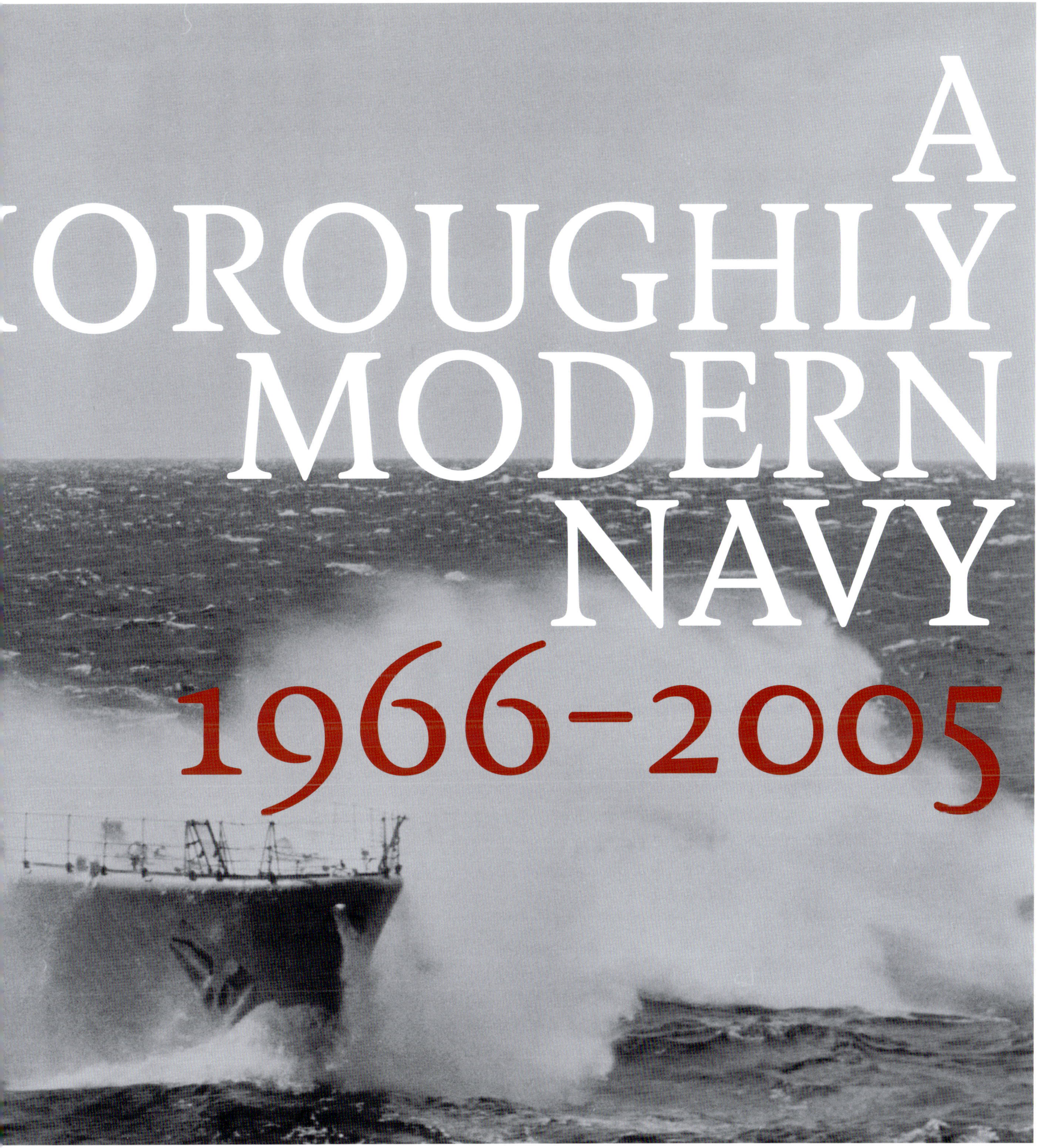

By the late 1960s the Royal New Zealand Navy's collective security obligations included the Canberra Pact, SEATO (South-East Asian Treaty Organisation), ANZUK, ANZUS and, from 1971, the FPDA (Five Power Defence Arrangement), which comprised New Zealand, Australia, Singapore, Malaysia and the United Kingdom. To meet these international commitments as well as its obligations in home waters and to various Pacific Island nations, the RNZN needed both ships and the personnel to crew them.

However, 1966 was a year of ship losses for the Royal New Zealand Navy. HMNZS *Royalist*, which had been due to be paid off and replaced with HMNZS *Waikato*, had sustained massive engine room damage due to salt-water contamination and had been paid off earlier than expected, leaving a gap between the cruiser's decommissioning and the commissioning of the brand-new purpose-built Leander-class frigate. In addition to *Royalist*'s demise, the two remaining Loch-class frigates, *Rotoiti* and *Pukaki*, were also paid off in the same year. As a result of these losses, the navy borrowed the frigate HMS *Blackpool* from the Royal Navy in 1966, for a term of five years, while its modest frigate-building program was coming to fruition. Apparently, when the RNZN crew arrived in the United Kingdom to commission *Blackpool*, they were faced with a completely stripped-down ship and had to spend a considerable time alongside at Chatham dockyard, making the vessel habitable.

The commissioning of what would eventually be four new frigates over a period of 15 years began with *Waikato* in September 1966, with the ship arriving in New Zealand waters in June of the following year. *Waikato* was immediately put on duty in a now long-established routine of exercises and patrols at home and with other navies, and duties in the South Pacific, at ceremonial events and in a maritime rescue capacity.

The arrival of *Waikato* spurred the redevelopment of a Fleet Air Arm of sorts for the navy. Such a move was not without precedent as the cruisers *Achilles* and *Leander*, whose working lives had spanned the decades before and during the Second World War, had been equipped with amphibious aircraft known as 'Pusser's Ducks'. These Supermarine Walrus aircraft were launched by catapult and recovered from the sea by an onboard crane following their flights. In addition, many New Zealanders had served in the Fleet Air Arm of the RN. Thus there was something of a

AAX 0006

The 1000th Mooloo beret knitted by 'Mum' Milnes for the crew of HMNZS Waikato *in the 1960s. Mrs Milnes was an elderly woman who 'adopted' HMNZS* Waikato *when it was first built and knitted hats in the Waikato football colours. It is believed that Mrs Milnes, who was from Cambridge, was blind. When she died the Navy sent a small representation to her funeral.* 1697/4

AK47 submachine gun of Chinese manufacture, used in Vietnam. JTD 0006

tradition of airborne Kiwi matelots before the arrival of the new frigate in 1966. Although the branch had lapsed through lack of need, with the commissioning of *Waikato* and its Westland Wasp helicopter, it became necessary once more to form a – albeit very small – naval air force. Because of its diminutive size but specialised needs, the navy air force joined with the other two services of the armed forces, with the Royal New Zealand Air Force providing training and aircraft maintenance for its land- and sea-borne compatriots.

The ways in which the navy operated changed dramatically in the decades following the end of the Second World War. Though ships and the men to crew them remained the bedrock of the navy, new opportunities and challenges were continually arising and the service faced ongoing restructuring in order to fulfil the requirements of a small modern navy. One major change was the end to the recruitment of seamen boys – youths aged between 15 years and three months and 16 years and three months – in 1996. This abrupt termination of what had been the mainstay of naval recruitment for the past 45 years was almost entirely the result of social

.30-calibre M1 Carbine (American). Weapon taken from a captured Viet Cong soldier by American troops and presented to Surgeon Commander J. Frew New Zealand Medical Team, January 1968. JTB 0003

A plaque from Z Force, Vietnam. GFG 0019

changes within New Zealand. There simply was no longer a demand for the seaman boy class, with potential recruits increasingly electing to stay on at school for longer than their counterparts in previous generations.

The 1960s also marked a watershed in how wars were waged and the use of international military personnel in them. From this period, United Nations peacekeeping forces began operating extensively in the world's hot spots.

In the wake of fighting between India and Pakistan over Kashmir in 1965, the United Nations was asked to provide international observers from its member nations. New Zealand's military contribution included a single naval officer, Lieutenant Commander Reg Hurden. Arriving in Kashmir in October 1965, Hurden spent a year in the Himalayan foothills investigating reported violations of the ceasefire and maintaining an independent presence in the region. The lack of roads meant that patrols were carried out either on horseback or on foot. Although a second naval officer, Lieutenant Commander Peter Oldham from the Naval Volunteer Reserve, relieved Hurden in late 1966, a year later Hurden volunteered for a second deployment to Kashmir.

Although the RNZN was involved in the Vietnam War in a medical capacity from the late 1960s to the early 1970s, it was not until 1992 that the navy once more began providing personnel for a variety of United Nations missions.

Following the Second World War, with French colonial rule finally at an end in Vietnam, nationalist sentiment came to the fore. As an ally of the United States, the New Zealand Government decided in principle to involve itself in the conflict. In the final third of the war, the RNZN played a part in New Zealand's contribution in terms of medical expertise. The First New Zealand Medical Team was formed as a result of the recommendations made in 1965 by the New Zealand Director-General of Health, Dr D. P. Kennedy, who saw the need for a team of military medics in South Vietnam to look after the medical needs of the civilian population, whose numbers had greatly expanded as refugees flowed down from the North. The team was to provide surgical and medical treatment for civilians, using the Bong Son Dispensary, located 97 kilometres north of Qui Nhon, as a base hospital and service centre for a number of outlying small clinics. The team would also be responsible for on-the-job medical training for Vietnamese hospital staff and the establishment of health and sanitation education and protocols.

The initial deployment of these 'Tan Tay Lan' medics, as the Vietnamese called the New Zealanders, included five naval personnel. Following pre-deployment training at Burnham Military Camp, the team arrived in Vietnam in mid-1967, taking over from the US army medical team that had been running the hospital at Bong Son. The hospital consisted of a small brick building that was the operating theatre, a small ward, X-ray unit and laboratory. The main wards, which could house approximately 100 patients, were under canvas in four large tents. In addition,

there were three outlying dispensaries, at Puy My, Tam Quan and Hoai An. At Tam Quan, on 1 March 1970, the medical team lost a member to a booby trap set in a local church. Although Royal New Zealand Air Force Sergeant Gordon Sutherland Watt survived the blast, he later succumbed to his injuries and was buried with full military honours at Ulu Pandan War Cemetery, Singapore. Petty Officer Dennis Manson of the RNZN was also injured in the blast, but recovered a few days later.

A more substantial hospital at Bong Son had been planned for some time and, soon after the New Zealand Medical Services team arrived, work began on the new building. For this first rotation and the others that followed them, one highlight of the project was the construction of a house for the New Zealand medics in the hospital grounds.

After the initial deployment, team members were regularly rotated in a staggered fashion. Nearly all the fresh food and fuel for the team was supplied by the US 173rd Airborne Brigade which had a large base nearby – apart from fresh bread, which was flown in from Singapore by the RNZAF at the team's own expense. Although official supply networks were in place, acquiring vehicles and medical supplies from the Americans was often an easier option.

Although, initially, the New Zealand team did the lion's share of the work at Bong Son, both in terms of medical work and organising supplies, by 1971 Kennedy's recommendations for the training of Vietnamese nationals had been implemented and the staff at the hospital had taken over clinical and administrative duties, most of the theatre work and all the x-rays. With a fragile peace in place by 1971 and the hospital running reasonably efficiently, it was decided that the New Zealand medical team should be withdrawn. The following year, however, the peace was shattered and the area the team had been based in was invaded by the North Vietnamese. The hospital at Bong Son was reduced to rubble, one of the many casualties of the fighting. It was not until the late 1990s that a hospital was built in Bong Son to replace the one that had been destroyed. This new hospital, built on a different site, boasts a 400-bed capacity and is the second largest in the province.

After two and a half decades of 'shipbuilding', the economic realities of the early 1970s, which included rising inflation and a substantial rise in fuel oil prices, slowed the growth of the RNZN and would set a precedent for the remainder of the century and into the next.

Apart from *Canterbury* and a handful of smaller vessels that replaced a diminishing motor launch fleet, there was a definite tightening of the purse strings in regard to ship acquisitions.

However, New Zealand's was by no means the only navy to be constrained by cost-cutting measures. This was brought home to the RNZN when the United Kingdom withdrew the RN from the Singapore Station towards the end of 1971, replacing it with an ANZUK force. In contrast to its previous leadership role in the region, the RN was now a minor player in this

Formica plaque showing the flags of USA and New Zealand over a temple. Presented to MCPO Cameron upon leaving Vietnam in November 1972. GFH 0011

Steel helmet with DPM cover as used in Vietnam. JGC 0029

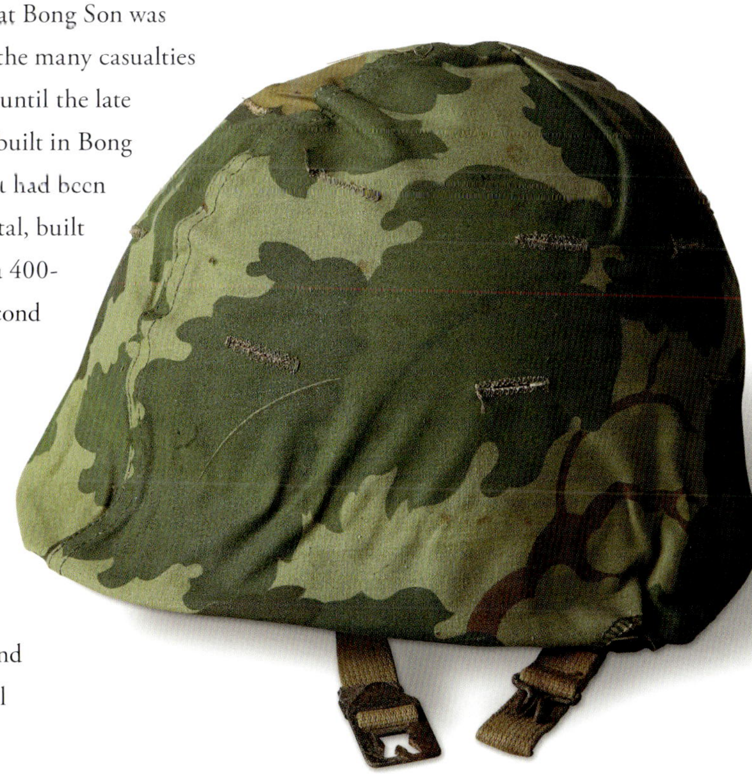

LEANDER-CLASS FRIGATES: HMNZS *Canterbury, Southland, Waikato* and *Wellington*

The Leander-class frigates commissioned into the RNZN over a period of a decade and a half were intended as replacements for the navy's existing Loch-class frigates. While *Canterbury and Waikato* arrived new, the two other ships built at the same time for the RN were considerably aged by the time they were commissioned into the RNZN fleet in the early 1980s. The frigates carried out a by-now-established routine of exercises - Pacific Island tours, ceremonial duties and supply runs. *Canterbury* was one of two ships sent to Mururoa Atoll in 1973 as part of the Government's protest against French nuclear testing there, and also had the honour representing the RNZN at the Silver Jubilee Review at Spithead in June 1977. The deployment of a RNZN vessel in the Indian Ocean during the Falklands War of the early 1980s saw both *Canterbury* and *Waikato* on patrol duty with the RN. The frigates were also on hand during periods of unrest in the Pacific, notably in Fiji in 1987 and at Bougainville in 1990 and 1997.

On 1 March 1995 *Southland* was decommissioned. Later that same year, *Wellington* and *Canterbury* saw service in the Persian Gulf from October through to November. By 1998 *Waikato* had come to the end of its operational life and was decommissioned in July. *Canterbury* was deployed to East Timor when violence erupted there in 1999, remaining on active duty despite its age. When *Wellington* was decommissioned in May 2000, *Canterbury* became the sole representative of the 'frigate navy' which had been the mainstay of the RNZN fleet for the previous three decades. Five years later, on 31 March 2005, *Canterbury* was decommissioned.

Class and type: **Leander-class frigates**
Name: **HMNZS *Waikato, Canterbury, Wellington* and *Southland***
Builder: ***Waikato* - Harland & Wolff Ltd, Belfast; *Canterbury* - Yarrow & Co. Ltd, Glasgow; *Wellington* - Vickers-Armstrong Ltd, Naval Yard, Newcastle; *Southland* - Yarrow & Co. Ltd, Glasgow**
Laid down: ***Waikato* - 10 January 1964; *Canterbury* - 12 April 1969; *Wellington* - 27 October 1966; *Southland* - 2 December 1959**
Launched: ***Waikato* - 18 February 1965; *Canterbury* - 6 May 1970; *Wellington* - 29 February 1968; *Southland* - 22 December 1961**
Commissioned RNZN: ***Waikato* -16 September 1966; *Canterbury* - 22 October 1971; *Wellington* - 1 October 1982; *Southland* - 21 December 1983**
Paid off/decommissioned RNZN: ***Waikato* - 3 July 1998; *Canterbury* - 31 March 2005; *Wellington* - 5 May 2000; *Southland* - 1 March 1995**

HMNZS *Waikato*.

Ikara missile launch from Southland.

General characteristics
Displacement: **2450–2500 tonnes standard**
Dimensions: **113.4 x 13 m**
Propulsion: **2-shaft double-reduction geared steam turbine engine, 30,000 shp**
Speed: **30 knots**
Complement RNZN: **243–260 officers and ratings**
Armament: ***Waikato* and *Canterbury* – Guns: 2 x 115-mm, 2 x 20-mm. Tubes: 6 x 324-mm AS TT; Missiles: 1 x quadruple Seacat launcher; Aircraft: 1 x Westland Wasp with HT. *Southland* – Guns: 2 x 40-mm; Tubes: 6 x 324-mm AS TT; AS – 1 x Ikara GWS40 launcher; Missiles: 2 x quadruple Seacat launcher; Aircraft: 1 x Westland Wasp with HT. *Wellington* – Guns: 2 x 115mm, 2 x 20mm; Tubes: 6 x 324-mm AS TT; Missiles: 1 x quadruple Seacat launcher; Aircraft: 1 x Westland Wasp with HT**

new strategic alliance. With its commitments to its ANZUS partners – Australia and the United States – in the South Pacific taking precedence over ANZUK, New Zealand too cut back its level of involvement in the area that had been known as the Singapore Station. This cooling of relations between the RNZN and the RN was symptomatic of a general distancing from Britain, both nationally and navally, that had been taking place in the years following the Second World War.

However, despite cutbacks in defence spending there were some new acquisitions to the fleet during this period. An additional research vessel was added in early 1970 in the form of a five-year loan from the United States. The *Charles H. Davies*, renamed HMNZS *Tui* on commissioning, was built as a specialist oceanographic research vessel. Despite the limited original loan period, *Tui*'s time in New Zealand waters would eventually span 25 years, so valuable was the ongoing research in which the ship was involved. In 1971, *Blackpool* was returned to the United Kingdom in accordance with the conditions of its loan agreement and paid out of the RNZN. The ship's crew travelled on to Scotland to commission HMNZS *Canterbury*, the second of the Leander-class frigates to join the RNZN fleet, in October of the same year. It took almost a year, after working up and sea-trails, before *Canterbury* finally saw the waters of its 'home' port of Lyttelton.

Four *Lake*-class patrol vessels named after the earlier Loch-class frigates, HMNZS *Pukaki*, *Rotoiti*, *Taupo* and *Hawea*, arrived in New Zealand in two lots as deck cargo on board a heavy-lift ship in 1975. The *Lake*-classes were immediately put into slip at the Devonport Dockyard where their fitting out was completed in a matter of weeks, before being named and commissioned into the RNZN. Although the Lakes were predominantly intended for use on fisheries patrol duties, patrolling the 200-mile exclusive economic zone in the waters off the New Zealand coast, they also took part in fleet exercises with the regular navy and Volunteer Reserve.

The survey ship, HMNZS *Lachlan*, was quietly paid off on 13 December 1974, and its eventual replacement, *Moana Roa*, a commercial vessel, was commissioned into the RNZN as HMNZS *Monowai* in July 1975.

The vessel was then taken to Scotland for its specialised refit later that same year. While in dry dock, being fitted with a helicopter deck and hangar and new propeller systems and crew accommodation, amongst other modifications, the ship had to contend with a serious fire in the cafeteria and cracks in the main engine. It would be two and a half years before the refitted *Monowai*, now a specialist survey vessel, sailed into Auckland in early 1978, and a little over three since the vessel it was replacing had been paid off.

In 1978 a decision to replace the remaining motor launches, including the Volunteer Reserve and Diver Branch tenders, involved a shipbuilding contract being awarded by the RNZN to a New Zealand company for the first time. Based on the design of the Australian navy's torpedo recovery vessels, these inshore patrol craft were built by the Northland-based Whangarei Engineering Company.

The Women's Royal New Zealand Naval Service was disbanded in 1977 and henceforth women entered the regular navy as near equals with their male counterparts – as, at this stage, women were still limited to the survey, research and support branches. The new intake

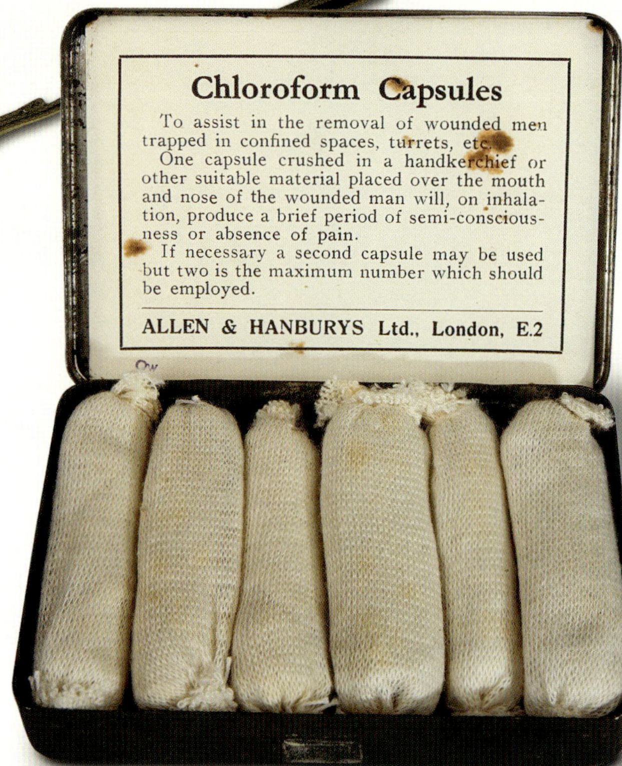

5.56 mm Colt M16A1 submachine gun. JTD 0011

Chloroform capsules in metal tin with instructions for use. Used by the medical team in Vietnam. IMA 0003

Four syrettes containing 1 cl of antropine injection. For use in cases of nerve gas attack as an antidote. Used in Vietnam by the medical team. IMA 0004

WARRANT OFFICER MEDICAL ASSISTANT E. J. FITZGERALD

Edward Fitzgerald, then a chief petty officer, volunteered for the first rotation of the First New Zealand Services Medical Team which left for Vietnam in 1967.

Edward Fitzgerald: I think it was 1966 when the Vietnam thing was first mentioned. They asked for volunteers. … It was about the beginning of April '67 when we went to Burnham [Military Camp] to do our group training.

INT: Was this the first team to go up?

EF: This was the first team. … It started off [when] the Government decided they should give extra support for Vietnam. … [T]hey decided we could send another civilian team of medics up there. … There were three doctors, one from each service. Albie Green, navy, was the Commanding Officer, Neil Officer was a T[erritorial] F[orce] Officer, army, and Doctor Graham, Squadron Leader Graham, he was a TF air force doctor. …

INT: Did you know by that time exactly where you were going and what your duties were going to be when you got there?

EF: Vaguely – the only photos we had seen had been taken by helicopter and didn't mean a damn thing. … We had a night in Saigon in the transit camp at Ton Son. The next day they flew us up to Qui Nhon. … The following day, when we flew out, they issued us all with 45s on the tarmac, but no ammunition. I scurried around some American MPs and got the ammunition for the boys, who had never seen an American 45 in their life. … We got to Qui Nhon, and … Geoff Braybrook, who was a WO2, met us in a Yank truck and piled us on … and he took us around to the civilian team house. … Eventually, we got an old Vietnamese villa right opposite the American Red Cross Centre – bare. Immediately we had to go scrounging beds and sheets, and most of those came from the American hospital. …

… Qui Nhon was the base area. Quite a big place, actually. The civilian team had been there for years, and there was a huge American support complex. … We had this shocking American meal and [went] up into their club and [were] quietly enjoying a Budweiser, and the Viet Cong put in an attack on the fuel dump about 200 metres down the road. All hell broke loose, and there were Americans diving everywhere with weapons. We had nothing, so we were told just to take cover. … North Vietnamese sappers had actually got into the fuel tank, so it was a good introduction actually. … Next day we scrounged up some more gear, and Albie arrived from Bong Song, and we started splitting the team up to go to the various sectors.

INT: What, into … villages?

EF: Sort of townships. Tom Palmer, an air force sergeant, Pete Quinn, a staff sergeant, and myself and Squadron Leader Graham went to Phu Vinh, which had quite a big dispensary. Of course, 'dispensary' to them was virtually a cottage hospital to us. We moved into this MACV compound. … We started off with virtually nothing. For an amputation saw we had an ordinary mechanic's hacksaw – no suture scissors, very little of anything. I got our allocated jeep and went down to Qui Nhon again, where I knew there was a detachment of the US Navy who ran a 'Market Time' base and went over and saw them. … You

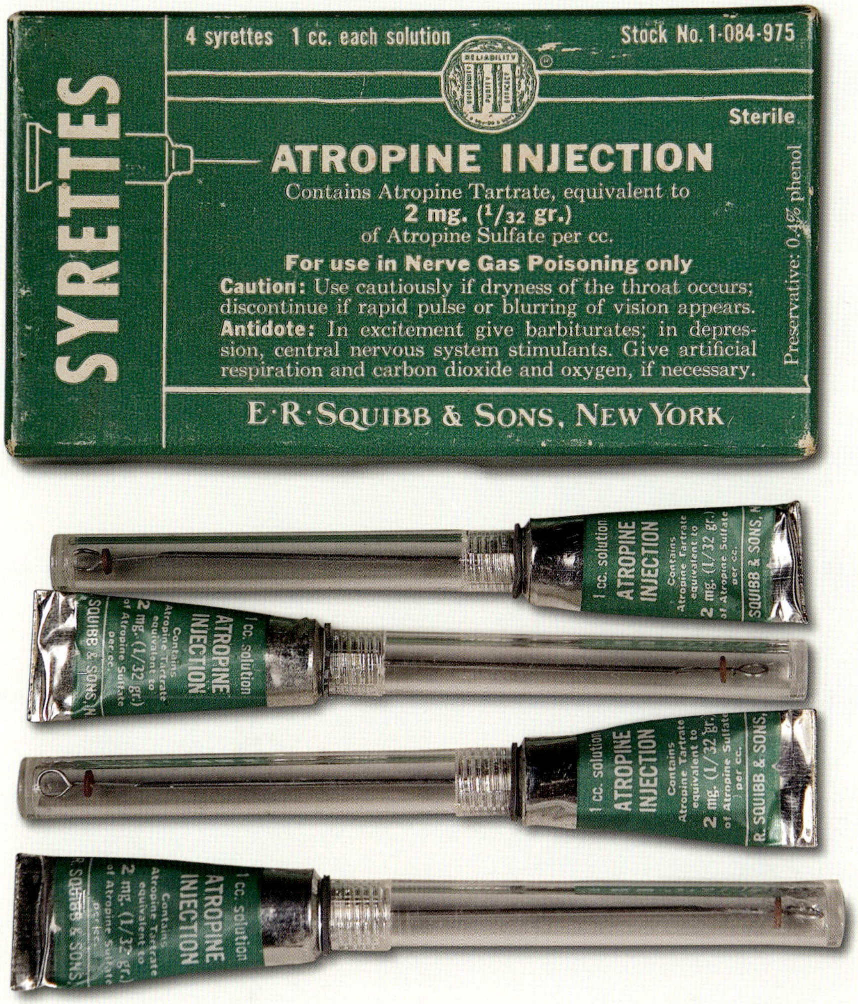

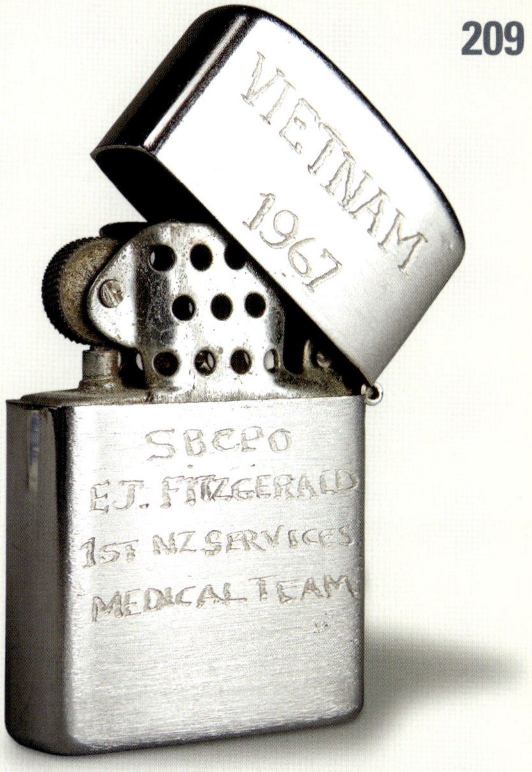

GSE 0009

name the instrument and the supplies – I brought those back, and we were home and hosed then.

INT: Can you just paint a little word picture of this cottage hospital, the dispensary?
EF: Well, there were two tents out the back. The main building was French-designed, everything was sort of square, ornamental, big façades in the front – it looked quite nice from the distance. … [We] would be treating gunshot wounds and minor amputations and treating burn cases. As well as that there was a maternity annex as well, and that is something out of the sixteenth century. The delivery table was a solid block of concrete with a drainage hole in it, which went to God knows where. The so-called maternity ward had straw mats on the concrete. So the woman was taken in and put on this concrete slab to deliver the child and then back onto the straw mat again, and that was their post-natal care. … It was primitive, no lighting.

The nicest part of the building was out the back, a separate building. … It was beautiful. It had two beds in it. It was clean. I tried to put a couple of infectious cases into it and found out then it was the morgue.

INT: How many beds were in the hospital, roughly?
EF: The patients were actually outside in tents. They were very big marquee types and you fitted 20 to 30 beds in them. …

INT: How many Vietnamese staff were there?
EF: There should have been about eight, actually … [and] four Kiwis.

INT: What were the main types of problems?
EF: Traffic accidents, because they used to run across the road like ducks, and there were convoys all day. A lot of petrol injuries, people burning themselves by buying our gas, and stuff like that, and putting it in their cookers. We never saw any Napalm victims – it was mainly cooking accidents. A lot of gunshot wounds. A lot of them weren't quite sure what had hit them. If they had been hit by 30/30, [it] didn't do a hell of a lot of damage – they were quite easy to take out. If people had been hit by an M16 or an AK47, you had one hell of a mess. … Higher velocity, and it shattered the bone and gored great hunks of meat out. … You got a lot of fragmentation wounds, we used to call them 'pepper-pot' wounds. They would hit the ground and you would see 20 to 30 wounds over the back and the thighs and that – so you cleaned those and got the metal out, if possible, and treat[ed] them.

INT: How did you work? Did you work on your own?
EF: Yes, we split up. Peter Quinn … was generally right at the door as they first came in, and he categorised them – he would send some into Tom Palmer and some into me. Depending on the severity of the wounds, we would work on them – you know, cutting dead flesh, setting minor fractures. We didn't have any x-ray facilities there. If you were worried about [something and needed] an x-ray, you had to go down to the American Air Base about 30 k[m] down the road …. [W]e used to get medical cases – meningitis and things like that, or tetanus cases. There was no point in sending a medical case down to the Impact Hospital at Qui Nhon, because they would never be seen. They were up to their eyeballs in blood down there. You did some real bush medicine.

ABD 0327

HMNZS *Endeavour*

As we have seen, *Endeavour* has been a popular name for both RNZN and RN ships. A total of five vessels working in New Zealand waters have borne the name, including Captain Cook's *Endeavour.* This particular vessel, an Antarctic tanker, was the fourth.

Built in the United States by Cargill Inc., the tanker was commissioned USS *Namakagon* in mid-1945 and operated in the Pacific until September 1957 when it was decommissioned and placed in reserve at San Francisco.

The tanker was taken out of reserve in early 1962 and had extensive ice-strengthening built into its hull and bows by Williamette Iron and Steel Co. It was commissioned, on a five-year loan term, into the RNZN as HMNZS *Endeavour* later that same year. This loan agreement would be extended for a further five-year period in 1967.

During *Endeavour*'s nine-year tenure with the RNZN, in addition to the Antarctic duties for which it was intended, the tanker worked tirelessly in a number of other areas. *Endeavour* undertook many scientific cruises for the Department of Scientific and Industrial Research in the waters around the Antarctic continent and the Pacific, playing a crucial role in ongoing oceanographic research voyages. Other duties included supply runs to the weather stations on Raoul and Campbell Islands, training voyages and search-and-rescue operations.

Endeavour was decommissioned in 1971 and returned to the United States, a year short of its second five-year loan term – a result of cuts to the defence budget. The vessel reverted to her original name for only a matter of minutes before being commissioned into the Navy of the Republic of China (Taiwan) as *Lung Chuan.*

Class and type: **Antarctic tanker**
Name: **HMNZS *Endeavour***
Builder: **Cargill Inc., Minnesota, USA**
Laid down: **1 August 1944**
Launched: **4 November 1944**
Commissioned as *Namakagon*: **June 1945**
Commissioned as HMNZS *Endeavour*: **5 October 1962**
Paid off RNZN: **30 June 1971**

General characteristics
Displacement: **1850 tons standard**
Dimensions: **94.7 x 14.8 m**
Propulsion: **2-shaft GM diesel-electric, 3300 bhp**
Speed: **14 knots**
Complement RNZN: **68 plus 14 civilians**
Armament RNZN: **Unarmed**
Pennant number: **A184**

ACZ 0163

Ceremonial bell impressed 'HMNZS TUI 1970', engraved on the rim with the names of persons christened onboard. It is tradition for children to be christened under the ship's bell or to use the bell as a christening bowl. SBC 0010

of female ratings trained alongside their male counterparts at HMNZS *Tamaki*. Despite these major advances, it was to be another 10 years – in 1986 – before women ratings were allowed to serve at sea, albeit in non-combat ships.

For its part, the Naval Volunteer Reserve was affected by a Defence Review in 1978 which emphasised the need for both the regular navy and the Reserve to undertake service rather than training for war. However, the concept of four geographically based divisions of reservists remained. And according to the Review's recommendations, in the closer alignment of regular and Reserve forces, reservists could serve in three naval branches: sea service, supply control and support services.

Patrol duties in the southern reaches of the Pacific continued through the late 1960s and into the 1970s, when the 'peaceful isles' became the site of protest over French atmospheric bomb testing in the Pacific Basin. Mururoa and its sister atoll, Fangataufa, in French Polynesia were the site of extensive nuclear testing by France, which administered the islands, from 1966 until 1974. Although France was not a signatory to

DLA 0156

LIEUTENANT L. R. HUNN

Lisa Hunn served in the frigates *Wellington*, from October 1995 to January 1996, and *Canterbury*, from September to November 1996, undertaking United Nations blockade duties against Iraq. In both ships she served as an Officer of the Watch. The following extract from her oral interview deals with her time on board *Canterbury*.

INT: How many female personnel [were there]?
Lisa Hunn: For the deployment, we had 20 on board plus two officers, a doctor, Surgeon Lieutenant Commander Drewry and myself.

INT: Did you act as their Divisional Officer, or are they split up amongst the branches?
LH: I have my own division, which is the Communications Division, and women that are in my division are under my divisional control. The rest of the girls are split up by branch.

INT: There is no split-up by [gender], or anything like that?
LH: Absolutely not. However, if the female personnel have any problems they are not happy talking to a man about, then they can come to me. I have already told them that they can come to me if it's serious.

INT: They have their own mess deck?
LH: Yes. …

INT: You obviously have a cabin of your own?
LH: Yes, I ha[d] my own cabin, fortunately. … The women [on *Canterbury*] have separate shower areas and they share toilets down aft. There are two designated toilets for the women. For the female officers, we share the shower facilities with the guys and put up a sign when we are in there. They just wait outside until we get out. We share the heads. They have pulled most of the urinals out of most of the places, and so there is no risk of walking in on anyone.

INT: It's just like a mixed flat, presumably, and it is [as] relaxed as that?
LH: Yes, it is pretty relaxed. The guys can tend to moan sometimes because they would have to wait for us. But we were not long showerers, so it's not as if we held them up, and we generally co-ordinated our showering times. As I [was] the only woman officer [on *Canterbury*], it [wa]s just hard luck on them. They ha[d] to wait. …

… On the way north from Darwin, we had just worked up and so were quite au fait on NBCD [Nuclear, Biological and Chemical Defence]. Then we had to get into the chemical side of NBCD, which I dread. I can't stand chemical warfare. Between Singapore and Bahrain, we started chemical training and running around in respirators and full suits. Doing cleansing training is quite an intensive procedure. I'm not keen on respirators, and I wouldn't have liked to have worn them for any long sort of period. I guess we kept them on for a maximum of one hour at a time during training exercises. … It was hard for me on the bridge trying to communicate, because there is a big mouthpiece that sticks out so you are unable to have a headset on.

INT: Don't they have microphones?
LH: Yes, they do, but you can't hear them, as it muffles your voice quite a bit. Also, for an Officer of the Watch, it restricts your sight because you have got tunnel vision. Yes, it was difficult. Definitely not the kind of thing I would have liked to have done in a real-time situation.

… [When we were in the Persian Gulf] we would patrol around our area at slow speed and have the helicopter ready to go. Any contact we spotted, we would take an interest in and investigate it. There are a lot of fishing vessels up there, so generally you would have a stationary fishing fleet over one side of the area. I would keep an eye on them, and the ops room would report when something was moving at a steady speed in a certain direction. They were responsible for tracking the traffic coming in and out of the two waterways [the straits of Homuz] and, if it had and [was] heading at a steady speed out of the area, then we would go and have a look. …

INT: What do female crew members get up to when they get ashore? What do you do? Do you go sightseeing, shopping?
LH: Yes, generally I would say that women, relative to all the men, would do a lot more shopping, because that is what women do. However, there are a lot of guys who go shopping and a lot of the times they would say: 'Come shopping with me, I want to buy this for my wife, my partner or whatever. Can I have your opinion?' I guess we did a lot of that. Generally, women do exactly what the guys do.

INT: In my day, sailors went ashore and chased liquor and chased girls.
LH: Absolutely, and I am pretty sure they still do that nowadays.

INT: Do the girls drink and chase boys?
LH: They definitely drink.

HMNZS Taupo. ABS 0043

Items used to board foreign fishing vessels around the coast of New Zealand. JGF 0011

Fisheries Protection Squadron ceremonial lifebuoy centre panel. SGB 0003

Fisheries Protection pennant. Flown by Te Kaha *in the Southern Ocean, 1999, when the ship was despatched to investigate fish poaching.* SFJ 0133

either the Limited Nuclear Test Ban Treaty of 1963 or the Nuclear Non-Proliferation Treaty of 1968, many South Pacific countries had signed these treaties and French testing in the area was seen to fly in the face of the principles underlying these multi-nation agreements. The two French atolls became the location for a growing flotilla of protest vessels, often including the Greenpeace vessel *Rainbow Warrior*, during the testing season.

In 1973, in a politically unprecedented act, the newly elected Labour Government sent a naval ship to join the annual migration of protest vessels to the test site. In June 1973, with the purpose of focusing international attention on atmospheric nuclear testing in French Polynesia, the frigate HMNZS *Otago* set sail for Mururoa where it joined a host of civilian vessels from around the region. Cabinet member Fraser

'The reorganisation marks a change from the traditional concept of training for war to one of service in peace and war ...'
Chief of Naval Staff Rear Admiral Neil Anderson on the impact of the 1978 Defence Review.

Cleman was on board the warship, reiterating New Zealand's disapproval of the tests, and a host of journalists were also included to ensure widespread publicity for the Government's stand. The Australian navy contributed to the action in the form of HMAS *Supply*, a fleet oiler that carried not only fuel oil but fresh food and supplies to the New Zealand frigate.

The first of the season's tests, which *Otago* witnessed from the support zone west of the Mururoa atoll, took place on 21 July and it was the New Zealand frigate which first informed the world of France's latest outrage in the Pacific. The recently commissioned *Canterbury* took over from *Otago* a few days later and the latter returned to New Zealand, leaving *Canterbury* to witness the second test on 13 August.

The international attention given to France's nuclear policy and practice brought an end to atmospheric detonations, forcing the testing underground. A total of 147 underground nuclear tests were subsequently conducted at Mururoa and Fangataufa. Shafts were drilled deep into the volcanic rocks underlying the atolls, where nuclear devices were detonated. This practice created much controversy as cracking of the atolls was discovered, resulting in fears that the radioactive material trapped there would eventually escape and contaminate the surrounding ocean and neighbouring atolls. The test site at Mururoa was dismantled following France's last nuclear test to date, on 27 January 1996.

Naval shore establishments, or 'stone ships', also underwent refits of sorts. The Naval Wireless and Telegraph Station which had been commissioned in 1943 to handle the communications traffic of

Flag with white H-Bomb cloud with words 'Norms [Norman Kirk's] Mystery Tours' flown by HMNZS Canterbury *at Mururoa Atoll July 1973 during nuclear testing by the French. Donated by Mr Michael Bell, 1993.* SFL 0002

Air Mail envelope showing a stamp of a mushroom cloud. The stamp was made by Leading Seaman Garthwaite onboard HMNZS Canterbury *in 1973 and the Captain gave approval for the stamp's use.* ELB 0017

HMNZS Canterbury.

both the RNZN and British Pacific Fleet during the final years of the war, and commissioned as HMNZS *Irirangi* in 1951, was still in operation, but its support buildings were showing their age by the early 1970s. Because the station was still performing a valuable service and would continue to do so, a decision was made to move *Irirangi*'s accommodation and administrative facilities to the Waiouru Military Camp. The facilities were closed in 1994.

The Devonport Dockyard has continued to develop to meet the navy's changing roles. The instalment of a concrete pontoon and a syncro-lift docking facility were notable innovations. As the Dockyard developed, so too did its capabilities and in 1975 it began a two-year half-life refit and modernisation of *Waikato*.

In addition to the RNZN fleet's more conventional duties in home waters and abroad, the 1980s began with *Monowai* monitoring the rocket splashdown tests conducted by the the People's Republic of China near Tuvalu. Later that year (1981), the survey vessel spent 115 days at sea on survey duty on the 8000-mile ANZCAN telecommunications cable designed to link Australia, New Zealand and Canada. In 1982, *Canterbury* and *Waikato* each did two tours of patrol duty in the Indian Ocean to allow RN vessels to be redeployed to the South American coast when war over the Falkland Islands broke out between Argentina and the United Kingdom.

The 1980s also witnessed another round in the continuing battle to keep the New Zealand Navy Fleet at operational capacity. Twenty years had passed since the commissioning of *Otago* and *Taranaki*, and they were beginning to show their age. While *Taranaki* was scheduled for a complete rebuild at the Devonport Dockyard under the supervision of English shipbuilding company Vosper Thornycroft, at a cost of $42 million, the offer of a pair of cheap ex-RN vessels scuppered this plan and the contract was cancelled in 1983. *Otago* was paid off in the same year. The RN replacement ships would prove to be nothing more than a stopgap, as the 'new' RNZN frigates were nearing the end of their economically viable lives and would provide little

more than a band-aid solution to the problem of maintaining a blue-water fleet. However, the price was right and the New Zealand Government, still feeling the economic pinch of the previous decade, agreed to the purchase.

The Falklands War intervened shortly before the proposed paying off and recommissioning of the first of these frigates, HMS *Bacchante*, and delayed the takeover of the vessel by a few months. In October 1982 *Bacchante* was recommissioned as HMNZS *Wellington* and joined the RNZN fleet. On the frigate's arrival in Auckland, the vessel was promptly entered into the Dockyard for major reconstruction and modernisation, which cost $27 million and took three and a half (instead of the proposed two) years to complete. The second frigate, HMS *Dido*, was renamed and commissioned into the

HMNZS Monowai.

HMNZS Southland. AAZ 0171

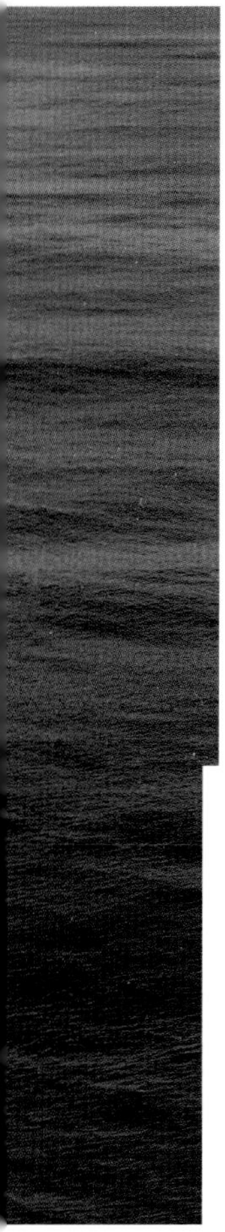

Rainbow Warrior *sinking at Marsden Wharf, Auckland, 1985.* AUX 0221

AUX 0071

RNZN as HMNZS *Southland* at Portsmouth in July 1983, after which it too underwent a refit and modernisation, at a cost of $14 million. Fortunately this took considerably less time than the work being done on *Wellington*, and *Southland* reached New Zealand waters in July the following year.

The navy's small ship flotilla also experienced a few changes in its complement during this period. The new inshore patrol craft being built in Whangarei began to arrive from 1980, with the first two going to the Hydrographic Branch. By early 1984 a further two patrol craft – HMNZS *Moa* and *Kiwi* – were delivered, both destined for the South Island's two Naval Reserve divisions. The two North Island divisions received their new vessels – HMNZS *Wakakura* and *Hinau* – the following year. Other new arrivals in this period included HMNZS *Endeavour*, a tanker, and a specialised diving vessel, HMNZS *Manawanui*, which was equipped with a diving bell and recompression chamber.

Under the New Zealand Nuclear Free Zone, Disarmament, and Arms Control Act 1987, the territorial seas and land of New Zealand became nuclear-free zones, effectively barring nuclear-powered and nuclear-armed ships from using New Zealand ports or entering its waters. After this Act was passed by the David Lange-led Labour Government, the United States, with its large fleet of nuclear propelled and armed naval vessels, suspended its ANZUS obligations to New Zealand, seeing New Zealand's rejection of its naval vessels as a betrayal of the ANZUS treaty. The popular mandate for the country's nuclear-free status was further illustrated by the national outrage which erupted when the Greenpeace protest ship, *Rainbow Warrior*, was blown up by French naval operatives on 10 July 1985, while moored alongside Marsden Wharf in Auckland. Navy divers surveyed the sunken wreck in situ, and the dockyard took responsibility for the raising, docking and subsequent inspection of the Greenpeace vessel. In addition to the ongoing problem of keeping ships on the water, during the 1980s the RNZN also faced the challenge of keeping them

HMNZS Endeavour *refuelling* Southland *in open sea.* ABE 0112

HMNZS *Endeavour*

HMNZS *Endeavour* is the RNZN's purpose-built fleet replenishment tanker, carrying supplies and fuel for RNZN, Commonwealth and Allied surface units. She can re-supply ships at sea or in overseas ports from the 7500 tonnes of fuel in her eight tanks, or the supplies held in the four containers on deck. HMNZS *Endeavour* can also provide fuel to helicopters fitted with in-flight refuelling. *Endeavour*'s motto 'Nil intentatum' means 'Nothing unattempted'. Her crest features a navigator's compass and the stars of the Southern Cross, symbolising the pioneering navigations and survey work of Captain Cook.

In August 1990, *Endeavour* was the neutral venue for Operation Big Talk. Peace talks were held on board between the Bougainville Interim Government and the National Government and the resulting agreement was known as the Endeavour Accord.

In 1997 the *Endeavour* was back in Papua New Guinea waters when the New Zealand-led Peace Monitoring Group was deployed to the island. *Endeavour*'s role was to provide logistics support to the naval task group as well as land and air forces based ashore. Initially *Endeavour* provided all the fuel required ashore, as well as fresh water. It was also used by NZDF troops as a place to relax and shower.

Endeavour was involved in operations in East Timor from September to October 1999 and January to February 2000. She served as a supply ship for fuel and stores to escort and amphibious ships as well as land and air units. She also supplied fuel to the coalition forces ashore, by refuelling road tankers embarked on landing craft brought alongside the ship.

Class and type: **Fleet tanker**
Name: **HMNZS *Endeavour***
Builder: **Hyundai Heavy Industries Co. Ltd, Uslan, South Korea**
Laid down: **6 April 1987**
Launched: **14 August 1987**
Commissioned: **8 April 1988**
Decommissioned: **Still in service**
Pennant No: **A11**

General characteristics
Displacement: **7300 tons standard**
Dimensions: **138 x 18.4 m**
Propulsion: **5300 shp**
Speed: **14 knots**
Complement: **50 officers and ratings**
Armament: **Unarmed**

crewed. Such was the shortage of seagoing men that the *Lake*-class patrol craft *Pukaki*, which had a complement of only 21 and had been commissioned new into the RNZN only the decade before, was placed in operational reserve. This was a symptom of the ongoing recruitment and retention problems that all three of the armed services faced throughout the period, and have continued to face into the present day.

Despite these problems, the ageing frigate fleet was kept busy through the 1980s on a well-worn routine of naval duties including regular tours to New Zealand's Pacific Island neighbours. As a consequence, the RNZN had a presence in Fiji in 1987 when two political coups occurred. *Wellington* was alongside in Suva during the first coup in May, and was ordered to leave by the Fiji Government, joining *Canterbury* and *Monowai* which were waiting off the coast in case they were needed to evacuate New Zealand residents. *Monowai* was again in Fiji during the second coup in September, and once again stayed in range in case it was needed for evacuation duties.

However, none of the vessels commissioned into the RNZN during these years addressed the issue of the unavoidable replacement of the four aged frigates, including the recent additions *Southland* and *Wellington*. In a joint venture with Australia, the Anzac Frigate Project (as it became known) began the search for a vessel that would fit the needs of both navies and a suitable contractor to undertake the work. Public opposition to the proposal was widespread, and there was a general belief that the armed forces were becoming increasingly obsolete. By the late 1980s there was doubt as to whether any frigates at all would be added to the RNZN fleet.

However, as a sop to public opinion, it was estimated that completing the frigates, which would be built to modular designs, would provide approximately $800 million worth of roll-on work for local contractors. A total of 147 businesses would eventually benefit from the Anzac Frigate Program by the time *Te Kaha* and *Te Mana* were commissioned in 1997 and 1999 respectively. The final contract, under which New Zealand agreed to buy two German-designed MEKO frigates, with the possibility

United Nations ID card complete with UN Driver's Permit secured to dog tags and issued at Trentham, February 1995. DGB 0010

UN peacekeeper's uniform. CDE 0004, CAH 0005, CBO 0003,

PETTY OFFICER MEDICAL ASSISTANT A. D. SMITH

Alan Smith was posted to Iraq with the UN Special Commission on Weapons of Mass Destruction.

Alan Smith: We were in a team, like the medical team [which] supported all the other teams. There was the Bravos, which was the biological team, Charlies, which was the chemical team, and there was the Deltas, they were a missile team – and a nuclear team, the Novembers, scientists, very strange people.

... You did two or three sites – land, get in the aircraft and go home again. At this place [a paper mill], industrial safety just did not exist. There was chlorine and hydrochloric acid lead leaking and mixing on the floor – which is a pretty dangerous sort of a mix – in concentrations that were enough to make you sick. You wore gas masks at the time. Holes in the ground, uncovered bits and pieces swinging off buildings and sheets of corrugated iron. On one site I was with, the chemical team and I came out of the building and I looked up. There is a sheet of corrugated iron, a three-and-a-half metre sheet held on by one nail, and it's flapping in the breeze. ...

INT: Did you do the testing for chemicals?
AS: Depending on what was happening in the site. In a place like Fetlujma 3, which was a chemical place where they actually made nerve agents – you would go to a warehouse there, and the guys would go in all suited up with the detector kits and I would have to stand at the door and watch them, and we were in radio contact. I had to keep them in sight at all times. They would use detectors to see whether it was a hot-spot zone. Once we got into this thing, the CAMs [chemical agent monitors] and the AP2C went crazy, and we were getting seven bars on the CAM. We actually got seven bars on the door – with the wind blowing behind us, we were getting three bars on the CAM about 20 metres away from the door, and so it was pretty strong in there. The Iraqis were wandering around in shorts, sandals, open T-shirts – no respirators or anything – and we were all suited up, and it was 55 degrees.

INT: How would you decontaminate out there in the desert?
AS: Everything gets washed with a mixture of bleach and stuff.

INT: You actually carried a wash?
AS: Yes, we carried all the equipment with us and set up a decom chain.

INT: Were you working every day of the week?
AS: Yes, we worked every day. Friday was a day that the Iraqis didn't work – it was like our Sunday ... but we did do inspections on those days [too]. If you weren't required for an inspection, you didn't actually have to go into work that day, but sometimes you did [anyway]. ... I once worked 14 days without a break and I was exhausted. We were starting at six in the morning and finishing at six at night in 55 degrees of heat, wearing chemical suits and stuff. ...

INT: You have spoken about finding sites with high chemical levels. Were most sites like that, or was that a rarity?
AS: There were a few sites that had quite a lot of stuff, and there were others that were places where we knew they manufactured things and where they stored stuff. They might have a store of cyanide and equipment to produce things. It might actually be canneries or dairy factories – places that had stainless steel tanks or glass-lined tanks and anodising equipment – where they had a missile factory. The equipment they had could be used for the manufacture of other things, and so this had to be checked. That is why we did spot checks to try and catch them out and to see if they had been using stuff. We did find a couple of instances where there was evidence that they had done something. ... I went to a lot of sites quite often like El Qaa, which was a place where they make explosives. Once again, it is a huge place. It had been bombed during the conflict. They were setting up a phosgene plant and that was quite a dangerous place, in fact.

INT: They were still setting it up?
AS: Yes, it had all been destroyed and they were rebuilding it and they were making phosgene, which is used to make explosives. It is another component of the various types of explosives that they made. There [was] a nitric acid plant. This orange plume [emitting from it] was full of nitrous

oxide and, when you breathe that, it turns to nitric acid in your lungs and so you mask up. This would be blowing down over the compound where you are trying to work and checking the monitoring and the air-sniffing gear, and just looking in the buildings at some of the stuff. We used to go there probably once a fortnight, and sometimes two or three times in a week different teams would go out. ...

... Tuwaitna, which was their major research facility ... was protected by huge earthen berms which was supposed to stop the bombs getting in. Laser-guided bombs are a bit more accurate than that. [We] would go there with the Charlie team and meet the nuclear team coming out and, when you are leaving, in would be coming the biological team. There would be three teams that would visit this one site in one day.

INT: Were you actually pushed out of the place? You were there when you were evicted?
AS: I was fortunate in November, as I was already out in Bahrain on ODO [occasional day off] and everybody came to join me.

INT: I see – so you weren't forcibly removed?
AS: No, I wasn't forcibly removed myself, but I went back with them on the 17th November when we went back ... into Baghdad. Then I left Baghdad on the 7th December, and they were finally kicked out on the 15th. So I missed that week.

INT: Did your quarters and things get disturbed whilst you were out [of the country]?
AS: No, they didn't. When we went out in November, previously, our rooms had been ransacked and our stuff was taken [in] previous evictions. This time, the hotel staff had put seals on the rooms and tape over the doors, and no one went in. ...

INT: What about the UN HQ?
AS: They were sealed up and, when they left, the last thing they did was rivet the doors closed, put plates over them. They had [also] gone around and they had spiked all the computers. They put screwdrivers through all the hard drives.

of securing a further two at a later date, was awarded to the Melbourne-based consortium Australian Marine Engineering Consolidated (AMECON) in 1988. AMECON later became Transfield and then Tenix.

In March 1995 *Southland*, the first of the Leander frigates, was decommissioned, followed by *Waikato* a few years later in July 1998.

The final decade of the century saw the RNZN as busy as ever, carrying out the myriad of duties that fall to a modern navy. In the mid-1990s, women were allowed to serve at sea in a combat capacity for the first time; in 1995, when *Wellington* was deployed to the Persian Gulf, there were 24 women on board.

The 1990s also marked a period when the RNZN, both as ships and as individual service representatives, began to contribute regularly to United Nations peacekeeping missions and, in the case of the Middle East, as weapons inspectors.

The island of Bougainville had long been a Pacific hot spot, and years of dissent over its failure to gain independence from Papua New Guinea finally erupted into civil war in the late 1980s. In 1990, the RNZN sent *Waikato*, *Wellington* and *Endeavour* to the island for the peace talks as Operation Big Talk. *Waikato* provided accommodation and support for representatives of the Bougainville Revolutionary Army and Bougainville's interim government, *Wellington* housed the government negotiators and *Endeavour* provided neutral territory for the talks themselves. Although the talks appeared successful, civil unrest continued for a further seven years and a peace of sorts was not finally brokered until 1997. The unarmed Peace Monitoring Group which was deployed to Bougainville in November that year on *Canterbury*, *Endeavour* and *Manawanui* managed to ensure that the area remained peaceful; and, when initial tensions caused by the arrival of navy ships and peacekeeping personnel evaporated, attention turned to reinstating the island's infrastructure such as the restoration of the power supply and rebuilding basic social services such as schools.

In 1991, the RNZN's 50th jubilee year, the United Nations negotiated for the warring factions in Cambodia to disarm and hold national elections, following over 10 years of guerrilla warfare by the Khmer Rouge against the Vietnamese Government which had displaced them in 1978. A 31-man naval contingent was sent to Cambodia to patrol the coast and waterways, observe troop movements and accept surrendered weapons in the lead-up to elections. For the most part, the RNZN personnel were based on a houseboat on Tonle Sap. The medical complement of the naval contingent set up a clinic for local people, with the remainder on patrol duty in Z-boats or old Cambodian Navy patrol vessels. In Phnom Penh, a rented house was acquired and used by the navy when not in the field. Kiwi House, as it was known, featured a large painted kiwi on its corrugated iron fence.

As the time drew closer for the Khmer Rouge to complete their disarmament and the elections to begin, animosity towards United Nations personnel increased markedly and three of the observers, including John Oxenham, a RNZN chief petty officer, were taken prisoner. After several tense days, the observers were released and Oxenham was subsequently awarded the New Zealand Gallantry Medal for his part in negotiating with the Khmer Rouge. The New Zealand peacekeepers were withdrawn when the elections were finally held in May 1993.

Class and type: **Anzac MEKO-200 frigate**
Name: **HMNZS *Te Kaha* and *Te Mana***
Builder: **Tenix Pty Ltd, Victoria, Australia**
Commissioned RNZN: ***Te Kaha* – 1997; *Te Mana* – 1999**
Decommissioned: **Still in service**
Pennant No: ***Te Kaha* - F77; *Te Mana* - F111**
Standard displacement: **3600 tons full load**
Dimensions: **118 x 14.8 m**
Propulsion: **CODOG, 1 x GE/LM 2500 gas turbine; 2 x MTU 12v 1163 TB 83 diesels**
Speed: **27 knots**
Complement: **164**
Armament: **1 x FMC 5′/54 Mk 45 Mod 2 automatic gun; 1 x GE/GD 20-mm Phalanx Mk 15 Mod 11; 6 x 324-mm Mk 32 Mod 6 torpedo tubes; 1 x Lockheed Martin Marietta Mk 41 Mod 5 octuple VLS firing 8 x Raytheon RIM-7P Sea Sparrow missiles**
Countermeasures: **Sea Gnat SBROC Mk 36 Mod 1 chaff launcher; SLQ-25 torpedo decoy**
Aircraft: **1 x SH-2G Seasprite**

ANZAC MEKO-200 FRIGATE: HMNZS *Te Kaha & Te Mana*

The two Anzac frigates *Te Kaha* and *Te Mana* were commissioned into the RNZN in 1997 and 1999 respectively. They were built in Australia by Tenix to a design of Blohm + Voss, the Hamburg-based firm with a reputation for tough warships from both world wars. After the war, Blohm + Voss developed a number of ship designs that were modular in construction. This design innovation, whereby a ship is constructed of self-contained units, had the advantages of reduced costs in addition to enhanced survivability and damage control. Blohm & Voss produced a number of these modular ships for both the domestic and international market.

The new frigates proved an immediate success. In 1999 *Te Kaha* joined the Australian-led force to intervene in East Timor (INTERFET), one of many warships that ensured the success of the operation. After two weeks *Te Kaha* sailed west to the Persian Gulf, to join the Multi-national Interception Force, enforcing UN sanctions against Saddam Hussein in Iraq.

Ongoing civil tensions in the Solomon Islands, which had been monitored by the RNZN since 1990, saw both *Te Mana* and *Te Kaha* working in the area from 2000 through to 2002. The escalation of tensions and the continuation of war in the Middle East after 'September 11' 2001 saw the two ships join the US-led task force, Operation Enduring Freedom, in the Arabian Sea from 2002 to 2004.

Te Mana.
Te Kaha.

French crystal decanter with two port glasses in a commemorative wooden box. Presented to HMNZS Te Kaha *by Transfield Ship Builders, 1997.* TKH 0008

New Zealand naval peacekeepers also served with the United Nations in Bosnia in the early 1990s. When the federation of Yugoslavia began to break up in the mid-1990s, a number of independence wars flared up, feeding off notions of religious and ethnic identity. In June 1992 the United Nations deployed an international force to Bosnia, one of the worst-affected areas, delivering humanitarian supplies and services. The initial New Zealand commitment to Bosnia consisted of five military observers including Gywn Rees, a commander in the RNZN. New Zealand continued to supply military personnel for the United Nations effort in the region until 1996 when the UN transferred responsibility for peace-monitoring activities in the former Yugoslavia to a NATO-led implementation force – which has regularly included a RNZN officer on the staff of the British delegation.

By the mid-1990s, following the First Gulf War (August 1990–February 1991), when a 34-nation coalition force authorised by the United Nations and led primarily by the United States mobilised against Iraq in order to liberate Kuwait, RNZN ships were working with the Multinational Interception Force in the Persian Gulf area. Their main task involved the inspection of shipping to and from Iraq in accordance with United Nations' sanctions. *Wellington*'s tour lasted from October 1995 to January 1996. Later that year, *Canterbury* was in the Persian Gulf, on a tour that lasted from September to November. In the three years between the second and third deployments to the Gulf, the two replacement Anzac frigates, HMNZS *Te Kaha* and *Te Mana*, were commissioned into the RNZN. *Te Kaha* took up the navy's third deployment in the region, serving from October to December 1999.

COMMANDER K. E. WOODHEAD, MNZM

Commander Karl Woodhead, who is still serving in the Royal New Zealand Navy, joined the navy in February 1990. Prior to being deployed to Afghanistan, he had served in non-operational deployments in South-East Asia and the Pacific and in operational deployments in the Arabian Gulf, Sinai and the Solomon Islands.

In late 2003 Woodhead, then a lieutenant commander, volunteered for an operational deployment to Afghanistan as part of the ongoing commitment to that area by New Zealand's joint defence forces. Woodhead and approximately 100 other NZDF personnel formed CRIB 2, the second rotation posted to Afghanistan. Based in Bamian, CRIB 2, which arrived in November 2003, spent six months working on reconstruction projects and building relationships with Afghan nationals – tasks initiated by the previous rotation.

Karl Woodhead: … Warlords and drug lords … provide the social services and other services that the Government can't, and in that way buy loyalty, and they are the ones that are causing the insecurity and instability. So it is really a pioneering thing for the military to be so close to the provision of aid and infrastructure and development in Afghanistan. It happened in Vietnam, I suppose, when they first tried out reconstruction teams. … Then with Afghanistan they decided on this provincial reconstruction team concept, which was to set up teams in provinces. They set about developing those areas and providing projects – anything from wells and clinics to training programmes, human rights to universities, and bridges for roading and telecommunications, or whatever.

Traditionally, the military hasn't been involved in that sort of thing. Their interface with the aid community has been very much about providing protection to convoys and providing for security and stability. The military are policing, in a sense, so the aid agencies can go and do their stuff, and that was partly what we were doing. … [It was] essentially a Kiwi team with about 100 Defence Force personnel. We employed between 30 and 40 Afghan nationals. That was largely to help us out on building the camp or services to the camp, but we also employed a number of interpreters [to] go out on patrol. We had a British aid representative from the Department for International Development, a US AID [Agency for International Development] representative and a US State Department representative: they were the international members.

… We had a lot of money, but we had no ability to actually get anything done. We had to find implementing partners to do it – and that was one

of the biggest obstacles, actually finding enough contractors … who could actually use our funds and work with us on a programme to get something done.

INT: What were your living conditions like?
KW: They were adequate … they had to expand the camp in a hurry. The logistic issues were nightmarish to get materials into there, and to do it quickly and to have reliable building materials and so on was a real problem. The first rotation spent most of their time building the camp just to look after the team and to provide a base so that we could actually start operating.

INT: Did you feel threatened at all while you were there?
KW: All the time there were some threats. There wasn't a lot of action as such. It was a bit like living in a cold environment – the cold is always there, and so the threat is always there. You were always on your guard. We were looking out all the time. We would be looking for signs of threats. We were guarded all the time by Afghan Militia Force guards as well as our own people, who were armed to the teeth on patrols. There are so many threats. There is an active threat from perhaps the Taleban or the warlords or drug lords, or whatever. There are less obvious threats, like the mines everywhere. … We had incidents there – children picking up mines and being injured by them.

… One of the best parts, for me personally, was doing the aid work and trying desperately to get an aid programme underway. New Zealand AID gave about $2.6 million, and didn't send anyone with it. So it fell upon me to create an aid programme as well as doing all the engineering tasks. I basically had two jobs, working flat tack, which was a real challenge. But I really enjoyed it. … Part of that was because we were in a relatively safe environment, and so we were able to get further ahead than others who were still, daily, dealing with rocket attacks. We were inventing a lot of things that hadn't been done before. I was right at the forefront of that process and loved it. It was fantastic.

In 1994 New Zealand sent two medical teams to Kuwait as part of the country's contribution to the Coalition Forces. The second group included two RNZN doctors and eight medical assistants. Later deployments included naval personnel with specialisations in much-needed fields like communications. New Zealand navy personnel also contributed on the ground in multinational United Nations weapons inspection missions in Iraq. This regular flow of naval and other personnel came to an end in 1998 when all the United Nations teams were expelled from Iraq. Continuing unrest in the region involved both *Te Kaha* and *Te Mana* returning to the Arabian Sea as part of Operation Enduring Freedom in 2002–03, working with the United Nations coalition naval forces in the area.

Violence erupted in East Timor in 1999, after a referendum indicating that the East Timorese wanted independence from Indonesia after 24 years of occupation. *Te Kaha* and *Endeavour* joined the Australian-controlled international intervention force to provide logistical support, *Endeavour* performing the crucial task of ferrying fuel from Singapore to the capital, Dili. *Canterbury* relieved *Te Kaha* around two months later. Subsequently, in the lead-up to and aftermath of the elections, RNZN personnel served on the ground in East Timor in a variety of capacities and, given the political instability of the region, may have to perform this role again in the future.

In the Solomon Islands, the fragile peace that had been established during Operation Big Talk began to deteriorate in the late 1990s as armed factions took to the streets and law and order began to collapse as the Government lost control. In late 2000, the Solomon Islands Government requested international help to regain control of the situation. The RNZN contributed personnel to the multi-force disarming teams working in the Solomons from December 2000 to March 2001. RNZN ships, *Te Kaha*, *Te Mana* and *Manawanui*, also maintained a presence in the area from 2000 to 2002.

Khaki brassard worn while on peacekeeping duties in the Solomon Islands. CMN 0007

The new HMNZS Canterbury.

Inshore patrol vessel HMNZS Rotoiti.

In the new century, the RNZN has continued to contribute to United Nations peacekeeping efforts in every part of the world. In 2008, for example, the 11th rotation of RNZN personnel was deployed to Afghanistan to continue with the ongoing task of attempting to establish an infrastructure in a country that, it seems, will never be at peace. And when trouble flares up in one of the other myriad hot spots scattered across the globe, New Zealand and its navy will be there, 'doing their bit'.

Meanwhile, back at home, the never-ending battle to keep the RNZN Fleet operational continued. In the late 1990s, the Westland Wasp helicopters were replaced with the Kaman Aerospace SH-2G Seasprite. Four of these helicopters were purchased second-hand and were in service on RNZN ships by 1998. The option to buy a third MEKO frigate lapsed towards the end of the century. The decision to forgo a third and fourth frigate left the RNZN with a blue-water fleet comprising the aged *Canterbury* and *Wellington*, the latter slated for decommissioning in May 2000, and the two new frigates *Te Kaha* and *Te Mana*. Although the Defence Review of May 2001 may have abandoned the idea of a third and fourth MEKO frigate, *Canterbury*'s days were numbered. In March 2005, *Canterbury* was paid off after spending 34 years in service with the RNZN.

With the necessity of maintaining an operational RNZN Fleet ever in mind, in 2002 a Maritime Forces Review – Project Protector – conducted by the government outlined the requirements for a modern fleet in consultation with MFAT, the Ministry of Fisheries, Customs, Maritime New Zealand and a number of other stakeholders. In mid-2004 a study was undertaken in conjunction with a number of civilian agencies in order to establish the number of vessels required and the most desirable fleet mix.

In April 2004, Tenix Defence Pty Ltd was chosen as the major contractor for the building of the Project Protector vessels. The first steel in this ongoing project was cut in early 2005. The new *Canterbury*, an amphibious sea-lift vessel, was commissioned into the RNZN in 2007. Included in the program are replacements for the navy's existing inshore patrol vessels, of which all but one – *Kahu*, the former *Manawanui* – have been decommissioned since 2000. Their eventual replacements will be two Protector-class offshore patrol vessels and four *Lake*-class inshore patrol craft. These seven new Project Protector vessels are ideally suited to the needs of a small modern navy with a myriad of commitments both in home waters and further afield.

The piupiu being welcomed on to Te Taua Moana Marae, 8 July 2005.

THE RETURN OF THE PIUPIU

The famous piupiu that served HMS *New Zealand* so well in the First World War was finally returned to the Royal New Zealand Navy on 4 July 2005. There was a short ceremony in the form of a powhiri, karakia and blessing in London in the presence of Rear Admiral D. I. Ledson, ONZM, and Lieutenant T. Ripia, RNZN. The piupiu was then handed over to the Navy Museum.

It was welcomed home to Te Taua Moana Marae at HM Naval Base Devonport on 8 July 2005.

While little is known of the true origins of the piupiu, it is believed to have been gifted to Captain Halsey of HMS *New Zealand* when the ship was in New Zealand in 1913 by either the Ngai Tahu or Te Arawa tribe.

The piupiu was conserved and preserved for future generations of New Zealanders in September 2005. Gaynor Duff, Textile Conservator, gave the following description:

> *This piupiu seems to have developed from a pihepihe (a type of shoulder cloak that could also serve as a piupiu). The pihepihe has a long kaupapa (twined solid backing) which could vary in length. There is a shortening of the kaupapa as time progresses and it finally disappears to leave the piupiu of today.*
> *The hukahuka (rolled flax strips) were also attached to the kaupapa as well as the belt area. It appears to be an early example of piupiu, in that the piupiu has a woven area that extends from the two toned woven belt to a black woven patterned area, the kaupapa, that extends to half thigh. The hukahuka extend from the belt area and the kaupapa, but are not as dense as earlier ones…*
>
> *The piupiu is in excellent condition for its age (c.92–120 years), and well worked. Made of harakeke, New Zealand flax, it has been dyed, most probably with natural dyes such as hinau bark for the red brown muka threads in the belt area, and possibly tanekaha bark which gave black brown. However, the black thread may have been dyed using other dyes such as black mud dyeing and futher research could determine this.*

The piupiu is now one of the New Zealand Navy's most treasured taonga.

GLOSSARY

ANZCAN	Australia, New Zealand, Canada
ANZUK	Australia, New Zealand, United Kingdom
ANZUS	Australia, New Zealand, United States
BMD	Bomb and Mine Disposal
CNS	Chief of Naval Staff
CO	Commanding Officer
DEMS	Defensively Equipped Merchant Ship
DFC	Distinguished Flying Cross
DPM	Disruptive Pattern Material
DSC	Distinguished Services Cross
DSO	Distinguished Services Order
FPDA	Five Power Defence Arrangement
HMNZS	Her/His Majesty's New Zealand Service
HMNZT	Her/His Majesty's New Zealand Troopship
HMS	Her/His Majesty's Service
LCI	Landing Craft, Infantry
LCM	Landing Craft, Mechanised
LCT	Landing Craft, Tank
MAC	Merchant Aircraft Carrier
MBR	Motor Boat Reserve
ML	Motor Launch
MP	Military Police
MSF	Minesweeping Flotilla
MTB	Motor Torpedo Boat
NBCD	Nuclear, Biological and Chemical Defence
NZNF	New Zealand Naval Forces
RN	Royal Navy
RNVR	Royal Naval Volunteer Reserve
RNZN	Royal New Zealand Navy
RNZNVR	Royal New Zealand Navy Volunteer Reserve
SEATO	South-East Asian Treaty Organisation
TF	Territorial Force
VC	Victoria Cross
WRNZNS	Women's Royal New Zealand Naval Service

BIBLIOGRAPHY

Barratt, Glyn, *Russophobia in New Zealand 1883-1904*, Dunmore Press, 1981

Bennett, Geoffrey, *Naval Battles of World War II*, David McKay, 1975

Brooks, John, *Dreadnought Gunnery and the Battle of Jutland*, Routledge, 2005

Campbell John, *Jutland: An Analysis of the Fighting*, Conway Classics, 1986

Cowan, James, *The New Zealand War: Volumes I & II*, Government Printer, 1922

Crawford, John, *Atlantic Kiwis: New Zealanders and the Battle for the Atlantic*, NZDF, 1993

Crawford, John, *New Zealand's Pacific Frontline: Guadalcanal – Solomon Islands Campaign 1942-45*, NZDF, 1992

Gash, Noel and Whittaker, June, *A Pictorial History of New Guinea*, The Jacaranda Press, 1975

Grove, Eric, *Big Fleet Actions*, Brockhampton Press, 1991

Harker, Jack S., *Almost HMNZS Neptune*, Moana Press, 1991

Harker, Jack S., *HMNZS Achilles*, William Collins Publishers, 1980

Harker, Jack S., *HMNZS Gambia*, Moana Press, 1989

Harker, Jack S., *Well Done Leander*, Collins Bros., 1971

Hintz, O., *The History of HMNZS Philomel*, Wilson & Horton, 1944

Howard, Grant, *Happy in the Service An Illustrated History of the Women's Royal New Zealand Naval Services 1942-1977*, Word Publishing, 1985

Howard, Grant, *Portrait of the New Zealand Navy: A Fiftieth Anniversary Celebration*, Grantham House Publishing, 1991

Howard, Grant, *The Navy in New Zealand: An Illustrated History*, A.H. & A.W. Reed, 1981

Hutchings, Megan (ed.), *Against the Rising Sun*, Harper Collins, 2006

Hutchings, Megan (ed.), *Last Line of Defence*, Harper Collins, 2007

King, Michael, *New Zealanders at War*, Heinemann Publishers, 1981

King, Michael, *The Penguin History of New Zealand*, Penguin, 2003

McDougall, R.J., *New Zealand Naval Vessels*, GP Books, 1989

McEwan, John, *Auckland Rockies: A History of Auckland's Naval Reserves, 1858-1995*, Pyramid Press, 1995

McGibbon, Ian C., *Blue Water Rationale: The Naval Defence of New Zealand 1914-1942*, Historical Publications Branch, 1981

McGibbon, I.C., *New Zealand and the Korean War Volume I, Politics and Diplomacy*, Oxford University Press, 1992

McIntyre, David W., *New Zealand Prepares for War*, University of Canterbury Press, 1988

Pugsley, Christopher, *From Emergency to Confrontation: The New Zealand Armed Forces in Malaya and Borneo 1949-66*, Oxford University Press, 2003

Rabel, Roberto, *New Zealand and the Vietnam War: Politics and Diplomacy*, Auckland University Press, 2005

Ross, J. O'C., *The White Ensign in New Zealand*, A.H. & A.W. Reed, 1967

Strachan, Hew, *The First World War*, Simon & Schuster, 2003

Taylor, T.D., *New Zealand's Naval Story*, A.H. & A.W. Reed, 1956

Templeton, Malcolm, *Ties of Blood and Empire*, Auckland University Press, 1992

Unknown, *Historic Fort Takapuna: O Peretu*, Department of Conservation, 2001

Waters, S.D., *Official History of the Royal New Zealand Navy in the Second World War*, Government Printer, 1956

Wright, Gerry, *A Kiwi on our Funnel: The Story of the HMNZS Ships Hickleton and Stanton*, Zenith, 2006

Wright, Matthew, *Blue Water Kiwis: New Zealand's Naval Story*, Reed Publishing, 2001

Wright, Matthew (ed.), *Escape! Kiwi POWs on the Run in World War II*, Random House, 2006

Wright, Matthew, *Quake – Hawkes Bay 1931*, Reed Publishing, 2001

Wright, Matthew (ed.), *Torpedo! Kiwis at Sea in World War II*, Random House, 2007

Yates, Keith, *Flawed Victory Jutland 1916*, Naval Institute Press, 2000

NEWSPAPER ARCHIVES

The Evening Post
The New Zealand Herald

UNPUBLISHED

'25 Years of Women in the RNZNVR', Maritime Museum, 2005

'Defensive Mining in New Zealand 1942-45', RNZN Museum Archives

Fleet Air Arm Operations 1942, 43, 44, RNZN Museum Archives

'HMNZS Dockyard: 1888-1945 Vol 1-4', RNZN Museum Archives

Mundie, Florence, 'The Sinking of SS *Rangitane*', RNZN Museum Archives

'New Zealand Personnel in the Far East: December 1941-March 1942', RNZN Museum Archives

'Operations of HMS *Achilles* August 1939-February 1946', RNZN Museum Archives

'Operations of HMNZS *Leander* August 1939-1941, RNZN Museum Archives

'Recruiting and Training: Schemes A & Y', RNZN Museum Archives

'Recruiting and Training: Schemes R', RNZN Museum Archives

'Recruiting and Training: Schemes B', RNZN Museum Archives

'Recruiting and Training: HMNZS *Tamaki*', RNZN Museum Archives

'Recruiting for Fleet Air Arm', RNZN Museum Archives

'Tales from the Beach: New Zealanders in Operation Neptune', RNZN Museum, 1994

'Tales from the Sea: The Royal New Zealand Navy in the Second World War', RNZN, 1995

'The Minesweepers' War', RNZN Museum Archives

Treanor, Ken (ed.), 'New Zealand Military Medics in Vietnam 1964-1971', 1997, RNZN Museum Archives

'War Diary: HMNZS *Gambia*, 1943-1945', RNZN Museum Archives

'War Diary: HMNZS *Leander* 1940-1944', RNZN Museum Archives

'War Diary: HMNZS *Monowai* 1940-1943', RNZN Museum Archives

'Women's Royal New Zealand Naval Service 1942-45', RNZN Museum Archives

RNZN FACT SHEETS

HMNZS *Achilles*

HMNZS *Bellona*

HMNZS *Chatham*

HMNZS *Leander*

HMNZS *Philomel*

HMNZS *Pukaki*

HMNZS *Royalist*

HMNZS *Waikato*

Sailors in Blue Berets: The Royal New Zealand Navy and Peacekeeping

The Battle of the River Plate

The Naval Battle for Crete

The Navigators

The Navy and the Napier Earthquake

The Navy and the North African Campaign 1940-43

The Navy Whaler

The Royal New Zealand Navy

JOURNALS

Navy Today (various)

The White Ensign: RNZN Museum Journal (various)

RNZN ORAL HISTORY ARCHIVE

Stanley Parslow, DLA 0026

Commander Charles Palmer, DLA 0039

Chief Electrician Robert Harvey, DLA 0078

Able Seaman Huia Beesley, DLA 0010

Commander S. F. Hermans, DLA 0074

Chief Petty Officer Ivan Brown, DLA 0032

Fourth Officer Barbara Macky, DLA 0215

Able Seaman G. C. Forrester, DLA 0206

Lieutenant A. W. Direen, DLA 0235

Laurence Charles Hurndell, DLA 0073

Able Seaman S. E. Coveney, DLA 0132

Royal Marine Sergeant A. F. Edwardson, DLA 0238

Warrant Officer R. W. Kirkwood, DLA 0079

Chief Petty Officer M. Smith, DLA 0027

Commodore B. E. Turner, DLA 0017

Lieutenant Commander C. V. Harris, DLA 0020

Leading Seaman N. J. Scoles, DLA 0208

Commander C. R. Vennell, DLA 0045

Leading Cook T. W. Abbot, DLA 0114

Rear Admiral D. B. Domett, DLA 0103

Captain T. M. O'Brien, DLA 0110

Warrant Officer Medical Assistant E. J. Fitzgerald, DLA 0104

Lieutenant L. R. Hunn, DLA 0156

Petty Officer Medical Assistant A. D. Smith, DLA 0174

Commander K. E. Woodhead, DLA 0213

INDEX